Cambridge Technicals

Level **3**

Business

Tess Bayley, Karen Tullett,
Dianne Wainwright and Leanna Oliver

HODDER
EDUCATION
AN HACHETTE UK COMPANY

Hachette UK's policy is to use papers that are natural, renewable and recyclable products and made from wood grown in sustainable forests. The logging and manufacturing processes are expected to conform to the environmental regulations of the country of origin.

Orders: please contact Bookpoint Ltd, 130 Park Drive, Milton Park, Abingdon, Oxon OX14 4SE. Telephone: (44) 01235 827720. Fax: (44) 01235 400454. Email education@bookpoint.co.uk Lines are open from 9 a.m. to 5 p.m., Monday to Saturday, with a 24-hour message answering service. You can also order through our website: www.hoddereducation.co.uk

ISBN: 978 1 4718 7479 6

© Tess Bayley, Karen Tullett, Dianne Wainwright and Leanna Oliver 2016

First published in 2016 by
Hodder Education,
An Hachette UK Company
Carmelite House
50 Victoria Embankment
London EC4Y 0DZ

www.hoddereducation.co.uk

Impression number 10 9 8 7 6 5 4 3

Year   2020 2019 2018 2017

Cover photo © plustwentyseven/Digital Vision/Getty Images
Illustrations produced by Barking Dog Art
Typeset in India
Printed in Dubai

A catalogue record for this title is available from the British Library.

Contents

About this book

This book helps you to master the skills and knowledge you need for the OCR Cambridge Technicals Level 3 Business qualification.

This resource is endorsed by OCR for use with the Cambridge Technicals Level 3 Business specification. In order to gain OCR endorsement, this resource has undergone an independent quality check. Any references to assessment and/or assessment preparation are the publisher's interpretation of the specification requirements and are not endorsed by OCR. OCR recommends that a range of teaching and learning resources are used in preparing learners for assessment. For more information about the endorsement process, please visit the OCR website, www.ocr.org.uk.

Using this book

ABOUT THIS UNIT

Without successful marketing, customers may not be aware of products and services. Businesses strive to ensure that their products or services are sold to customers at the right price and in the right place, always ensuring that customers can access them.

Know what to expect when you are studying the unit.

LEARNING OUTCOMES

The topics, activities and suggested reading in this unit will help you to:

1 understand the impact of legislation, concepts and principles on accounting processes
2 understand the reporting requirements of private limited companies and public limited companies
3 be able to prepare final accounts for sole traders
4 use ratios to assess the performance of businesses.

Prepare for what you are going to cover in the unit.

How will I be assessed?

This unit will be externally assessed via a test set and marked by OCR.

Find out how you can expect to be assessed after studying the unit.

How will I be graded?

You will be graded using the following criteria, which are in the specification produced by OCR for the qualification.

Find out the criteria for achieving Pass, Merit and Distinction grades in internally assessed units.

LO1 Understand who customers are and their importance to businesses *P1 P2 P3 M1 D1*

Understand all the requirements of the qualification, with clearly stated learning outcomes and assessment criteria fully mapped to the specification.

LO1 Understand different types of businesses and their objectives

GETTING STARTED

(5 minutes)

List ten businesses. Include a range of different types of businesses, e.g. some that produce or grow a product and some that provide a service.

You will use this list in later activities.

Try activities to start you off with a new learning outcome.

INDIVIDUAL ACTIVITY

PAIRS ACTIVITY

GROUP ACTIVITY

Carry out tasks that help you to think about a topic in detail and enhance your understanding.

CLASSROOM DISCUSSION

(5 minutes)

Does the most appropriate form of ownership depend on the activities carried out by the business?

Take the opportunity to share your ideas with your group.

KEY TERMS

Budget – planned income and expenditure over a period of time.

Favourable variance – where the actual figure is better than the budgeted figures, e.g. if costs are lower than budgeted or revenue higher than budgeted.

Adverse variance – where the actual figure is worse than the budgeted figures, e.g. if costs are higher than budgeted or revenue is lower than budgeted.

Understand important terms.

KNOW IT

1 State two reasons why a sole trader might want to become a private limited company.
2 State two differences between a private limited company and a public limited company.
3 State one advantage and one disadvantage of being a government-owned corporation.
4 Explain three factors that might influence the decision to form a partnership.
5 Explain three aims and three objectives a sole trader might have.

Answer quick questions to test your knowledge about the learning outcome you have just covered.

Unit 1 assessment practice questions

Below are some practice questions for you to try.

Try the types of questions you may see in your externally assessed exam.

LO1 assessment activities

Activity 1 Pass criteria *P1 P2 P3 P1 P2* and *P3*

TOP TIPS

✔ Check with your tutor that your business choice is suitable.
✔ Ensure your choice of business gives you appropriate opportunities to meet the requirements of P1.
✔ Spend equal time and produce similar amounts of evidence for each of the pass criteria.

Start preparing for your internally assessed assignments by carrying out activities that are directly linked to Pass, Merit and Distinction criteria. Top Tips give you additional advice.

Read about it

Suggests books and websites for further reading and research.

Acknowledgements

Every effort has been made to trace and acknowledge ownership of copyright. The publishers will be glad to make suitable arrangements with any copyright holders whom it has not been possible to contact. The authors and publishers would like to thank the following for permission to reproduce copyright illustrative material:

Front cover © photocreo/Fotolia; **page 3** © WavebreakmediaMicro /Fotolia; **page 17** © Adam Gilchrist/Shutterstock; **page 64** © Africa Studio/Shutterstock; **page 108** © Rawpixel.com/Shutterstock; **page 112** © Monkey Business Images/Shutterstock; **page 120** © Trueffelpix/Shutterstock; **page 124** © Ribah/Shutterstock; **page 130** © Frederic Lewis/Getty Images; **page 140** © Martyn Evans/Alamy Stock Photo; **page 155** © donaveh/123RF; **page 159** © martin berry/Alamy Stock Photo; **page 178** © Gregg Vignal/Alamy Stock Photo; **page 183** © kasto/123RF; **page 198** © ariadna de raadt/123RF; **page 215** © Kheng Guan Toh/Shutterstock; **page 216** © Constantin Stanciu/123RF; **page 294** © Kevin Britland/Alamy Stock Photo; **page 305** © ScreenGem/Everett/REX/Shutterstock; **page 314** © SWNS/Photoshot /Getty Images; **page 316** © Elena Larina/Shutterstock; **page 322** © Elena11/Shutterstock

This book contains public sector information licensed under the Open Government Licence v3.0.

Unit 01

The business environment

ABOUT THIS UNIT

Businesses don't exist in isolation. They are influenced not only by the people who own them and work for them, but also their suppliers, competitors, local communities, the government, and many other groups and individuals.

In this unit you will find out how businesses are run and the reasons why particular decisions are made. You will learn about different types of business and how they are structured. You will discover how different functions work together within a business and how businesses can respond to external factors in order to remain competitive. You will also find out how financial and performance information can help a business plan for success.

LEARNING OUTCOMES

The topics, activities and suggested reading in this unit will help you to:

1 understand different types of businesses and their objectives
2 understand how the functional areas of businesses work together to support the activities of businesses
3 understand the effect that different organisational structures have on how businesses operate
4 be able to use financial information to check the financial health of businesses
5 understand the relationship between businesses and stakeholders
6 understand the external influences and constraints on businesses, and how businesses could respond
7 understand why businesses plan
8 be able to assess the performance of businesses to inform future business activities.

How will I be assessed?

This unit will be externally assessed via a test set and marked by OCR.

LO1 Understand different types of businesses and their objectives

List ten businesses. Include a range of different types of businesses, e.g. some that produce or grow a product and some that provide a service.

You will use this list in later activities.

1.1 Different types of business activity

There are several different types of **business activity**, as described below.

> ### 🔑 KEY TERM
>
> **Business activities** – tasks completed by a business to achieve its objectives, e.g. buying, selling and producing products or services.

Primary activity

The key purpose of primary activity is the extraction and harvesting of raw materials. This includes mining, agriculture, fishing, and oil and gas extraction.

In countries in the early stages of industrial development, most of the population is employed in primary activities.

Secondary activity

The key purpose of secondary activity is to manufacture products. These can be finished products sold to **retail customers**, or components sold to **business customers** and used in the production of other products.

> ### 🔑 KEY TERMS
>
> **Retail customers** – customers who buy finished products, e.g. frozen peas from a supermarket.
>
> **Business customers** – businesses that purchase products or services from another business.

As a country becomes more industrialised, employment in secondary activities increases.

Tertiary activity

The key purpose of tertiary activity is the provision of services. These can be services to the public, such as hairdressers, schools, banks and supermarkets, or services to businesses, such as transport.

As a country becomes more industrialised, the demand for services increases. This leads to growth in the provision of, and employment within, service industries.

1.2 Different sectors of operation

Private sector

Businesses operating in the private sector aim to make a profit. They range from small local businesses, such as an electrician, to large multinational corporations, such as Walmart Stores, Inc. Examples of private sector businesses in the UK include Next plc, Britvic plc and Iceland Ltd.

Public sector

The UK public sector is responsible for providing a wide range of public services, such as health care, education, libraries, the armed forces, maintaining public roads and refuse collection.

A range of public corporations are also owned by the public sector, including the Royal Mint, Forestry Commission, Ofsted and the Student Loans Company.

The public sector is financed via sources including taxation, council tax payments, business rates, licence fees (e.g. BBC), and selling products and services (e.g. Ordnance Survey).

Third sector

These are organisations that do not aim to make a profit and are not government owned. They rely on donations, fundraising, and grants from sources such as charitable foundations and the government. Registered charities such as the NSPCC and Oxfam, self-help groups such as Alcoholics Anonymous and community groups such as Grow Wild all operate within this sector.

Refer back to your list of ten businesses. For each business decide:

- which type of business activity it performs
- which sector of operation it belongs to.

1.3 Different forms of legal business ownership

▲ **Figure 1.1** Becoming a private limited company can involve lengthy legal discussions

Table 1.1 explains the pros and cons of different types of business.

Type of business	Advantages	Disadvantages	Most appropriate for ...
Sole trader • Owned by one person, although the owner may decide to employ others to work alongside them. It is the most common form of ownership in the UK	• A sole trader can often start a business with limited finance, e.g. a window cleaner • There are few legal requirements to consider when starting compared with other forms of ownership • Sole traders are solely responsible for decision making • Sole traders can choose their own working hours and holidays • A good relationship is likely to be built with their customers as they deal with them directly • Sole traders do not have to share profits with other owners	• Sole traders are personally liable for any debts incurred by the business (**unlimited liability**). This may result in, say, their home being sold to raise finance • Sole traders do not have co-owners to discuss ideas and decisions with • Sole traders often work long hours and take few holidays as there is no one to take responsibility when they are not there; similarly, if they are ill the business can suffer and customers may be let down • A lack of finance may restrict the business, e.g. not being able to invest in new equipment or expand	Individuals who have an enterprising business idea or people wishing to start a business alongside employed work, e.g. a wedding cake maker The risk of unlimited liability means that this form of ownership is better suited to businesses where there is no large initial financial outlay

Type of business	Advantages	Disadvantages	Most appropriate for ...
Partnership • A business with a minimum of two partners. It can be straightforward to set up, although a Deed of Partnership is advisable. This summarises details of the owners, e.g. the capital each has invested into the business and how profits will be shared • In a limited liability partnership, the partners aren't personally liable for debts the business can't pay; their liability is limited to the amount of money they invest in the business. Different partners may have different liabilities.	• There are others to discuss decisions with, and to cover for holidays and sickness • As each of the partners contributes capital there is more finance available for investment • Partners may have different areas of expertise that will be beneficial to the business, e.g. one may have ICT expertise and another financial expertise • There are few legal requirements when starting the business	• Decision making may take longer as more people are involved • If partners disagree, arguments could affect the service provided • All profits are shared • The partners have unlimited liability • If one partner works longer hours than others or one partner takes longer holidays, this may cause resentment • The business does not have a separate legal identity; therefore if one of the partners dies the partnership would end	Partnerships are commonly used by professional services such as doctors' surgeries, solicitors and accountants
Private limited company (Ltd) • A company is a separate legal entity to the owners. It is a form of ownership where shares in the business are sold to raise finance. Those purchasing the shares (the shareholders) are the legal owners. The individual(s) who set up the business are likely to become the majority shareholders, although shares may be sold to people approved by these owners • A private limited company can usually be identified by 'Ltd' or 'Limited' after its name	• As the company is a separate legal entity, the owners/shareholders have **limited liability** • Shares can be sold to raise additional finance • The owners can choose to whom shares are sold • The owners can keep control of the business as long as they limit the number of shares sold to others, i.e. they remain the majority shareholders	• Becoming a limited company can be an expensive and lengthy process. The Articles of Association and the Memorandum of Association (AOA), along with Form 12 and Form 10, are legal documents that must be completed and sent to the Registrar of Companies, who will issue a Certificate of Incorporation • Shares cannot be sold to the general public; this limits the finance that can be gained via selling shares • Shares cannot be transferred or sold unless permission is gained from the other shareholders; some people may therefore be reluctant to invest in the company	For a small business, becoming a limited company provides the owners with less risk than being a sole trader or partnership due to having limited liability; however, additional costs of the legal process may be off-putting Some large businesses, such as Coca-Cola Enterprises Ltd, are still private limited companies with the benefit of limited liability and control over decision making
Public limited company (plc) • A plc is a separate legal entity from its owners, the shareholders. Unlike a private limited company, the shares in public limited companies can be bought and sold via the stock market. The business has limited liability, must have share capital of more than £50,000, at least two shareholders, two directors, a qualified company secretary and, usually, a wide spread of shareholders. It has the letters 'plc' after its name • Plcs are subject to costly regulations, including an annual general meeting (AGM), and strict auditing	• Shareholders benefit from limited liability • As shares can be sold via the stock market, large amounts of capital can be raised if required • Shares can be bought, sold and transferred easily • A plc has a high profile so may find it easier to attract new customers and reliable suppliers; banks may also be more willing to lend them money as they are seen as a lower risk than businesses with other forms of ownership	• The accounts of plcs are in the public domain so anyone – even competitors – can view them • Due to the size of plcs, the decision-making process may be lengthy, particularly if shareholders need to be consulted, and may concentrate on short-term profit rather than long-term strategy • The legal process to become a plc is lengthy and costly; it is only once the legal certificate is issued that the company can begin trading • Issuing further shares can be costly as this includes legal costs, producing a prospectus and advertising the sale • The original owners are unlikely to retain full control over decision making, although they may personally benefit from the first share issue, e.g. Mark Zuckerberg, the founder of Facebook • There is a greater risk of takeover	Businesses that need to raise large amounts of capital, e.g. Tesco plc, may require capital to build new stores, or an oil extraction company could require capital due to high investment costs

Type of business	Advantages	Disadvantages	Most appropriate for ...
State/government owned (public sector) • In the UK a range of organisations are still under government control, such as Ordnance Survey and the BBC • The government identifies the aims and objectives of the organisation and appoints a board of directors to run it	• Some businesses/ industries are vital. Support from the government ensures that these industries survive • In some industries it would be inefficient to have more than one provider of a product or service, e.g. the Royal Mint; if there were multiple producers of UK currency it would be difficult and costly to maintain security • The government can support large businesses that are struggling to survive, e.g. the bank Northern Rock was nationalised in 2008 after suffering financial problems	• Large businesses/industries may be inefficient due to **diseconomies of scale** and higher prices may be charged to customers • Businesses that are not answerable to shareholders regarding profits may not prioritise cost control • These businesses can be used for political gain, e.g. if unemployment is high, additional jobs can be created; however, this would increase costs and inefficiency	Large organisations that provide a vital product or service to the population and that may not exist without government support
Charity/not for profit (third sector) • Includes voluntary and community groups, trade unions, charitable trusts and charities (limited companies with charitable aims). They have charitable aims other than making money. They may make a profit but invest any money they receive in the cause they support	• Advantages of small charitable groups are the same as those for sole traders • Such groups are quick and easy to set up and can make an immediate impact • Advantages of being a charity are the same as those as for a limited company	• Disadvantages of small charitable groups are the same as those for sole traders • They often depend on volunteers, which can make it difficult to maintain support in running the group • Disadvantages of being a charity are the same as those as for a limited company • Setting up a formal charity is expensive as it is regulated by Companies House and the Charity Commission • Annual accounts must be provided to both Companies House and the Charity Commission • Some larger charities use aggressive commercial tactics to raise money, which may put off potential supporters	Groups with social, cultural, political, environmental and welfare aims and objectives, especially where people are willing to work on a voluntary basis
Community interest companies (CIC) • Limited companies that aim to benefit the community or trade with a social purpose rather than earning high profits for shareholders. Although shareholders may get a small return, most profits are invested into the community or a social enterprise	• The company has its own legal identity • The reputation of the business may be enhanced	• The Articles of Association and the Memorandum of Association must be completed and sent to the Registrar of Companies • Tax must be paid on profits	Companies of all sizes that have social/community benefits at heart, and that are familiar with the structure of and running of a limited company

KEY TERMS

Unlimited liability – when the owners of a business are personally liable for all debts incurred by the business if the business itself does not have the funds to repay them.

Limited liability – when the owners of a business are liable for the debts incurred by the business only to the value of their investment in the business.

Diseconomies of scale – when a business becomes too large, the cost per unit may increase and the business may become more inefficient, e.g. communication becomes slower as more employees join the hierarchy.

INDIVIDUAL ACTIVITY

(5 minutes)

You plan to start your own business. Choose one of the following:

● pizza takeaway
● jeweller
● newsagent
● pensioners' lunch club.

Which form of ownership would you choose? Why do you think this is the most suitable?

GROUP ACTIVITY

(5 minutes)

Join together with others who have chosen the same business. Do you all agree on the same method of ownership? If not, can you all agree on one method?

What are the advantages and disadvantages of the form of ownership you have chosen?

CLASSROOM DISCUSSION

(5 minutes)

Does the most appropriate form of ownership depend on the activities carried out by the business?

1.4 Factors which inform business ownership

Legal status

Legal status will have an influence on the form of ownership as some forms will result in the business being a separate legal entity from the owner(s) (e.g. a limited company or charitable company), whereas others will not (e.g. sole trader or partnership). This means that, in a limited company, the business rather than the individual owner would be sued if there were an issue such as damage to a customer's property.

Liability

Business owners must consider the financial risk involved when choosing a form of ownership. For example, becoming a sole trader or a partnership will result in higher personal financial risk due to unlimited liability, whereas becoming a limited company will lower the risk due to the business having a separate legal identity.

The owner's personal situation may also influence this choice as an individual without commitments such as children or a mortgage may be more likely to accept this risk.

Funding

Some forms of ownership require more paperwork and legal expense. For example, a sole trader needs to register for tax and send annual self-assessment forms to HM Revenue and Customs (HMRC) but there is no legal process that they must follow to maintain their business. On the other hand, becoming a public limited company is costly. This usually requires a merchant bank to facilitate the process, which will charge a commission fee, plus the costs of producing a prospectus and advertising the share sale. Each year, accounts must be produced and published, often as an expensive glossy brochure.

A business must consider whether this financial outlay is outweighed by the benefits of becoming a public limited company as well as whether there are funds within the business to finance the process.

Control/decision making

The form of ownership chosen will influence the level of control the owner(s) have with regard to decision making. A sole trader will have sole responsibility for making decisions; in a partnership the decisions can be discussed among the partners; whereas in a limited company it is the shareholders who control the business. In a public limited company, the shareholders elect a board of directors to make the decisions on their behalf, but ultimately these shareholders are the owners, who direct and control the business.

Legal/administrative requirements

It is much simpler to start up as a sole trader than it is to start up as a limited company, from both a legal and an administrative view. This may influence the type of ownership chosen, depending on the timescale in which the owner(s) wishes to commence trading.

Similarly, once the business is trading, there are different requirements for different forms of ownership. For example, a public limited company must produce and publish audited accounts and submit them to Companies House, whereas a sole trader simply completes an income tax self-assessment form.

GROUP ACTIVITY

(1 hour plus time to perform presentations)

1 Working in small groups, research a local business. Investigate:
  - the type of business ownership
  - the reasons why that form of ownership is appropriate.
2 Once your research is complete, prepare a presentation that includes:
  - a brief introduction to the business including its type of activity, its sector of operation and its form of legal business ownership
  - an explanation of the advantages and disadvantages for this business of its form of ownership
  - an explanation of the factors that may have influenced its decision as to choice of ownership
  - in your opinion, is this the most appropriate form of ownership for this business? Why? Why not?
3 As a class, discuss the businesses researched. Are there similarities between businesses with the same type of ownership? Are there differences? Can conclusions be drawn between business activities and their choice of ownership?

1.5 Differing business aims and objectives

Survival

Survival is an important aim for all businesses, but particularly a new business. The chances of survival will be influenced by factors such as the finance available within the business, the economy – many businesses fail to survive a **recession** – and the number of competitors in the market.

Financial

Businesses may have a range of financial **aims** and objectives. These include to:

- break even – covering costs; in the short term a business can survive as long as costs are covered, even if it is not making a profit
- increase revenue – a business that is moving forward should aim to increase revenue, e.g. by introducing additional products/services, expanding the number of stores or attracting customers from competitors; as long as costs are kept under control, increasing revenue should lead to an increase in profits
- reduce costs – in a competitive market, businesses must control or reduce their cost; benefits include the option to pass this cost saving on to customers via lower prices, which may improve competitiveness or the ability to earn higher profits
- make a profit – most types of business exist to make a profit, therefore aims and objectives relating to profits, if achieved, will provide the business with funds for investment as well as providing remuneration for the owners; if a business does not make a profit in the long run, the owners are unlikely to continue trading as they are receiving no benefit from their investment.

Growth

Growth can be measured in terms of number of employees, increasing the value of sales or increasing output. Reasons why a business may aim to grow include:

- wanting a greater market share
- wanting physical expansion, e.g. opening more stores or building a new factory
- increasing provision, e.g. a bus company purchasing additional buses to operate more routes
- benefiting from **economies of scale**
- spreading risk by diversification
- a larger business may find it easier to obtain external finance such as bank loans.

KEY TERMS

Business aims – a summary of what the business wants to achieve in the future.

Recession – a period of economic decline where demand and output fall.

Economies of scale – cost advantages gained when the size of a business increases, e.g. suppliers may offer discounts to those placing larger orders.

Reputation

A business may choose aims and objectives that will improve its reputation and therefore the success of the business. For example, producing good-quality products, providing excellent customer service and acting in an ethical and socially responsible manner can all provide a business with a **unique selling point (USP)**, which should enable it to stand out from the competition.

Being enterprising

Entrepreneurs are often sole traders trying to build their own business as they want to be their own boss and pursue a career that interests and challenges them.

A business that is enterprising is likely to take risks to pursue an idea. Such a business is likely to keep trying to identify gaps in the market, remain competitive and use its experience to produce products or provide services that customers find new and exciting.

PAIRS ACTIVITY

(30 minutes)

Consider the businesses listed below. For each one:

- state two objectives you think this business should have
- state two objectives you do not think are appropriate for this business (but that would be realistic for an alternative business)
- ensure that you can justify your decisions.

Business organisations to consider:

a local hairdresser
b B&Q plc
c Poundstretcher Group
d your school/college.

KNOW IT

1 State two reasons why a sole trader might want to become a private limited company.
2 State two differences between a private limited company and a public limited company.
3 State one advantage and one disadvantage of being a government-owned corporation.
4 Explain three factors that might influence the decision to form a partnership.
5 Explain three aims and three objectives a sole trader might have.

LO2 Understand how the functional areas of businesses work together to support the activities of businesses

GETTING STARTED

(15 minutes)

- In groups, consider one of the **functional areas** in a business. Produce a spider diagram that identifies the tasks you think that staff within that functional area will be responsible for.
- Your group could feed back to the rest of your class. Can your peers make other suggestions? A volunteer should write any additional suggestions onto your diagram. These can be referred back to during your LO2 studies.

KEY TERM

Unique selling point (USP) – a specific factor that makes a business stand out from its competitors, e.g. excellent customer service.

Functional area – a division of a business where employees have similar roles, skills and expertise, e.g. marketing function, human resource function.

2.1 Key tasks of functional areas of businesses

Finance

Employees within the finance function (also known as accounting or accounts) are responsible for controlling the finance of the business. Their roles and duties include:

- making and receiving payments on behalf of the business, and recording financial transactions
- preparing annual financial accounts, including the **statement of financial position** and **income statement**
- monitoring and analysing financial performance, e.g. **cash flow forecasting**
- paying employees.

🔑 KEY TERMS

Statement of financial position – a summary statement on a particular date that shows a business's assets, liabilities and owner's equity.

Income statement – a financial statement that shows the revenue and expenses a business has received and paid over a period of time; the statement will show the profit the business has made during this time.

Cash flow forecasting – estimating the expected cash inflows and outflows for a period of time in the future to identify likely surpluses or shortages.

Pricing strategy – the method used to determine the price of a product/service, taking into consideration the market, competitors' pricing, customer incomes, etc.

Marketing

Employees within the marketing function are responsible for identifying customer needs and working with the research and development function to ensure that products and services are designed that satisfy these needs. Based on their research they will also decide on the most appropriate distribution channel (e.g. in stores or online) and an appropriate **pricing strategy**.

Marketing employees are also responsible for promoting the business and its products/services using different forms of media, including social media, to create awareness and generate sales.

Sales

Employees within the sales function are responsible for communicating with existing customers and potential new customers. They are the representatives of the business in direct contact with customers, and therefore must provide excellent customer service and be knowledgeable about the products/services offered.

Many businesses will have sales targets included in their objectives and the sales function is key to achieving these.

The sales function can take different forms. For example, in a jewellers the sales staff work in the store and deal with customers face to face. However, in a manufacturing business the sales function is likely to be based at head office, and will deal with customers via the telephone and email.

Human resources

Responsibilities of employees within the human resource (HR) function (also known as personnel) include:

- recruiting new employees
- identifying training needs and organising training
- planning recruitment needs, e.g. considering business objectives and the impact these will have on the number of staff and the skills required
- ensuring that appropriate pay and benefit systems are in place
- overseeing redundancy procedures and other dismissals
- ensuring that human resource legislation is met, e.g. equality legislation
- establishing company policies such as **disciplinary** and **grievance procedures**
- administration tasks, e.g. ensuring that employee details such as addresses and bank details are up to date.

🔑 KEY TERMS

Disciplinary procedure – a specified process for dealing with alleged employee misconduct, e.g. poor performance.

Grievance procedure – a specified process for dealing with a complaint made by an employee about their treatment at work, e.g. discrimination or receiving lower pay than stated in their employment contract.

Operations management

Employees within the operations management function (also known as production) are responsible for transforming raw materials (inputs) into finished goods/services (outputs).

In some businesses this process relies on labour, whereas in other businesses technology and machines are used. Employees in the operations management function are also responsible for ensuring that quality standards are met.

Customer services

Employees within the customer services function are responsible for liaising with customers on a day-to-day basis. Today most businesses have customer service helplines that function via telephone, online messaging or online chats.

Contact Onlineshop.com

Email	Phone	Chat
Send us an email	Call us	Start chatting

▲ **Figure 1.2** Modern businesses offer many ways of contacting the customer service function

Customer service staff should be knowledgeable, helpful and calm as not only do they need to be able to answer customer queries, they are also likely to be the first contact if a customer has a complaint. They need to manage the expectations of customers (for example, by not promising what cannot be delivered) and to resolve any queries promptly.

Business support services

Employees within the business support services function (also known as IT or administration) are responsible for the administration relating to the day-to-day running of the business. This includes:

- producing contracts
- maintaining equipment, e.g. photocopiers, and arranging maintenance visits if necessary
- arranging meetings
- organising travel plans
- providing technical IT support.

Research and development

Skilled employees within the research and development function are responsible for developing new products and services in response to market research findings. Their role is key to ensuring the success of a business as they must develop products/services that customers want and need if the business is to remain competitive and profitable.

Purchasing/procurement

Employees within the purchasing function (also known as procurement) source and provide the raw materials, goods and services needed in the day-to-day running of a business.

A manufacturing business such as Cadbury's requires raw materials, e.g. sugar, as well as goods, e.g. packaging. A service business such as Bibby Distribution requires vehicles and IT equipment. Most businesses also need goods such as stationery, and services such as water and electricity. It is the role of the purchasing function to source these resources at the lowest cost while ensuring acceptable quality.

Public-sector procurement is governed by regulations to ensure that the best value is obtained from the supplier and that the purchasing process is transparent and fair.

2.2 How business functions interrelate with other business functions

The functional areas must communicate effectively with one another if a business is to operate successfully.

GROUP ACTIVITY

(30 minutes)

- Copy the table below on to a large sheet of paper. In groups discuss how and why you think different functional areas need to communicate, then complete the table. An example is given for 'Finance', however there are other possible examples for this function.

- Feed back your ideas to other groups in your class.

Functional area	Other functional areas that the stated function should liaise with	Reasons why good communication is important between these functional areas
Finance	Finance will need to liaise with the sales function to gain accurate sales figures.	Accurate sales figures are vital if the finance function is to produce accurate financial accounts
Marketing		
Sales		
Human resources		
Operations management		
Customer services		
Business support services		
Research and development		
Purchasing		

Consequences of poor interrelationships

All private-sector businesses should aim to satisfy their customers as this is how they will make a profit. Poor interrelationships between business functions may affect the service provided to customers. For example, if the sales function receives a large order from a customer but does not inform the operations management function that production needs to be increased, there may not be sufficient products available for delivery on the agreed date. This will adversely affect the business's reputation and it is unlikely to receive further orders from this customer.

INDEPENDENT RESEARCH ACTIVITY

(1 hour plus time for interviews)

- Research a business that has different functional areas. You could visit, or talk to, people who are employed there.
- Investigate:
  - how and why the functional areas within this business communicate with one another
  - the impact on the business if communication were poor or didn't exist between these functional areas.
- Produce a report or a presentation that summarises your findings.

KNOW IT

1 State three responsibilities of the finance function in a business.
2 State three responsibilities of the human resources function in a business.
3 How might the role of the customer services function differ in a bank compared to an online retailer such as Amazon?
4 State two consequences of poor interrelationships between functional areas.

LO3 Understand the effect that different organisational structures have on how businesses operate

GETTING STARTED

(10 minutes)

In pairs, write down or sketch the organisational structure you might expect for a:

- local restaurant employing 10 people
- car hire company employing 50 people in five locations
- school or college employing 100 people.

3.1 Different organisational structures

Structures can be influenced by elements like an organisation's size, its function (what it does), its products or services, and its geographic location. A business can take on a particular structure to suit its situation. Some examples are given in Table 1.2.

KEY TERM

Flat structure – a company structure containing few levels.

Table 1.2 The advantages and disadvantages of different organisational structures

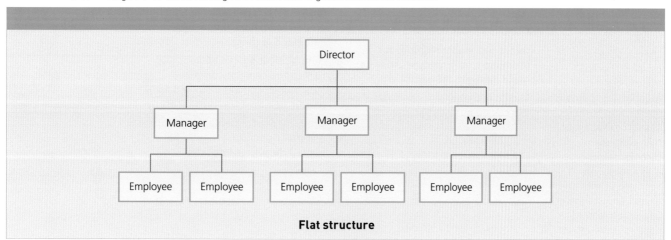

Flat structure

	Advantages	Disadvantages	Best suited to ...
There are very few layers between the top level and the bottom level. The chain of command tends to be short and **span of control** tends to be wide	Due to the short chain of command, communication flow tends to be good. Information can be passed on more accurately and there is generally more interaction between the top and bottom levels, improving understanding Authority is delegated to employees so decisions can be made more quickly as information and orders are more direct Due to the wide span of control employees are empowered and motivated to make decisions Fewer management levels keep staff costs down, improving efficiency	Wider span of control may mean that employees at the bottom level are not supervised closely, which could lead to mistakes Fewer levels reduce the opportunities for promotion, which might cause more ambitious employees to leave	Smaller businesses with fewer job roles and division of functions unnecessary

Hierarchical/tall structure

	Advantages	Disadvantages	Best suited to ...
Many layers of management, resembling a pyramid with fewer people at the top than the bottom. The chain of command is clearly defined, instructions are passed down from the top to the bottom. At each level there is a person in charge of several people. There is usually clear division of functions, e.g. finance, marketing, human resources, operations management. Directors and managers with specialist skills and expert knowledge are appointed to ensure each function is run smoothly	Everybody knows their job roles and to whom they are **accountable** At each level, authority is delegated from above so that employees are empowered to make decisions in their areas of work. Decisions can be made quickly, which speeds up the response to problems A narrow span of control enables supervision to be closer, leading to fewer mistakes Offers more opportunities for promotion, so employees may be more motivated to work harder Middle management can specialise, increasing business efficiency	Responses to problems can be slow as information is passed down from one level to the next Whilst authority can be delegated, responsibility cannot. People higher up the hierarchy are responsible for the actions of those under them even if they didn't make the decisions. This has implications for the selection and training of employees before authority is delegated to them Communication can be poor due to the long chain of command; information can get distorted as it travels up and down the hierarchy Different departments can compete and make decisions that do not benefit the whole business	Medium to large businesses with a large number of employees, and the armed forces

	Advantages	Disadvantages	Best suited to ...

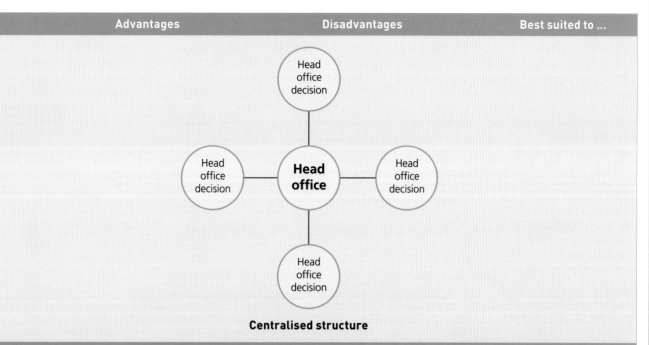

Centralised structure

	Advantages	Disadvantages	Best suited to ...
In a centralised structure, decisions for the whole business are usually made by people at the top of the hierarchy. Information and instructions flow from the top to the bottom	Useful in unforeseen circumstances or times of uncertainty. Strong leadership allows quick responses to potential threats People at the top tend to be more experienced with specialist skills so mistakes are less likely Decisions made tend to benefit the whole business rather than individual departments Responses to problems can be quicker as only a few people at the top of the hierarchy are consulted	People lower down the structure may feel demotivated as decisions are made for them without consultation There may be better understanding lower down the structure regarding customer and employee needs, which is not taken into consideration when decisions are made at the top	Small businesses, e.g. a haulage company's owner makes all operations decisions, which are passed on to drivers, telling them where to pick up goods and where to deliver them

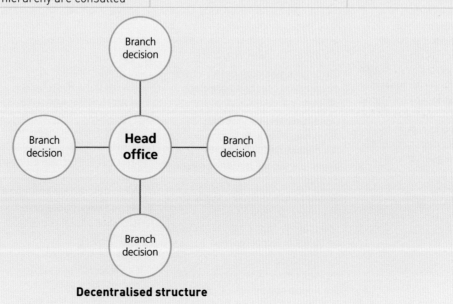

Decentralised structure

	Advantages	Disadvantages	Best suited to ...
People at the bottom of the organisational structure are given authority to make certain decisions relating to their day-to-day activities. A decentralised structure relies on the delegation of authority. While it encourages employees to take more responsibility, it is crucial that there is a high level of co-ordination for it to work	Employees feel more empowered and motivated as they have more responsibility and are able to make certain decisions for themselves People at the top can have more time to focus on important decisions that affect the whole of the business Quicker response to customer feedback as people lower down the structure tend to have a better understanding of customer needs and wants For a business with branches in different locations, decisions can be made to satisfy local demand, improving competitiveness	Decisions made might not reflect those valued by the whole business, sending confusing messages to stakeholders The quality of decisions made relies on the expertise and experience of the people lower down in the structure. Training is crucial to the success of this model Conflict might arise as people who are authorised to make decisions do so based on their own needs	Certain supermarket chains allow their store managers to make decisions based on local needs and wants, to increase sales and customer satisfaction

	Marketing	Operations	Finance	Human Resources
	Marketing manager	Operations manager	Finance manager	HR manager
Project A Team leader	Marketing Team A	Operations Team A	Finance Team A	HR Team A
Project B Team leader	Marketing Team B	Operations Team B	Finance Team B	HR Team B
Project C Team leader	Marketing Team C	Operations Team C	Finance Team C	HR Team C
Project D Team leader	Marketing Team D	Operations Team D	Finance Team D	HR Team D

Matrix structure

	Advantages	Disadvantages	Best suited to ...
Teams from different departments are created to run different projects, to focus on different products or services, or to serve customers in different locations. Team members often have to report to their departmental manager as well as the project manager	It is a very flexible arrangement – teams can be removed as a project is completed relatively easily without causing major disruption to the organisational structure Close collaboration between the departments leads to greater efficiency and productivity Communication is good as employees work as teams across the departments. The collective expertise allows better and quicker decisions Greater motivation among team members as they have the opportunity to contribute their ideas as they work together A cross-functional team can be formed for each location so that the needs and wants of customers in a specific location can be served better	Team members may not know who their immediate line manager is, leading to miscommunication Team members might be given conflicting instructions from their departmental and project managers, which might lead to lower productivity and efficiency Managers can have different leadership styles, which could demotivate employees Having two managers is costly, which reduces profitability Sharing employees can lead to unhealthy competition between departments, e.g. each project manager will look for the best employees from other departments	A business with multiple products or operating in different countries. It draws together the expertise of the functional departments to create different projects or products so the end result is of a higher standard A manufacturing company can form different teams based on the different products made. Each product will have expert knowledge from the marketing, finance, human resources and operations management department, so that it has a better chance in the market. As the company introduces a new product, a new cross-functional team could be formed without having to take on new employees. If a product is unsuccessful, its team can be removed relatively easily and the employees reassigned to other products

Hierarchical/tall structure – a pyramid-shaped structure with many levels.

Centralised structure – a structure where decision making is kept at the top of the hierarchy.

Decentralised structure – a structure where decision making is more spread out and filtered down the hierarchy.

Matrix structure – where employees are grouped by function and product/project.

Span of control – the number of subordinates a supervisor manages.

Accountability – the responsibility that someone has for actions that are carried out.

GROUP ACTIVITY

(40 minutes)

Research a business you are interested in. Find out its organisational structure, the advantages and disadvantages of the structure, and the impact of the organisational structure on how it is run. You can present your findings in a poster or PowerPoint presentation.

The use of organisation charts
Showing elements of the organisational structure

Elements of organisational structures include division of work, span of control and chain of command. Organisational charts show these elements so that everybody is clear about what their job role is, who is in charge of whom and how communication flows in a business. It is important to show these elements clearly so that a business runs smoothly and, in case of an emergency, everybody knows who to report to. It is especially useful in a large organisation where there are a lot of employees.

The status of different levels of job role

In a medium-sized to large business, there are different job roles at different levels of authority. Typically, these are:

- supervisors
- assistants/operatives
- directors
- managers
- chief executive.

PAIRS ACTIVITY

(10 minutes)

By drawing arrows on Table 1.3, match the job roles with the tasks that might be undertaken by different roles.

Table 1.3 Tasks associated with different roles

Chief executive	Assign duties to employees, explaining how these are to be carried out
Directors	Decide what work needs to be done to meet departmental aims and objectives
Managers	Lead and develop a business's long-term strategy
Supervisors	Oversee a department, ensuring the company policies are implemented
Assistant/operative	Complete tasks as directed

Chief executive

The chief executive is the person with the most authority in a business. With authority comes responsibility, so the chief executive is responsible for the success or failure of a business. He or she is answerable to all the stakeholders, e.g. employees, customers, government, local community.

The chief executive makes the most important decisions that affect the whole business. These could be any future plans, the direction a business is following or how a business presents itself to the world.

Directors

Directors report to the chief executive. In a medium-sized to large business there may be several directors, each in charge of a function (e.g. finance, sales, HR). Directors are leaders who oversee all activities undertaken within their function. They plan departmental strategies and take part in the overall strategic decisions of a business. Their main role is to make sure that the areas under their leadership contribute to achieving the overall aims of a business.

Managers

Managers make sure that their department achieves the aims and objectives identified by their directors, to whom they report directly. Managers are in overall charge of the activities in their department, ensuring that it is run smoothly. Decisions concerning the whole department are made by managers.

Supervisors

Supervisors are usually in charge of team members in a specific area of a department, e.g. a golf course supervisor would be responsible for maintaining the golf course by ensuring that grass is cut and trees managed. Supervisors make day-to-day decisions to ensure that the area they are in charge of is run smoothly.

Assistants/operatives

Assistants or operatives are at the bottom of a hierarchy and are responsible for carrying out instructions given by their supervisors.

KNOW IT

1 Understand the concepts of chain of command, span of control, authority, delegation, empowerment and accountability.
2 Know the different organisational structures that a business could adopt.
3 Know that businesses can be organised in terms of function, product/service and geographical location.
4 Understand the advantages and disadvantages of different organisational structures, and how they impact on the operations of businesses.
5 Understand that different structures suit different businesses.

LO4 Be able to use financial information to check the financial health of businesses

GETTING STARTED

(10 minutes)

In pairs, discuss what profit is and why it is important. When might an organisation not prioritise making profits for shareholders?

4.1 Financial terms used to check the financial health of businesses

Business costs

Accountants are concerned with the monetary cost of business resources, but economists consider costs as **opportunity costs**.

KEY TERMS

Opportunity cost – a benefit, profit or other advantage that must be given up to acquire or achieve something else.

Costs – the expenses a business incurs when producing and supplying products and services to customers.

Depreciation – the cost of an asset consumed over its useful life, e.g. due to wear and tear.

Businesses split their accounting costs into categories. These may include those described below.

Fixed costs

These are **costs** that have to be paid even if the business produces or sells nothing. Examples include:

- rent
- office salaries
- advertising
- insurance
- **depreciation**.

▲ **Figure 1.3** Graphical representation of fixed costs

Variable costs

These are costs that vary directly with the level of output. If output doubles, the variable costs double. If the output halves, the variable costs halve. If output were zero, no variable costs would be incurred. Examples include:

- direct labour (cost of paying employees involved in production)
- raw materials
- packaging costs
- royalties paid.

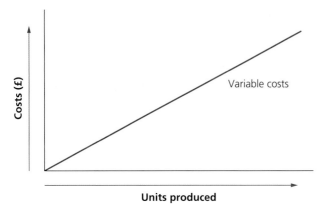

▲ **Figure 1.4** Graphical representation of variable costs

Revenue

Revenue (also called sales, total revenue or turnover) is the income that a business earns over a period of time – for example, over one month or one year. Examples include cash sales, credit sales, interest, royalties received, dividends from business investments. The amount of revenue earned will depend on the number of items sold or services offered, and the selling price of each.

Revenue = Selling price × Quantity sold

> 🔑 **KEY TERM**
>
> **Revenue** – the money earned from selling manufactured output, goods purchased or services offered; the total revenue of a business is based on both the level of output and the selling price per unit.

> 👥 **PAIRS ACTIVITY**
>
> **(20 minutes)**
>
> Work in pairs to discuss and write down two fixed costs, two variable costs and two sources of revenue for a business of your choice. Draw a symbol that represents each of your six key words. Share these with the rest of the group, and explain how you have categorised your costs and revenues.

Cash flow

▲ **Figure 1.5** It is important for a business to maintain cash flow

Cash inflows will include all receipts of money. Examples include:

- cash received from selling products/services
- loan receipts
- commission received
- rent received.

Cash outflows will include all payments made by the business. Examples include:

- wages
- insurance
- payments to suppliers
- loan interest.

Net cash flow and profit

Net cash flow is the difference between cash inflow and cash outflow.

Profit and **cash flow** are closely linked but very different (see Table 1.4). Profits are the main objective for most businesses. It is the reward a business owner or investor gains for risk taking. Businesses use profit to:

- reward owners in the form of drawings or dividends
- invest for future growth
- save for a contingency.

> 🔑 **KEY TERMS**
>
> **Net cash flow** – the difference between money coming into a business and money going out of a business.
>
> **Profit** – the surplus left over from revenue after paying total costs.
>
> **Cash flow** – the movement of money into and out of a business.
>
> **Loss** – the deficit of revenue after paying total costs.
>
> **Insolvent** – when a business is unable to pay its debts.

Businesses do not always generate a profit. A **loss** is made when business revenue is not sufficient to cover the total costs. To eliminate a loss, a business needs to cut costs (by using cheaper suppliers, reducing staff levels, etc.) or increase revenue (by increasing product sales, charging higher prices, etc.).

If a business runs out of cash and is unable to pay its day-to-day expenses, it is classed as **insolvent**. Business owners have the choice of raising extra finance or to cease trading. By constructing a cash flow forecast, business owners can plan ahead and identify when they may require additional funding.

Table 1.4 Profit versus cash flow

Profit	Cash flow
Profit = total revenue - total costs	Net cash flow = cash inflows - cash outflows
Considers costs incurred and revenue received, but does not consider when money changes hands	Cash is the physical money that a business has at a particular time; it includes all monetary payments, including bank transfers, direct debits, notes, coins and money in the bank
Calculated in the income statement	Shown in the cash flow forecast
Required for long-term business survival	Required for short-term business survival

Break even and margin of safety

Most businesses will want to maximise their profits, but being profitable is not always possible. New and small businesses and businesses facing an economic slowdown may find that they cannot generate profits at all. In this situation, it may be a more realistic objective for businesses to aim to simply **break even**.

🔑 KEY TERMS

Break even – the point at which the level of sales allows total costs to equal total revenue; at the break-even point a business makes no profit or loss.

Margin of safety – the amount a business sells in excess of its break-even point.

The break-even point is the level of sales where total costs equal total revenue, so there is no profit or loss. It has a number of applications and is used by businesses to:

- calculate the level of sales and unit price of each item needed to cover total costs
- see how changes in sales or costs affect profits.

There are a number of assumptions made when calculating break-even output. These include:

- all output is sold
- the business makes only one type of product
- all costs can be classified as either fixed costs or variable costs.

If a business is generating a profit, its output level will be higher than the break-even output level. The business may wish to know how far output can fall safely before it begins to experience losses.

The **margin of safety** measures how far output can fall before the business begins to make a loss. It is measured by the number of units of output between the current level of production and the break-even level of production.

Margin of safety (in units) = Actual output in units − Break-even output in units

4.2 How to calculate profit/loss and break-even point/output

Key formulae

These are:

Profit = Revenue − Costs

Break-even output = Fixed costs ÷ (Selling price − Variable costs)

Calculating the break-even point/ output and profit/loss

Dolphin's Bakery Sells a range of biscuits.
The biscuits sell for £1.20 each.
This reflects their unique selling point of low sugar content.
The bakery sells 5,500 biscuits on average per month.

↓

Variable costs
The ingredients, boxes and staff wages cost 60p per biscuit.

Fixed costs
The biscuits are sold from a small retail outlet on Deansgate in Manchester. This costs £800 per month for rent, £450 per month for heating and lighting, and £250 per month for insurance.

↓

Break-even output
Break-even output = Total fixed costs ÷ variable costs
Break-even output = £1,500 (per month) ÷ £0.60
Break-even output = 2,500 biscuits per month

↓

Profit / Loss
Profit / loss = total revenue − total costs
Profit / loss = total revenue − (total fixed and variable costs)
Profit / loss = (5,500 × £1.20) − (£1,500 + [2,500 × £0.60])
Profit / loss = £6,600 − £3,000
Profit = £3,600 per month

▲ **Figure 1.6** Case study: calculating the break-even output and profit

Table 1.5 Financial information for five businesses

	Alpha	Beta	Gamma	Delta	Omega
	£ per unit	£ per unit	£ per unit	£ per unit	£ per unit
Raw materials	8	8	16	32	4
Variable labour	2	9	4	8	4
Other variable costs	1	2	2	4	1
Fixed costs	4	6	8	16	3
Selling price	20	32	40	80	16
Number of units produced and sold	10,000	25,000	20,000	40,000	12,500

INDIVIDUAL ACTIVITY

(35 minutes)

Use the information in Table 1.5 to calculate for each business:

1 break-even point/output
2 profit/loss per unit
3 total profit/loss
4 margin of safety.

4.3 How to interpret financial statements

Income statement

An **income statement** is produced by a business for a specific period of time. This is usually 12 months and produced at the end of the business's financial year. The income statement will include:

● *revenue* (see page 17) – this is the money that comes into a business as a result of the ordinary activities of the organisation; in the income statement revenue is recognised either as the receipt of cash in a cash sale or at the point of sale for a credit sale

● *expenses* are the operating costs of a business; examples include wages, heat and light, rent, advertising and telephone costs.

KEY TERMS

Income statement – a financial statement that shows the revenue and expenses a business has received and paid over a period of time; the statement will show the profit the business has made during this time.

Gross profit – revenue minus cost of sales.

Cost of sales – the total amount the business has paid to create or make available a product or service that has been sold.

Net profit – gross profit minus expenses.

Assets – resources owned by a business, e.g. cash, motor vehicles, premises, machinery.

J Simpson

Income Statement for the year ended 31st December 2015

	£	£	£
Revenue		8,462	
Less Returns inwards		300	
			8,162
Less cost of sales			
Opening inventory	200		
Purchases	4,629		
Carriage inwards	100		
Less returns outwards	49		
		4,880	
Closing Inventory		2,548	
Cost of sales			2,332
Gross profit			**5,830**
Less expenses			
Salaries		1,150	
Motor expenses		520	
Rent		670	
Insurance		111	
Depreciation of premises		150	
Depreciation of motor vehicles		120	
Bad debts		50	
General expenses		105	
			2,876
Net Profit			**2,954**

▲ **Figure 1.7** Example income statement for a sole trader

The first line of the income statement details the revenue a business has gained from its goods and services. To calculate the **gross profit** for a period, a business will deduct the **cost of sales** from the revenue. The cost of sales are all costs directly related to the production of the goods and services.

Businesses need to account for their selling and administrative expenses (for example, distribution costs and advertising expenses). These are deducted from gross profit to calculate the **net profit** for a period of time.

It is often useful for business managers and owners to compare income statements over a period of several years. Businesses will analyse changes in revenue, cost of sales and expenses, and make adjustments to their business practices as required.

Statement of financial position

This is a snapshot of a business's financial health at a particular moment. The statement is a representation of the accounting equation, where the total assets will equal the total liabilities and owner's equity. The two sides must always balance.

The statement of financial position communicates information about the financial health of the business and indicates the relative liquidity of the assets. The statement can be compared over time and with other similar businesses. It must be remembered, however, that it needs to be reviewed alongside a business's income statement and cash flow forecast to make informed decisions.

It is split into different sections, as follows.

Assets

Assets are resources that are owned by a business. They are used to help the business survive and function.

Non-current assets are acquired for use within the business and are likely to be used for a considerable amount of time (usually more than 12 months). Examples include motor vehicles, premises and machinery.

Current assets are part of a business's operating cycle and are likely to be converted into cash within a 12-month period. There are five main categories of current asset:

1 cash in the bank
2 cash in hand (or stored on the business premises)
3 trade receivables (debtors: people, or organisations, that owe money to a business)
4 inventory (stock)
5 prepayments (where the business has paid in advance for an item, e.g. rent).

Liabilities

Liabilities represent the debts owed by an organisation. There are two main categories of liability.

Current liabilities are amounts falling due within one year that arise through day-to-day trading. Examples include bank overdraft, trade payables (people, or organisations, that the business owes money to), accruals (debts for which an invoice has not yet been received), corporation tax and dividends payable.

Non-current liabilities are amounts falling due after one year – sources of long-term borrowing – and will exist for more than 12 months. They will appear in a number of consecutive statements of financial positions. Examples include long-term bank loans, mortgages and debentures.

Equity

Equity, or capital, is the term used to describe how much a business is worth. It represents how much the owner(s) have invested in the business.

J Simpson

Statement of Financial Position as at 31st December 2015

Non-current assets	Cost	Depreciation	Net book value
	£	£	£
Premises	1,500	150	1,350
Motor vehicles	1,200	120	1,080
	2,700	0	2,430
Current assets			
Inventory	2,548		
Trade receivables	1,950		
Cash at bank	1,654		
Cash in hand	40		
		6,192	
Amounts falling due within one year			
Trade payables	1,538		
		1,538	
Working capital			4,654
Net assets			7,084
Financed by:			
Capital / equity			5,025
Net profit / loss			2,954
			7,979
Drawings			895
			7,084

▲ **Figure 1.8** Example statement of financial position for a sole trader

Cash flow forecast and cash flow statement

A **cash flow forecast** is a management accounting document and a form of budget. The forecast will show when cash is expected to come in to and go out of a business. The forecast is made up of three sections:

1 receipts – any money that a business expects to receive
2 payments – any money that a business expects to spend
3 net cash flow – the difference between receipts and payments; the net cash flow will give an indication of how much money is remaining at the end of each month.

> ### 🔑 KEY TERMS
>
> **Cash flow forecast** – a management accounting report that outlines predicted future cash inflows and cash outflows per month over a given period of time.
>
> **Cash flow statement** – a financial accounting statement that shows the actual cash inflows and outflows for a business over the previous 12 months.

Money should be recorded only when it is predicted that the cash will change hands. The closing balance from one month will become the opening balance of the next month. The cash flow forecast does not inform managers about profits or profitability. A profitable business can have a poor cash flow.

Accurate cash flow forecasting helps a business to:

- identify problems before they happen
- plan how to use excess cash
- plan a project with minimal borrowing
- support an application for finance.

The cash flow forecast should be compared with actual cash flows included in a **cash flow statement**. By comparing the two documents, owners and managers are able to identify any variances and put corrective actions in place.

Cash flow problems that have been identified can be resolved in a number of ways, including:

- holding less inventory within the business
- improving credit control – reducing the credit period allowed to customers, chasing non-paying customers and asking for longer credit periods from suppliers
- increasing sales levels
- selling non-current assets, e.g. old computers or business vehicles
- reducing costs.

GROUP ACTIVITY
(45 minutes)

Select a plc in the UK and download its financial accounts for the past two years from its website. In small groups, review the accounts, and identify their strengths and weaknesses. For any weaknesses, consider action(s) the business could take to improve.

KNOW IT 💡

1 Define the following terms:
   a fixed costs
   b variable costs
   c cash flow
   d net cash flow
   e profit
   f break even
   g margin of safety.
2 Name three variable costs.
3 Explain the difference between revenue, profit and cash flow.
4 State the formula for calculating break-even output.

LO5 Understand the relationship between businesses and stakeholders

GETTING STARTED
(10 minutes)

Think about the last product that you purchased and where you purchased it; it could be a drink, a piece of fruit, or another type of snack from a local shop or a large supermarket. Write a list of all the people or businesses that have an interest in that organisation. They are its stakeholders. Discuss your ideas with the rest of the class.

5.1 Who the main stakeholders are and their objectives

What is a stakeholder?

A **stakeholder** is an individual or group who has an interest in a business and may be directly affected by the activities of that business.

Every business has many different stakeholders with different objectives. For example, if a large bakery opened in a quiet residential area selling freshly made produce from 6 am seven days a week, the local residents may welcome the idea of having fresh bread every day, but be less pleased at the prospect of deliveries and employees arriving in the early morning. In this situation the stakeholders are the local community but also the employees, the suppliers, financial institutions and the customers.

Types of stakeholder

Stakeholders have varied interests and involvement in the business, and are either **internal** or **external** **stakeholders** (Table 1.6). This enables businesses to focus on the different needs and wants of the identified stakeholders. Internal stakeholders are identified as being involved directly within the business.

KEY TERMS

Stakeholder – any person, group or organisation that has an interest in a business because they are, or may be, affected by the activities of that business.

Internal stakeholder – an individual or group who are involved in a business directly by being or representing members of the workforce; this includes owners (sole trader, partners), employees (e.g. chief executive, directors, managers, supervisors, assistants) and trade unions.

External stakeholder – a person or group of people with links to the business, e.g. because of their personal location or that of the business they are connected with the organisation directly. They can be shareholders, customers, suppliers, potential investors, lenders, local community, pressure groups, and central and local government (e.g. HMRC, environmental health, planning department).

Table 1.6 Types of stakeholder

Stakeholder	Type	Example objectives	Why this stakeholder is important
Employee (staff and managers)	Internal	For business to succeed and remain profitable to retain salary and job security Be fairly paid and receive benefits Have a long and fulfilling career Get rewards and recognition for work, e.g. bonus, promotion Enjoy good working conditions	Business depends on employees to function
Owner/founder	Internal	For business to succeed and remain profitable Have skilled, loyal and hard-working staff to contribute to business's success Set aims and objectives to help business to grow Ensure the business remains competitive	They decide on the direction of the business
Customer	External	Be treated fairly Get good value for money, etc. Get quality products/services	Without consumers purchasing products or services, the business will not survive. If quality products or services are not gained, they may take their business elsewhere
Suppliers	External	Commitment to a fair contract Be paid within the agreed timescales	Supply products and services to the business on a regular basis
Financial businesses	External	Advise the business financially Fund or retain the financial aspects of the business	Provide financial and investment advice Provide finance when and if required
Local residents/communities	External	Purchase the products/services Respect the local community Inform the local community of any major changes that may impact on the local residents	Purchase the products/service Promote the business locally by supporting the business They can determine the success of the business

Stakeholder	Type	Example objectives	Why this stakeholder is important
Local and central government	External	Ensure business abides by the laws and regulations, e.g. HMRC, Environmental Health, planning departments Encourage and support economic development and growth	Support local businesses
Trade unions	External	Support employees to ensure working conditions, pay, etc., are fair Aid conflict resolution	A group to ensure that the business acts and treats employees fairly If conflicts arise, support workers
Shareholders	External	Support the business Investing funds in exchange for shares with the business paying out dividends to shareholders	Invest regular financial funds to the business Aid the business in moving forward according to its aims and objectives
Pressure groups	External	Monitor business activities and processes Influence alternative business decisions	Can improve and influence business operations and methods

▲ **Figure 1.9** Examples of internal and external stakeholders

GROUP ACTIVITY

(30 minutes)

Take part in a debate discussing the topic 'External stakeholders are more important to a business than internal stakeholders'. You can research and make notes in pairs or groups beforehand. After the debate, discuss the issues raised with the whole class.

Decide if you are for or against this. Join the group that shares your opinion and discuss your thoughts with other members before the debate takes place.

5.2 The ways in which different stakeholder groups attempt to alter business behaviour

Stakeholders can influence a business's decisions and processes.

INDEPENDENT RESEARCH ACTIVITY

(2 hours)

Research the controversial topic of HS2 (High Speed Two), the planned high-speed railway line linking London to the Midlands. Consider all the stakeholders who are involved in this potential new service. Research the stakeholders, write an article on your findings and conclude with your view on this new proposal. Focus on three main areas of impact: business, environmental and potential users.

5.3 How businesses respond to the different and sometimes conflicting objectives of different stakeholders

Each stakeholder will have different objectives. For example, they may:

- be concerned about the environmental impact of the organisation on the local countryside
- want the business to expand to improve its economic prospects
- want to make the organisation's manufacturing processes more cost efficient.

Conflicts can arise when the needs of some stakeholder groups clash with or compromise the expectations of other stakeholder groups. This means a business has to make choices that some stakeholders might not like. All viewpoints should be discussed and communicated in an appropriate way, considering the importance and impact that the issues that have been highlighted will have on the business.

Conflict resolution using amicable methods will avoid negative responses that could escalate into bad publicity. This could damage the reputation of a business, which could take months or years to rebuild, if indeed this is ever possible! Sometimes a third party could be a mediator. They must remain impartial and focus on the immediate issues. A mediator will need to:

- identify the facts
- review the evidence
- assess the impacts
- agree the issues to be resolved based upon the main stakeholder objectives.

 KEY TERM

Conflict resolution – the methods a business may implement to resolve any major issues that affect the way in which business is performed.

A mediator will also need to listen to both parties, understand the issues and, above all, facilitate the negotiation process towards some sort of resolution that both parties can agree.

See LO5.4 for more details on this.

Stakeholder analysis

A stakeholder analysis can identify the needs and wants of the stakeholders. This could help a business to focus on different elements of the stakeholder to understand them better, reducing any potential conflicts and resolutions. The key elements of a stakeholder analysis include:

- stakeholder name
- communications approach
- key interests and issues
- current status – advocate, supporter, neutral, critic, blocker
- desired support – high, medium, low
- desired project role
- actions desired
- messages needed
- actions and communications.

INDEPENDENT RESEARCH ACTIVITY

(1 hour)

Visit this website and read the article there: http://tinyurl.com/hezyr26

Consider the stakeholders at your school or college and perform a stakeholder analysis for the senior management team. Devise and complete a table using the above headings.

Meeting stakeholder needs could have both benefits and drawbacks for a company (Table 1.7).

Table 1.7 Benefits and drawbacks of meeting stakeholder needs

Benefits	Drawbacks
Gaining a better understanding of each stakeholder's individual objectives	Listening to all stakeholder groups can take time. Businesses may therefore have to select which groups they discuss issues with. It is important to understand the needs of all the different stakeholders, as certain aspects of business will not affect or directly affect all stakeholders
Communicating with stakeholders, listening to their thoughts and concerns, and involving them in decisions will build up trust, better understanding and appreciation of the decisions that will be made from both sides	
Understanding and appreciating which stakeholders could have the most influence on the business	If the advice is not implemented, stakeholders may become annoyed, which could distract from business activities
Stakeholders may have access to different resources, which could enable a business to benefit from these contacts	

5.4 The consequences to a business of not listening to its stakeholders

Stakeholders can influence and change the way a business operates in a competitive world. They can be a key element in decision making, but if a business gets things wrong, there may be consequences for its stakeholders.

Access to technology and the popularity of social media mean that any mistakes can be viewed worldwide in a very short time. This can have huge implications for both immediate and future business prospects, so it is important to be proactive rather than reactive to stakeholder needs and objectives. Any controversial decisions should be clearly justified, when and if required, to the various stakeholder groups.

KNOW IT

1 Who might be the external stakeholders of a car repair business?
2 What is the role of a mediator?
3 What are the key elements of a stakeholder analysis?
4 What are three consequences of a business not listening to its stakeholders?

LO6 Understand the external influences and constraints on businesses and how businesses could respond

GETTING STARTED

(10 minutes)

Think about your favourite shop. It could be online, a big chain or a small independent store. What do you think are the main factors beyond its control – the **external influences** – that impact on its success?

6.1 The factors which comprise the external business environment

Social factors

As a society, we are continually changing the way we work, the way we play, and our values and beliefs. In particular, we are going to investigate the following **social factors**.

KEY TERMS

External influences – factors outside of a business that are beyond the owner's control.

Social factors – things that affect our lifestyle, e.g. demographic issues, attitudes to work, disposable income, social trends, cultural beliefs.

Demographic issues

This refers to the study of a population based on age, race, gender, economic status, level of education, income level and employment, etc. In the UK the main demographic issue is the ageing population; this has implications for businesses in terms of choice of goods and services to provide, and how to reach their target market.

Here are some examples of how manufacturers tap into the ageing population.

- Fashion brand Sotto e Sopra uses materials that help women to feel comfortable during temperature changes that come with age.
- Harley-Davidson, the iconic motorcycle manufacturer, launched a three-wheeled motorcycle in Europe.
- In Europe, it was found that the main demographic group that eat out are the over-fifties. This influences not just what food to serve in restaurants, but also the design and font size of the menu itself.

Attitudes to work

The following paragraph shows the findings of recent research carried out by the government on people's attitude to work:

> Managers and professionals were more likely to agree that it was usual for people to work when they are feeling quite unwell (77 per cent) and also less likely to say that it was usual for people to call in sick when there was nothing the matter with them (24 per cent). For respondents in manual and routine roles the comparative responses were 67 per cent and 42 per cent, respectively.

Source: www.gov.uk

What are the implications for businesses looking to get the most from their employees? The result seems to suggest that perhaps making the work less routine may improve attendance.

Another finding suggests that, if businesses take an active role in helping people with long-term illnesses back to work by adapting the working environment, then they are likely to get a positive result.

Further results of the survey are presented in Figure 1.10.

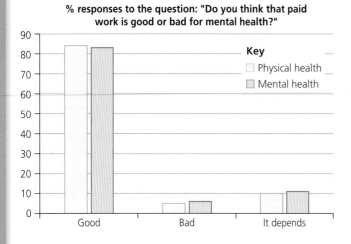

% responses to the question: "Do you think that paid work is good or bad for mental health?"

Key
☐ Physical health
▨ Mental health

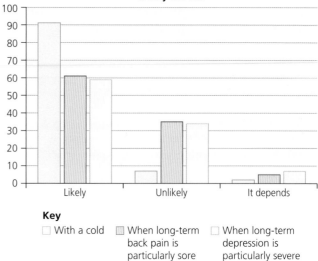

% responses to how likely respondents were to go to work if they were ill

Key
☐ With a cold   ▨ When long-term back pain is particularly sore   ☐ When long-term depression is particularly severe

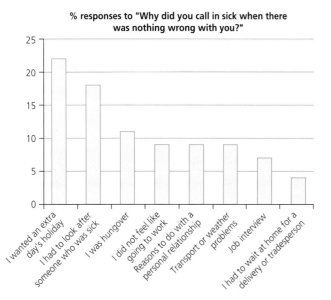

% responses to "Why did you call in sick when there was nothing wrong with you?"

▲ **Figure 1.10** The results of a government survey of attitudes into sickness and work

Source: www.gov.uk

The conclusions we can draw from these findings are that there is generally a positive attitude to work, with the majority interviewed considering it good for people's physical and mental health. The majority also would consider going to work if they were ill. The last diagram is perhaps the most important one for businesses as it suggests actions that employers could take to reduce absenteeism.

Disposable income

A person's disposable income is the total income earned less all the taxes that person pays. It is the amount of money people have available to spend on goods and services.

Knowing how much their customers have to spend helps businesses to decide:

● what type of product to stock or service to provide – if the disposal income of their customers is relatively high, high-end or branded goods can be stocked
● which pricing strategy to use – a fish and chip shop in an affluent area will be able to charge a much higher price than one in an area of high unemployment
● where to locate a shop – this depends on the product/ service being sold, whether it is high end or not; a business selling cheap plastic household goods would expect to be located where people have low disposable incomes.

Social trends

Social trends relate to the value system, beliefs and practices of a population as a whole. They show what our society is like and how it is changing in the long term. Businesses should identify social trends for long-term survival.

For example, Nintendo's Wii Fit was developed because we are more concerned about children spending too much time on their computers and not getting enough exercise. Other examples include the growth in sales of organic and 'free from' foods, as we are now more aware of the benefits of eating healthily. More businesses turn to social media to market their product/service as social media usage continues to increase.

Kodak, once a big name in image technology, went bankrupt because it failed to adapt to the changing trend in digital photography technology. This can also be seen as an example of technological change - often, more than one factor influences a company's success.

PAIRS ACTIVITY

(20 minutes)

Find out why and how farmers markets have become so successful, in terms of social trends. Share your findings with the rest of your class.

Cultural beliefs

To succeed, businesses must have a thorough understanding of the cultural beliefs of their target market. This is especially important when a business invests overseas. Extensive research on language, values and cultural practices must be carried out before decisions are made on product/service, as well as on how the product/service chosen is marketed. For example:

- Dunkin' Donuts had to apologise and redesign its 'charcoal' doughnuts campaign completely when it was deemed to be racist
- eBay lost out to Taobao, a local competitor in China, because it failed to understand that sellers and buyers there want the chance to establish personal contact via instant messaging before a deal is struck.

GROUP ACTIVITY

(20 minutes)

Investigate the secret of Starbucks' success in China using this link: http://tinyurl.com/z33r87j

You can present your findings in a poster or as a PowerPoint presentation.

Technological factors

We live in an era where technology is advancing at lightning speed. Compared with just 20 years ago, we learn differently, we play differently, we shop differently, we work differently and, most of all, we communicate differently. Businesses need to take into account these changes – **technological factors** – and adapt the way they operate in order to succeed.

> ### KEY TERM
>
> **Technological factors** – these include machines used to automate the production process in a factory, hardware and software used for communication, purchasing and sales, and mobile technology.

Automation

This can be easily seen in factories where machines are used for repetitive tasks. The advantages are significant as machines are more accurate, reducing waste and thus minimising costs. Machines are also faster and can be set to work 24/7 to meet demand. In the developed world it is much cheaper to use machines than employ workers. Apart from the initial investments, running costs are much lower, enabling businesses to compete on a global scale. However, the main disadvantage besides the high initial costs is the human cost of fewer jobs and redundancies when a factory introduces automation.

Communication

Good communication is vital to the smooth running of a business, especially if it is a large multinational with headquarters, branches and employees across the world. Businesses need to have good communication networks not just within and among employees – it is also important to have effective communication with suppliers, contractors and customers.

For example, Jaguar Land Rover transformed its IT from a UK-based operation to a globally scaled facility, providing secure IT resources to its engineers worldwide. Its new communication system means engineers all over the world can work collaboratively.

Purchasing/sales

Many businesses have an inventory control system that triggers a need to re-order stock. This is translated into orders, which are transmitted to suppliers automatically. This system ensures a continual supply of stock to meet demand. Businesses also need to be aware of how technology has changed the way consumers purchase goods and services, and adjust how they market and distribute their products accordingly.

According to the Consumer Barometer Tool, 60 per cent of consumers in the UK and USA carry out research on the internet before making their purchasing decisions. The implication of this for businesses is clear, as it has become essential not only for businesses to have a web presence but that their websites are browsed before those of their competitors.

> ### ? THINK ABOUT IT
>
> Consider the findings from a recent survey:
>
> - 59 per cent of respondents say they would consider allowing retailers to know where they are in-store in exchange for promotional offers
> - 73 per cent use promotional offers they receive via email
> - 42 per cent use promotional offers they receive via social media
> - 62 per cent say their desktop computer is the device they use most often to redeem digital promotions, 27 per cent their phone and 10 per cent their tablet.
>
> Imagine you are a retailer selling branded trainers, how would you advertise your products given the findings above?

Mobile

There has been a surge in mobile service providers. Banks now provide mobile contactless payment systems, where consumers can pay for goods and services by merely tapping their mobile phones onto a reading device. Will this new technology end debit and credit cards? Businesses must consider the growing popularity of this new technology and change the way they accept payments.

Besides using their mobile phones to make purchases, consumers are also increasingly using them to carry out research before making a decision. A 2015 survey by Blackhawk Engagement Solutions suggested that 38 per cent of customers go to Amazon first when comparing prices on their smartphone, 32 per cent use Google and 17 per cent other retail websites. This has serious implications for businesses, especially e-commerce businesses.

Economic factors

Economic factors affect consumer spending, which in turn has an impact on demand for goods and services.

If economic factors are favourable, businesses can look forward to high levels of revenue and profit. At the same time, businesses need to be prepared for times when economic factors are unfavourable so the ability to forecast economic trends is vital in long-term decision making.

> ### 🔑 KEY TERM
>
> **Economic factors** – changes in the economy that affect the price and cost of goods and services – the level of interest rates, exchange rates, unemployment rate and taxation.

Interest rate

This is the cost of borrowing money from financial institutions such as banks. It is also the return or reward on savings. The rate of interest is set by the Bank of England based on the level of economic activities in the UK. Businesses want interest rates to be as low as possible so they pay less in interest repayments on the loans they borrow, thus keeping running costs down and increasing profits. However, individuals or businesses with money invested in savings benefit from higher interest rates because they get more of a return on their money.

The level of impact depends on how highly geared (this is the amount of debt) a business is, and whether the business is selling high-end or low-end goods/service.

INDIVIDUAL ACTIVITY

(15 minutes)

Describe and explain the impact of high interest rates on the following businesses:

- estate agent
- travel agent
- budget retailer.

Exchange rates

This is the value of one currency as compared with another. The impact of changes in exchange rates depends on the type of business activity undertaken. For a UK manufacturer hoping to export its goods overseas, a weak pound is favourable as it means that its goods are cheaper on the global market and therefore more competitive. For a business that imports goods from abroad a strong pound is favourable as it means they are able to buy more goods with the same amount of money.

In 2011, even though McDonald's sales in Europe increased, its yearly profits were actually down as a result of a weakening euro. This is because when the amount of profit was converted to US dollars it was worth less than it had been.

Inflation

This is the rate of increase in the price of goods and services. The rate of inflation is calculated by looking at how the prices of hundreds of things we usually buy, including food and entertainment, have changed over time.

When inflation increases this is generally unfavourable for businesses and consumers. Businesses will find that the costs of providing their goods and services such as gas and electricity will rise, reducing their profits. Consumers, having to pay a higher price for everyday goods and services, will have less money to spend on anything else. This in turn reduces demand and is bad news for most businesses.

Unemployment

This is the situation of people who do not have a job but are able to work. The rate of unemployment affects businesses in two ways. When unemployment is high people generally have less money to spend. This will decrease demand and sales revenue. However, businesses will also have more people to choose from when recruiting. This means that they have a wider pool of labour supply to choose from and, at the same time, wage levels will tend to be lower than when unemployment is low.

Long-term unemployment can have serious effects on businesses. If the unemployment rate is high over a prolonged period of time, businesses will start making their workers redundant due to lower sales and profit. This will increase the unemployment rate, which will lower sales and profit further.

Taxation

This is the amount of money paid to the government on earnings (income tax, national insurance, corporation tax) or goods and services purchased (VAT, import duties). An increase in income tax and national insurance will mean that people generally have less money to spend on goods and services. This is bad news for businesses as they will see a fall in demand and sales, especially if they are selling non-essentials. An increase in corporation tax means that businesses will have less **retained profit** to invest in the future, which is again an unfavourable condition for them.

Environmental factors

Environmental factors are all the issues that businesses need to consider to reduce the impact of their business activities on the environment. These issues are becoming more important as we become aware of the damage we have done to our planet. The UK government has imposed legal constraints that require businesses to cut down on energy consumption, reduce waste and dispose of waste responsibly. Businesses also face pressure from consumers and pressure groups to strive for sustainability.

Energy management

This basically means saving energy in the workplace. Businesses need to save energy not just to meet legal requirements but because effective energy usage leads to lower costs, especially when energy prices are high. So how can businesses save energy?

PAIRS ACTIVITY

(20 minutes)

Suggest ten ways in which a business can save energy in the workplace.

Share your ideas with the rest of your class.

Carbon emissions

This refers to the amount of carbon dioxide that is released into the atmosphere as a result of business activities. This greenhouse gas causes global warming. The most effective way of reducing carbon emissions is to cut down on the use of fossil fuel. The UK government has introduced environmental taxes, reliefs and schemes to encourage businesses to reduce their carbon footprint.

Waste reduction

A business can reduce waste by getting things right first time (quality control). Waste reduction can take place in the office environment, such as by using less paper or printing on both sides. Manufacturers could find ways of reducing packaging materials.

The benefits to a business of reducing waste are not just cutting costs – it can also potentially improve the reputation of the business as one that cares about the environment.

Recycling

This is the process of converting waste into useful materials. For a business, there are many advantages to recycling. It can reduce the cost of handling waste, reduce spending on buying materials and even decrease landfill tax imposed by the government. Businesses should recycle as much as possible to increase profitability and improve their reputation in the eyes of their customers.

Pollution

This can take the form of air, land, water and noise pollution, depending on the nature of the business activity. While cost saving is one of the main reasons for reducing pollution, businesses can benefit from a better reputation as well as reducing the risk of paying compensation as a result of pollution.

 INDEPENDENT RESEARCH ACTIVITY

(15 minutes)

Read about how Somerset cheese producer Wyke Farms has become the first national Cheddar brand to be 100 per cent self-sufficient in solar and biogas energy. You can find out more from the link below or by searching on the internet.

http://tinyurl.com/hojkkvz

Political factors

Political factors are government policies and practices that affect a business.

Political instability

This refers to the chances of the collapse of a government. Businesses prefer to operate in a politically stable country as instability could lead to riots, demonstrations, strikes or a coup d'état. Political instability can cause economic downturns, affecting business revenue and profits.

Many businesses' suppliers are located in countries where there is political instability. This is risky as if riots or violence break out in these areas there could potentially be a disruption to the supply chain, halting business operations. This could lead to businesses

not meeting demand, and losing revenue and profit. To minimise the risk of this eventuality, businesses must have contingency plans in place to reduce the damage of any potential crisis.

Change of government

Businesses tend to be concerned about a change of government – for example, before a general election. With a new government come new policies and new practices, which might not favour certain businesses. New policies mean changes and changes can be costly, reducing profits for businesses.

Another example of the possible impact of a change in government is when Royal Bank of Scotland and Lloyds Banking Group threatened to move out of Scotland if it became independent.

Government initiatives

These can be legislation, actions or projects introduced by the government to benefit the population. A recent example of a government initiative is the 2015 Enterprise Bill, which included:

- new measures to speed up insurance payments to business and give further powers to government for broadband investment
- the introduction of a Small Business Commissioner to help small businesses resolve late payment disputes with larger firms
- using regulators to contribute to cutting £10 billion of administration costs.

PAIRS ACTIVITY ·······························

(20 minutes)

Read the following article about the New Enterprise Bill: http://tinyurl.com/punvkeq

Identify and explain:

1 who the winners are and how they benefit
2 which businesses will lose out, and in what way.

···

Legal factors

Legal factors are laws that affect how businesses are run.

 **KEY TERM**

Legal factors – anything to do with the law.

Business framework

Business framework legislation shows how a business is structured and organised, including how it is run. Here are two examples.

1 Companies Act – elements relevant to private companies include reducing the amount of administration – for example, by making annual accounts available to shareholders electronically. Companies must state their name, place of registration, registered office and registered company number on their website, order forms and emails. Smaller companies benefit from not having to appoint a company secretary and not having to hold an AGM.

2 Partnership Act 1890 – a business partnership can be formed through working together, oral agreement or a written contract. The minimum number of partners is two and there is no maximum. Each partner is allowed to participate in management and get an equal share of profit. In England partners are jointly liable for the debts and obligations of the firm. The partnership is dissolved if one partner dies. The Partnership Act can have a huge impact on anyone wishing to run a business with other people.

Consumer protection

This involves ensuring the rights of consumers are upheld. Laws aim to make sure that goods supplied by businesses are safe to use, are of reasonable quality, and that consumers are not misled by the description of goods and services before making a purchase.

● The Sale and Supply of Goods Act and the Supply of Goods and Services Act were replaced by the *Consumer Rights Act* in October 2015. This act covers what should happen when goods are faulty, there are unfair terms in a contract and what should happen when a business acts in a way that isn't competitive. As before, businesses must not give misleading prices. A business may have committed a criminal offence if it gives false or misleading information about a price for goods or services or if the price is not displayed but is key to making a decision to buy. The act gives consumers a clear right to the repair or replacement of faulty digital content, such as online films and games, music downloads and ebooks. If a service is not provided with reasonable care and skill, or as agreed, the business that provided it must make sure the service meets what was agreed with the customer or give some money back.

● *Consumer Protection Act* – the law states that:
  • businesses must not manufacture and supply unsafe goods
  • the manufacturer or seller of a defective product is responsible for the damage it causes
  • local councils have the right to seize unsafe goods and temporarily stop the sale of goods that might be unsafe.

❓ THINK ABOUT IT

Case study: Volkswagen

In 2015, the German car manufacturer Volkswagen (VW) admitted cheating emissions tests in the US. Some cars had devices in diesel engines that could detect when they were being tested, changing the performance accordingly to improve results.

When this was discovered, group chief executive Martin Winterkorn resigned and said his company had 'broken the trust of our customers and the public', and recalled 500,000 cars in the US alone.

VW can be fined up to $37,500 for each vehicle that breaches standards, so it may have to pay $18 billion in fines, as well as being sued by consumers and shareholders.

It is unclear whether managers wilfully misled others internally or outside the company. More managers could resign.

Although diesel vehicles were thought to be better for the environment, the latest scientific evidence suggests that is not the case and diesel car sales have already fallen.

Although the American diesel car market is proportionally tiny, there may be a big impact in Europe if customers switch to petrol cars in large numbers.

1 What issues emerged when VW launched a huge marketing campaign trumpeting its cars' low emissions?
2 Summarise the consequences to VW of this scandal.
3 Analyse the effects of the scandal on stakeholder groups of VW, to include customers, shareholders, employees and suppliers.

Employee protection

The UK government has passed laws aimed at protecting people at work. These ensure that employees are treated equally, the working environment is safe, employees are not forced to work beyond 48 hours a week and that they are paid a minimum wage. Here are some examples.

- *Equality Act*: this encompasses equal pay, sex discrimination, disability discrimination, age equality, race relations, religion or beliefs, and sexual orientation. There are implications for employers during recruitment, training, development and transfer, during dismissal, as well as the day-to-day management of employees. Employers risk financial penalties and damage to their reputation, as well as worsening employer–employee relationships.
- *Health and Safety at Work Act*: this ensures that the workplace is safe and healthy for employees, customers, visitors and the general public. It sets out the duties that employers have towards their employees, as well as the general duties of employees while at work. For example, employers must start with a risk assessment of the workplace to identify potential hazards. Protective clothing must be provided if necessary and hazardous materials must be stored properly. Employees are expected to take reasonable care at work.
- *Working Time Directive*: according to this law no one is allowed to work for more than 48 hours a week, but you can opt out if you want to work more hours. For under-18s, working more than 40 hours a week is not allowed. The law protects employees from stress and illness as a result of too much work. The law also specifies that employees are entitled to an uninterrupted 20-minute break if the daily working hours are more than six. In addition, almost all workers are legally entitled to 5.6 weeks' paid holidays every year.
- *National Minimum Wage Act*: the main purpose of this law is to ensure that employees are not exploited by earning low pay. It is against the law for an employer to pay its employees below the minimum wage level. The rate of minimum pay depends on an employee's age.

Data Protection Act

This is designed to protect personal data kept by organisations for different purposes. It states that the data should be:

- used fairly and lawfully
- used for limited, specifically stated purposes
- used in a way that is adequate, relevant and not excessive
- accurate
- kept for no longer than is absolutely necessary
- handled according to people's data protection rights
- kept safe and secure
- not transferred outside the European Economic Area without adequate protection.

Everyone has the right to find out what data organisations hold about them. Every organisation processing personal information has to register with the Information Commissioner's Office (ICO), unless they are exempt. Businesses should have a policy on what data is kept, how it is stored and a procedure should be put in place to ensure that it is updated regularly. Good information handling improves a business's reputation, while non-compliance may lead to criminal charges and huge fines.

Copyright, Designs and Patent Act

This deals with the legal rights granted to the designer and creator of a piece of original work. Only the person owning the copyright will be able to use and distribute it in any way. This protects the interests of the creator, who has invested time, effort and money in creating an original piece of work. Copyright law applies to music, books, videos, software or artistic work. An infringement of the law may lead to prosecution and fines.

The most obvious implication of this law for businesses would be when photocopying or scanning into a computer, a common day-to-day activity in many offices. Businesses need to make sure they have licences for software before it is installed on their intranet.

Planning permission

Businesses need to apply to their local council before making alterations to their premises. Alterations could include change of use (e.g. from shop to office), extensions, changes to shop fronts, erecting signs, and installing new external security shutters or grilles.

Making alterations without prior permission could lead to an enforcement notice being issued by the council requiring things to be put back to how they were.

Ethical factors

Ethical factors are moral issues that businesses should take into account when carrying out their business activities. It has become more and more important for businesses to do beyond what the law requires to build on their reputation and meet stakeholder expectations. Some of the ways in which a business can act ethically have been covered earlier.

> **KEY TERM**
>
> **Ethical factors** – moral issues, doing what is right.

Ethical employers do not exploit their workforce, do not use child labour, pay above minimum wage or, even better, a living wage, and have fair working practices such as making sure employees have a good work–life balance or offering flexible working arrangements for employees with a young family.

6.1 The factors which comprise the external business environment

and welfare schemes actually improves attendance and productivity, leading to higher profit levels. Offering sport or educational sponsorships to people in the local community helps to improve customer relations and enhances a business's reputation. Supporting cultural events locally shows that a business cares about its stakeholders, not just about its bottom line.

> ## ? THINK ABOUT IT
>
> ### Case study: People Tree
>
> OUR MISSION
>
> People Tree is a pioneer in Fair Trade and sustainable fashion.
>
> People Tree aims to be 100 per cent Fair Trade throughout our supply chain. People Tree purchases Fair Trade products from marginalised producer groups in the developing world. We guarantee the majority of all our purchasing is Fair Trade and is committed to the World Fair Trade Organization Fair Trade standards.
>
> WE ACHIEVE THIS THROUGH THE FOLLOWING:
>
> - TO SUPPORT producer partners' efforts towards economic independence and control over their environment and to challenge the power structures that undermine their rights to a livelihood.
> - TO PROTECT the environment and use natural resources sustainably throughout our trading and to promote environmentally responsible initiatives to create new models to promote sustainability.
> - TO SUPPLY customers with good quality products, with friendly and efficient service, and build awareness to empower customers and producers to participate in Fair Trade and environmentally sustainable solutions.
> - TO PROVIDE a supportive environment to all stakeholders and promote dialogue and understanding between them.
> - TO SET AN EXAMPLE to business and the government of a Fair Trade model of business based on partnership, people-centred values and sustainability.
>
> *Source: www.peopletree.co.uk/about-us/mission*

> ## ? THINK ABOUT IT
>
> ### Case study: BT
>
> Telecommunications giant British Telecom (BT) is considered a beacon for implementing many positive changes in its workplace mental health policy and practice. BT has developed a three-tiered mental health framework, as follows.
>
> 1 Level one: promoting employee well-being and preventing distress, including tips on the company intranet and management training.
> 2 Level two: identifying distress and intervening early through online stress risk assessment and companion training for line managers.
> 3 Level three: support and treatment for people experiencing mental health problems, including producing 'advance directives' to identify early warning signs and establish a plan of action for how someone can be supported if becoming distressed.
>
> BT's approach has seen stress and anxiety sick leave fall significantly, by 24 per cent in one area. BT has also launched a cognitive behavioural therapy (CBT) service for staff that has been used by around 200 people, with a very high satisfaction rate.
>
> *Case study from Time to Change: www.time-to-change.org.uk*

> ## ? THINK ABOUT IT
>
> ### Case study: BSkyB
>
> Read about entertainment and media company BskyB's activities to reduce its staff's car use: http://tinyurl.com/jdubu68
>
> Having read about BSkyB's green campaign, answer the following questions.
>
> 1 Identify and explain how the following stakeholder groups of BSkyB benefit:
>   a employees
>   b managers
>   c shareholders
>   d local community.
> 2 Evaluate the advantages and disadvantages to BskyB of implementing the scheme.

Another ethical behaviour is being environmentally friendly in all aspects of business operation; this has been covered in earlier sections such as waste management, recycling, carbon emissions, transport miles and energy use (see above).

Many businesses organise corporate social responsibility (CSR) activities, e.g. charitable donations and humanitarian aid. Within the organisation, many businesses have found offering their employees health

Consequences for a business and its stakeholders of not operating ethically

Here are some consequences of businesses being seen not to operate ethically.

● Loss of customers and sales: as more consumers are critical about what they buy and from whom they buy things, any unethical behaviour will cause them to shop elsewhere. This leads to a decrease in sales revenue and market share. The impact is more severe if competitors adopt ethical practices.

● Damage to reputation: if a business is discovered to operate unethically and this is publicised, as seen in recent cases, the damage to reputation is more long term and can affect the continued success of a business. Not only does it affect a business's ability to attract new customers and keep existing ones, it will be difficult and costly to regain the trust that customers once had.

● Damage to employee motivation and productivity, especially if it directly affects the working environment or arrangement: unproductive employees mean higher costs and lower efficiency, affecting a business's ability to compete. Demotivated employees lead to absenteeism and high staff turnover, pushing up costs and decreasing profits.

Competitor factors

A competitor analysis could include research into issues such as the strength of the competition, market share of a business, competitor behaviour and position in market. The purpose is to find out the impact of competition and how a business can respond to the actions of its competitors.

One way of finding the strength of a business's competitors is to draw up a grid, like the one in Table 1.8, in this case using the example of product features for mobile phones.

Table 1.8 Comparing competitors' products

Competitors	A	B	C	D
Features:				
Operating system				
Size				
4G				
Front and back cameras				
Benefits:				
Ease of use				
Price				
Quality				
Guarantee				

Information from the grid will provide an insight into each competitor's strengths and weaknesses, which could be used to inform marketing decisions regarding the marketing mix.

Market share is the proportion of the total market that a business sells to. This information is useful for judging the popularity of a business in the market it operates. Market share over a period of time provides vital information on a business's performance as compared with its competitors. For example, Tesco's market share decreased significantly between 2009 and 2014, in favour of discount supermarkets. The management must investigate why market share has decreased by such a huge amount, and appropriate strategies be put in place to regain its market position.

Some typical types of competitor behaviour are described next.

Conflict

This is when the major players are very aggressive in their strategies in the face of competition. There will be price wars, extensive promotional campaigns and continual innovations, as in the electronics industry. The main interest of the dominant businesses in the market is to get rid of competition in order to increase their own market share and achieve economies of scale. The casualty of intense competition is usually the smaller businesses that are unable to compete on price. However, consumers benefit from the lower prices.

Competition

The main purpose is to outperform competitors rather than get rid of them. Strategies are less aggressive and price wars avoided as they do not benefit the industry in the long term.

Co-existence

Businesses avoid going into competition with one another. This might be because a business has difficulty defining its own market, or does not realise that there are other competitors operating in the same market. This could also be a result of having different geographical areas or slightly differentiated products.

Co-operation

This is where a few businesses in the same market come together to pool skills and resources so that economies of scale can be achieved. There is a growing trend towards joint ventures, sharing of research and development contracts so that competitive advantage is achieved in the global market. This benefits businesses as, together, they are able to become stronger and more efficient. There will be a positive impact on job opportunities and job security. Consumers also benefit from this co-operation as the cost savings from achieving economies of scale can be passed on as lower prices to them.

Collusion

Businesses work together to agree on prices so that consumers cannot shop around. This usually happens in a market where there are a small number of suppliers who collude on prices to improve profitability. While this means businesses can earn high profits, the impact on consumers is undesirable as they are likely to face limited choice and higher prices. It is also illegal in most circumstances.

6.2 Identify how the external environment can impact on a business and its stakeholders

Throughout this learning outcome, we have seen both the positive and negative impacts that changes in external environment can have on businesses and their stakeholders. There is more detail about how businesses can plan for these impacts by, for example, carrying out a SWOT analysis, in LO8 (page 43).

6.3 How businesses can respond to changes in their external environment

We have also investigated the different ways in which businesses can respond to these changes. More often than not, businesses that respond and adapt to their external environment are more successful than businesses that do not, especially where technological factors are involved.

> **KNOW IT**
> 1 Understand the factors that make up the external business environment.
> 2 Be able to identify how the external environment can impact on a business and its stakeholders.
> 3 Know how businesses can respond to changes in their external environment.

LO7 Understand why businesses plan

> **GETTING STARTED**
> **(10 minutes)**
> In pairs, discuss something that you planned recently – for example, a party, holiday or night out. Why did you plan? What might have happened if you hadn't planned?

7.1 Why do businesses plan?

There are many reasons why businesses need to plan, at all stages of their existence. Here are some examples:

- to survive and avoid business failure
- to develop business ideas
- to avoid unnecessary risk
- to meet key objectives.

▲ **Figure 1.11** Can you think of any other reasons why businesses plan?

On a more detailed level, planning could involve:

- setting objectives for managers
- explaining business objectives to management and employees
- sharing a business strategy, priorities and specific action points with other people
- deciding whether to buy/rent extra space
- ascertaining personnel requirements

- developing new business alliances
- supporting an application for finance for business growth.

Planning reduces the chances of failing. Businesses can fail due to:

- flawed business plans
- poor financial control
- lack of knowledge of the market and competition
- concentration risk (for example, by relying on a single customer to provide the majority of their income)
- lack of a clear and unique selling point.

All entrepreneurs are classed as 'risk takers'. However, they are prepared to take only a certain level of risk. Business planning will allow individuals to consider their own attitude to risk and uncertainty. Some people are known to be risk averse and unwilling to take any risk.

7.2 Determining appropriate sources of finance for businesses

All businesses require finance and funding to exist as a business organisation, in order to:

- start up as a business organisation, to pay for premises, equipment, machinery and advertising

- operate on a day-to-day basis, and have sufficient cash to pay wages and suppliers
- expand and grow the business.

New businesses can find it difficult to raise finance as they are deemed to be high risk to lenders as they have few customers and many competitors. If the business fails, the lender will be unable to regain their finances.

A range of sources of finance are available to businesses. These are often categorised as short term (must be paid back within a year) or long term (paid back over many years). Businesses can choose:

- *internal* sources of finance – funds found inside the business, e.g. retained profit
- *external* sources of finance – funds from outside the business, e.g. bank loans.

The source of finance chosen by a business will depend on a number of factors, such as the purpose or use of the finance, the length of time for which the finance is required, the amount of money the business requires, and the ownership and size of the business.

There is a range of different sources of finance for a business to choose from (see Table 1.9), each with its advantages and disadvantages.

Table 1.9 The advantages and disadvantages of different sources of finance

Source of finance	Definition	Advantages	Disadvantages
Savings	An owner of the business may provide their own money as part of the start-up capital when a business is being set up Savings can also be used as a form of additional capital, e.g. for expansion Savings are normally a long-term source of finance	Savings contributed by the owner do not have to be repaid. No interest is payable to the owner(s)	There is a limit to the amount of money an owner can afford to invest
Retained profit and reserves	Reserves are generated when profits are ploughed back into the business They are available for a business that has been trading for more than one year, and are generally a medium- or long-term source of finance	Reserves do not have to be repaid No interest is payable	New businesses will not have built up reserves yet Businesses may not have made sufficient profit to reinvest in the business
Overdraft	This is where a business is allowed to overdraw a current bank account, i.e. withdraw money even if it does not have enough money in the account, up to the overdraft limit It is a short-term source of finance	It can be used for day-to-day running costs, and to cover the period between money going out of and coming into a business On a short-term basis, it is usually cheaper than a bank loan	Interest is payable on the amount overdrawn It can be expensive if used over a long period of time

Source of finance	Definition	Advantages	Disadvantages
Loan	A loan is an amount of money borrowed at an agreed rate of interest for a set period of time Depending on the use and amount of the loan, a lender may ask for security (e.g. a house) in case the loan is not repaid A loan is usually a medium- or long-term source of finance	Payments are spread over a long period of time, which is good for budgeting	A loan can be expensive due to interest payments making the repayment much more than the initial amount Banks may require security on the loan
Mortgage	A mortgage is a long-term loan secured on a property; it is repaid in instalments over a period of time, typically 25 years On payment of the final instalment, the business will own the property	Throughout the mortgage period the business will have the use of the property Payments are spread over a long period of time, which is good for budgeting	This is an expensive method of financing compared to buying with cash If the business fails to keep up the repayments the property will be repossessed
Credit card	A plastic card issued by banks, building societies or other providers to purchase goods or services on credit	It is a convenient source of finance for smaller purchases Credit cards provide consumer protection (if there is a problem, the money may be claimed back) If repaid within the payment period, a credit card allows free borrowing	Interest charges are high if not repaid within the interest-free period Consumers and businesses need to avoid entering a debt spiral – getting into more and more debt that can never be paid off
Hire purchase	Hire purchase allows businesses to obtain assets without the need to pay a large sum of money up front The business pays an initial deposit to acquire the item and makes regular payments for a set period of time Unlike leasing, after all of the repayments have been made the business owns the assets	Businesses can use up-to-date equipment immediately that it might not otherwise be able to afford Payments are spread over a period of time, which is an effective way of budgeting Once the final repayment has been made the business will own the asset	Due to the extra charges and interest, hire purchase is more expensive than paying cash in full
Trade credit	Trade credit is a short-term source of finance; it is often referred to as 'buy now, pay later' Typical trade credit periods are 30, 60 or 90 days	Businesses are able to buy the goods and pay for them later Trade credit aids cash flow No interest is charged if money is paid within the agreed timescale	Discounts offered for early payment will be lost if it is not paid back on time
Venture capital	A venture capitalist is a person who invests in a project in which there is a substantial element of risk; they usually fund new or expanding businesses	In addition to financial backing, venture capitalists often offer considerable business advice, as the venture capitalist usually has considerable business expertise Additional resources are often offered in relation to legal, tax and personnel matters Venture capitalists usually have business connections that will assist with business growth	Loss of control for the business owner, as the venture capitalist typically wants to shape the business's decisions Depending on the venture capitalist's share and stake in the business, the owner could lose management control

Source of finance	Definition	Advantages	Disadvantages
Share issue	Share issues are available only for limited companies and are a long-term source of finance A share issue involves issuing further shares to family, friends or the public	The funds received from a share issue do not have to be repaid No interest is payable	Profits leave the company because they will be paid out as dividends to all shareholders There is a possibility that ownership of the company could change hands because a new shareholder buys more than 50% of the shares
Crowdfunding	This is the practice of funding a project by raising many small amounts of money from a large number of people, often via the internet; it is most widely used by musicians, artists and film-makers	Crowdfunding provides an alternative to funding from conventional means Ability to raise finance relatively quickly, usually without upfront fees Crowdfunding can raise awareness of a new business	Crowdfunding is mostly unregulated Money raised will usually be returned to investors if the funding target is not met Individual ideas could be copied if they are not protected with a patent or copyright Crowdfunding puts an obligation on a business to provide the 'free' products and services funders are promised, e.g. a local vintage B&B raised £50,000 for an extension but now has to provide 'free' overnight stays and afternoon tea for hundreds of people

? THINK ABOUT IT

Case study: Jazzy Jumpers Ltd

- Jazzy Jumpers Ltd sells unique and customised jumpers for children aged 3–12 in three retail outlets across the north-west of England
- The company was founded in 2012 by Amina and Philip, who at the time agreed to each own 50 per cent of the shares.
- Jazzy Jumpers Ltd has decided that the time is right to expand. Amina and Philip have set the objective of doubling their turnover in the next three years, while improving day-to-day cash flow.
- To meet the objective, they need to purchase a £50,000 printing machine that will enable them to double their current output, print multiple designs at the same time and print more sophisticated designs.
- The printer will allow Jazzy Jumpers to launch a premium range of jumpers, which can be sold at a high price.
- Although profitability has been increasing, Philip is worried about their cash flow position as the company has already had to extend its overdraft with the bank twice.
- Over the past 12 months, more competitors have entered the market, so Amina and Philip need to

raise the finance for the new machine as soon as possible in order to protect their market share.

Amina and Philip have researched possible financing options. These are:

- loan – five-year term with 5 per cent interest per annum
- venture capital – an individual is prepared to lend the money required in return for 3 per cent of the shares in the company
- hire purchase – £500 per month for five years with a deposit of £20,000.

Jazzy Jumpers would like you to act as their financial adviser and recommend the best course of action for their company.

The company's current financial performance is documented in Table 1.10.

Table 1.10 Jazzy Jumpers: selected financial data for 2015–2016

Net profit	Outstanding debtors	Bank balance	Share capital
£100,000	£200,000	(£100,000)	£50,000

7.3 What may be included in a business plan

A business plan is a formal document produced by a business that sets out how it will succeed. The plan indicates how much money the business will need and where this money is going to come from.

By producing a comprehensive business plan, an entrepreneur is likely to reduce the risks involved in setting up a business. The plan should also be used to persuade a bank or finance provider to lend money, and any other shareholders and partners will use the plan to decide if they wish to invest.

Contents of a business plan

A business plan will normally contain the following elements.

Executive summary
- What is the business?
- What is the business potential?
- What is the market?
- Funding requirements
- Prospects for attracting investors/lenders
- Predicted profit data
- Priority of business objectives

General business description
- Brief description of the business idea
- Previous history, if relevant
- Information about the owner's qualifications, experience and financial status
- Business location

Products and services
- Identification of the product or service
- Unique selling point
- How the product/service is to be protected, e.g. patent or copyright

Financial plan
- Break-even calculation
- Cash flow forecast
- Forecast income statement
- Forecast statement of financial position
- Plans for growth and development

- Contingency plans
- Possible sources of finance to approach

Resource requirements
- Location
- Finance
- Number of employees
- Premises requirements
- Fixtures and fittings
- Equipment

Marketing
- Size and predicted growth of the market
- Results of market research
- Analysis of market segments
- Identification of target segments
- Competitor analysis
- Potential customers
- Distribution channels

Operational plan
- Physical location
- Production process
- Facilities
- Equipment
- Quality control measures
- Material requirements

Management and organisation
- Organisational structure
- Senior management details
- Staffing requirements
- Key personnel
- Recruitment and selection
- Training
- Labour relations

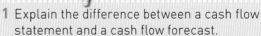

KNOW IT

1 Explain the difference between a cash flow statement and a cash flow forecast.
2 Explain why it is important for businesses to plan.
3 Identify and explain three sources of finance suitable for a sole trader.
4 List the resource and financial requirements for a business plan.

LO8 Be able to assess the performance of businesses to inform future business activities

Factors affecting the success or failure of a business

A business should regularly analyse how it is performing, not just in a financial sense but in all areas. This will ensure that the business:

- is still relevant in the marketplace
- maintains a real competitiveness within the market
- can identify if there are any potential trading issues
- strives towards future plans within the overall business aims and strategic business objectives that have been set.

The factors affecting the performance of business can be split into two main different categories – financial and non-financial – with short- and long-term elements being present in both categories.

Financial factors

Businesses consider the results of their performance in the market by focusing on their profit, the turnover and the amount of capital employed within the business. This gives businesses an overall understanding of their current position, but it does not guarantee that they will continue to succeed in the long term.

All businesses are susceptible to failure. Businesses will not only focus on their profit and turnover but also their investments and plans for the future in terms of expansion, breaking into new markets and **diversification**.

All the factors for the future will be determined by their financial situation. For some businesses, future planning will not be possible if they are failing in their current market. The business must ask itself the following questions.

- What is the current profit and turnover?
- Which areas are currently failing?
- Are the business's pricing strategies suitable for our current target markets?
- What is the business's current debt position?
- Which areas could be scaled down in terms of cost-saving measures?

If a business is failing, managers and owners must take a realistic approach to their position to try to save it. By answering such questions and forming a plan, it is to be hoped that, with a team-based approach, the business could continue in some capacity.

Governments may encourage businesses to continue and may offer them support. Governments can, however, put up tax rates and introduce new laws with a financial impact – for example, the introduction of the minimum wage in 1999. This was good for employees as they had to be paid a minimum amount, but small businesses had to adjust to the new law, often by putting this newly incurred cost onto the products/services they sold to customers, which could reduce sales. Some businesses could not continue.

Non-financial factors

If a business does not understand its market – including the most important aspect, its customers – it will almost certainly fail. A number of high-profile businesses have ceased trading since 2010 (see 'Think about it'), partially because they had not kept up with the changes in retail shopping habits, with the increase in online shopping.

▲ **Figure 1.12** 'Barriers to growth' is another way to describe the difficulties and issues a business may face if it wants to grow

8.2 How to conduct a SWOT (Strengths, Weaknesses, Opportunities and Threats) analysis

A **SWOT analysis** is a tool that was created to help a business analyse its current and future position to aid decision making. It has four sections, forming the acronym SWOT (Table 1.12).

Table 1.12 A SWOT framework

Strengths [internal]	Opportunities [external]
Weaknesses [internal]	Threats [external]

🔑 KEY TERM

SWOT analysis – a tool that enables a business to analyse the Strength, Weaknesses, Opportunities and Threats of its current operations.

The SWOT analysis focuses on internal elements of a business and the external parts of its operations. Due to its simple form, a SWOT analysis can be performed quickly by individuals or teams, but is a very effective business tool.

Strengths

A business will focus on all the positive aspects of its operations. Any points made can be expanded and quantified further for clarification.

Weaknesses

The weak elements of the business must be identified so that they can be turned into strengths. This aspect of the process can be seen as negative, but all those involved must be honest in their responses. All businesses are vulnerable, so the team must identify these vulnerabilities with a view to making them positive in the future.

Opportunities

Opportunities can be seen as another opening or potential in which the business could also be successful. Examples include the increased popularity of the internet, and social trends towards healthy eating. Identifying gaps in the market to be exploited depends on the business spotting such opportunities. Seeing the potential is key when identifying opportunities.

Threats

This section of the analysis focuses on the external factors that a business cannot usually control – for example, new laws and regulations, changes in government, market changes and new competition. These elements can be difficult to predict but still have to be 'managed'.

INDIVIDUAL ACTIVITY

(30 minutes)

● Apricot Dance Studio opened five years ago in your area, employing a small team of specialised dance teachers.
● The studio operates from 7.30–11.00 am and from 2.30–8.30 pm, which has proved popular.
● The studio is now in a position to expand due to increased demand from all age groups for dance classes.
● It is considering diversifying into new markets to compete with other dance-related businesses and general fitness organisations.

The business will need to review its current provision. Complete a detailed SWOT analysis to provide evidence of where you consider it is appropriate for the business to diversify. Research local dance studios, which will enable you to include enough detail to persuade the business to take on your ideas.

8.3 How to interpret business performance

A business should complete performance assessments at certain times, to review how it is performing both internally and externally in terms of achieving its set aims and objectives. **Business performance** can be measured in three main ways. By:

1 financial analysis
2 assessment of non-financial information
3 comparisons with industry and business in various forms.

🔑 KEY TERMS

Business performance – how a business judges if it is succeeding and in which areas it needs to improve, to maintain or gain in terms of market share.

Financial analysis – a variety of different tools that enable a business to review its current financial arrangements, make improvements and future plans for the organisation.

Financial analysis

Businesses use a variety of different financial equations and ratios to assess how they are performing, focusing on turnover, profit and capital employed in the business. Completing such **financial analysis** can enable a business to focus on particular areas where their performance may be lacking.

Assessment of non-financial information

An understanding of the business as a whole is needed to continue to compete and improve performance in its markets.

Assessments enable a business to focus on its short- and long-term strategies and its ability to achieve profitability, as well as overall competitive strength to achieve its long-term goals. Using indirect and quantitative indicators – for example, customer loyalty and intellectual capital (e.g. employees) – can enable a business to determine its position in the market. By combining the accounting knowledge and non-financial data with regard to its position and performance, businesses can communicate their objectives and hopefully implement relevant strategies to address the overall business aims.

Critics of traditional measures argue that drivers of success in many industries are 'intangible', such as intellectual capital and customer loyalty, rather than the 'hard assets' allowed on statements of financial position. Although it is difficult to quantify intangible assets in financial terms, non-financial data can provide information about a firm's intangible assets.

Comparisons with industry and business in various forms

Key performance indicators (KPIs) determine how the business is doing against its set objectives or goals. For example, a business may have an overall objective to 'increase its sales', however it could make this more specific by stating that it will 'increases sales by 6 per cent in the next quarter by doubling the average value of orders'. This gives clear goals to be achieved by employees, which can be monitored and measured.

🔑 KEY TERM

Key performance indicator (KPI) – a measure that a business judges itself against based upon the goals it has set itself.

Businesses can also compare (benchmark) themselves to others within the same industry by using industrial average data, to ensure that they remain competitive, reacting to industry change, trends over time, customer influence, and supply and demand.

If a business identifies any necessary improvements, it needs to make specific recommendations that can be implemented within its future objectives.

However, focusing purely on one element of business performance will not give an overall picture. A business may be profitable over a number of years, but if its customer interest fades due to changes in the market, or if it has not kept up with the competition, it becomes vulnerable very quickly. Having an all-round understanding of business performance is important, no matter how hard the outcomes and reality may be.

Read about it

Stakeholder management: www.mindtools.com/pages/article/newPPM_08.htm

Consumer pressure group story: http://tinyurl.com/zu3w6k8

Organisational strategy information: http://bookboon.com/en/organization-ebooks-zip

Details on businesses that have ceased to trade: www.retailresearch.org/whosegonebust.php

Further factors that can affect the success or failure of a business: http://tinyurl.com/zeudt3a

Article helping to explain the reasons why businesses may fail: http://tinyurl.com/ltu9pdj

Further information on KPIs: http://tinyurl.com/zhh65e8

Other background reading:

Accounting, Costing and Management (2nd rev. edn), by Riad Izhar and Janet Hontoir, Oxford University Press, 2001

Advanced Accounting for A2, by Ian Harrison, Hodder Arnold, 2004

Business Accounting Volume 1 (10th edn), by Frank Wood and Alan Sangster, FT Prentice Hall, 2005

Business Accounting, by Rob Jones, Causeway Press, 2004

Complete A–Z Accounting Handbook (2nd rev. edn), by Ian Harrison, Hodder Arnold, 2003

Designing Your Organization, by Amy Kates and Jay R. Galbraith, Jossey-Bass, 2007, p. 1

Introducing Accounting for AS (2nd edn), by Ian Harrison, Hodder Arnold, 2008

Unit 1 assessment practice questions

Below are some practice questions for you to try.

Section A

1 Which of the following statements describes the main difference between a private limited company and a public limited company? (1 mark)
   a Private limited companies have limited liability but public limited companies do not.
   b Public limited companies can sell shares on the stock exchange but private limited companies cannot.
   c Private limited companies have shareholders but public limited companies do not.
   d Public limited companies are owned by the government but private limited companies are owned by private individuals.

2 Which of the following best describes the functions of a customer service department of a hospital? (1 mark)
   a It sources raw materials.
   b It pays suppliers.
   c It deals with patient complaints.
   d It organises recruitment and selection.

3 What does a cash-flow statement show? (1 mark)
   a Profit and loss
   b The profit margin of a product
   c The flow of money into and out of a business
   d Margin of safety

4 Which of the following is not an economic factor? (1 mark)
   a Level of consumers' disposable income
   b Unemployment rate
   c Exchange rate
   d Taxation

5 Mark runs a market stall selling flowers. On a particularly busy Saturday, his revenue was £600 and he paid £50 for renting the stall for the day. Calculate the amount of profit he made on this Saturday if the cost of his stock was a third of his revenue. (1 mark)
   a £150
   b £250
   c £350
   d £450

Section B

All of the questions in this section should be answered in relation to businesses that you have researched.

1   Describe the main purpose of a third-sector organisation you have researched. (2 marks)

Name of business:

Purpose of business:

2   Explain the key features of a public-sector business you have researched. (2 marks)

Name of business:

Key features:

3 a   Describe how a business you have researched is organised by geographic location. (2 marks)

Name of business:

How business is organised:

   b   State one advantage and one disadvantage of organising a business by geographic location. (2 marks)

Advantage:

Disadvantage:

4   Explain two possible impacts on a business that you have researched of not listening to the concerns of its local community. (4 marks)

Name of business:

Activity of business:

Impact 1:

Impact 2:

5   For a business you have researched, analyse one legal implication and one non-legal implication of failure to comply with the Consumer Protection Act. (6 marks)

Name of business:

Activity of business:

Legal implication:

Non-legal implication:

Section C

Mark has been running a successful market stall selling flowers for five years. He has now saved up some money, which he would like to invest in a shop at a local shopping mall. The more upmarket location will allow Mark to experiment with fair trade flowers, which he anticipates to be increasingly in demand by the type of customers he is trying to sell to.

He estimates the start-up cost at £20,000, which means he will either have to take out a bank loan or raise the capital needed by taking on a business partner. Steve, a friend that Mark has known since secondary school, is running an online business selling garden ornaments that he imports from China. Steve is keen to sell his products through a traditional channel and Mark is wondering whether going into partnership with Steve is better than remaining a sole trader.

1 a   What is meant by the term 'break even'? (2 marks)

   b   Explain two advantages and two disadvantages to Mark of calculating the break-even level of output required before deciding whether to invest in a shop. (8 marks)

2 a   Besides fair trade, identify two ways in which Mark could operate ethically. (2 marks)

   b   Analyse the advantages and disadvantages to Mark of operating as an ethical trader. (9 marks)

3   Suggest whether Mark should go into a partnership with Steve, justifying your answer. (12 marks)

Unit 02

Working in business

ABOUT THIS UNIT

This unit considers the skills, knowledge and understanding required when undertaking many day-to-day roles in a business. You will develop a practical awareness of the skills that are needed by employees if a business is to be successful. These include understanding the protocols to be followed in the workplace, how to make meeting and travel arrangements, how to complete business documents, how to prioritise tasks and how to communicate effectively.

LEARNING OUTCOMES

The topics, activities and suggested reading in this unit will help you to:

1 understand protocols to be followed when working in business
2 understand factors that influence the arrangement of business meetings
3 be able to use business documents
4 be able to prioritise business tasks
5 understand how to communicate effectively with stakeholders.

How will I be assessed?

This unit will be externally assessed via a test set and marked by OCR.

LO1 Understand protocols to be followed when working in business

GETTING STARTED 👤 ....

(10 minutes)

1 Individually, write a definition of the term 'protocol'.
2 Compare this with definitions written by your peers to agree a class definition.

1.1 Authority protocols

Authority **protocols** provide a framework for employees to follow. These are usually associated with the different levels of responsibility that employees and managers have in the business hierarchy (see Unit 1, LO3, page 3).

> 🔑 **KEY TERMS**
>
> **Protocol** – procedures or rules that must be followed.
>
> **Line manager** – the superior to whom an employee reports; usually this is the person directly above the employee on an organisation chart.

Authority in the workplace

On decision making

Employees are trained to carry out their day-to-day tasks, such as providing customer service. However, sometimes a task or problem needs to be escalated to their **line manager** because they have greater authority. For example, if a customer has a complaint that the employee has failed to resolve to the customer's satisfaction, the manager could have the authority to provide financial recompense such as gift vouchers.

On authorisation

Employees may not have the authority to carry out certain tasks, such as signing letters or authorising payment. In this case, responsibility sits with their manager, e.g. an employee may agree a lease for new premises but will refer this to the line manager for final authorisation.

Reasons for authority protocols

Authority protocols enable a manager to delegate tasks to a subordinate while still overseeing the outcome. This provides a checking procedure. For example, if the employee makes an error either in a document or a payment calculation, then the manager acts as a double-check to ensure that the information is accurate.

Authority protocols also lower the risk of fraud if more than one person is involved in the preparation and authorisation of payments.

1.2 Confidentiality protocols

Organisational procedures to maintain confidentiality

Businesses can introduce a range of organisational procedures with the aim of maintaining confidentiality, including:

- ensuring that only those who need to see specific information have access to it
- using the blind copy (bcc) line in emails to several external recipients so that email addresses are not shared
- requiring employees to sign a non-disclosure agreement (NDA) if they have access to confidential information, i.e. they will not discuss this information with anyone who has not also signed the agreement
- businesses can include in a job description that disclosing confidential information will be deemed gross misconduct.

Storage of data and documentation

- *Manual storage* includes the use of secured filing cabinets for hard copies of documentation and ensuring that confidential documents are not removed from the premises.
- *Electronic data* can be stored securely by password-protecting computers. This ensures that only the individual that the computer belongs to is able to access the data and documents, as long as the password is not shared. Network passwords can be used so that only those employees provided with the password can access certain documents. In addition, passwords can also be used to protect data back-ups from unauthorised access.

Implications of breaching confidentiality

If confidentiality is breached there are implications for the individual(s) concerned, as well as the business itself.

- Breaching confidentiality is considered gross misconduct, which may result in an employee's dismissal. They would also be unlikely to receive a reference, so future employability may be affected too. Legal action could be taken by the business against the individual were there a breach of legislation such as the Data Protection Act (see page 34).

- If the breach reveals confidential information about an employee or customer (such as personal or bank details) this could have serious implications such as the risk of identity theft and loss of trust in the business.
- The implications of revealing business information depend on who sees it. For example, a competitor discovers plans for expansion then it will have an opportunity to react by bringing forward its own expansion plans, prior to the details being made public. Alternatively, if employees access plans for large-scale redundancies staff morale and productivity are likely to fall.

Reasons why confidentiality may need to be breached

Some employees may attempt to utilise confidentiality protocols for personal gain. For example, an employee who has access to payment systems may believe that they can access these funds without other staff becoming aware. If, however, they are suspected of fraud or **embezzlement**, it may be necessary to access their emails and documents to identify whether this is the case.

Alternatively, there may be times when an employee must be contacted in an emergency (e.g. a store manager if the store has flooded during the night) and therefore their home telephone number needs to be

> **🔑 KEY TERM**
>
> **Embezzlement** – theft by an employee of assets that belong to the employer; this may include money, stock and stationery.

provided so they can be contacted.

GROUP ACTIVITY

(20 minutes)

NHS data breaches: Between April 2011 and April 2014, there were at least:

- 50 instances of data being posted on social media
- 143 instances of data being accessed for 'personal reasons'
- 124 instances of cases relating to IT systems
- 103 instances of data loss or theft
- 236 instances of data being shared inappropriately via email, letter or fax
- 251 instances of data being inappropriately shared with a third party.

Source: adapted from NHS Data Breaches: A Big Brother Watch Report (http://tinyurl.com/mmgds7e)

1 List the potential consequences of these breaches for the NHS and the individuals concerned.
2 Recommend how these breaches could have been avoided.

1.3 Constraints on document content

Voluntary constraints

- Organisational: businesses may have specific requirements to ensure consistency across all employees, e.g. all staff may be required to conclude an email with their signature, job title and contact details.
- Ethical: businesses may have guidelines relating to stereotypes, whistle-blowing or privacy that affect how some documents are worded, so as not to offend or betray confidences.
- Codes of practice: some job roles and businesses have codes of practice to follow. For example, the Code of Practice for Social Care Workers requires that workers maintain clear and accurate records. Similarly, Asda Mobile has devised a code of practice for complaints handling. This states the complaints procedure, which should be followed by all staff, as well as clarifying the process for customers.

Legislation

- Copyright: works protected by the Copyright, Designs and Patents Act include music, books, leaflets, newsletters, films and software. Businesses must ensure that relevant permissions are gained, e.g. if a song is to be included in a TV advertisement or if an extract from a book is to be included in a newsletter. Sources should be quoted for any extracts used in documentation or presentations to avoid accusations of **plagiarism**. Similarly, if the business itself has such works, e.g. technical drawings of car engines, then any individual or business wanting to reproduce these must ask for permission from the copyright holder and pay a fee if necessary.
- Data protection: the Data Protection Act requires personal information to be protected (see page 34). Any documents that contain these details must therefore be secure. Personal details should be included in documents only when relevant.
- Consumer protection: legislation such as the Consumer Protection from Unfair Trading Regulations (see page 291), impacts on the content of documents produced, e.g. a newspaper advertisement stating special offer prices when no products are available at these prices would breach this legislation.

- Equal opportunities: the Equality Act (see page 34) protects individuals from discrimination, e.g. a business cannot produce a job advertisement requesting a 'barmaid' as this is gender discrimination, or request a 'young' person as this is age discrimination.

KEY TERM

Plagiarism – using someone else's work and leading others to believe that it is your own.

1.4 Checking protocols
Checking of documents

Documents should be checked for errors or possible misinterpretation. These checks may be carried out by, for example:

- more senior employees (e.g. to check financial figures)
- specialists (e.g. a solicitor for a legal contract)
- those to whom the document refers (e.g. a manager's report)
- a proofreader (e.g. to ensure the professionalism of a report for shareholders)
- external communications company (e.g. a press release).

The checks may take time or cost money in the short term but could prevent problems in the long term, as well as preventing damage to the business's reputation.

Checking of arrangements

When arrangements are made (e.g. for meetings, training or travel), arrangers must ensure that all relevant staff have received the details and that the details themselves have been copied accurately.

Implications of poor checking

The repercussions of not checking could be serious. For example, if travel arrangements have been provided incorrectly then a flight or train could be missed, wasting time, money and possibly business opportunities. If the wrong meeting location has been provided to one of the participants, it may not be possible to make an important decision without them. Similarly, if an inaccurate report has been sent to shareholders, the reputation and professionalism of the business could be questioned.

1.5 IT security protocols
Protection of information against unauthorised access

A range of protocols can be used to protect against unauthorised access, including:

- password-protecting documents, computers and networks (see Section 1.2)
- installing anti-virus software that constantly searches a computer to identify (and attempt to rectify) any activity or threats from a computer virus
- installing anti-spyware software, which monitors incoming data from emails, websites and downloads to prevent spyware programs from accessing the computer's operating system
- granting staff different levels of access rights, e.g. the administrator for the network server will have greater access rights as they will require the ability to access other employees' files
- having a screen saver time-out for when computers are left unattended, which requires a password to unlock the screen
- positioning computer screens so that the general public cannot view them, e.g. in a GP's surgery.

Inappropriate use of IT equipment and software

The inappropriate use of IT equipment and software might include:

- using workplace computers for non-work activities, e.g. accessing social media
- installing unauthorised software, e.g. games
- installing software that is licensed only for business use on home computers.

The consequences of inappropriate use could range from wasted business time to charges of gross misconduct and fines for breaking the law.

1.6 Employment protocols
Health and safety legislation

The Health and Safety at Work Act, along with legislation such as the Workplace (Health, Safety and Welfare) Regulations and the Health and Safety (Display Screen Equipment) regulations detail protocols that must be followed. These include providing adequate lighting and ventilation, providing regular eye tests for employees who use computer screens and ensuring that risk assessments are carried out.

Equal opportunities legislation

All staff must be aware of legislation such as the Equality Act (see page 34). Many businesses offer induction and ongoing training in factors such as what can or cannot be said, how to act, and what can or cannot be included in communications, to ensure that discrimination does not occur.

Contractual obligations

Once a contract of employment has been signed by employer and employee it becomes legally binding, so both parties must obey what is stated, such as working hours, annual leave, pay and benefits.

Minimum standards of professional behaviour

These include the following.

- Punctuality: all employees are expected to arrive at work on time. Repeated lateness is unprofessional and may result in a disciplinary procedure. If an employee is unable to attend work due to sickness or a medical appointment, they must inform their employer promptly.
- Appearance and dress code: requirements for appearance and dress vary from business to business – for example, a lawyer would dress smartly to create a professional impression, an assistant in a fashion store would wear clothing from the store and a fire-fighter would wear a uniform. Some businesses also have rules about not displaying tattoos or body piercings, as some customers may perceive these as unprofessional.
- Use of appropriate language: swearing, slang words and open complaints about the business should be avoided, particularly when dealing with customers or third parties. Employees should be aware that, when talking among themselves they are still representing the business. This also applies outside of the workplace.

KNOW IT

1 Explain why a business may have authority protocols.
2 State three organisational procedures used to maintain confidentiality.
3 Explain how data protection legislation impacts on document content.
4 State two methods used to maintain IT security.
5 Why does a business have minimum standards of professional behaviour?

● ●

LO2 Understand factors that influence the arrangement of business meetings

GETTING STARTED

(10 minutes)

1 Imagine that you are employed in the head office of a discount supermarket. You have been asked to arrange a meeting next week, which will involve the managing director, the sales director and six regional managers, who are based at depots around the UK.
2 List the factors that will influence your arrangements.

2.1 Factors that influence meeting arrangements

Meeting criteria

When organising a meeting, a range of factors should be considered including:

- whether the people involved are internal, external or a combination, e.g. if the meeting involves internal staff the meeting could be held that day, especially if all people involved work in the same location; however, if external people are involved then travel arrangements need to be considered
- whether the meeting is urgent, e.g. a fire at a supplier's factory means that an urgent decision must be made about a replacement supplier
- senior staff are likely to attend numerous meetings and regard some as a greater priority, e.g. a meeting with a new customer regarding a large order is likely to take priority over a scheduled weekly sales update
- the purpose of the meeting, e.g. if the meeting is to discuss the purchase of a new warehouse then the meeting could take place there or at the property agents; a performance appraisal meeting is more likely to take place in the workplace
- the location of personnel may impact the choice of venue or choice of media, e.g. if the people required are worldwide then video-conferencing or a telephone conference may be a more cost-effective and time-efficient option than a face-to-face meeting.

Personnel availability

When a meeting is being arranged, it is necessary to check when the required personnel are available.

Electronic diary systems can be synchronised on smartphones, tablets and computers, and reminders sent. Maintaining an electronic diary system also means that other personnel, such as a personal assistant, can monitor a manager's diary and arrange suitable times for meetings without discussing it with the manager.

Some email software can check personnel availability, e.g. if a manager wants to arrange a meeting for Monday at 4 pm and inputs the staff involved, the system will flag who would and would not be available and enable the manager to enter the meeting into colleagues' diaries.

Venue/room

Factors influencing the venue/room for a meeting include those listed below.

- Availability: some businesses have meeting rooms that can be reserved, or meetings may take place in managers' offices. An external venue such as a hotel or serviced offices may be used if the business does not have a suitable meeting room.
- Location: if people are travelling from around the UK, for example, then arranging a centrally located venue would be beneficial.
- Resources: if, say, a presentation is to be shown access to a projector will be needed, therefore the venue must offer this facility.
- Refreshments: an all-day meeting, for example, may need lunch to be provided. The choice of venue may depend on whether catering services are available.
- Shared office space: for instance, it is unlikely that a confidential meeting would be held in an open office; an external venue may be more appropriate.

Resource packs

If attendees require copies of documentation, this must be produced/photocopied beforehand, especially if it is to be distributed prior to the meeting.

If people external to the business are to attend then it may be necessary to provide travel information. On the day of the meeting it may be necessary to arrange visitor badges and parking spaces, and to ensure reception staff have been informed of their arrival.

Business costs

A meeting could have cost implications, e.g. if people have to travel long distances then alternative options could be telephone conferences and web conferences, which not only reduce travel costs but also mean that time is not wasted travelling that could be spent more productively.

There are instances, however, where a face-to-face meeting is a more professional approach, such as when meeting with a potential new client, irrespective of the cost.

2.2 Factors that influence business travel arrangements

Travel criteria

Business travel arrangements will be influenced by the following factors.

- Destination: different modes of transport are likely to be chosen depending on the distance to be travelled. The decision will be based on the convenience, cost and the time taken for each option. If a meeting needs to be held with a client in France then one option would be to book a flight and a second would be to drive, or use the train, travelling either by ferry or Eurostar. If the meeting is in the UK then car or train are likely options.
- Dates/times: dates and times of the transport options should also be considered, e.g. local airports operate flights to some destinations only at certain times of the year. Similarly, if the earliest train of the day would not allow an attendee to reach their destination for the meeting start time then they would have to consider driving.
- Personnel: if a group is travelling together then driving will be the most cost-effective mode of transport as they can travel in one car, i.e. the cost for four people would be the same as the cost for one person. If they travelled by train, then each individual would need to purchase a ticket. The level of seniority of the personnel will also have an influence on travel arrangements. For example, the managing director of a business is likely to require a more luxurious hotel than an employee on the lower levels of the hierarchy. Similarly, some CEOs of large corporations may choose to fly first or business class rather than economy.
- Special requirements: for example, if an individual has not passed their driving test then travelling by car would not be an option. Similarly, if an individual does not have their own car then the cost of hiring a rental car may be greater than the cost of travelling by train.

If a business has employees who travel regularly there may also be the requirement to have a business travel insurance policy. This may cover trip cancellation as well as providing cover for lost/stolen sample products or business equipment.

Mode of transport timetables and schedules

When making a decision as to the mode of transport, consulting timetables and schedules will reveal whether certain travel options are available, e.g. if a train departs at a convenient time. Figure 2.1 shows an extract from a train timetable.

| 05:48 | Edinburgh Waverley (Plat 2) | 4h 53m |
| 10:41 | London Kings Cross (Plat 1) | Direct |

| 06:26 | Edinburgh Waverley (Plat 19) | 4h 26m |
| 10:52 | London Kings Cross (Plat 2) | Direct |

| 06:55 | Edinburgh Waverley (Plat 11) | 4h 47m |
| 11:42 | London Kings Cross (Plat 7) | Direct |

| 07:30 | Edinburgh Waverley (Plat 8) | 4h 21m |
| 11:51 | London Kings Cross (Plat 3) | Direct |

| 08:00 | Edinburgh Waverley (Plat 19) | 4h 43m |
| 12:43 | London Kings Cross (Plat 5) | Direct |

▲ **Figure 2.1** Which train would be best for a meeting starting near King's Cross at 12.30 pm?

If an individual working in Edinburgh needs to be in London for a meeting tomorrow starting at 10 am then the train would not be suitable, unless they travel today and pay for overnight accommodation. However, if the meeting started at 12.30 pm, then the 6.55 am and the 7.30 am trains would both be suitable.

Calculation and comparison of costs

A business must ensure that all costs are considered, e.g. when choosing to fly there are additional costs for luggage and airport parking as well as a time cost to arrive two hours before the flight. When booking a train ticket online there is a booking fee to add to the price.

When comparing costs, it is essential that all of these costs are included and also that consideration is given to timescales, e.g. driving to Brussels may be cheaper than flying, but if it takes five hours longer then this represents time when the employee is not being productive.

Flights – Manchester Airport – Amsterdam
Outbound 1 August   15.25   17.40   Cost £133 each + £30 each for luggage
Inbound 3 August   14.25   14.40

Outbound 1 August   17.40   19.55   Cost £133 each + £30 each for luggage
Inbound 3 August   13.40   16.00

Additional costs – Car from the office in Stockport to the airport 9.6 miles (approx. 22 mins)
Airport parking – £29.99.
Taxi from the office to the airport (return) - £48.00

North Sea Ferries – Hull to Rotterdam
Outbound 1 August   20.30   9.00
Inbound 2 August   21.00   11.30
Two adults, two cabins, one car and breakfast = £677.00

Additional costs – 109 miles from the office to Hull ferry terminal (approx. 1 hr 55 mins)
68.1 miles from Rotterdam ferry port to Amsterdam (approx. 1 hr 21 mins)

Stena line Ferries – Harwich to Hook of Holland
Outbound 1 August   23.00   8.00
Inbound 2 August   22.00   6.30
Two adults, two cabins, one car = £406.00

Additional costs – 255 miles from the office to Harwich (approx. 4 hrs 29 mins)
52.3 miles from Hook of Holland ferry port to Amsterdam (approx. 1 hr 10 mins)

▲ **Figure 2.2** A summary of travel options to a meeting in Amsterdam

1 Discuss the advantages and disadvantages of each option.
2 Recommend which option should be chosen. Justify your answer.

2.3 Factors that influence business accommodation arrangements

Accommodation criteria

Location, rating and meal arrangements when booking accommodation will all influence the cost. Close proximity to the meeting venue and major roads or station is beneficial, even if this is more expensive than hotels further away.

In an unfamiliar location, the hotel grading, star rating or guest reviews may influence the decision. Hotels with high official ratings are likely to be more expensive, but paying for a good night's sleep may be important if employees need to be well rested for a meeting.

Payment may also be a consideration, e.g. if the employee has to pay for the accommodation themselves and then claim this back as expenses they may not have the funds available. Similarly, if a business has an account with a specific hotel chain then employees will be expected to book one of these hotels where possible.

Personnel requirements

Staff may have particular considerations, e.g. an adapted room if they have a disability, or accommodation that caters for special dietary requirements. This may reduce the choice of accommodation.

Most hotel rooms today have Wi-Fi access if staff need to work in the evening, but this is not always free. Other facilities, such as a gym or swimming pool, are attractive but not vital, so any additional cost may not be warranted.

Calculation and comparison of costs

Online booking websites allow easy comparison of the basic cost of accommodation. However, additional costs may need to be considered, e.g. some city-centre hotels require guests to pay for car parking. If people are not driving to the hotel, then a location close to the railway station and the meeting venue would reduce taxi fares even though the hotel itself may be more expensive.

? THINK ABOUT IT

Case study: Proctor & Son

Proctor & Son plc is an automotive components manufacturer. Its head office is in York, where it also has a factory. It has two additional factory sites, in Lancaster and Reading.

You have been asked to arrange travel and accommodation for three colleagues who are due to attend a meeting in York on 12 March. They need to arrive the evening before as the meeting starts at 8.30 am. Two of the colleagues live in London and one in Lancaster.

In pairs:

- recommend travel and accommodation arrangements
- calculate the total cost, including any additional costs such as taxi fares, car parking or petrol costs (assume 45p is paid per mile as expenses)
- justify why you have recommended your chosen accommodation and form of travel rather than the alternative options.

KNOW IT

1 Explain three factors that will influence meeting arrangements.
2 Is cost always the main factor when choosing travel arrangements?
3 How might any special requirements influence the choice of accommodation?
4 State one benefit and one drawback of using a price comparison website when booking overnight accommodation for business purposes.

LO3 Be able to use business documents

GETTING STARTED 👤

(15 minutes)

- Your tutor will provide each group with a business document. In groups decide what you think the purpose of this document is.
- Feed back your ideas to your class.

A range of documents are used in the day-to-day running of a business, including financial recording documents and order forms. These can be paper based and completed by hand, or they can be electronic and completed on a computer.

3.1 The purpose, interpretation and completion of business documents

Transaction documents

A transaction document records a transaction (financial exchange) between two parties, such as a supplier and a customer. It can be printed or electronic. It may contain the following terms and abbreviations.

- COD (cash on delivery): pay for goods on delivery rather than before or after delivery.
- E&OE (errors and omissions excepted): a disclaimer on an invoice or similar transaction document showing that the supplier is attempting to reduce any legal liability due to administrative errors or inaccuracies.
- T&Cs (terms and conditions): restrictions or statements relating to delivery charges, delivery arrangements or payment terms.
- Terms (e.g. Terms 30 days): the time by which payment is expected.

Typical types of document include the following:

- Purchase order: this is a legally binding document between a supplier and a customer/buyer. It lists the items that the buyer has ordered and the agreed purchase price. It may also state the delivery date and **payment terms** for the buyer.
- Invoice: this is a document that a business issues to customers requesting payment for goods and services. For an example, see page 68.
- Credit note: this is sent by a seller/supplier to a customer if, for example, goods received by a customer have been damaged in transit, an error has been made on the invoice such as an incorrect discount being applied or a customer returns an item. The credit note can be offset against future purchases or a refund can be given. For an example, see page 68.
- Statement of account: this is issued by a supplier to a customer, usually at the end of each month. This states all transactions over the last period including details of invoices issued, payments received and credits applied. The final balance shows the total amount owed by that customer on that date. For more information, see Unit 11.

> ### 🔑 KEY TERM
> **Payment terms** – when payment should be made by the buyer/customer to the supplier.

Employee documents

Travel expense claim form

When employees travel as part of their role, they can claim expenses. This includes petrol costs, train fares, taxi fares, car parking and sometimes refreshments. If an employee uses their own car they must record the journey mileage as petrol costs are usually reimbursed at 'x' pence per mile. Travel expense claim forms often need to be signed by a line manager to confirm that the journey was necessary and that only allowable expenses are being claimed for.

Ernest Barten Ltd Shore Court Derby DE219XY		
Travel expenses claim form		
Date of claim:	Claim reference (office use only):	
Mileage Journey details:		
	Total @ 45p per mile	
Fares Details:		
	Total	
Accommodation and subsistence Details:		
	Total	
Miscellaneous Details:		
	Total	
Total expenses claimed		

▲ **Figure 2.3** An example of a travel expenses claim form

Other internal documents

Typical internal documents may include the following.

- Petty cash voucher: petty cash is held to reimburse staff for small purchases made on behalf of the business, e.g. buying stamps. A petty cash voucher is a form that records the amount removed from the petty cash float by an authorised person. Usually the employee will need to provide a receipt, which will be attached to the petty cash voucher as proof of purchase.
- Stock requisition form: this is completed when goods need to be ordered for relevant use, e.g. printer paper or a filing cabinet. The completed form is sent to the purchasing/procurement department, which then, if the requisition is authorised, orders the goods on behalf of the employee/department.

- IT requisition form: this is a request for IT equipment to be ordered/purchased, including laptops, printers and portable hard drives. The form is similar to a stock requisition form and is completed by the employee or manager requesting the equipment and then forwarded to the purchasing function once authorised by a senior member of staff.
- Reprographics requisition form: this is completed by an employee requiring either photocopying to be done or other reprographic services, e.g. booklets being produced or signs being laminated.

3.2 The purpose and interpretation of other business documents

 CLASSROOM DISCUSSION

(5 minutes)
Why is it vital that a business keeps accurate records of all financial transactions?

Bank statement

This summarises transactions into and out of a bank account over a period of time, usually a month. The accounts function will monitor the business's bank accounts by carrying out bank reconciliations by checking the inflows and outflows recorded on the bank statement against the business's own financial records. The bank statement also indicates the funds available for making purchases or paying bills.

Budget variance report

A **budget** variance (e.g. **favourable** or **adverse variance**) is the difference between budgeted income and expenditure and the actual income and expenditure figures. The budget variance report summarises these differences and is useful in the decision-making process, e.g. do costs need reducing? Why is revenue falling?

KEY TERMS

Budget – planned income and expenditure over a period of time.

Favourable variance – where the actual figure is better than the budgeted figures, e.g. if costs are lower than budgeted or revenue higher than budgeted.

Adverse variance – where the actual figure is worse than the budgeted figures, e.g. if costs are higher than budgeted or revenue is lower than budgeted.

Delivery note

This is a document that accompanies a shipment of goods. It details the products and the quantities delivered. The customer will sign the delivery note to confirm that the correct items/number of items were delivered. Any issues, such as missing or damaged products, will be highlighted. The supplier then refers to the delivery note when issuing the invoice for this delivery.

Goods received note

This is a document used by the customer for checking items received to ensure that they match the purchase order. Once checked and any discrepancies highlighted, a copy will be returned to accounts staff, who check the goods received note against the invoice from the supplier to ensure that payment is made for the correct number of items. Today, many businesses use electronic systems to check deliveries and transfer this information to the accounts function.

Payslip

This is an employee's record of the pay they have received. Gross pay is the amount before deductions and net pay is the amount the employee will actually be paid after deductions. Any deductions will be listed, including income tax, national insurance contributions, pension contributions, charity donations and student loan repayments.

Receipt

This is evidence that goods or services have been purchased and the amount paid for these. It is also likely to detail the date, the business that the goods or services have been supplied by, and the payment method used.

Remittance advice

This is a notification sent by a customer to a supplier informing them that their invoice has been paid. Traditionally when payments were made by cheque the remittance advice was sent in the post accompanying the cheque. Today the remittance advice is more likely to be sent to the supplier once electronic payment has been made.

Request for repair form

This can be an internal document – for example, if a projector breaks down then a request for repair form can be completed and sent to the maintenance team.

It can also be an external document that is completed and then sent to an external repair company, e.g. if a business **leases** a photocopier and the contract includes maintenance, then a request for repair form may be sent to the leasor detailing the issue. A form sent to an external business will require additional details to an internal form such as the company name and address.

> **🔑 KEY TERM**
>
> **Leasing** – a method of financing a fixed asset whereby the lessee pays to rent (lease) the asset from the leasor.

3.3 How to make payments, and the advantages and disadvantages of each payment method

INDIVIDUAL ACTIVITY

(5 minutes)

List ways in which customers pay for goods and services. Consider retail customers and business customers.

Different payment methods can have advantages and disadvantages to both the payee and the payer. This may also depend on who the payee and payer are, e.g. the business, suppliers, customers, travel providers. Table 2.1 summarises some of these advantages and disadvantages.

▲ **Table 2.1** Advantages and disadvantages of payment methods

Cheque	Advantages to the payer	Disadvantages to the payer
A document requesting that a specified sum of money be paid from one person's/business's bank account (the drawer) into another person's/business's bank account (the drawee)	Cheques can be sent via post Large amounts of cash do not need to be handled The drawer has a record of the payment being made	Cheques for business accounts often need to be signed by two people, which can be time consuming
	Advantages to the payee	**Disadvantages to the payee**
	It is safer to carry a cheque than large amounts of cash to the bank	Cheques must be paid in to a bank, which can be inconvenient Any errors on the cheque delay payment Cheques have to 'clear' before the funds can be withdrawn or spent Cheques can 'bounce', i.e. the payer may not have sufficient funds in their bank account to make the payment; the payee may not be aware of this until after goods have been received by the drawer
Credit card	**Advantages to the payer**	**Disadvantages to the payer**
Enables an individual or business (payer) to make payment for goods or services but in effect they are borrowing the money from the credit card company. The credit card company transfers the money to the payee and the payer then owes that amount to the credit card company. If this debt is repaid when requested then no interest is charged, however if the full amount is not repaid interest is charged on the outstanding balance	Payment can be made even if there are insufficient funds in the payer's bank account to pay the full amount There is a degree of protection from fraud when paying by credit card Credit cards can be used for online payments, which benefits customers and suppliers	The payer is charged interest if the full amount is not repaid to the credit card company when requested Some businesses charge the payer a fee if payment is made by credit card
	Advantages to the payee	**Disadvantages to the payee**
	The credit card company authorises the payment, therefore the payee knows that they will receive payment Payments can be made online	Payees must pay a processing fee which reduces the amount received (unless this is passed on to the payer)

Debit card	Advantages to the payer	Disadvantages to the payer
Can be used for payment online or where there is a debit/credit card payment machine. Funds are transferred from the payer's bank account directly into the payee's bank account	Large amounts of cash do not need to be handled Can be used for online payments	Some businesses charge an additional fee to the customer if paying by debit card Fraud is a growing issue when using debit cards If sufficient funds are not in the payer's bank account, their bank may not authorise the payment
	Advantages to the payee	Disadvantages to the payee
	Once authorised via the card payment machine, the payee is guaranteed to receive the payment Can be used for online payments	Payees must pay a processing fee Appropriate technology must be purchased to enable transactions to be processed

PAIRS ACTIVITY

(20 minutes)

An employee needs to book overnight accommodation before attending a conference the next day. He also needs to book a train. He has decided to book both of these online using his credit card as his employer will then refund the money once an expenses claim is submitted.

Explain the advantages and disadvantages for this employee of booking using a credit card.

Online/digital payment methods

Online payments via credit and debit cards, and digital payment methods such as PayPal, have become increasingly popular with internet shoppers. PayPal Checkout buttons on a website enable customers to access a gateway to complete the payment process for goods.

Digital payment methods offer ease of use to customers as once an account is set up they need to log in only when purchasing rather than entering credit/debit card details each time. It is also beneficial to small businesses that want the security of knowing that, once authorised, payment will be received. However, the fees increase costs for the business receiving the payment.

Bank payments

- Paying in slip: if an individual/business needs to pay cash or cheques into their bank account they often need to complete a paying in slip to accompany the payment. This details information such as the date the deposit was made, the bank account for it to be paid into, the amount paid in, and whether this was cash or cheques or a combination of both.
- Electronic transfer is the electronic movement of funds between one bank account and another. No physical cash changes hands. Electronic transfers include transferring funds between an individual's/business's own accounts, e.g. from a current account to a savings account, from an individual's account to a business account, e.g. to pay a mobile phone bill, or via credit/debit card transactions in a shop. For regular bill payments customers can set up a **standing order** or a **direct debit**. Transfers are convenient, quick and easy to use, although internet access will be necessary to complete these transactions online.

KEY TERMS

Standing order – an instruction given by an account holder to the bank to pay a specific amount to another account on a regular basis, e.g. annually or monthly – for example, to pay a monthly gym membership.

Direct debit – an instruction given by an account holder to the bank to allow another account holder (usually a business) to withdraw funds from that account.

3.4 Purpose, completion and checking of meeting documentation

The relevant participants must be aware of a planned meeting and its content. A record should be made of the discussions.

Notice of meeting

This can be formal or informal depending on the purpose of the meeting and the people involved. For example, the Annual General Meeting for shareholders of a public limited company will require a formal notice, which is likely to be sent by letter. However, a performance management meeting between two members of staff is likely to use a more informal method, e.g. email.

Whatever the format used, the notice should include the date, time, location and purpose of the meeting. If any information needs to be brought to the meeting or read beforehand this should also be stated in the notice.

Agenda

The agenda lists, in order, items for discussion in a meeting or activities to be undertaken. It will also reconfirm the date, time and location of the meeting. Everyone involved in the meeting should be provided with a copy of the agenda.

Minutes

The minutes are a summary of what is discussed and agreed during a meeting. They begin with the date, time and location of the meeting, plus the names of the people attending and those sending their apologies. Each item listed on the agenda is a section within the minutes. After the meeting a copy of the minutes will be distributed to all attendees.

Conference documentation

A conference is a large meeting that can be used to provide information to a large group of people. The attendees at a conference are known as delegates.

Figure 2.4 describes some of the documents that might be needed at a conference.

Documentation for delegates	• If a conference is internal to a business then details may be emailed to delegates, however if it is a conference to discuss, for example, changes to health and safety processes within a specific industry, then the event will need to be publicised. This could be via brochures or leaflets sent to businesses within that field.
	• Invitations may be produced and sent to potential delegates. This can give the impression that it is an honour to attend the conference and make an invitation more desirable.
	• Once delegates have accepted a place at the conference instructions will be produced and provided to them. These will include confirmation of the date, time and location as well as directions and information such as the nearest train station.
	• Evaluation forms will be provided to all delegates at the end of the conference. These give delegates the opportunity to provide feedback on the success of the event.
Documentation for staff	• Staff facilitating the conference will require appropriate documentation to have been produced and available for them on the day e.g. an attendance register which delegates should sign on arrival.
	• Any information sheets or resources needed by delegates need to produced and provided to staff for distribution at the appropriate time.
Documentation for presenters	• Presenters require documentation for use during their presentations including copies of presentation slides and prompt notes. If copies of slides are to be provided to delegates, these will also need to be produced.
	• It is important that all documentation produced for conferences is checked for errors as any inaccuracies will appear unprofessional.

▲ **Figure 2.4** Types of conference documentation

KNOW IT

1 State three pieces of information included on a purchase order.
2 What is the purpose of a credit note?
3 What is a budget variance?
4 State three possible deductions shown on an employee's pay slip.
5 What is the difference between a direct debit and a standing order?

LO4 Be able to prioritise business tasks

GETTING STARTED

(5 minutes)

How do you prioritise the tasks that you have to carry out in a week?

4.1 Reasons for prioritising business tasks

Workload

Employees have a limited number of hours within the working day, therefore it is necessary to prioritise tasks to decide which need to be completed first.

Conflicting demands on time

Employees, particularly senior managers, have their own tasks to carry out but their role is also to support and advise others. This may cause conflicting demands on their time, e.g. if a manager needs to prepare for a presentation to the executive board the next day but a **direct report** is struggling to deal with a customer complaint and requires help. The manager must decide which should take priority.

KEY TERM

Direct report – a subordinate to a member of staff.

Importance of meeting deadlines

Internal/external deadlines

In both of the following examples it is important that these tasks are prioritised over tasks that do not have an imminent deadline.

- Internal: a sales manager is holding a training session for employees tomorrow at 2 pm. Any documentation for the session must be completed prior to this time. If this internal deadline is not met, her reputation may be adversely affected as the session will appear unprofessional and poorly planned.
- External: a new customer must receive a delivery by 5 pm today. If this external deadline is not met, then the business will appear unreliable and may not gain further orders from this customer.

Interim/final deadlines

Large projects will often have **interim deadlines** as well as a final deadline. Interim deadlines are planned so that, if met, the final deadline will also be achieved. However, there are instances where the interim deadline may not be given the same level of priority as the final deadline, resulting in an increased workload as the final deadline approaches.

KEY TERM

Interim deadline – projects can be broken down into smaller tasks/targets, each of which can be allocated a deadline; these interim deadlines, if completed on time, will help to meet the final deadline.

Impacts of missing deadlines

This will in part depend on the importance of the task, e.g. if an employee has not completed a self-appraisal form prior to a performance management meeting their line manager may not be pleased but it will not impact on the overall running of the business. However, if a project to extend a factory is not completed by the deadline then this may impact on the business's ability to meet customer orders.

4.2 Factors that influence task prioritisation

Figure 2.5 describes some of the factors that may influence the order in which tasks are completed.

4.3 How to use information to inform prioritisation

Internal sources

Business objectives

A business with an objective to provide excellent customer service is likely to prioritise tasks that will help it to meet this objective, e.g. customer enquiries or complaints will be prioritised over tasks such as a monthly review with suppliers.

Stakeholders' resources and budget

Complex tasks may have a long timescale and require a range of resources. If funding is not available then the task/project will become a lower priority at that point in time, e.g. if a business aims to expand by opening a new factory but calculations show that funding is not available until next year, then the process of identifying a suitable site will not currently be high priority.

External sources

Changes in the economy

If interest rates rise a business may need to reassess its current borrowing. If the business relies on loans and mortgages for financing projects, then this will be of higher priority than for a business that utilises retained profit.

▲ **Figure 2.5** Factors that influence task prioritisation

Similarly, a business that buys materials from abroad or sells its products/services abroad will be affected by fluctuations in the exchange rate. In this instance meetings to discuss how to minimise the effect of fluctuations are likely to have a higher priority than in a business that operates locally or nationally.

External stakeholders' requirements, feedback and availability

This will vary depending on the stakeholder. For example, if the local community raise a complaint regarding pollution in a river then resolving this will be a high priority because media attention will adversely affect the reputation of the business, and if laws have been broken then legal action could be taken and fines imposed. The quicker the business is seen to be taking action and the issue resolved, the less serious the repercussions may be.

Sometimes a stakeholder wants to pass on information that they claim is urgent – for example, a supplier may have identified an issue with its materials that will affect the product. The supplier and the customer will need to deal with this as a high priority. The supplier should discuss changes to company procedures as soon as all parties are available, to ensure that this is not repeated.

Data sources

Numerical

Numerical data such as sales figures can inform prioritisation, e.g. if sales fall dramatically then assessing the reason for this fall and deciding on remedial action becomes a priority.

If issues are identified with the cash flow forecast then the level of priority may be determined by when the problem is likely to arise – for example, if the business is likely to require an overdraft next month then arranging this will become a priority, however if the overdraft is required in eight months' time then it will currently be a lower priority.

Graphical

Graphical data is used to illustrate information such as the results of customer satisfaction surveys. If the data highlights an issue, e.g. with the quality of services provided, then discussions to devise a plan of action to resolve this will become a priority.

Tabular

Tabular information is often produced using a spreadsheet. This includes costings, financial accounts, project timescales and survey results. If this information highlights an issue which needs to be dealt with immediately, this will become a priority, e.g. if a project has missed an interim deadline then remedial action may become a priority if the final deadline is to be achieved.

4.4 How to assign priorities and identify appropriate actions to complete tasks in accordance with their priority

Levels of priority

Examples of levels of priority:

- high – an urgent task, e.g. a product recall
- medium – must be completed but is not urgent, e.g. a skills audit

- low – must be completed but other tasks can take priority first, e.g. completing a self-appraisal form for a meeting in two weeks.

GROUP ACTIVITY

(20 minutes)

Discuss the business tasks listed in Table 2.2 and imagine all of them are on your 'to do' list. Decide whether each task should be assigned high, medium or low priority.

Table 2.2 Assigning priorities to tasks

Task	High/ medium/ low priority	Justification for level of priority chosen
A performance appraisal meeting		
A telephone call from your line manager		
Responding to an email enquiry from a customer		
A meeting to review last year's sales figures		
Ordering printer cartridges		
A meeting to sign the lease on a new store		
Telephoning an ICT consultant as the computer system has crashed		
A meeting with a supplier to agree raw material prices for the next six months		
The cleaner's store room has flooded		

4.5 Need to change priorities when necessary

Change deadlines

The business environment is constantly changing and, as such, priorities will also change, e.g. if contamination is found in a food production plant, resolving this will take priority over other tasks, even if the deadlines for other tasks then have to be changed.

Delegate tasks

Tasks with different levels of priority must all still be completed. If a manager has an urgent request from a director to complete a task, then lower-priority tasks may be delegated to the manager's subordinates.

LO5 Understand how to communicate effectively with stakeholders

5.1 Characteristics which inform the design of business communications

Clear and informative communication is key to the smooth running and success of a business. Business communication takes many forms including advertising, presentations, emails, agendas and packaging.

Audience

The **audience** must be considered if it is to be clearly understood, e.g. if a product is aimed at children then any advertising must be appropriate for this age group. Similarly, if a product is aimed at doctors then any advertising will use medical terms that most consumers would not understand.

KEY TERM

Audience – the people or other businesses that communication is aimed towards.

Communications may be more informal for internal audiences, e.g. emails between peers, however if the communication is a presentation to a potential new client then it should be more formal.

Purpose

Business communications for different purposes – for example, to inform, persuade, thank or deal with a complaint – will have different tones. A line manager may have an informal meeting with a new member of staff to find out whether they have settled in, whereas a meeting to discuss a legal issue with lawyers would be more formal, with an agenda and minutes taken.

Business communications that inform customers about a problem should clearly make a point in few words so that the message is easily understood, e.g. a product recall notice due to a danger being identified. However, advertising, which is aimed at persuading customers to buy, will be more descriptive and detail the benefits to the customer of buying a product.

Content

The content of business communications will influence the method of communication, e.g. if information is complex (sales figures or financial documents) then a report would be a useful method as recipients can read through the information at their own pace and they can refer back to it. If a meeting were used to verbally share this information, then it would be difficult to remember and understand the key points.

Business function

The functional area producing the business communication will impact on the design and the purpose. For example, the marketing function is responsible for selling the potential benefits of a product or service. Any communication is likely to be eye-catching and informative. The human resources function will deal with matters regarding employees. This communication is likely to be more formal, e.g. providing employees with a pay slip or issuing a contract of employment.

INDEPENDENT RESEARCH ACTIVITY

(30 minutes)

Research three contrasting examples of business communication.

For each example:

- consider who is the audience
- think about the purpose of the communication
- consider how clearly the message is conveyed to the audience
- identify how the communication has adapted the communication to meet the needs of the audience
- recommend one improvement, justifying your reasoning.

Available resources

Resource availability will influence the choice of business communication in some situations. For example, if a business is selecting which form of advertising to use to communicate with potential customers, then the budget available will influence its decision, e.g. TV advertising is costly, so lower-cost options such as radio advertising may have to be considered if insufficient funds are available.

5.2 How the characteristics of business communications design impact on the use of resources

Quality of paper/card

Card and high-quality paper will cost more. To ensure that resources are used effectively, businesses should consider when it is necessary to use high-quality materials and whether a hard copy is required at all, e.g. if a survey is to be sent to all employees, this could be emailed rather than printed. However, a quotation for a client could be printed on high-quality paper to create the impression that the business provides a quality service/products.

Colour/black and white

Colour printing and photocopying cost more than using black ink alone. A decision should be made as to whether colour is necessary, e.g. if a report is produced for shareholders that includes graphs and diagrams, then a glossy colour brochure may make these easier to interpret. However, a notice for the staff kitchen should be printed in black ink only.

Hard copy/electronic copy

Some documentation does not need to be printed, e.g. a spreadsheet summarising the mileage of a company's vehicles can be saved electronically and emailed to the relevant staff. However, a worksheet to be used in a training session would need to be produced as a hard copy so that delegates can refer to it easily.

Cost of consumables

Consumables are office supplies like paper, pens, staplers, ink and toner cartridges and postage.

🔑 KEY TERM

Consumables – resources that will be used and replaced on a regular basis, e.g. printer cartridges, stamps and paper.

▲ **Figure 2.6** Examples of consumables

The cost of consumables may impact on decisions such as whether to send invoices by letter/post or electronically.

Ease/cost of distribution

Most businesses use email to notify customers of special offers because it is cheaper and more direct than producing and posting leaflets or booklets. However, a local pizza delivery shop will produce leaflets detailing offers as these can be easily and cheaply delivered through the doors of people living in the area, i.e. their target market.

Timescales

Copying or printing in black and white on white paper is a task that employees in most businesses are able to complete themselves, although printing large quantities can be time consuming. More complex requirements, such as printing on card, laminating and producing booklets, may be done by the reprographics department or an external organisation. Each request will be prioritised by reprographics staff and the timescale for completion is therefore likely to be longer.

PAIRS ACTIVITY

(20 minutes)

Considering the factors listed in Section 5.2, how would you recommend that each of the documents listed below be produced, e.g. colour, paper, card, laminated, glossy, electronic?

- employee survey
- self-appraisal form
- brochure to send to prospective clients
- annual accounts
- notice advertising the office Christmas party.

5.3 How and when to use different types of communication

Formal communication

- Letters are likely to be printed on headed paper, which clearly identifies the sender. Although electronic communication is now overtaking the use of letters, letters are still used in formal situations, e.g. when detailing legal contracts. Once produced and signed, letters can be sent via the post, attached to an email or delivered by hand.
- Reports are used when detailed information needs to be presented. Reports contain narrative but can also include tables, graphs and figures that support the information being conveyed. The standard elements of a written report include:
  - title
  - introduction
  - body
  - conclusions
  - recommendations
  - appendix and references (if required).
- Notices will be used as an internal method of communication, e.g. to inform colleagues that an employee is running a marathon for charity.

Verbal communication

- Telephone calls are more personal than sending an email or text. They enable discussions and questions. Telephone conferences are used when a group of people, not in the same location, need to discuss a problem, make a decision or receive an update.
- Message: voicemail and answerphones allow verbal messages to be left; these are usually short and provide basic information, e.g. a request to return the call.
- Face-to-face communication can range from a formal meeting to a casual conversation at a colleague's desk. Being able to observe body language can be a useful tool when holding a face-to-face discussion (see page 330).

Electronic communication

- Email can be used for a variety of purposes, including informing customers about a special offer, sending a report to a line manager or confirming the time of a meeting. It is a quick and easy method of communication, which can be sent to multiple recipients at the same time.
- Text message/short message service (SMS) provides a limited amount of information quickly and easily.

It is therefore an inappropriate method if detailed information is required.
- Picture message/multimedia messaging service (MMS) can be a useful tool for providing visual information quickly, e.g. if the serial number on a printer is required by the maintenance team.
- Social media is a communication, advertising and promotional tool. However, negative feedback via social media can adversely affect the business's reputation.
- Web pages are a form of promotion the business can control, i.e. it can select the information that appears on its website. The website should follow the corporate branding and have a professional format. The purpose may vary – it might attract customers to either buy via the website or visit in person; other websites just provide information.
- Presentation slides may have a house style that should always be followed. The format should also be professional and slides checked to ensure that there are no inaccuracies prior to the presentation taking place.

Marketing documentation

- Business cards are a method of promotion that enables potential and existing customers to be provided with contact details. The quality of a business card may influence the customer's perception of the business.
- Press releases are a form of promotion used when a business wants to make an announcement to the media, e.g. a technological breakthrough or a new environmental policy.
- Promotional literature includes annual reports, brochures and leaflets. These should be professional and informative as they will influence a customer's or potential shareholder's perception of the business.
- Questionnaires can be used to gather market research data. They should be professional in appearance but also clear for recipients to understand as this is more likely to result in accurate data being collected.
- Data collection sheets are often for internal purposes and as such do not need to be as colourful or glossy as some forms of promotional literature. They may be used for tallying survey results or for checking stock levels in a warehouse.

Recruitment documentation

- A job description summarises the key tasks of a job role. It is also likely to state the person's line manager and whether the role has any direct reports.

- A person specification states the essential and desirable skills an applicant will require to successfully undertake the role. As this is provided to applicants prior to submitting their application, it should be clear, concise and accurate to convey a professional appearance to those interested in the role.
- A job advertisement's format may vary depending on whether it is inserted into a newspaper or added to the business's website, for example. The advertisement should summarise the key tasks of the role, the method of application and the closing date. If it is in a third party location, e.g. a newspaper, there may also be a brief introduction to the business. This will influence the applicant's first impression of the business and must therefore be professional and accurate.
- Application forms must be straightforward to complete, while enabling the business to collect sufficient information about each person to shortlist people for interview.

5.4 How to review business communications to make sure they are fit for purpose

Appropriate type of communication for audience

Any communication must be understood by the intended audience to achieve its objective, e.g. a report for internal staff using technical jargon to explain product specifications will be suitable for this audience but it may need to be simplified if a customer is to understand it.

Tone

Often what is communicated relies on tone as much as the actual words used. This includes facial expressions, body language, the volume of speech and the way in which something is expressed, e.g. a **press release** will usually be upbeat and promote positive aspects of a business, even if there are negatives.

KEY TERM

Press release – an announcement that issues information to the media, e.g. regarding an award or a new innovation.

Layout/design

- Logo: most written or electronic business communications will incorporate the corporate logo. This provides consistency as there are often guidelines about how it should be used.
- Letterhead: many businesses will purchase pre-printed headed paper. This means that all letters sent by the business will have the same format detailing contact information for the business.
- Font: it is advisable to use a standard font when writing formal communications, to ensure consistency. Some fonts, e.g. Arial, are more formal than others, e.g. Comic Sans MS.
- Corporate colours: corporate colours on all business communications from letterheads to websites help to establish a corporate identity that customers, suppliers and other stakeholders recognise, e.g. blue and white for the NHS.
- Images: images can be used in business communications to illustrate points made. All images should be relevant and used only if appropriate permissions have been granted, e.g. if a supermarket wants to use a photograph of checkout staff on its website, permission will have to be obtained from them.

Relevance of information

All information should be relevant to the purpose of the communication, e.g. if a document is produced to provide a customer with product specifications, then detailed cost information would not be relevant.

KNOW IT

1 Explain two examples of how the intended audience will influence the design of business communications.
2 State one example of when it would be most appropriate to use verbal communication in a business context.
3 State two benefits of using electronic business communication.
4 Describe one advantage and one disadvantage to a business of using social media as a marketing tool.
5 Why is it important to ensure that business communications are fit for purpose?

Read about it

7 C's of effective business communication: http://tinyurl.com/kffqbjm

Business forms and templates: www.entrepreneur.com/formnet

Confidentiality protocols – University Hospitals Bristol: http://tinyurl.com/jmo6ne9

How do I prioritise my workload? http://tinyurl.com/zcjezco

Intellectual Property Office (Copyright, Designs and Patents Act): http://tinyurl.com/l7kohn6

Making travel arrangements for executives: http://tinyurl.com/hyn4ne3

Six things you would do when proofing and checking a business document: http://tinyurl.com/zejoucx

The essentials of effective business communication: http://tinyurl.com/zm7a3l4

Unit 2 assessment practice questions

Below are some practice questions for you to try.

1 Descuento Ltd is a supermarket with 110 stores throughout the UK. Its head office and main warehouse are near Loughborough (Leicestershire) and it also leases warehouses in Basildon (Essex) and Wakefield (West Yorkshire). Recently it has expanded into the London area, opening 18 new stores in six months.

The business aims to offer customers excellent value for money, and therefore the quality of both the products sold and the service provided is key to its success.

Tomas Jensen has been the managing director for five years. He has initiated many changes, including the recent introduction of own-label products and the expansion into London. He, and the other members of the executive board, are planning to take over a smaller competitor called Value Haven, which is based in south-west England. This would enable Descuento Ltd to open 35 new stores within the next year by converting the Value Haven stores into Descuento stores.

Tomas and the executive board have access to confidential information regarding the planned takeover of Value Haven.

a Outline two methods of maintaining the confidentiality of this information. (2 marks)

b Explain two implications for Descuento Ltd if the confidentiality of this information were breached. (4 marks)

c Recommend two IT security protocols that Descuento Ltd could use to protect against unauthorised access to information. Give reasons for your choice. (6 marks)

2 Carmen Simpson is the marketing co-ordinator at Descuento Ltd. She has overseen the design and production of new own-label packaging for products including yoghurts, frozen vegetables and tinned soups.

Next week, Carmen has a meeting with Andrew Stanley at Jay Media to discuss design ideas for packaging a new range of own-label ready meals. Carmen needs to travel from Loughborough to Newcastle for the meeting.

Carmen can either:

- use her own car to drive to Newcastle upon Tyne from home; it is 188 miles each way and should take three hours 45 minutes to get there. Descuento Ltd pays employees 45p per mile when using their own vehicle for work purposes

- travel by train; a standard return train ticket will cost £96 and the journey to Newcastle should take three hours 9 minutes.

  a State two additional expenses Carmen may have if travelling by train that would not apply if she travelled by car. (2 marks)

  b Explain one benefit to Carmen of choosing to travel by train. (2 marks)

  c The Administration Department at Descuento Ltd has booked Carmen a hotel eight miles from Newcastle train station and two miles from Jay Media. Explain how this might influence Carmen's travel decision. (4 marks)

3 When Descuento Ltd orders products such as baked beans, pasta, coffee and washing powder from its suppliers, business documentation will be produced by both Descuento Ltd and its suppliers as part of the ordering and payment process.

  a Outline the purpose of a purchase order. (2 marks)

  b Look at the copy of the invoice sent to Descuento Ltd by Cleanz plc, a supplier of washing powder (Figure 2.7). Identify three errors on the invoice. (3 marks)

Descuento Ltd
Croby Park
Loughborough
LE11 4LV

INVOICE

Invoice to:	Delivery address:
Descuento Ltd	Descuento Ltd
Croby Park	Centurion Way
Loughborough	Basildon
LE11 4LV	SS15 9EH

| Customer account: CL492 | |

Invoice number: 6493	Delivery date: 29/09/16
Invoice date: 25/09/16	Payment terms: 30 days

Quantity	Description	Unit price	Amount
100	Non-bio washing powder 2.6 kg	£5.00	£500.00
200	Washing powder 4.2 kg	£70.00	£1400.00
	Subtotal:		£1900.00
	VAT (10%):		£380.00
	Total:		**£2280.00**

▲ **Figure 2.7** Find the errors in the invoice

c Twelve boxes of 4.2 kg washing powder were damaged in transit. Using information on the invoice in Figure 2.7, complete the shaded boxes on the credit note in Figure 2.8. (4 marks)

Cleanz plc
Ashlee Road
Bristol
BS16 8TR

CREDIT NOTE

Customer:	Date: 6/10/16
	Credit note number: CRN614
	Invoice number:

| Customer account: CL492 | Invoice date: 30/09/16 |

Quantity	Description	Unit price	Amount
	Subtotal:		
	VAT (20%):		
	Total credit		

▲ **Figure 2.8** Complete the credit note

d Analyse the benefits and drawbacks of two payment methods that Descuento Ltd could use to pay the invoice. Which payment method do you recommend? Justify your decision. (12 marks)

4 On Monday morning, Tomas Jensen looks in his diary and sees that he has two meetings today: a weekly sales update with the executive board at 10 am and an annual performance review for Sarah Farther, the finance director, at 4 pm. Tomas lists other tasks he aims to complete today, as follows.

● Task 1: Read through paperwork sent by the company lawyers regarding the takeover of Value Haven. He has a meeting with the lawyers tomorrow at 1 pm.

● Task 2: Prepare for a meeting with Vincent Welsh, the chairman of Descuento Ltd, on Thursday in the boardroom at the Loughborough head office. Tomas needs to produce an update on progress with the takeover as well as projected sales figures and profits for the next year. The finance director needs to provide him with the financial information.

● Task 3: Book a hotel room in London for Thursday night.

  a Identify three factors that influence task prioritisation. (3 marks)

  b Explain one reason why Tomas may have to change the level of priority assigned to a task. (2 marks)

  c Identify two methods of business communication Tomas could use to provide the information requested by the chairman. (2 marks)

  d In the centre column of Table 2.3, write the task number of one task that you believe to be of high priority, one task that is of medium priority and one that is low priority. (3 marks)

  e Complete the right-hand column to justify your reasoning for allocating that level of priority. (3 marks)

Table 2.3 Assigning priorities to tasks

Level of priority	Task	Reason for level of priority chosen
High		
Medium		
Low		

5 The takeover of Value Haven by Descuento Ltd is to go ahead in June. This means that Descuento Ltd

will be able to open 35 new stores in the south-west in time for the busy Christmas trading period. Some local people are concerned about rumours that Value Haven is to close, because they like its value for money and good customer service.

a Using the information given in the first paragraph of this question and in question 1, above, write a press release that will be given to the local media in the south-west to announce the take-over. (12 marks)

You will be assessed on the content, tone and layout of your press release. Ensure that it addresses the concerns of the local community.

Use the letterhead in Figure 2.9 to write your press release. You may want to draft your press release on separate paper first. You will not receive marks for the draft.

Descuento Ltd

**Croby Park
Loughborough
LE11 4LV**

▲ **Figure 2.9** Letterhead

Unit 03

Business decisions

ABOUT THIS UNIT

All businesses make decisions. Key decisions might include extending a product range, a business changing direction and targeting a new market, or deciding if it should expand. The decisions made could affect the day-to-day operational activities of the business and could also impact on its short- and long-term success.

The ability to make decisions depends on the effective collation, processing and analysis of relevant information. In this unit you will develop your skills of business decision making using multiple sources of information. You will explore the criteria on which business decisions should be based, and methods to interpret and analyse this information. You will learn to consider the many variables involved and be encouraged to analyse possible solutions, investigating each for potential drawbacks and benefits, before reaching your preferred decision. The learning contained within this unit will provide a framework that you will be able to apply in a business setting.

LEARNING OUTCOMES

The topics, activities and suggested reading in this unit will help you to:

1 understand factors to be taken into account when making business decisions
2 be able to use financial data to inform business decisions
3 understand how human resource information informs business decisions
4 understand how marketing information informs business decisions
5 be able to use resource, project and change management information to inform business decisions
6 be able to use information to make and justify business decisions.

How will I be assessed?

This unit will be externally assessed via a test set and marked by OCR.

LO1 Understand factors to be taken into account when making business decisions

(10 minutes)

Imagine the fashion and home furnishings retailer Next is planning to expand its product range. What sort of information would managers need to decide what new products to introduce?

1.1 Different types of business decision

A business continually makes decisions at three levels: **strategic**, **tactical** and **operational** (Table 3.1).

KEY TERM

Strategic decisions – decisions made by top management that affect the long-term direction of a business.

Tactical decisions – decisions made by middle management that aim to meet strategic objectives.

Operational decisions – day-to-day decisions made by staff at all levels that help the business to run smoothly.

Table 3.1 Types of business decision

Type of decision	Description	Questions	Taken by	Impact	Examples
Strategic	Business-wide complex and multi-dimensional choices of identity and direction May involve large sums of money	Who are we? Where are we heading?	Senior managers	Long term	Expand product range Relocate headquarters Diversify
Tactical	How to manage performance to achieve the strategy These decisions may involve significant resources but within clearer boundaries, and may not affect the whole business	What resources are needed? What is the timescale?	Senior or middle managers	Medium term	Carry out research on suitable product for development Look for suitable locations for headquarters
Operational	Routine decisions that follow known rules, involve more limited resources, can be carried out quickly and have a shorter-term application	How many? To what specification?	Staff at all levels	Short term	How much stock to order Which suppliers to use

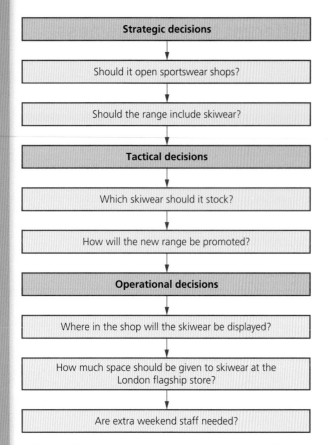

▲ Figure 3.1 How types of business decision are linked

1.2 Different criteria used when making business decisions

Just like individuals, businesses make decisions using different criteria, which are determined by internal and external factors.

Internal factors

Attitude to risk

If a business is said to be risk averse this means that it is reluctant to take risks. As the level of risk increases, the potential for reward, which can either be profit or loss, also increases. A risk-averse business may be less likely to gain high rewards or suffer great losses than a business that is more likely to take risks. Eastman Kodak spent $500 million per year to develop digital photography products that it hoped would change the way people create, store and view pictures. The company took a huge risk but it didn't pay off as Kodak's forecast of customer behaviour was inaccurate and it failed to keep up with technological advancement in its sector.

Risks can be the effect on a business's reputation and the likelihood of success of a project. Ansoff's Matrix is a tool businesses use to measure risk (see page 161).

Organisational objectives

These are targets that have a direct impact on the decisions taken by a business. For example, if the business objective is to reduce running costs by 10 per cent, it is unlikely that more staff will be employed. The decision regarding a marketing mix will depend on marketing objectives set.

Core competencies of a business

These are the things that a business is good at, making it stand out from its competitors and enabling it to do better. Facebook's core competence is social networking, while Apple's is product design. You would not expect Facebook to start making handheld tablets, for example. However, Tesco's tablet equivalent – Hudl – was well received. The product might have been outside Tesco's core competencies but the company took a risk and succeeded.

Writing in 1990, business management experts Prahalad and Hamel (see 'Read about it' at the end of this unit) stated that, 'managers will be judged on their ability to identify, cultivate, and exploit the core competencies that make growth possible – indeed, they'll have to rethink the concept of the corporation itself'.

According to Prahalad and Hamel, in order for a business to grow, it needs to develop areas of expertise unique to them. Businesses need to constantly adapt their core competencies to changes in the external environment, and to be able to evolve and develop as opportunities arise.

Impact on internal stakeholders

For example, a business deciding on whether to automate a production line will need to consider subsequent job losses and its impact on employees. Before deciding whether to extend its opening hours, a business will need to think about the effect on its employees, especially those with young families.

Business ethics

Consumer trends dictate that businesses take a strong ethical stance in their activities. Doing the right thing is not always the most natural choice, as ethical business practices cost money. A restaurant choosing to use local organic supplies for its ingredients is showing strong business ethics even though it is more costly. A manufacturer choosing to locate in the UK to benefit the local community puts ethics before profits. A business also needs to consider its corporate social responsibility when making decisions. For example, US company Ben

& Jerry's uses only fair trade ingredients and has developed a dairy farm sustainability programme in its home state of Vermont. Actions such as this can also provide a business with a unique selling point that appeals to customers and improves its reputation.

Financial considerations

The decisions that a business makes often depend on the funds available. Whether to buy or rent premises depends on what the business can afford. Available funds could be internal (e.g. retained profit, owners' funds) or external (e.g. bank loan, mortgage, selling shares, debentures).

Businesses often decide it is cheaper to use outside contractors for a task instead of doing the task in-house. A prime example is using a distribution company to deliver products. By outsourcing deliveries, huge capital investments and the running costs of maintaining the vehicles are avoided.

Time

Complex decisions require more time to consider than simple, straightforward ones. In addition, a choice could depend on the amount of time it takes for a business to reap its rewards. For a business that prioritises cash flow over long-term profit, a project with a shorter payback period is preferred.

Opportunity cost

This refers to the consequences of decisions and alternatives. For example, due to limited resources, a business has to choose between two projects, A and B. By choosing project A, the business will lose out on the benefits of project B, and vice versa.

> ### 🔍 INDEPENDENT RESEARCH ACTIVITY
>
> **(10 minutes)**
>
> Improve your understanding of this important concept by searching on YouTube for the video 'Opportunity cost definition and real world examples'.

External factors

Level and nature of risk

Examples of risks that are beyond a business's control are natural disaster, terrorist attacks, war, changes in consumer trends and changes in economic factors. Before a major strategic decision is made, businesses need to identify the likelihood of these risks and consider their options; this is the first step of the risk-management process.

Impacts on external stakeholders

These are important considerations as external stakeholders such as customers, local community and pressure groups can have a serious impact on a business's reputation. If you were an energy provider, would you consider fracking?

> ### PAIRS ACTIVITY ⋯⋯⋯⋯⋯⋯⋯⋯⋯
>
> **(20 minutes)**
>
> Read the following articles:
>
> - www.bbc.co.uk/news/uk-14432401
> - http://tinyurl.com/j7fd3hb
>
> Identify the stakeholder groups that will be impacted by fracking activities and explain how they will be impacted.

Degree of uncertainty

The next step is to assess the level of risk – the likelihood of the risks actually happening. Some risks may be likely and difficult to control (e.g. when a particular competitor is known to be developing a similar product), while others are less likely or can be controlled (e.g. an online shop could be hacked).

Before making a major strategic decision that requires lots of borrowed funds, businesses need to consider the risk of a rise in interest rates and how likely it is that this will take place. Businesses looking to expand their operations into China will need to predict the economic conditions there.

The decision will of course depend on the business's attitude to risk and how important change is to the long-term survival of the business.

Changes in market

These refer to changes in the demand and supply of certain goods or services in the market, mainly as a result of social factors such as changing consumer preferences. Businesses need to respond quickly to any changes in the market they operate in, in order to maintain or gain market share.

? THINK ABOUT IT

Case study: McCain

McCain (known for its oven chips) experienced a slowdown in sales as a result of campaigns to encourage healthier eating. McCain responded to this challenge by:

- improving the nutritional make-up of its potato products, which are now pre-cooked in sunflower oil instead of vegetable oil to reduce saturated fats; salt is not added to oven chips and added salt was reduced by up to 50 per cent in other potato products
- reducing quantities of salt and oil throughout its potato products range – McCain argued that these figures were very low already
- conveying the message that its chips are not unhealthy and are made from simple ingredients such as whole potatoes and sunflower oil.

Because McCain is a market-focused company, it recognises that it has to respond to what its consumers want.

Source: © Business Case Studies LLP. Reproduced by permission of the publisher: www.businesscasestudies.co.uk

Changes in external environment

These could be any changes in external factors including economic, legal, political and technological. The McCain case study also shows how the company responded to the external environment.

? THINK ABOUT IT

Legal factors

Responsible businesses not only abide by the law but also seek to create standards above minimum requirements.

Economic factors

These include inflation, unemployment, interest rates, exchange rates and economic growth. In McCain's case, they include changes in buying patterns as people's incomes rise. For example, as incomes go up people may buy what they see as superior varieties of a product type, e.g. ready meals like oven chips.

Political factors

The UK government has increased the pressure on food suppliers to sell healthier foods and supports healthy eating initiatives, e.g. through higher taxation.

Technological changes

Food technology involves researching, developing and finding technical solutions to problems like retaining the flavour and nutritional content of frozen food. McCain found a solution by switching to sunflower oil, which not only reduced salt and fat saturated fats by 70 per cent, but also kept the taste its customers enjoyed.

Source: adapted from www.businesscasestudies.co.uk

1.3 The use of different types of information when making business decisions

Internal information

This is information that can be found in the different functional areas – finance, sales, marketing, production, human resources, etc. The use of financial information will be covered in detail in LO2.1. For example, trends in sales revenue inform production and development decisions, and the purchase of raw materials; production costs and running costs of different products can be used to measure the profitability of each product; productivity, absenteeism and staff turnover are measures of how motivated employees are and these figures can be compared across departments or over time.

External information

Information outside of a business includes all the external factors covered earlier in this unit. Besides carrying out market research on consumer preferences, a business also needs to compare its current activities and performance with those of its competitors.

Qualitative information

This is data based on people's opinions, attitudes and feelings, collected to gain a deeper understanding of consumer behaviour. Qualitative data is usually collected using unstructured or semi-structured questions, giving people opportunities to express their opinions.

Quantitative information

This is numerical data that can be quantified and analysed mathematically. Quantitative information is usually translated into statistics, e.g. the proportion of people who spend 30 per cent of their income on entertainment, the percentage of population who prefer to eat out rather than have takeaways.

Historic information

This refers to using past data to make decisions, e.g. on competitors, the market, past consumer trends. Historic information can be found across all functional departments and can also be gathered outside the business. The internet provides a rich source of historical information, which can be assessed relatively easily and quickly.

Forecasted information

This is based on internal or external prediction and forecasts. For example, sales forecasts can be used to inform human resource needs, while consumer trends are useful for making strategic decisions regarding product development. Businesses need to constantly look ahead when planning for the medium and long term.

Primary research information

This is data collected through primary research – the collection of new data and information specific to a business's need when the information does not already exist. Examples could include a business wanting to find out how many people living in the local area smoke or the number of similar businesses operating within a five-mile radius.

Secondary research information

Secondary data already exists and is readily available to businesses from many sources, such as data agencies, government statistics, journals and magazines, computer databases, etc. Examples include population make-up, consumer buying habits and lifestyle changes.

Table 3.2 outlines the advantages and disadvantages of these different types of information.

Table 3.2 Advantages and disadvantages of different types of data

Type of information	Advantages	Disadvantages
Internal	Readily available Less costly to collect than external information Generally contains fewer errors than information collected externally through market research	Requires a culture of keeping accurate information within a business Only using internal information to make decisions fails to consider the external environment Does not help with consumer trends Does not provide opportunities for benchmarking across the sector Cannot prepare a business from impending or future threats
External	A large amount of information is available It is easy to obtain online	The quantity of available data can be confusing It can be very costly, especially to small businesses, to obtain information from external research companies
Qualitative	Allows a deeper understanding of consumer behaviour by looking in detail at their opinions, attitude and feelings Allows people to elaborate on their answers so that more detailed and meaningful analysis can be made	Difficult to analyse as the answers vary according to opinions It can be time-consuming to organise focus groups and face-to-face interviews It takes longer to analyse the results; the quality of the data collected depends heavily on the skills of the interviewer/observer Fewer people can be researched and therefore the results cannot be accurately generalised to apply to the whole population
Quantitative	Easy to analyse using statistical methods Consumer trends and preferences can be deduced from a large amount of data Results collected are more objective than qualitative data Results can generally be applied to the whole population Research methods are much easier, cheaper and less time-consuming to implement than those for collecting qualitative data; these methods can be repeated easily in another location or with other samples of population, and the results compared	It does not answer the question 'Why?', e.g. while it is useful to know that more women than men work part-time, it is more useful to find out the reason for this The use of structured questions might lead to bias and false answers, rendering the findings unreliable The options presented to interviewees might not be the options they truly prefer, only the closest match The data can appear to be more scientific and factual than it actually is

Type of information	Advantages	Disadvantages
Historic	If things remain more or less the same, historic information can be used to forecast the future relatively accurately Future sales of a product can be forecast using past sales figures It does not require a lot of skill to collect historic data and it can be collected quite quickly It ensures consistency, and reinforces the attitude, value and culture of a business; this leads to continuity and stakeholders know what to expect	If there have been changes to the internal and external business environment, the use of historic information could impede growth; this could lead to loss of market share and failure
Forecasted	If reliable, it allows businesses to be prepared e.g. contingency plans can be put in place if the interest rate is forecast to go up, or if the economy is forecast to slow down then appropriate plans can be made for reducing human resources Cash flow forecasts can be used to predict shortages of cash so that a loan can be arranged before it is a problem	A forecast is simply a prediction, an educated guess, that might not be useful in the face of changes Inaccurate forecasts may lead to disastrous decisions and huge losses Predicting the future is not easy, especially for new businesses with little historic data Forecasting requires a high degree of skill, knowledge and experience – even professionals can get it wrong
Primary	Questionnaires can be tailored to a business's specific needs; the results can then be used to solve particular problems that a business faces	Large-scale primary research can be very costly and time-consuming Time and money need to be spent on designing the research methods, which will then need to be carried out over a period of time A lot of skills and knowledge are required when designing the questionnaire and in subsequent interpretation of the results
Secondary	Easier, quicker and cheaper to collect than primary information Existing information collected by professional organisations can be very accurate and reliable, as data is usually collated from a large sample	It can be costly to obtain, making it beyond the reach of small businesses Free secondary information can be very confusing, and it is time-consuming to sift through the different sources to reach a conclusion Different sources might present conflicting information It is difficult to find secondary data that fits the specific needs of a business It can be hard to tell how reliable a secondary source is

1.4 How to judge the validity of information used to make decisions

When using information to make decisions, it is vital to make sure that the information used is valid – does it tell the 'truth'? The validity of information can be judged using the criteria described below.

Reliability

If a piece of research is to be repeated, will the researcher get the same result?

Of course it is impossible to get exactly the same result again and again, but there should be a strong correlation between results. Information is said to be reliable if the same response is obtained when a question is given to the same sample at different times, or when the same question is given to different samples.

Bias

Has the researcher, in the process of collecting the information, somehow influenced the outcome?

This could be the way the questions are asked, e.g. their tone of voice or body language, the way the sample is chosen or the way the research is carried out. For example, not giving people enough time to fill out a questionnaire tends to produce biased results.

Relevance

Can the information selected be used to answer the question or solve the problem?

For example, in a survey on spending habits, it would be irrelevant to ask people what time they usually get up in the morning. Great care must be taken when deciding on what questions to ask to ensure the questions will enable you to collect the information you set out to obtain.

Complexity

Is the information too difficult to understand?

Results should be expressed in clear language. Diagrams and flow charts can be used effectively to describe a system or a process, but they should not be so complicated as to impede understanding.

Degree of detail

Does the level of detail match the type of decision being made?

Some decisions require detailed personal information on consumers, e.g. to build an accurate profile. However, the decision on whether to discontinue a product line does not require detailed information on consumer spending; a study of the sales trends of the product should be sufficient for the decision to be made.

Currency

Is the information up to date?

Outdated information should not be used to inform the future, e.g. consumers are becoming more aware of food miles and sustainability. Information in this area has to be up to date otherwise the decision made may be the wrong one.

Intended use

Is the information appropriate to what it will be used for?

Information gathered for psychologists to explain a certain behavioural pattern is usually not intended for marketing purposes. In this case the information would contain more details than needed and the level of complexity would be too high. It is therefore important to choose information that is gathered for the purpose intended, in order not to waste time and effort.

Quality

Is the quality of the information chosen up to standard?

The internet has become the main source of information for most people, but sometimes it is hard to tell if that information is reliable and authoritative. The first check for quality is the source: does the information come from a well-known and reliable organisation? Other criteria include whether it is complete, up to date or comprehensive enough for the task to be performed.

1.5 The purposes, benefits and importance of communication

With internal and external stakeholders

Effective communication between stakeholders eases the decision-making process. Communication should take place before, during and after decisions have been made. Communication allows stakeholders of a business to know why change is necessary, the options available to them and the rationale behind a particular course of action.

Customers and the local community also need to be informed of a decision that has a direct impact on them. For example, informing customers, the local community and employees of a proposal to extend the working hours of a noisy industrial dry-cleaning business would convey an image of a caring business that is prepared to listen to their views.

If the decision involves huge financial commitment or a business finds itself having cash flow problems, lenders need to be informed in the first instance to avoid confusion and distrust.

With the media

The media need to be dealt with sensitively, especially if a crisis is involved. By being seen to be open and sincere, carrying out swift remedial actions, a business can avoid damage to its reputation.

PAIRS ACTIVITY

(15 minutes)

In early January 2006, Salmonella Montevideo, a bacterium that can cause severe food poisoning, was found in a factory of food manufacturer Cadbury Schweppes. The company decided not to inform health authorities as senior management felt that it posed only a minor risk. When the information was leaked in late June 2006, the Food Standards Agency (FSA) declared Cadbury's products to present an unacceptable risk to the public. It was only then that the company decided to recall more than a million affected products.

Cadbury's failure to deal with the crisis of food poisoning led to a loss in sales and consumer confidence. Even though Cadbury's market share recovered, the long-term effect was substantial damage to the image of the company.

In pairs, discuss what Cadbury Schweppes should have done.

Cadbury's experience illustrates the importance of communication. In a crisis, the business concerned must be seen to be open and willing to take remedial action. Cut for space. Stakeholders need to be reassured and informed of the steps that the business has already taken to deal with the problem, and that the situation is under control.

1.6 Factors affecting the quality of decision making

The quality of a decision made could mean the success or failure of a business. A sound decision requires the following elements.

Access to relevant information

Sometimes it is difficult to obtain information that could be useful, e.g. competitors' sales figures and strategies. Equally, too much information could be overwhelming or introduce inaccurate data.

Access to decision-making tools

Depending on the kind of decision to be made and the availability of personnel, these tools could help speed up the decision-making process and improve the quality of the decision made.

For example, multi-voting could be used to reduce a long list of options according to a business's priority and objectives. This involves getting a team of people to vote on a list of options identified via brainstorming. A decision tree could compare the probability of success or failure of options available. It sets out different options in a visual format, starting with a box containing the decision that needs to be made. Lines from this box lead to possible solutions; squares represent decisions and circles uncertain outcomes. Eventually, all possible solutions and decisions should be mapped out. Then, for each circle, estimate the probability of each outcome, to a total of 100%. For example, if an outcome is very likely, it could be 90%, making the other outcome 10%. Then you need to calculate the value of the outcomes. For uncertain outcomes, multiply the value by their probability. Finally, the most desirable course of action can be chosen.

Availability of finance

The more funds a business has access to, the more options can be adopted, which ultimately improves the quality of decision making. Paying to seek advice from consultancy companies with expert knowledge and guidance should improve the quality of the decision. Having the funds to carry out large-scale research also helps to improve the quality of the information collected, which increases the probability of a business adopting the right course of action.

Key personnel

Staff with knowledge, skills and experience not only ease the decision-making process, but the outcome chosen is also likely to be more successful. Having personnel with the analytical skills to understand the information collected is key to accurate interpretation of data. Being able to follow a solution-focused approach, coupled with problem-solving abilities, will certainly improve the quality of the final decision.

Training of managers in decision-making skills

If managers are familiar with the decision-making process, then a business is more likely to adopt a systematic approach to solving problems and finding solutions.

Power differentials and potential for bias

This is the concept that people with power (i.e. senior management) are more likely to pay attention to information that confirms their beliefs and favour decisions that appear to benefit only those in power. The focus should be on making decisions to benefit the whole business, including staff at the bottom of the hierarchy, based on the aims and objectives set.

Consultation

Internal and external stakeholders should be consulted where appropriate. Seeking advice and expertise from consultancies can benefit businesses that do not have this internal skill and experience. Consulting firms can provide help and guidance in the different functional areas, and can also provide in-house training courses, workshops and seminars to help the decision-making process.

> **KNOW IT**
> 1 Describe the difference between strategic and tactical decisions.
> 2 Define the term 'opportunity cost'.
> 3 Define the term 'business ethics'. Explain two reasons why it is important to take business ethics into consideration when making business decisions.
> 4 Explain the benefits and drawbacks of using quantitative and qualitative data in decision making.
> 5 Explain how a business benefits from communicating with internal and external stakeholders before, during and after decisions are made.

LO2 Be able to use financial data to inform business decisions

(10 minutes)

Working on your own, match the following financial terms with their definitions to find out how much you know about financial data.

Financial terms	Definitions
Gross profit	The flow of money into and out of a business
Net profit	The point where total revenue equals total costs
Break even	The money left over after all expenses have been taken away from the revenue
Cash flow	The money left over after the cost of producing goods or services has been taken away from the revenue

2.1 How to use profitability data

Businesses exist to make profit, at least in the private sector. Without profit a business cannot grow; it does not have surplus funds to invest in improving itself, to develop new goods and services, or satisfy the needs of stakeholders such as employees and shareholders.

More information about accounting can be found in Units 12 and 13.

Costs and revenues

Costs

Costs are the amount of money businesses spend on goods and services. For a business that is already established, costs can be classified as fixed or variable:

- fixed costs do not change according to sales, e.g. rent, rates, insurance
- variable costs change depending on the level of output, e.g. raw materials, direct labour.

Since costs are the amount of money going out of a business, they must be closely monitored to ensure that there is enough working capital to keep the business running smoothly. The formula for calculating total costs is:

Total costs = Fixed costs + Variable costs

Revenues

This is the money earned by a business primarily through selling goods and services. It is money flowing in to the business and so can be used to judge its success. Ideally sales revenues should follow an upward trend year on year. The formula for calculating total revenue is:

Revenue = Selling price $\times$ Units sold

Gross and net profit/loss

Gross profit or loss

This is the money left over after taking the costs of goods and services (variable costs or cost of sales) from the sales revenue. This figure indicates how profitable a good or service is. For example, supermarkets may pay dairy farmers 48p for two litres of milk and sell it for 94p. If a supermarket sells 100 two-litre bottles of milk every day, then gross profit can be calculated using the formula:

Gross profit = Revenue − Total variable cost

First we calculate the total revenue for selling 100 units:

Revenue = Selling price $\times$ Units sold

= 94p $\times$ 100 = £94

Then we calculate the total variable cost of selling 100 units:

Total variable cost = Variable cost per unit $\times$ Units sold

= 48p $\times$ 100

= £48

Gross profit = Revenue − Total variable cost = £94 − £48
= £46

The greater the difference between revenue and cost of sales, the higher the gross profit.

Net profit/loss

This calculates the money left over after taking away expenses (fixed costs) from gross profit, e.g. salaries, rent and insurance – expenses that cannot be directly linked to the production or purchase of goods and services. It shows how profitable a business actually is. Besides paying dairy farmers for the milk, the supermarket needs to pay rent, salaries, insurance, utilities, etc. If the total expenditure of stocking the milk is £15 per day, then the net profit of selling the milk in the supermarket can be calculated using the formula:

Net profit = Gross profit – Expenses

= £46 – £15 = £31

Profitability ratios

Profitability ratios measure a business's ability to make profits, so are good indicators of business performance. These ratios can be used by management to show how well departments keep costs down. Shareholders base their decision as to whether to invest in a business on examining these figures. There are two types of profitability ratio: net profit ratio and gross profit ratio.

Net profit ratio

This is a comparison of a business's net profit with its sales revenue, expressed as a percentage. It measures a business's ability to generate profit and can be used to indicate efficiency. The net profit ratio of a business can be calculated and compared over a period of time or it can be compared with those of its competitors.

Net profit ratio = (Net profit/revenue) $\times$ 100

Using the example of the supermarket:

Net profit margin = £31 ÷ £94 $\times$ 100 = 33%

To determine whether 33% is a good figure, a business needs to compare it with the industry average.

Gross profit ratio

This measures the profitability of the goods and services provided by a business. It compares the gross profit made from selling goods and services to the total sales revenue received, expressed as a percentage.

Gross profit ratio = (Gross profit/revenue) $\times$ 100

Using the example of the supermarket:

Gross profit margin = £46 ÷ £94 $\times$ 100 = 49%

The gross profit margin is usually much higher than the net profit margin as it is a simple calculation of the proportion of profit made by selling goods and services before taking expenses into account. As with net profit margin, whether it is a good figure or not depends on its change over time and it should be compared with similar businesses in the same industry. Gross profit margins tend to be much higher than net profit margins because of high costs of employing workers, renting premises, marketing campaigns, etc.

Business performance data

Profitability ratios are key indicators of a business's performance. Other key indicators can include:

- customer satisfaction – by finding out how satisfied the customers of a business are with the quality and price of goods and services provided, the quality of the shopping experience and after-sales services, we will know how a business is performing and can predict its long-term performance; this data can also be used to compare across the industry to assess the competitiveness of a business
- employee satisfaction – satisfied employees work harder and better, improving productivity; rates of absenteeism and staff turnover tend to be low, keeping costs down; wastage level will be low, with better employee performance due to high levels of motivation.

INDIVIDUAL ACTIVITY

(20 minutes)

The following income statement has been prepared for a veterinary centre.

	£
Revenue from selling goods	30,000
Revenue from selling services	324,000
Total revenue	354,000
Less: cost of sales	54,000
Gross profit	
Expenses	
Wages	156,000
Overheads	120,000
Repairs and maintenance	6,600
Total expenses	282,600
Net profit	

Calculate:

1 the gross profit
2 the net profit
3 the gross profit margin
4 the net profit margin.

Comment on the performance of the veterinary centre based on your calculations.

2.2 How to use break-even analysis

Break even is when a business's revenue equals total costs – it is the point where neither profit nor loss is made. It determines the minimum number of units that need to be sold not to make a loss. This information can be used to plan production, including stock control and purchasing raw materials. It can also be used as a modelling tool to find out the effects of different selling prices on the break-even level. For a new business start-up, the break-even point indicates the viability of a business idea.

Break-even analysis is also covered in Unit 13, LO2 (page 239).

Advantages:

- it can be used to work out the minimum amount of sales needed not to make a loss
- it can be used as a modelling tool to work out a suitable pricing strategy using different prices
- the effects of changes in variable and fixed costs can be worked out and contingency plans put in place
- break-even analysis can be used to support an application for a loan.

Disadvantages:

- the model assumes that all output produced is sold, not taking waste into account; in many businesses this is unrealistic
- it assumes that costs increase at a constant level – for example, a business might negotiate a discounted price if materials are purchased in bulk; this means that the total costs do not increase at a constant rate and therefore the total cost line is unlikely to be straight
- it also assumes that selling price is constant, with no special offers or discounts; it is unrealistic to assume that sales revenue increases at a constant rate.

How to draw, label and interpret a break-even graph

The break-even graph consists of three lines, showing:

- fixed costs
- total costs
- sales revenue.

The vertical (y) axis shows the amount of costs or revenue. The horizontal (x) axis shows the number of units sold or produced.

The fixed cost line is usually presented as a horizontal line, as fixed cost does not change in response to the level of output.

▲ **Figure 3.2** Break-even analysis: fixed cost line

The sales revenue line starts from zero, as there is no revenue when no units are sold. The line increases at a constant rate.

▲ **Figure 3.3** Break-even analysis: sales revenue line

The third line is worked out by adding fixed costs and variable costs at different levels of production or quantity, using the formula:

Total costs = Fixed cost + Variable cost

The total costs line starts from the point where the fixed costs line meets the y-axis because, at zero production, there are no variable costs.

As indicated in Figure 3.4, the break-even point is at the intersection between the sales revenue and total costs line. The break-even quantity can be read off the x-axis, while the y-axis shows the total costs and revenue from selling the break-even quantity.

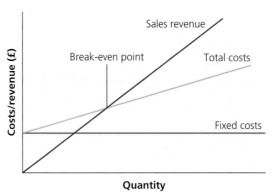
▲ **Figure 3.4** Break-even analysis: total costs and break-even point

Using the break-even graph, the amount of profit made at Q2 can be worked out by taking C1 away from R1; C1 being the total costs of producing Q2 and R1 being the total revenue of selling Q2.

▲ **Figure 3.5** Break-even analysis: calculating profit

How to calculate profit/loss

The break-even point can be calculated using a simple formula:

Break–even point =

Fixed costs / (selling price – variable costs) = per unit

For example, at a market stall selling T-shirts:

- selling price of each T-shirt = £10
- cost of each T-shirt = £5
- cost of market stall = £40

Break-even point = £40/(£10 – £5) = 8 T-shirts

This means the stallholder needs to sell eight t-shirts to not make a loss.

In the absence of a graph, the amount of profit made at a particular level of output or sales can be worked out using the following formula:

Profit = Sales revenue – Total costs

So what profit is made if 100 T-shirts were sold?

First, work out the sales revenue of selling 100 T-shirts:

Sales revenue = Selling price × Quantity sold = £10 × 100 = £1,000

Then work out the total variable cost of producing 100 T-shirts:

Total variable cost = Variable cost per unit × Quantity sold = £5 × 100 = £500

The total costs of selling the T-shirts can then be calculated:

Total costs = Fixed cost + Total variable cost = £40 + £500 = £540

Finally, the amount of profit made if 100 T-shirts were sold:

Profit = Sales revenue – Total costs = £1,000 – £540 = £460

Margin of safety

This is defined as the difference between the quantity at a certain output level and break-even level. This can be worked out by the formula Q2 - Q1.

Using the example above, the break-even point will need to be worked out first:

Break-even point = Fixed costs/(Selling price – Variable cost per unit) or Fixed costs/Unit contribution

= £40/(£10 – £5) or £40/£5

= 8 T-shirts

Margin of safety if 100 T-shirts are sold = 100 – 8 = 92

Profit = Margin of safety × Unit contribution = 92 × £5 = £460

INDIVIDUAL ACTIVITY ·······················

(20 minutes)

1 Using the above information on the T-shirt market stall, complete Table 3.3.

Table 3.3 Working out profits and margin of safety

No. of T-shirts	Sales revenue (No. of T-shirts x selling price)	Fixed cost	Variable cost (No. of T-shirts x variable cost per T-shirt)	Total cost (Fixed cost + variable cost)	Profit/ loss (Sales revenue - Total cost)
2					
4					
6					
8					
10					
12					
14					

2 Draw and label a break-even chart for the market stall.

Factors affecting the break-even level of output

These are related to costs and revenues. Costs could be a rise in rent, pay rises, spending on a marketing campaign, investing in technology, spending more on raw materials, etc.

An increase in costs increases the break-even level, while a decrease in costs lowers it.

An increase in revenue decreases the break-even level, while a decrease in revenue raises it.

PAIRS ACTIVITY ·······························

Consider the factors in Table 3.4 and explain the effect of changes of these factors on the break-even point of a business.

Table 3.4 Factors affecting the break-even point

Factors	Effect
Selling price reduced to stimulate sales	
Cheaper suppliers found overseas	
Rent increases	

Ways to lower the break-even level of output

Finding ways to lower the break-even point will increase profit level. As profitability is an important indicator of performance, businesses should explore ways of achieving a lower break-even output. This usually involves weighing up the effects of a lower fixed cost, a higher selling price or a lower variable cost.

Lowering fixed cost:

- negotiating a cheaper rent
- moving to smaller premises
- shopping around for cheaper insurance premiums and utility costs.

Increasing selling price:

- the product or service must be price inelastic – it has a unique selling point that customers will pay for – for example, top branded perfumes and trainers can enjoy price increases and yet their sales volume will not be affected because consumers are willing to pay more for the perceived benefits of using these products
- prices can increase when there is a shortage in supply, e.g. popular toys that are short in stock at Christmas.

Lowering variable costs:

- switching to a cheaper supplier
- buying stock in bulk at a discounted price
- using less or poorer-quality material
- if direct labour is involved, paying lower wages.

2.3 How to use contribution data

Unit contribution = Selling price − Variable cost per unit

This calculates how much profit (gross) each unit sold makes and therefore how many units need to be sold in order to cover the fixed cost. For example, if a retailer sells bottles of glue for £1 each, while they cost 30p to stock:

Unit contribution = £1 − £0.30 = £0.70

Knowing the unit contribution of a product allows a business to calculate the minimum price of the product. In this case, selling the glue at 30p per bottle would mean the unit contribution would be zero and the product would not contribute to covering the fixed cost.

> **? THINK ABOUT IT**
>
> ### Case study: ABC Ltd
>
> ABC Ltd is considering whether it should accept a special order for 15,000 units of printers from a customer, at £48 per unit. The following data relates to the volumes, prices and costs for the year.
>
> | | |
> |---|---|
> | Production capacity | 80,000 units |
> | Forecast revenues volume | 60,000 units |
> | Selling price | £62.00 |
> | Materials | £36 per unit |
> | Direct labour | £10 per unit |
> | Fixed overheads | £820,000 |
>
> The first step is to work out the unit contribution of each printer:
>
> Unit contribution = £48 − £46 (materials + direct labour) = £2.00
>
> By selling the printers at a reduced price of £48 per unit, ABC Ltd is making only £2 per unit. This figure may seem very low compared with the normal unit contribution of £62 - £46 = £16 per unit. However, the production capacity is 80,000 units and it is forecast to sell only 60,000 units. ABC Ltd could use the spare capacity of 20,000 units to generate more revenue. The extra profit from selling 15,000 printers at £48 is £2 x 15,000 = £30,000. This is a substantial income stream that ABC Ltd cannot afford to ignore and therefore it is a good idea to accept the special order.

However, there might be an argument for selling the glue at 30p if it is a bulk order from an important customer. The order could be accepted to improve customer relations, as the important customer might repeat-purchase in the future. This is known as a special order decision.

2.4 How to use cash-flow data

Cash flow is the movement of money into and out of a business, as revenue from selling goods and services or as loans from banks or dividends received from shares.

When money is spent, cash flows out of the business, so a healthy amount of cash should be available. The net cash flow, which is the difference between cash coming in and cash going out, needs to be positive for a business to survive.

Cash flow does not indicate profit; it is a snapshot of whether a business is spending more or less than it is receiving in terms of cash inflow.

How to interpret cash-flow position

Look at Table 3.5.

The only source of income was from sales of food and drinks, except in April, so the total inflow is the same as the sales figures.

Total outflow is calculated by adding all the cash outflow together.

Net cash flow is calculated by taking total outflow from total inflow.

The opening balance for January is £500. You will see that the opening balance for each month is the same as the closing balance of the previous month.

Closing balances can be calculated using this formula:

Closing balance = Total inflow - Total outflow + Opening balance, or

= Net cash flow + Opening balance

e.g. for May:

= £5,500 – £5,230 + £200 = £470

Indications of good cash-flow position:

- net cash flow is positive – total spend is less than total income
- the closing balances are positive – at the end of each month there is cash left over to run the business in the following month
- opening balances are positive – cash is available for paying bills at the beginning of every month.

Using the closing balances as a criterion, the café is in trouble in February and March, with negative closing balances. Net cash flow is negative for most months, except April and May. The loan has allowed the café to meet its expenditure in April, as indicated by the positive net cash flow. The closing balance in April is also positive, which means the business has some money to pay for its expenditure in May.

Table 3.5 Simple cash-flow statement for a café

	January	February	March	April	May	June
Cash inflow						
Sales	4,500	4,600	4,800	4,900	5,500	5,200
Loan	0	0	0	1,000	0	0
Total inflow	4,500	4,600	4,800	5,900	5,500	5,200
Cash outflow						
Stock	2,300	2,100	2,400	2,500	2,530	2,600
Rent	500	500	500	500	500	500
Wages	1,200	1,200	1,200	1,200	1,200	1,200
Overheads	1,000	1,000	1,000	1,000	1,100	1,100
Total outflow	5,000	4,800	5,100	5,200	5,330	5,400
Net cash flow	(500)	(200)	(300)	700	170	(200)
Opening balance	500	0	(200)	(500)	200	370
Closing balance	0	(200)	(500)	200	370	170

However, the loan increased overheads by £100 in May and June, presumably because of loan repayments. Although this has not affected the business's cash flow position much in May, the effect is felt in June when the net cash flow is again negative. Overall, the cash-flow position of the café is weak. The main problem is its inability to generate enough sales to pay for stock and its bills.

Ways to improve cash flow

Ways to improve cash flow include:

- increasing cash inflow, e.g. improve sales revenue, get a loan
- decreasing cash outflow, e.g. reduce spending.

As seen in the example of the café, a loan can increase cash inflow. However, this is a short-term solution. To survive in the long term, the café will need to improve its sales revenue. This can be achieved through increasing the prices charged for food and drinks. However, this strategy will work only if it does not drive customers away.

The café can try to reduce spending, e.g. by buying cheaper supplies. However, this might compromise the quality of food and drinks, and lose customers. It could also find cheaper premises, use less gas and electricity by reducing waste, reduce the number of staff, etc. All these methods have negative consequences that need to be weighed against the benefits to find the appropriate solution.

PAIRS ACTIVITY

(15 minutes)

Humm, a manufacturer of electric bikes, has the following financial figures:

- selling price £400
- cost of production £200 per bike

- overheads £20,000 per month
- 1,500 bikes were sold in June.

Complete the cash-flow statement in Table 3.6 using the information provided.

Table 3.6 Cash flow statement for Humm

	April	May	June	July
Cash inflow				
Sales revenue	400,000	480,000		720,000
Total cash inflow	400,000	480,000		720,000
Cash outflow				
Cost of production	200,000	240,000		360,000
Overheads				
Total cash outflow				
Net cash flow				
Opening balance	0			
Closing balance				

2.5 How to use investment appraisal

Investment appraisal is the process of evaluating how attractive a business project or idea is. There are three main techniques commonly used by businesses:

1 payback
2 accounting rate of return (ARR)
3 net present value (NPV).

These are summarised in Table 3.7. See Unit 13, LO4 (page 249) for more detailed information that will help you to calculate investment appraisals.

Table 3.7 Advantages and disadvantages of investment appraisal methods

Method	Description	Advantages	Disadvantages
Payback	The time it takes to recoup the initial investment in a project. Estimated net cash flow is worked out over time and payback period is the point where the cumulative net cash flow equals the initial investment. Payback period can be used to compare projects; the shorter the payback period, the more desirable the project	Widely used as it is easy to understand. Focuses on liquidity, which is important if a business has limited funds. The risk of a project with a short payback period is lower than that of a longer payback so is preferred by businesses that are risk averse	Cash flow is not discounted so the time value of money is not recognised. Payback emphasises liquidity and ignores profitability. Calculation ends as soon as payback is reached. Projects with longer payback might be more profitable than those with a shorter payback. It is a short-term approach; cash flow after payback is not considered

Method	Description	Advantages	Disadvantages
Average rate of return (ARR)	This calculates the average profit made over the lifetime of a project and expresses it as a percentage of the initial investment ARR = Average profit/Initial investment x 100	Takes profitability into account, which is an important performance indicator Takes into account cash flow throughout the lifetime of the project	Ignores the time value of money The calculation of average profit does not take into account the timing of cash flow, which can be a priority for businesses with limited funds
Net present value (NPV)	Recognises the time value of money by calculating the net cash flow over the lifetime of a project The NPV figure can be calculated for each project and comparisons made	Takes into account time value of money Considers all the cash flow in the whole lifetime of a project Can be easily compared with a target	The choice of discount factor might not reflect accurately the rate at which it has depreciated over the lifetime of the project Cash flow is estimated, so accuracy requires skills and experience

INDIVIDUAL ACTIVITY

(45 minutes)

The case study at http://tinyurl.com/h34obce describes the factors influencing a decision to expand a chemical plant at Grangemouth.

1 Using Table 3.8, and referring to Unit 13, LO4 (page 249), calculate:
   a payback period
   b average rate of return (ARR)
   c net present value, assuming a discount rate of 10 per cent in Table 3.9.

Table 3.9 shows factors for discount rates of 10 per cent and 20 per cent.

Table 3.8 Estimated cash flow for the Grangemouth expansion project

Year	Net cash flow (£ million)
0	(150)
1	80
2	185
3	210
4	210
5	210
6	210
7	210
8	210
9	210

Table 3.9 Discount rate factors for the Grangemouth expansion project

Discount factor	Year 0	Year 1	Year 2	Year 3	Year 4	Year 5	Year 6	Year 7	Year 8	Year 9
10%	1.00	0.91	0.83	0.75	0.68	0.62	0.56	0.51	0.47	0.42
20%	1.00	0.83	0.69	0.58	0.48	0.40	0.34	0.28	0.23	0.19

2 If a discount rate of 20 per cent were felt to be more appropriate, calculate the net present value based on this rate. Explain the difference this has made to your answer to question 3.

3 Based on your calculations above, would you approve the expansion project? Justify your decision.

KNOW IT

1 Explain what the following ratios measure:
   • gross profit ratio
   • net profit ratio.
2 Explain the meaning of the following terms:
   • margin of safety
   • unit contribution
   • special order decisions.
3 Analyse different ways an ice cream manufacturer could lower its break-even point.

4 Analyse how a small business like a builder could benefit from cash flow management.
5 Describe the advantages and disadvantages of each of the investment appraisal methods listed below:
   • payback
   • average rate of return
   • net present value.

LO3 Understand how human resources information informs business decisions

(10 minutes)

Look at the list of buzz words below. They are qualities employers are looking for in an employee. Discuss with a partner what they actually mean.

Initiative

Proactive

Team player

Dynamic

Self-motivated

3.1 Factors involved in workforce planning

Workforce planning is a management process that focuses on making sure there are enough workers with the right skills, knowledge and experience to perform the different functions to fulfil aims and objectives of a business. Several factors need to be taken into account, as described below.

Size of workforce

- How many employees are currently employed?
- Are there enough employees to perform all the tasks to a good standard?
- Is there a need to recruit more to take on a new project?

Conversely, a business could have recruited too many employees and now needs to consider reducing the size of its workforce to improve efficiency, or a project has been completed and the team is no longer required.

The size of a workforce depends on the nature of the business's activity. In a labour-intensive industry such as hotels, restaurants and agriculture, more employees are generally required than in an automated factory. Where the workforce is more affordable, such as China and India, the number of people employed also tends to be larger than it would be where wages are much higher.

Skills of workforce

These are the qualities that employees should possess to work productively and the skills needed to meet the requirements of the business. An important skill relates to employees' ability to communicate effectively, verbally or in a written form. Employees need to communicate information accurately and appropriately according to who they are communicating with. Employees also need to communicate with external stakeholders, especially in the service industry. Other useful skills are planning and organisational skills, analytical and problem-solving skills and good time management to enable deadlines to be met. This requires the ability to plan, organise and prioritise tasks.

Availability of workforce

This is about having the right people with the right skills at the right time. Start with a **skills audit** to find out the workforce's current skills to see whether there are enough employees with the right skills to carry out the tasks required. Plans can be made to fill the skills gap either through training or recruitment.

> **KEY TERM**
>
> **Skills audit** – a review of the existing skills of employees, which is then compared to the skills the business needs currently and expects to need in the future.

Training requirements of workforce

This follows a skills audit. A skills gap analysis will provide information on the training needs of employees. Different types of training can be planned and arranged according to different needs.

Induction

This is introducing the business to new employees, e.g. the aims and objectives, culture and values, as well as more practical things like who to contact when ill, etc. Effective induction training helps new employees to be productive as soon as possible.

On-the-job training

This benefits both employees and the business as the training programme can be specific to particular roles. By working and training at the same time, no working time is lost and there is no extra cost of sending employees to be trained outside. Methods of on-the-job training include:

- coaching – using an experienced member of staff to provide instructions or demonstrations
- mentoring – assigning a knowledgeable member of staff to guide a trainee through a task, offering personal support when required
- job rotation – employees work on different jobs to learn new skills and knowledge

- 'Sitting next to Nellie' – working alongside an experienced member of staff to learn how a particular job is done; questions can be answered straight away, so this can be a fast way of learning to do a job.

Off-the-job training

This is provided away from the usual job – either by doing the training elsewhere on site instead of carrying out normal duties, or offsite at a college or training centre. It may be necessary for employees to learn to use a new piece of equipment, a new piece of software or to find out about changes in the business environment, e.g. new legislation on payroll management. This type of training is more expensive as employees are sent away to another organisation.

Internal training

Internal training is when employees are trained within an organisation. This could be on the job or off the job. Please refer to earlier sections for more information.

External training

External training takes place outside of an organisation. The employees could be attending conferences, training sessions or even taking classes provided at a college. External training is more expensive than internal training but it may be necessary if there is no expertise within an organisation to provide the training needed for the employee to perform a job effectively.

3.2 How to use workforce performance data

Calculate and interpret measures of workforce performance

Workforce performance data measures how productive and effective employees are, as well as how happy they are in the workplace.

Absenteeism

This relates to the number of days lost due to employees not turning up for work. Absenteeism is costly for a business, so management should understand its causes, which could include low morale, low pay, inappropriate leadership style, repetitive job, etc.

$$\text{Absenteeism} = \frac{\text{Number of days employees are absent}}{\text{Total number of working days}} \times 100$$

If a business employs 100 workers who work five days a week for 50 weeks, the total number of working days can be calculated as follows:

$$\text{Total number of working days} = 100 \times 5 \times 50 = 25,000 \text{ days}$$

The number of days employees were absent is 580. So:

$$\text{Absenteeism} = 580/25000 \times 100 = 2.32\%$$

High absenteeism is usually a sign of an unhappy workforce. The causes must be investigated so that remedial action can be taken. Absenteeism can often lead to low productivity as replacement workers might not be as experienced as skilled workers.

Labour turnover

This expresses the number of employees who leave a business as a percentage of the total workforce employed, usually over a one-year period. A high labour turnover may be an indicator of an unhappy workforce due to poor working conditions, low pay, lack of promotional opportunities, inappropriate leadership style, etc. Replacing employees is costly in terms of recruitment and selection, as well as training new replacements. High labour turnover can also lead to low morale among employees.

$$\text{Labour turnover} = \frac{\text{Number of employees leaving}}{\text{Total workforce}} \times 100$$

For example, in a business that has a total workforce of 80, the number of employees leaving over a one-year period is ten:

$$\text{Labour turnover} = 10/80 \times 100 = 12.5\%$$

Productivity

This is a measure of how efficient a workforce is and shows output per employee. In a labour-intensive industry, the consequences of low productivity are high unit costs leading to low profit margin; customers could be lost if orders are not met on time. Common causes of low labour productivity are lack of training, low morale and poor working conditions. Productivity can be improved through financial incentives such as higher pay and piece rates, or non-financial incentives such as a better working environment and training.

$$\text{Labour productivity} = \frac{\text{Total output}}{\substack{\text{Total no. of workers} \\ \text{(or Total no. work hours)}}}$$

For example, a small manufacturer of bouncy castles employs five machinists and they make 25 bouncy castles a day.

$$\text{Labour productivity per day} = 25/5 = 5 \text{ bouncy castles}$$

Wastage

As a measure of workforce performance, wastage is the amount of defective items produced compared to the total output, expressed as a percentage. High wastage levels could be caused by low employee morale as a result of a poor working environment, lack of training or a flaw in the production process, meaning closer quality control is needed. High wastage levels lead to low efficiency and profitability, and must be investigated fully. The formula for wastage level is:

$$\text{Wastage level} = \frac{\text{Quantity of waste}}{\text{Total output}} \times 100$$

Using the example of a cake factory that produces 2,500 cakes a week, if 250 cakes had to be scrapped a week due to poor quality, then

Wastage level = 250/2500 × 100 = 10%

 **PAIRS ACTIVITY**

(20 minutes)

1 Calculate the absenteeism rate if in a month there were 25 absences in a business that employs 30 workers five days a week.
2 Calculate labour turnover if ten employees annually left a business with an average workforce of 100.
3 Suppose a business produced 25 units of product in two hours. Calculate labour productivity.
4 A factory manufacturing trainers found that, for every 500 pairs of trainers produced, five pairs were defective. Calculate the wastage level.

▲ **Figure 3.6** Sickness absence rates by occupation group (2013)

Interpreting trends in workforce performance over time

How does a manager decide whether a figure is good or bad and when action needs to be taken?

To make sense of workforce performance figures, a business needs to compare them over time to discover the trend. Historic data is very useful as it can be compared to see whether labour turnover has increased over the past ten years. For example, some fast-food chains employ students, who are transient workers. For these branches a high labour turnover figure might not be alarming but it does need to be compared with figures for the past few years to see whether it has changed.

To use industrial averages to make comparisons with other businesses/industries

Businesses in different industries can compare their figures with the industrial averages to see whether there is a huge difference. A high variance in the wrong direction indicates further investigation is needed, followed by remedial action.

It is interesting to note from Figure 3.6 that the sickness figure tends to be high in occupations requiring lower skill levels than those in professional positions.

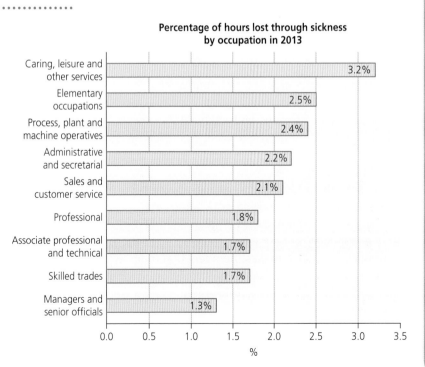

Percentage of hours lost through sickness by occupation in 2013

Occupation	%
Caring, leisure and other services	3.2%
Elementary occupations	2.5%
Process, plant and machine operatives	2.4%
Administrative and secretarial	2.2%
Sales and customer service	2.1%
Professional	1.8%
Associate professional and technical	1.7%
Skilled trades	1.7%
Managers and senior officials	1.3%

The causes of, effects of, and solutions for poor workforce performance

The causes of poor workforce performance have been suggested throughout LO3. Staff may be unhappy with their hours, pay, conditions, manager or benefits, they may call in sick regularly or not have the right skills or attitude to perform their jobs well. This can have a direct effect on the business's financial performance and reputation.

Here are some suggestions for ways of tackling this issue.

Appropriate leadership style

A caring management that values employees' contributions will lead to a happy, productive and efficient workforce. A manager needs to find time to interact with employees, listen to their problems and suggestions, and treat them with respect. Leading by example sets a standard for employees to follow, and rewarding employees when they have achieved a target motivates them to work towards goals set. A good manager understands the strengths and weaknesses of their staff.

Fair pay and benefits

Businesses such as Birmingham City Council, Barclays Bank and British Gas have embraced the 'living wage'. They recognise the importance of paying their employees salaries that will enable them to pay all their bills and still have some money left over. Their workforce is more likely to perform better if they feel that they are being rewarded fairly.

Some businesses go a step further. Admiral Group awards £3,000 worth of shares each year to every staff member.

At Innocent, the fruit juice and smoothie producer, employees start every morning with a free breakfast, they get private health care, and a scholarship worth £1,000 helps some employees realise their dreams.

Training programmes

These ensure that employees know exactly what they are doing, including how to work safely and responsibly. Training empowers employees, making them feel confident at their job, increasing motivation and productivity. It also makes them feel that their employers are prepared to invest in their future, giving them the prospect of career advancement.

Corporate image

If employees feel they are working for an ethical business that cares about its impact on stakeholders, they are more likely to feel proud of being part of it and are therefore less likely to leave.

All of the solutions cost businesses money but provide long-term benefits of improving workforce performance.

> ### KNOW IT
>
> 1 Define the following terms:
>   • induction
>   • on-the-job training
>   • off-the-job training
>   • skills audit.
> 2 Explain two reasons why workforce training is important to a business.
> 3 Explain two reasons why a skills audit is important to a business.
> 4 Define the following terms:
>   • absenteeism
>   • labour turnover
>   • labour productivity
>   • wastage level.
> 5 Explain two ways in which workforce performance data could be used to judge a business's performance.
> 6 Identify and explain three different causes of poor workforce performance.
> 7 Evaluate possible solutions for improving workforce performance within a call centre.

LO4 Understand how marketing information informs business decisions

GETTING STARTED

(15 minutes)

With a partner, discuss your knowledge of market research.

● Have you ever participated in market research?
● What did you need to do?
● What information was being gathered?
● Did you know how that information was going to be used?
● Can you give any examples of market research information being used in advertisements?
● Did this information encourage you to buy the product or service?
● Why? Why not?

4.1 How to use market research information

Marketing information refers to data collected from primary and secondary research. Businesses spend a lot of time and money carrying out research on consumer preferences before decisions are made about the design of a new product. Competitive analysis is carried out to compare one business with another and to see whether there is a gap in the market for a product.

Research data comes in different types, as described below.

Text

This is qualitative non-numerical data, e.g. the reasons why more consumers prefer local organic produce. Text enables in-depth analysis of consumer behaviour. Textual information could also come in the form of reports and articles from academic, commercial and government sources. The advantages and disadvantages of this type of data are discussed in more detail in LO1.3 (page 74).

Data

Numerical data can be analysed statistically, e.g. the number of people who prefer diesel cars. See Section 1.3 (page 74) to read about its advantages and disadvantages.

Tables

Data is displayed in rows and columns showing a mixture of numerical and non-numerical types. Tables allow information to be displayed clearly in a simple, easy-to-understand manner. Data can be analysed using simple statistical methods.

Graphs and charts

A graph is a diagram showing the relationship between two variables; bars and lines are typically used but a scatter graph shows relationship by using clusters of points.

Line graphs

These are used to show two sets of continuous data, effectively showing the relationship between the two factors. These are easy to read and show trends clearly, allowing estimations to be made of future figures.

Pie charts

A pie chart is a graph in which a circle is used to represent the whole population. The circle is then divided into different sectors to show the different proportions.

Scatter graphs

These can be used to show correlation. By looking at the pattern created by the scattered points, inferences can be drawn as to how or if two variables are related. For example, it is useful for businesses to find out whether there is a significant correlation between sales and the amount spent on marketing. Ideally it will be a highly positive correlation to prove that the marketing campaign has successfully generated sales.

PAIRS ACTIVITY

(20 minutes)

Look at Figure 3.8. Can you work out which scatter graphs the following statements describe?

1 There is no reason to believe that the increased sales of a product are due to a billboard advertisement.
2 As interest rates increase, profits decrease.
3 In most cases, average salary earned increases with higher qualification.
4 A product is moderately price elastic. An increase in price will result in a slight decrease in sales.

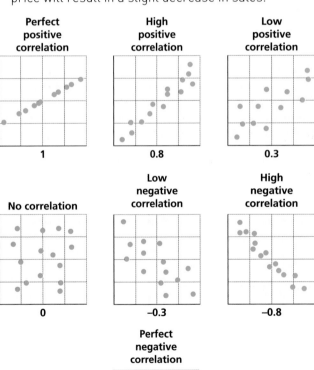

▲ **Figure 3.7** Types of scatter graph

Use Time Series Analysis to calculate and interpret moving averages

The two main purposes of Time Series Analysis are to:

1 analyse and interpret trends that exist within the historic data
2 extrapolate and predict future data based on the trends observed.

It is often used by businesses to predict future sales figures so that production plans can be drawn up. For example, a supermarket has compiled sales figures from the past ten years with the aim of figuring out the underlying trend and predicting future sales. The first step is to work out the three-year moving average as shown in Table 3.10. This is to smooth out the fluctuations from year to year so that the underlying trend can be observed more readily.

Table 3.10 Time Series Analysis example

Year	Sales revenue (£m)	3-year moving average
2005	65	
2006	72	(65+72+66)/3=68
2007	66	(72+66+57)/3=65
2008	57	(66+57+60)/3=61
2009	60	60
2010	62	62
2011	65	62
2012	60	66
2013	73	70
2014	77	

These figures are plotted on a graph (Figure 3.9).

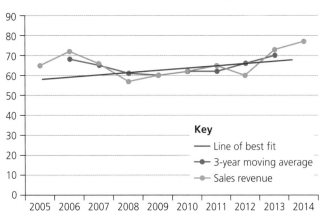

Key
— Line of best fit
—●— 3-year moving average
—●— Sales revenue

▲ **Figure 3.8** Time Series Analysis showing line of best fit

The blue line in Figure 3.9, representing the three-year moving average, is much smoother than the orange line representing the raw sales revenue figures. The next step is to draw a line of best fit through the three-year moving average line to predict future sales revenue. As it shows an upward trend, the supermarket is likely to experience an increase in sales revenue.

The line of best fit can help to predict the sales revenue for 2015 to be around £70 million. As sales revenue is predicted to go up in 2015, the supermarket can plan ahead, such as getting more supplies, as sales revenue is predicted to go up, or start recruiting more staff to meet increased demand.

For more detailed information on market research, refer to Unit 5, LO3 (page 137) and LO4 (page 143).

4.2 How to use marketing decision-making tools

In this section we will look at the marketing tools commonly used by businesses to make decisions. See also Unit 6, LO5 (page 160) for descriptions of the Boston Matrix and Porter's Generic Competitive Strategies.

Porter's Five Forces model

This is a tool for analysing the competitive power of a business in the market in which it operates. The more competitive power a business has, the more profitable its products.

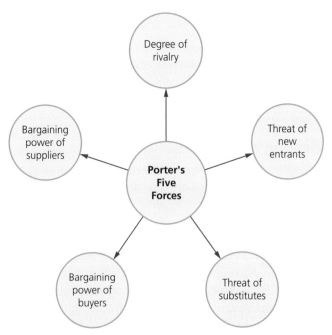

▲ **Figure 3.9** Porter's Five Forces model

First force: threat of new entrants to the market

● How easy is it for a competitor to operate in the same market?

- Is there a high set-up cost?
- Does a business need specialist knowledge to start operating in the market?
- Do you have any protection for your product, e.g. patent and copyright?

If it is difficult for a rival business to start up in the same market, you are in a strong position and will be able to dictate the pricing strategy to improve profitability.

Second force: threat of substitutes

- Are there other products in the market that can easily replace your product?

For example, if the price of rice goes up, consumers can buy pasta or potatoes instead. Suppliers do not have a lot of say in the pricing strategy of rice as it can be substituted easily. In fact, prices have to be competitive or else business will be lost.

Third force: bargaining power of buyers

- How easy is it for your buyers to ask for a discount?

A few powerful customers can get together and ask for a lower price, e.g. supermarket chains have significant bargaining power and can dictate prices at which milk is supplied to them. Most dairy farmers cannot afford to lose their custom and will have to accept low prices – some even selling at a loss.

Fourth force: bargaining power of suppliers

- Does your business have a choice of suppliers or do you buy only from a few suppliers because of the uniqueness of the product?
- How easy is it to switch suppliers and is it costly to switch?

If your suppliers are able to dictate the terms of sales such as prices, then you are in a weak position and will have to accept the prices set. This greatly reduces your ability to set competitive prices as the cost of stock could be high.

Fifth force: degree of rivalry

This is the number of competitors in the market and the level of competition. When a large number of competitors sell similar products then it is difficult for you to increase the price and profitability of your product. Customers can easily buy the product somewhere else.

Table 3.11 shows the advantages and disadvantages of the three models.

Table 3.11 Advantages and disadvantages of three marketing decision-making tools

	Advantages	Disadvantages
Boston Matrix	A simple, visual representation of the market position of each product Gives an overall picture of a business's product portfolio in their current positions By placing products in different categories, it is easier to see where decisions about future strategies should be made	It is too simplistic to use for strategic decision making; factors other than market share and market growth need to be taken into account High market share does not automatically mean high profitability Market growth is not the only indicator of how attractive an industry is; other factors, such as low barriers to entry and the number of existing suppliers, need to be taken into account 'Market' can be defined in different ways, e.g. total market or segment of a market; the position of a business can be different depending on how 'market' is defined
Porter's Five Forces	Allows an insight into the profitability of a market, so can be used to determine the attractiveness of a market before entering or exiting it Can be used to compare the impact of competitive forces on a business as well as on its rivals Using the model to analyse a business's competitive power, strategies can be developed to increase a business's ability to compete, e.g. redesigning a product to reduce the number of substitutes	As qualitative analysis, it must be combined with quantitative methods to gain a full understanding of the market structure Provides a snapshot of a business's current position so it is not suitable for long-term planning The model is more suitable for use in a simple market Does not provide a comprehensive understanding of a market
Porter's Generic Competitive Strategies	A simple framework for businesses to understand how to become competitive Suggests that businesses should either choose a cost focus or differentiation focus, and avoid being stuck in the middle	It can be risky to focus on cost reduction as a competitive strategy; cheap prices do not necessarily sell products – businesses have to get other aspects right, such as good customer service Differentiated products do not necessarily lead to high market share It is possible to achieve differentiation and cost leadership; technology can lead to lower unit production costs, as well as improving the quality of a product

4.3 Considerations when making marketing decisions

If the key focus of marketing is on satisfying customer requirements (see Unit 5, page 137), the needs of the target market are at the centre of any marketing decision. By identifying the needs and requirements of the target market through market research, the marketing mix – which comprises the product/service features, the place or channels of distribution, the price and the method of promotion – can be designed to reach these customers effectively. Table 3.12 shows an example.

Table 3.12 Examples of marketing mixes for different customer segments

	Product	Price	Promotion	Place sold
Mobile phones targeting teenagers and young adults	High-resolution screen Front and rear camera Smart or Android technology Great speakers Big RAM and storage Sleek and high-tech spec	Price skimming if newly launched with latest features Price is not as important as product features	During soaps on TV Billboards Pop radio Search engines	Phone shop Online
Mobile phones targeting older customers	Durable Easy to use Big buttons or screen Practical	Low to medium Price is as important as product features	Newspapers Specialist magazines, e.g. *Good Housekeeping* Classical music radio channels	Shops Supermarkets

Corporate image

A business must take its corporate image into account when deciding on the marketing mix. For example, Samsung is known for its high-end flagship phones. Would it affect its corporate image to sell cheap Android phones? It would send a mixed and contradicting message to its customers, who might find it difficult to associate the business with quality.

Divine Chocolate, a fair trade chocolate producer, focuses on promoting its ethical corporate image in its marketing campaigns. The unique selling points of its chocolate are good quality, fair trade and owned by farmers. Any deviation from this corporate identity will send a confused message to its target market.

4.4 How constraints on marketing impact business decisions

Marketing constraints are potential problems that might be encountered when planning and implementing a marketing campaign.

External constraints

These include the following.

- Legal constraints – e.g. the Trade Descriptions Act, which states that it is against the law to make false claims or describe a product inaccurately. For example, a jacket described as leather must be made of leather. The marketing team must make sure that any descriptions of the product must be accurate.
- Ethical constraints – a business must keep the well-being of its customers and the environment in mind, e.g. it is no longer acceptable to promote smoking and drinking, or include sexual innuendo in marketing campaigns. Electronic spam and telemarketing can be seen as unethical, and a product with planned obsolescence goes against sustainability.
- Social constraints such as changing consumer attitude and lifestyle cannot be ignored when designing a marketing mix. For example, a marketing campaign must not contain any discriminatory messages. Globalisation means that different cultural values need to be considered so that the messages and images in a marketing campaign are not offensive.

Internal constraints

These include the following.

- Financial constraints influence how a business can afford the type of promotion used. Television advertising and billboards can target the mass market effectively, but are often too expensive for small businesses. Cheaper methods are social media, local newspapers, local radio stations and leaflets.

- Time available to conduct market research, or to design and organise a marketing campaign can have an impact on the method used and the quality of the end product. Large-scale market research can take months to organise. Television advertising can take a long time to create from storyboard to filming and editing the final version. Cheaper methods, such as leaflets, could be produced professionally in a few days and can be just as effective if planned carefully.
- Corporate policy can contain guidelines for product design, the importance of charging a fair price, as well as emphasis on honesty and accuracy when creating marketing messages. Increasingly the focus is on sustainability and ensuring that business activities have a positive impact on the environment. Kingfisher, a multinational retailer, has its 'responsible marketing' corporate guidelines online, showing its commitment to sustainable practice, and offering customers honest and accurate information.

KNOW IT

1 Discuss the usefulness of Time Series Analysis to a business such as Tesco.
2 Analyse the strengths and weaknesses of each of the following tools for making marketing decisions:
   - Boston Matrix
   - Porter's Five Forces model
   - Porter's Generic Competitive Strategies.
3 What might be the external and internal constraints on a small company that designs and sells greetings cards featuring pictures of the local area?

LO5 Be able to use resource, project and change management information to inform business decisions

GETTING STARTED

(10 minutes)

Have you ever wondered what a bar code is and what information it contains? Look at Figure 3.11.

Source: www.infinigeek.com

Discuss with a partner how a business can make use of the information contained in a bar code.

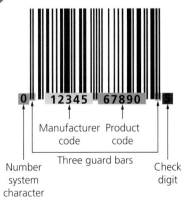

▲ **Figure 3.10** Bar code elements

5.1 The issues and key tasks involved in resource management

Resource management is the process of identifying a business's needs for resources, obtaining and allocating them, as well as monitoring their use in an effective way. This ensures that resources are available in the right quantity, at the right place and at the right time.

The management of physical resources

First, an audit on the resources required by the different functional areas, which will have different needs for rooms, furniture, etc. – for example, the production department would require more space for the production line than would a marketing department. The next step is to compare different suppliers in terms of price and quality, depending on company policy. Once resources have been allocated, the process of monitoring use and maintenance can begin.

The management of IT resources

This is similar to the management of physical resources, but it can require more skills and knowledge than managing physical resources. The manager should have some knowledge of IT hardware and software to be able to identify and match requirements. For example, which is the most suitable printer for marketing purposes as opposed to general administrative use? What is the latest software available for managing payroll and the type of system required in order for it to work effectively? Technology is advancing at such a pace that constant monitoring of needs and requirements is essential if the business is to manage its IT resources effectively.

Inventory management

This is the process of making sure that a business does not run out of stock or raw materials. This can be carried out effectively using different methods.

Stock control charts

These are used to control the flow of stock by setting a maximum (e.g. 300 units), minimum (e.g. 100 units) and reorder stock levels (e.g. 200 units). The quantity and frequency of order depends on sales and the length of time between order and delivery, known as the lead time (e.g. two weeks). The reorder quantity can be worked out by taking the reorder level from the maximum stock level to give 100 units. Buffer stock (e.g. 100 units) is the amount of stock a business is willing to hold; the quantity is a balance between the cost of holding stock and the loss of sales through insufficient stock.

Stock control chart

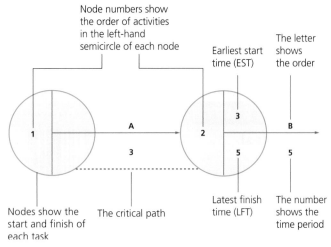

▲ **Figure 3.11** Example stock control chart

Electronic point of sale (EPOS) data

EPOS combines the data gathered by different electronic methods. It can be used to record sales levels, update stock levels and provide pricing information. From sales records a business will be able to work out the demand for each product for stock control and pricing purposes. Information on products that are often bought together can be used to create promotions such as 'buy item A and get item B half price'.

EPOS provides information such as average spend per customer, the type and number of items bought, as well as the time of visit, enabling a business to get a thorough understanding of spending habits, which can help with stock control and promotional decisions. For retailers with several branches, EPOS information can be used to benchmark and judge the performance of the stores. Differences in buying habits can be used to adapt the stores to appeal to customers more.

Radio-frequency Identification (RFID)

This is a small electronic device for tracking objects. RFID tags can be attached to stock on the production line, in the warehouse or in the store so that its location can be tracked at a distance as long as it is within the range of a reader. RFID tags can be programmed to hold detailed information about a product, including its shelf life. This information is especially useful in pharmaceutical and food industries. An RFID system can be used to inform the decisions regarding order quantities and order frequencies, as well as choice of suppliers.

5.2 How to use project management tools

See Unit 16, LO4 (page 285) for detailed information about project plans and Gantt charts.

Risk register

A risk register lists potential risks during the planning and execution of a project. Potential risks need to be assessed for the likelihood of their occurring, and the consequences analysed.

A contingency plan can then be drawn up to minimise the damage if the risks occur. Resource needs will be identified and plans put in place for securing them just in case.

5.3 How to use and interpret critical path analysis (CPA)

Critical path analysis (CPA, or network diagrams) is a tool for planning all the tasks for a project in the right order, with a clearly stated earliest start time (EST) and latest finish time (LFT) for each task. CPA can be used to plan the shortest time in which a project could be completed, by scheduling tasks that can be carried out at the same time. It helps to identify the float time for each activity (time available to do each task without causing delay to subsequent tasks) and the activities that are critical to completing the project on time.

CPA is valuable for resource planning and allocation. It allows just-in-time to be practised when allocating resources as the diagram shows clearly the tasks to be carried out and the length of time allotted to them. Tasks with float time that are not on the critical path are of lower priority when it comes to resources so that the focus could be put on tasks on the critical path. Any delays on the critical path will lengthen the project finish time.

Node numbers show the order of activities in the left-hand semicircle of each node

Earliest start time (EST)

The letter shows the order

A

B

Nodes show the start and finish of each task

The critical path

Latest finish time (LFT)

The number shows the time period

▲ **Figure 3.12** Key for critical path analysis diagrams

Table 3.13 shows an example of a project that consists of tasks A–G. The number of hours required to complete the tasks are given in the second column. A network diagram can be drawn up using this information.

Table 3.13 Data for CPA

Tasks	Duration (hours)	Preceding task
A	4	None
B	6	A
C	7	A
D	8	B
E	10	C
F	9	D, E
G	5	F

The circles are known as 'nodes'; the EST and LFT for the first node are always zero because there are no preceding tasks. The next step is to work out the ESTs for all the tasks, working from the first node in order of activity until you get to the last node. Task A takes four hours, so the earliest time B and C can start is 4; this is inserted in the top right-hand section of the second node. This process is repeated to find out the EST for D which is 4 (duration for A) + 6 (duration for B) = 10. The process is repeated to find out the EST for all the tasks.

Care has to be taken when working out the EST for task F because it is preceded by tasks D and E. If F cannot

start before D and E are complete, then the EST for F will have to be the EST for E (11) plus the duration for E, which is 10, the longer route.

The total amount of time to complete the project is worked out by adding the EST for G (30) to the duration for G (5) which is 30 + 5 = 35.

Table 3.14 EST for each task

Tasks	Duration (hours)	EST
A	4	0
B	6	0 + 4 = 4
C	7	0 + 4 = 4
D	8	4 + 6 = 10
E	10	4 + 7 = 11
F	9	11 + 10 = 21
G	5	21 + 9 = 30

To work out the LFT, the process is 'reversed'. Start by inserting the LFT for the last node, which is always the same figure as the EST. Then work backwards by subtracting the duration for G(5) from the LFT in node 7 (35).

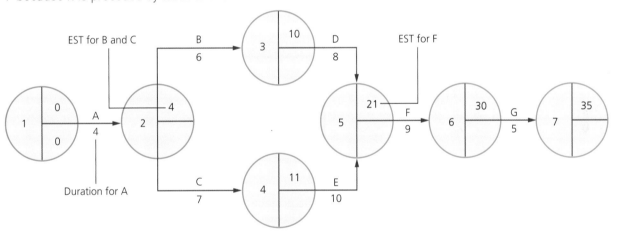

▲ **Figure 3.13** Critical path analysis diagram using data from Table 3.13

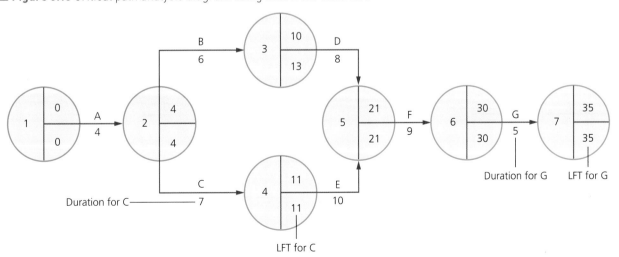

▲ **Figure 3.14** Critical path analysis diagram including the LFT

LFT for F = 35 - 5 = 30. The working is repeated in the same way until we arrive at node 2. To work out the LFT for A we have to consider the fact that C and E together take longer to complete than B and D, so LFT for A = LFT for C (11) - duration for C (7) = 4.

Table 3.15 LFT for each task

Tasks	Duration (hours)	LFT
A	4	11 - 7 = 4
B	6	21 - 8 = 13
C	7	21 - 10 = 11
D	8	30 - 9 = 21
E	10	30 - 9 = 21
F	9	35 - 5 = 30
G	5	35

The critical path is the longest route through the network, which in this case is A, C, E, F, G. Any delays in these tasks will lengthen the total project time. It is therefore critical to complete these tasks on time.

It is useful to work out the float time for activities that are not on the critical path, as shown in Table 3.16.

Table 3.16 Calculating the float time

Tasks	Duration (hours)	EST	LFT	Float = LFT - EST - duration
A	4	0	4	4 - 0 - 4 = 0
B	6	4	13	13 - 4 - 6 = 3
C	7	4	11	11 - 4 - 7 = 0
D	8	10	21	21 - 10 - 8 = 3
E	10	11	21	21 - 11 - 10 = 0
F	9	21	30	30 - 21 - 9 = 0
G	5	30	35	35 - 30 - 5 = 0
	Total float			6

Only B and D have float time (three hours each). With this information the project manager could deploy the resources from B and D to those on the critical path to ensure that they are completed on time.

Advantages of CPA:

● it provides an overview of the whole project, allowing the shortest completion time to be worked out
● helps identify activities on the critical path so that they can be prioritised in terms of resource allocation
● helps identify activities with float time, which helps resource allocation
● enables just-in-time to be practised as ESTs indicate when resources are needed for specific activities; this improves cash flow.

Disadvantages of CPA:

● the duration for each activity is only an estimate and can be inaccurate
● CPA can be very complicated when there are many activities
● it does not take into account changes in external or internal factors, e.g. adverse weather conditions can slow down deliveries of raw materials.

🔍 INDEPENDENT RESEARCH ACTIVITY

(20 minutes)

A project consists of the tasks shown in Table 3.17, with their respective durations.

Table 3.17 Data for CPA exercise

Tasks	Duration (hours)	Preceding task
A	3	None
B	5	A
C	6	A
D	8	B
E	2	D
F	9	C, E
G	5	F

The project can be represented in the network diagram in Figure 3.16.

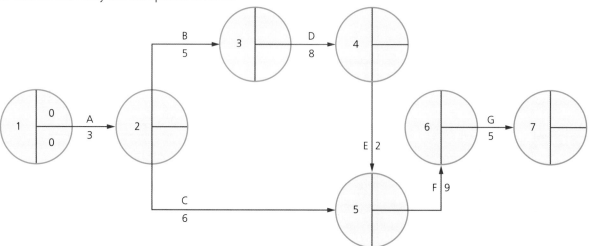

▲ **Figure 3.15** Network diagram for CPA exercise

1 Complete the nodes by working out the ESTs and LFTs.
2 Calculate the float time for activity C.
3 Identify the critical path.

5.4 How change is managed

The business environment is dynamic and change can be due to both internal and external factors. Businesses have to respond and adapt to change in order to survive and succeed.

Causes of change

Internal causes

Structural changes to how a business is organised via expansion, mergers or acquisition may result in changes to the way layers of command are organised.

Strategic change, a change in a business's overall direction, could be due to a decision to sell a new product, enter a new market, relocation or merging with a new partner. It will bring about changes in business operations, production methods and new ways of communicating with stakeholders. With a new location comes new culture and, most significantly, new policies and a change in the basic values and principles in response to changes in the external environment.

External causes

External factors are those beyond a business's control such as the state of the economy. In an economic downturn, businesses might have to scale down production due to a slowdown in sales. Spending cuts and a tighter budget might mean making some employees redundant, delayering to save costs.

A change in government usually leads to new legislation and initiatives that might favour some businesses over others. For example, a compulsory national living wage may force some smaller businesses to cut back on the number of employees or reduce recruitment, to maintain efficiency.

Technology is advancing at such a pace that, for some businesses, it is a case of keep up or risk losing market share. Social media influences how we work, how we play and especially how we shop. Developments in mobile technology mean that businesses have to change the way they accept payments in order to compete.

Social factors such as the changing consumer attitude towards sustainability have led to changes in how some businesses operate. Also, not only are consumers more concerned about eating healthily, they are more sceptical about 'health claims' made by food manufacturers. These changes have an impact on the decisions as to what products should be sold and how.

Resistors to change

In a business, resistors to change can come from individual employees, teams of employees or even the management. Some people resist change because they fear the unknown; change might affect their working environment and arrangements. Some employees might feel threatened by change as it might mean having to adopt a new way of working that they might not enjoy.

Resistors to change could also be caused by poor management where the employees do not understand how the new process works. Employees need to be informed of what needs to be changed and how it will be carried out. Lack of good communication about change will lead to confusion, mistrust and resistance.

The importance of encouraging a positive response from the workforce to change

The consequences of a failure to remove resistors to change are a demotivated workforce, leading to low productivity, high absenteeism and labour turnover.

Change management is about convincing the workforce that change is necessary to improve efficiency, to become more competitive and to survive in the long term. Without a positive response from the workforce to embrace the changes that are about to be introduced, the process will take longer and it will be harder to succeed.

The importance and impact of change

Change is necessary. Without change a business could be breaking the law, and risk facing fines and criminal charges. Failure to adopt new technology and new practices will lead to loss of revenue and market share. It might be necessary to change the product that a business sells due to changing consumer demand.

The impact of substantial change will be felt throughout a business across the hierarchy. The introduction of new technology in manufacturing might lead to redundancies or employees learning new skills. Social media can change how a marketing department operates. The impact of change depends on how drastic the change being introduced is. A change in the strategic direction of a business will have a significant impact on employees at all levels.

5.5 The factors involved in contingency planning

The purpose, importance, benefits and drawbacks of contingency planning

A contingency plan is a substitute plan if the original one does not work so that the effects of the original plan failing can be minimised. It is not just about planning for disaster; a business could face problems such as a loss of data, late deliveries, fluctuation in exchange rates and employees not turning up for work.

Benefits

- It is a good exercise for managers to identify potential problems.
- It is proactive, as plans are already in place before problems are encountered.
- By minimising the impact of problems that might occur, a business suffers less financial and non-financial damage.
- All employees know what to do if there is a problem so that it can be overcome more quickly and effectively.

Drawbacks

- The problems identified might never occur, so the process can be a waste of time.
- It can be a lengthy process that involves many employees who could be getting on with their jobs.

How to create contingency plans

A contingency plan can be created in four easy steps.

1 Identify problems by carrying out a risk assessment. Make a list of all potential problems that might occur. For example, businesses importing goods from abroad constantly face the problem of fluctuations in exchange rates.
2 Prioritise problems by putting them in order of the chance of occurrence. Assuming limited resources in terms of time and funds, this step helps to prepare for the problems that are most likely to be encountered.
3 Draw up a contingency plan to minimise the effects of the potential problem. This should include a human resource plan allocating roles and responsibilities in times of emergencies. A communication plan is also important to make sure that key personnel are informed of problems and actions taken to overcome them at every stage of the process.
4 Execute and review. Changes are made if necessary to improve the effectiveness of a contingency plan.

(30 minutes)

You are a restaurant owner employing ten waiters who are mainly students. Create a contingency plan to minimise the impact of waiters not turning up for work.

KNOW IT

1 Explain how a business could use the following for managing inventory:
a stock control charts
b electronic point of sale data
c radio-frequency identification.
2 Explain how each of the following could be used to manage a project:
a Gantt charts
b project plan
c risk register.
3 In the context of critical path analysis, define the following terms:
a EST   b LFT   c float time.
4 Discuss the usefulness of Critical Path Analysis to a building/construction firm.
5 Identify and explain the internal and external causes of change that could be faced by a business importing clothes from abroad.
6 Identify and explain three possible resistors to change.
7 Evaluate the usefulness of contingency planning for a business that is about to move its headquarters overseas.

L06 Be able to use information to make and justify business decisions

GETTING STARTED

(10 minutes)

Even the biggest companies in the world make bad decisions!

Blockbuster was the world's leading video and DVD rental company in the 1980s and 1990s. At one point, it had nearly 10,000 stores and made almost $6 billion a year. However, it failed to keep up with changing customer tastes and new technologies, so that when Netflix began a mail-rental DVD service in the late 1990s, Blockbuster did not recognise the danger of this new competitor. It even turned down Netflix's offer of a joint venture. Blockbuster finally went bankrupt and ceased trading in 2010, and Netflix is the best-known worldwide TV and film-streaming brand.

6.1 How to use business decision-making tools

Internal organisational audit

This identifies the key strengths and weaknesses of a business before decisions are made. An internal audit could include a business's attitude to risk, its core competencies, portfolio analysis (Boston Matrix), information gathered from market research, and SWOT analysis. All these topics are covered in Unit 1, this unit and later units.

External business environmental audit

This involves examining all the external factors that might have an impact on a business e.g. legal, ethical, economic, political, social, environmental and technological factors. These have been covered in Unit 1, this unit and later units in this book.

> ## INDEPENDENT RESEARCH ACTIVITY
>
> ### (45 minutes)
>
> Use the following link to read about a SWOT analysis of Coca-Cola: http://tinyurl.com/gro3d4u
>
> Using the same format, carry out a SWOT analysis for a company of your choice.

Competitor analysis

A competitor analysis is a study on a business's competitors by investigation of issues such as the strength of competition, market share of a business and its competitors, competitor behaviour and position in market. These are covered in detail in Unit 1 (page 36). The purpose of a competitor analysis is to find out the strengths and weaknesses of a business's competitors so that strategies can be formed to improve the business's competitive advantage.

Stakeholder analysis

Stakeholder analysis is covered in detail in Unit 1 (page 26). The information gained from studying stakeholder interests and potential conflict between stakeholder groups, especially between the business owners and customers, can be used to create strategies that will enable businesses to better meet different stakeholder needs. This is vital for a business's long-term survival.

Ansoff's Matrix

This is covered in Unit 6, LO5 (page 161).

6.2 How different strategies are used to help a business achieve a competitive advantage in different circumstances

Different strategies are used depending on a business's position in a market and whether it is in an emerging, maturing or declining position.

Table 3.18 Strategies to achieve competitive advantage

Strategy	Description	Examples
Joint venture	Businesses teaming up to share one another's advantages	Walmart entered the Indian retail market with Bharti Enterprises due to stringent regulatory restrictions imposed by the Indian government
		Costa Coffee entered the Chinese market with a local company, the Yueda Group, to gain local knowledge and expertise
Diversification	Very high-risk strategy for businesses entering a new market or existing ones in a mature or declining market; both product and market are new so there will be huge R&D costs to develop and create the new product, followed by marketing campaigns to enter the new market Involves a change in the strategic direction so the business needs to gain a thorough understanding of the new market and enter the market with a product that is either innovative or with a unique selling point to achieve a competitive advantage	Samsung – known for its mobile phones, televisions and tablets – has successfully diversified into making military hardware, building apartments and ships, and operating an amusement park Virgin's decision to diversify to the soft drink market is an example of how even multinationals can get it wrong – Virgin Cola failed and had to be dropped

Strategy	Description	Examples
Horizontal and vertical integration	Can be adopted by businesses entering a new market to gain new knowledge and skills, or in a mature or declining market to regain market share and growth Could involve merging, acquiring or taking over other businesses, either in the same (horizontal) or in a different stage (vertical) of production, primarily to achieve economies of scale	The acquisition of Volkswagen by Porsche to increase its product portfolio, with the Porsche brand targeting the high end and the Volkswagen brand the middle and lower end of the market Starbucks buying a coffee farm in China is an example of a vertical integration to ensure the quality of the coffee beans is of a high standard; it also guarantees the continuous supply of coffee beans at a constant price
Change product or service provision	A business operating in a mature or declining market changes the way its product or service reaches its customers through different channels of distribution	A retailer selling carpets on the high street decides to sell its carpets door to door from the back of a van Heinz, in a bid to maintain its market share in a highly competitive market, uses different packaging to suit different needs
Change market positioning	Changing customers' perception of a business's image through brand manipulation in a mature or declining market position; often involves comparative advertisements to persuade consumers that one brand is better than another	Supermarkets such as Aldi and Lidl adopt a value positioning strategy to gain market share from other supermarket brands; they have also exploited consumer perceptions of 'German quality' to reduce the association of value with poor quality Marks & Spencer adopts a 'quality positioning' strategy, fully utilising the quality brand image that it has built over many years; highly effective TV marketing campaigns gained the company a 38% market share in the party food market in 2014 Demographic-related positioning is used by companies such as Vitabiotics to target their vitamin supplements to, e.g., men, pregnant women, children and babies
Rebranding	Changing consumer perception of a brand in a mature or declining market position through extensive marketing campaigns	By using celebrities such as Emma Watson, Burberry turned its brand around from one associated with gangs into a luxury brand
Retrenchment	Cutting expenses, e.g. by withdrawing from less profitable markets or downsizing operations It can involve a change in strategic direction	Nokia's closure of some factories to focus on its partnership with Microsoft Thorntons sold off some of its stores to cut running costs, with a view to increasing its franchises, which are more cost effective as a growth strategy

6.3 How to make business decisions

A structured approach to business decisions involves identifying a problem and finding its solution. It is a process of identifying, prioritising, analysing and matching the best solution to a problem.

The identification of issues/causes

Before decisions can be made, the issues or causes of why change is necessary need to be identified, e.g. a slowdown in sales due to economic factors, a change in the strategic direction of a business in order to survive, or increased competition due to new rivals entering the market. A list of issues and causes needs to be made as a first step. Contingency planning usually starts with a brainstorming session on potential problems that a business might encounter in a given situation.

How to identify and prioritise decision-making criteria

Given the fact that most businesses aim to increase profitability, the use of resources such as time and money needs to be prioritised. A risk register, as described in LO5, can be used to prioritise problems to be overcome. This could either be based on the likelihood of a problem occurring or the severity of the likely consequences.

The analysis and synthesis of supporting information

Information collected from primary and secondary research needs to be analysed and synthesised. Quantitative information can be analysed using tables and charts, while qualitative information is more difficult to analyse systematically. You are looking for meaning: what is the information telling you? What conclusions can you draw? Can you spot a trend?

Synthesising information is the process of combining information collected from different sources to form a conclusion. For example, the result of a SWOT analysis could be combined with an internal audit of a business's budgets to see what opportunities the business can afford to exploit.

The use of decision-making tools to investigate solutions

Decision-making tools such as Ansoff's Matrix, the Boston Matrix and Porter's Five Forces can be used to provide solutions. However, these tools are best used with market research data, and internal and external audits, to reach a well-informed decision.

How to match solutions to decision-making criteria

The best solution is not always the cheapest option, depending on a business's circumstances. A business with cash flow problems might favour projects with a short payback, while an ambitious business may favour diversification into a foreign market. Internal constraints such as funding and skills, or external constraints such as legislation and economic factors, have to be taken into account when selecting the most suitable solution.

Respect other people's contributions to the decision-making process

For a decision to be accepted internally, managers need to listen to and respect contributions from employees. If employees feel they are not part of the decision-making process, they are less likely to embrace the change, which is likely to result in low motivation and productivity. The views of external stakeholders such as customers, local community and shareholders should be respected. A business that changes to create a better product for its customers in a responsible and sustainable way is more likely to succeed in implementing the change.

Present rationale and conclusions

When presenting the rationale for a decision, you are explaining why the decision has been chosen over others, in relation to business objectives. Reasons for the choice could be to do with finance, skills or culture, or because of constraints imposed by external factors. Rationale can persuade stakeholders that the right conclusions have been drawn, and the decision made is more likely to be accepted.

6.4 How to justify a business decision

A decision can be justified in different ways, indeed it should be a combination of different methods.

Appropriateness

This can be based on a feasibility study, e.g. is it a practical idea? Is the project viable? A feasible project is able to generate enough cash to fund its costs and make a profit. A project will also need to be desirable – will it help the business to meet its long-term goals? Will it help the business to improve its reputation and its relationship with its stakeholders? A decision should always be based on its chances of success. This could be arrived at using a decision tree or Ansoff's Matrix. High rewards might come with taking risks, but the final decision should be based on the likelihood of success, otherwise a business risks losing a huge amount in investment.

Awareness of other perspectives

A business should be aware of the perspectives of its internal and external stakeholder groups regarding a decision. Being knowledgeable about the interests of stakeholder groups allows a business to weigh up the consequences of not meeting stakeholder needs. It is not always possible to please all stakeholders so a business needs to take the decision that is most likely to be accepted by the most influential stakeholders.

Evidence based

Evidence drawn from primary and secondary research should be used to make business decisions; there should be a balance of qualitative and quantitative data gathered internally and externally. Provided that data from research is valid and reliable, the decision should be the right one.

> **KNOW IT**
>
> 1 What is an internal organisational audit and what should it include?
> 2 What is an external environmental audit and what should it include?
> 3 Evaluate the usefulness of a SWOT analysis in helping businesses make decisions.
> 4 Define the following terms:
>   • horizontal integration
>   • vertical integration.

Read about it

'The core competence of the corporation', by Coimbatore Krishnarao Prahalad and Gary Hamel, *Harvard Business Review*, 68, 3, 1990, pp. 79–91

Unit 3 assessment practice questions

Below are some practice questions for you to try.

The food industry is very competitive and major food manufacturers are constantly looking for ways to differentiate their products. Corporate social responsibility is essential to all the decisions made by Delany Foods Ltd, a large food manufacturer based in Wales. It is considering whether to invest in green energy as a way of combating rising energy prices as well as enhancing its reputation as an ethical company. The two options under consideration are wind turbines and a biodigester (see Table 3.19).

Table 3.19 Potential green energy investments

	Wind turbines	Biodigester
Capital required	£10 million	£2 million
Source of finance	Bank loan of £8 million	Reserves
Time required for installation	1 year	2 years

1 a What is meant by the term 'corporate social responsibility'? (2 marks)
   b Besides using green energy, describe three different ways Delany Foods Ltd could operate ethically. (3 marks)
   c Evaluate likely benefits and drawbacks to Delany Foods Ltd of operating ethically. (12 marks)

2 Define the different types of business decision in Table 3.20, describing their features, and give an example for each type. (9 marks)

Table 3.20 Potential green energy investments

Business decision	Definition	Features	Example
Strategic			
Tactical			
Operational			

3 a Describe Porter's Generic Competitive Strategies. (4 marks)
   b Analyse the likely benefits and drawbacks to Delany Foods Ltd of using Porter's Generic Competitive Strategies when making strategic decisions. (8 marks)

4 A decision tree has been drawn up to help evaluate the two strategic options under consideration (see Figure 3.17).
   a Complete the decision tree by entering the appropriate value into each of the nodes and boxes labelled a–g. (7 marks)

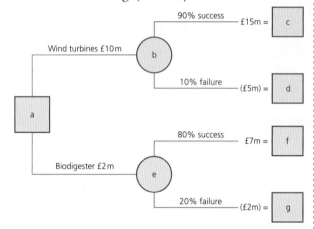

▲ **Figure 3.16** Decision tree for Delany Foods Ltd

   b Evaluate the usefulness of this decision tree to Delany Foods Ltd when make strategic decisions. (12 marks)

5 Table 3.21 shows the net cash flow for the two options.

Table 3.21 Net cash flow for the two options

Year	Wind turbines (£) millions	Biodigester (£) millions	Discount factor 10%
0	10	2	0
1	0	0	0.91
2	2.5	0	0.83
3	2.7	1.32	0.75
4	2.9	1.34	0.68
5	3.0	1.36	0.62

For both options, calculate:
   a the NPV (4 marks)
   b the payback period (4 marks)
   c the ARR. (4 marks)

6 a Identify two examples of quantitative data and two examples of qualitative data relevant to Delany Foods Ltd when deciding between the two options. (4 marks)
   b Using both quantitative and qualitative information, evaluate which of the two options Delany Foods Ltd should take. (16 marks)

Unit 04

Customers and communication

ABOUT THIS UNIT

Customers are vital to the success of any business, so businesses must consider the importance of the customer experience and ensure that they communicate effectively with them, whether internally or externally. Repeat business is crucial for future revenue and financial certainty. Businesses depend on customer satisfaction and customer loyalty by knowing who their customers are and what influences their behaviours.

In this unit you will learn the purpose, methods and importance of business communication, and the appropriateness of different forms of communication for different situations. You will develop the skills that help you create a rapport with customers, and have the opportunity to practise your business communication skills. You will also learn about the legal constraints, and ethical and security issues that affect how businesses store, share and use information.

LEARNING OUTCOMES

The topics, activities and suggested reading in this unit will help you to:

1 understand who customers are and their importance to businesses
2 understand how to communicate with customers
3 be able to establish a rapport with customers through non-verbal and verbal communication skills
4 be able to convey messages for business purposes
5 know the constraints and issues that affect the sharing, storing and use of information for business communication.

How will I be assessed?

You will be assessed through a series of assignments and tasks set and marked by your tutor.

How will I be graded?

You will be graded using the following criteria, which are in the specification produced by OCR for the qualification.

Learning outcome	Pass	Merit	Distinction
You will:	To achieve a Pass you must demonstrate that you have met all the pass assessment criteria	To achieve a Merit you must demonstrate that you have met all the pass and merit assessment criteria	To achieve a Distinction you must demonstrate that you have met all the pass, merit and distinction assessment criteria
1 Understand who customers are and their importance to businesses	**P1** Explain who the customers of a specific business are and what influences their behaviour		
	P2 Describe actions that a specific business has taken in response to the differing needs of its customers		
	P3 Explain the range of customer services a specific business provides and how each area of the business has responded to the need to provide customer service	**M1** Analyse the benefits to a specific business and to its customers of maintaining and developing customer service	**D1** Recommend and justify changes to the customer service provided by a specific business to improve the customer experience
2 Understand how to communicate with customers	**P4** Assess whether or not the form, style and layout of different communications are suitable for the intended audience and purpose		
	P5 Summarise the corporate standards and corporate profile of a specific business and explain their importance to that business	**M2** Explain how a specific business manages its corporate profiles through media activity	
3 Be able to establish a rapport with customers through non-verbal and verbal communication skills	**P6** Demonstrate non-verbal and verbal skills when communicating with a specific customer	**M3** Review own use of non-verbal and verbal skills when communicating with a specific customer and suggest improvements	
	P7 Explain the importance of listening skills in building a rapport with specific customers		
4 Be able to convey messages for business purposes	**P8** Structure and deliver a verbal business communication so that its content and type of communication is appropriate for its audience and purpose	**M4** Review use of own verbal and written skills when communicating business messages and recommend improvements	**D2** Justify how to adapt the structure, method of delivery and any other considerations to convey a business message for differing audience requirements
	P9 Structure a written business communication so that its content and type of communication is appropriate for its audience and purpose		
5 Know the constraints and issues which affect the sharing, storing and use of information for business communications	**P10** Describe the legal constraints, ethical and security issues faced by a specific business in relation to sharing and storing business communications		

LO1 Understand who customers are and their importance to businesses *P1 P2 P3 M1 D1*

GETTING STARTED 👤

(20 minutes)

Working in small groups, select a business in your local area. Discuss the types of customers who visit the business you have chosen, and identify the goods or services they may wish to purchase.

1.1 Different types of customers

Customers are the most important people in any business. They allow an organisation to achieve its business aims and objectives.

External and internal customers

There are two main types of customer. These are:

1 **external customers** who come from outside of the business providing a product or service
2 **internal customers** who are in the same organisation as the person who is providing a product or service.

🔑 **KEY TERMS**

External customers – those who do not belong to the business but conduct a transaction with the business to purchase its products or services, e.g. a customer visiting a supermarket.

Internal customers – a member of a business or organisation who relies on others within the business to do their job, e.g. an employee is an internal customer of the IT function.

Most businesses will have a mixture of internal and external customers. Regardless of the type of customer, a number of characteristics apply to all customers, including those listed below.

1 Demographics:
   • gender – male/female
   • age – pre-school children, school children, teenagers, young adults, middle-aged adults, elderly people

   • status – individuals, couples, groups, families with children
   • other – culture, ethics and religion.
2 Location:
   • local area
   • wider city/town
   • urban
   • rural
   • other parts of the country
   • other parts of the world.
3 Service access requirements:
   • weekdays
   • weekends
   • seasonal
   • term times
   • school holiday periods
   • before 9 am
   • after 5.30 pm
   • mornings
   • lunchtimes
   • afternoons
   • evenings.
4 Travel:
   • car
   • van
   • bus
   • train
   • tram
   • taxi
   • on foot
   • bicycle
   • motorbike.
5 Method of communication:
   • face to face
   • in writing
   • telephone
   • online.
6 Behaviour and demeanour:
   • demanding/undemanding
   • patient/impatient
   • confused
   • unsure
   • familiar/unfamiliar with the product/service
   • aggressive
   • assertive
   • specialist knowledge.

▲ Figure 4.1 Customers are individuals with different needs

Table 4.1 Customer types and characteristics

Type of business	Type of customers and their characteristics
Local hairdressing salon	Females Young adults Middle-aged adults Elderly people Car Bus Walk Individual customers Face to face From the local area
Tourist information centre	
Local bank	
Call centre	
Builder's merchant	

In addition to internal and external customers, businesses will come into contact with other customer groups.

Returning customers

These form the backbone of selling. Repeat or returning customers will help to provide revenue and certainty for the business.

One-off customers

These are people who purchase an item or service only once from a business. This can be because the customer does not live in the same area as the business, the purchase is required only once or the customer prefers a competitor's product.

Potential/new customers

These customers will allow the business to expand and diversify into new markets. Once the new customer has purchased a product or service the business should try to retain them.

1.2 What influences customer behaviour?

There are a number of things that influence a customer's behaviour when sourcing and purchasing goods and services. Some of these are described below.

Customer needs and expectations

Customer needs and **expectations** are important factors in influencing customer behaviour – for example, individuals who expect businesses and products and services to be environmental and ethically friendly may spend time researching energy efficiency ratings before purchasing new white goods for the home.

> **KEY TERMS**
>
> **Customer needs** – the solutions to problems that a customer is aiming to solve with the use of the product or service.
>
> **Customer expectations** – the perceived value a customer will gain from the purchase of a product or service.

Customer demographics

For example, the age of the customer will affect their behaviour – a young person is more likely to use online shopping than an elderly person. Individuals on a low income are likely to purchase from budget ranges, whereas high earners are more willing to purchase premium brands.

Cultural differences

People from different places or ethnic origins may look for different products or services, or have different expectations. For example, someone of a particular ethnic origin may shop for certain ingredients at a specialist supermarket or online provider.

Location

An individual's location will significantly affect their consumer behaviour. For example, if an individual lives in the city centre, they are more likely to visit businesses and retail outlets personally. A person who lives in a rural area with limited transport links is more likely to use online or telephone services, and arrange for goods to be delivered to their home.

Level of satisfaction

Customers who are extremely satisfied with a product or service are likely to return to the business and become a regular customer, making repeat purchases.

How often they need to interact with the business

Many businesses are used by a customer only occasionally. These include car dealerships, estate agents and solicitors. When making an expensive purchase customers are using a service relating to a specific event – for example, moving house. Other businesses, such as supermarkets, are frequently visited by consumers because food is a basic need. A customer's behaviour will change depending on how frequently they interact with a business.

1.3 Actions businesses may take to manage the customer experience

In a competitive environment, businesses need to manage their customer experience. There are a number of actions that most businesses will complete to ensure customers are satisfied with the experience they receive. Many of these actions interlink with one another (see Figure 4.2).

Creating a customer service offer to manage customer expectations

Customer service is the experience a customer receives when using products or services produced or received from a business. Customers want to purchase goods and services that meet their needs and wants. Ideally, the customer needs the goods and services to be at a price that they can afford.

▲ **Figure 4.2** Actions businesses may take to manage the customer experience

Creating a customer service offer to manage customer expectations

Businesses need to ensure their customer service allows customers to satisfy their needs but at the same time manage expectations that any customer may have.

Prioritising business needs

Balance how to meet an objective to deliver high-quality customer service with an objective to reduce business overheads. A business needs to review the financial cost of delivering an effective customer service. The business will need to balance the costs of this service with the costs of other business expenses (rent, wages, etc.).

Prioritising customers' needs

When different customers have competing needs and not all of them can be met, businesses may have to choose whose needs are to be met. Businesses are required to identify their target market and customers. If a business is not able to meet the needs of all of these customer groups, it may need to prioritise certain groups to differentiate its product or service.

Maintaining contact with the customer

A business needs to have continual contact with its customers. In particular, it will aim to promote customer loyalty, inform existing customers of new products, educate them on new initiatives and potentially provoke a response.

1.4 Why customer service is important

Effective customer service is often seen as a 'unique selling point' for a business and can ensure business survival in the longer term. Research from many businesses has shown that effective customer service will lead to:

- a competitive advantage over similar businesses that don't offer such good customer service; the business is more likely to succeed in the business environment
- public- and third-sector organisations (see Unit 1, LO1.2, page 2) providing the best value for the money that has been invested; as a public- or third-sector organisation is funded from public money or donations, the trustees have a responsibility to spend this money wisely, with specific aims and objectives

- an increase in public image and reputation
- higher customer numbers, greater customer diversity and improved customer loyalty
- satisfied customers who make repeat purchases and recommend the product or service to family and friends; this may lead to an increase in 'word of mouth' sales
- increased sales, and therefore the possibility of increasing profits and market share
- increased job satisfaction and motivation for the workforce.

> ### KNOW IT
>
> 1 State two types of business customer.
> 2 Explain the difference between customer needs and customer expectations.
> 3 Describe the difference between internal and external customers.
> 4 List three factors that influence customer behaviour.
> 5 Explain why customer service is important to business success.

LO1 assessment activities

Below are suggested assessment activities that have been directly linked to the Pass, Merit and Distinction criteria in LO1 to help with assignment preparation. These are followed by top tips on how to achieve the best results.

Activity 1 Pass criteria *P1 P2 P3*

Choose a business in the local area for which you already have knowledge of its operations and customer base. Then write your answers to the following questions.

P1 Using your chosen business, explain who its customers are and what influences their behaviour when using the business.

P2 Describe any actions it has taken in response to the differing needs of its customers.

P3 Explain the range of customer services provided and, giving examples, show how each area of the business has responded to the requirement of providing customer service.

TOP TIPS

- ✔ Check with your tutor that your business choice is suitable.
- ✔ Ensure your choice of business gives you appropriate opportunities to meet the requirements of P1.
- ✔ Spend equal time and produce similar amounts of evidence for each of the pass criteria.

Activity 2 Merit criteria *M1*

M1 Reflect on the work you have produced for P3. Using the business you have chosen and studied, analyse the benefits to the business and to its customers of maintaining and developing customer service.

TOP TIPS

- ✔ Ensure you are focusing on both the business and its customers.
- ✔ You can present your response in one or more format, e.g. in an assignment, in a recorded discussion, as a presentation to the rest of the group.
- ✔ Ensure you provide detailed evidence that meets the command verb 'analyse'.

Activity 3 Distinction criteria *D1*

D1 Using your chosen business, prepare a report for its senior management that recommends and justifies changes to its customer service to improve the customer experience.

TOP TIPS

✔ Ensure you understand the requirements for a business report.
✔ Ensure the business you are using has sufficient scope for you to make suitable recommendations.
✔ Give practical recommendations, with examples where appropriate.

LO2 Understand how to communicate with customers *P4 P5 M2*

GETTING STARTED

(10 minutes)

Working in pairs, construct a list of personal skills that you think are needed by a customer services assistant in a local bank.

Communication skills are a person's ability to process, receive and send information. When communicating in a business setting, individuals need to consider a range of styles and methods that meet the communication needs of their customers, including verbal and non-verbal communication skills. By using these effectively, staff will build positive and potentially profitable business relationships.

2.1 Audience requirements

An instant image when seeing the word 'audience' is a group of people listening to music at a concert or attending a theatre performance. In a business context, however, 'audience' has a much broader meaning.

What is an audience?

In previous units, you will have considered the idea of stakeholders: those with an interest in an organisation or who are affected by what it does. At a local sandwich shop, the customers who buy the sandwiches, the employees in the shop, and the bakeries, butchers and farmers who supply the shop with its raw materials are all types of audience.

Audience requirements

Irrespective of the method or style of communication, it is vital to show awareness of your audience. When planning your communication method, you need to consider the following in relation to your customers:

- age
- gender
- special needs
- accessibility
- knowledge
- customer type (e.g. internal or external customer).

The questions in Table 4.2 would apply to verbal, non-verbal and written communication methods, as well as media advertisements.

Table 4.2 Questions to ask when planning communications

Verbal communication (e.g. meetings, business presentations, interviews)	Can the audience see and hear? Is the audience comfortable? Is there sufficient seating? Is the temperature in the room appropriate? Are refreshments available? Is there a need to consider cultural differences in the audience? Are all issues addressed?
Non-verbal communication (e.g. meetings, business presentations)	Are facial expressions welcoming and friendly? Do gestures support verbal communication? Is there an appropriate level of eye contact with the audience? Is the presenter's posture relaxed? Is the presenter showing respect to the audience? Is the presenter's dress appropriate and in accordance with any cultural differences?
Written communication (e.g. sales letters, email newsletters)	Is the intended recipient identified for contact? Is the recipient addressed appropriately? Is the message clear and easy to understand? Is the content focused on topics of interest to the recipient?
Media advertisement (e.g. magazine ad, TV ad)	Is the message short and concise? If appropriate, are the details of the product and price clear and easy to understand? Are terms and conditions or any offers stated clearly?

Working in pairs, choose an advertisement from the internet, in a magazine or newspaper, or on the television. Analyse the advert and assess whether it meets its intended audience's requirements.

Working individually and considering your school or college, identify one communication example to illustrate each of the five purposes of business communication.

2.2 Purposes of communication in business situations

Before selecting the type of communication, a business needs to identify its purpose. There are five main purposes:

1. to inform – for example, staff or customers about new products or inform staff of changes to working conditions
2. to confirm – for example, arrangements for a staff meeting or a product delivery to a customer
3. to promote – for example, a particular product or service to a selected customer group
4. to make a request – for example, for information or data
5. to instruct – for example, a group of workers on the process of completing a particular task.

If the purpose is not clearly identified, the business risks damaging relationships with staff, customers and the general public. For example, recipients of a monthly email newsletter with no specific purpose or information could be irritated by it wasting their time and associate that business with 'junk' email.

2.3 The advantages and disadvantages of various forms of communication

There are a number of advantages and disadvantages of different forms of communication that need to be considered (Table 4.3). These are of particular importance when considering the purpose, content and audience of a business message.

▲ **Figure 4.3** Consider the purpose, content and audience of a business message when choosing how you will communicate it

Table 4.3 Advantages and disadvantages of different communication channels

Communication method	Advantages	Disadvantages
Face to face	Preferred communication channel if clarity of the message is the main aim Allows for interaction between all parties Enables discussions to take place Uses non-verbal gestures such as facial expressions, eye contact and body language	Conflict could become more heated and emotional in a face-to-face environment Tension and stress is more evident in face-to-face communication than in remote interactions Some people may prefer to write down what they want to say rather than having to respond verbally straight away If they are using a second language, the individual may require time to understand the conversation

Communication method	Advantages	Disadvantages
In writing (e.g. letters, contracts, handwritten notes)	Easy to preserve and store for future reference Complex material can be presented in a readable format Written documents provide a permanent record that can be kept for future reference Formal written documents maintain the image of the business There is less possibility of distortion of the information in the document Limited opportunities to misinterpret the information in the document Written documents are easy to verify	Expensive in comparison to email and text messaging due to the cost of paper, printing and postage. Considerably more time consuming to produce and to deliver than other forms of communication. It assumes a level of literacy that not everyone possesses Delayed response and decision making Lacks personal contact and the ability for a discussion to ensure understanding
By telephone	Instant responses to comments made No expensive hardware or software required Messages can be left if the person is unavailable Appropriate for long-distance conversations where travel is not appropriate Mobile phones and internet phone services like Skype have allowed businesses the ability to communicate with distant workers and business sites Calls can be made and voicemail left 24 hours a day, 365 days per year, which prevents issues with regional holidays and hours of working	May be difficult to find a mutually convenient time to hold the telephone conversation Messages are not always checked regularly or before being deleted Telephone conversations are less personal that face-to-face meetings There is a lack of non-verbal expressions, which inhibits the ability to interpret the context or emotion of the person delivering the message
Text message	Fast delivery of message, if both people have a mobile signal Appropriate for long-distance communication Allows for messages to be sent and received when internet access is not available Enables the receiver time to consider the message before responding There are low costs of sending and receiving text messages Can be sent 24 hours a day, 365 days per year, which prevents issues with regional holidays and hours of working	Excessive numbers of messages can be overwhelming and so are often ignored The information could be distorted as it is so short It is not always possible to know if a person has received the text message As a text message is seen as an informal method of communication, individuals may not use appropriate language
Email	Extremely fast delivery – usually instantaneously Can be sent 24 hours a day, 365 days per year, which prevents issues with regional holidays and hours of working Web-based emails can be sent and received from any computer where there is an internet connection Emails can be sent to multiple people at the same time Allows the inclusion of files such as documents and images	The recipient requires internet access to view the message, so the sender may assume the recipient has read the email when they haven't Viruses can easily be spread via email attachments Emails are less personal than face-to-face communication or telephone conversations The missing context of the message may lead to misunderstanding or misinterpretation of the communication There is a risk of phishing, spam and viruses when sending and receiving emails

Communication method	Advantages	Disadvantages
Websites, social media and networking	Allows businesses to reach a wider audience across the world for no additional cost There is easy access to business information, anywhere, anytime and anyone Can be regularly updated, and allows access to up-to-date business documents and information Allows a business to increase brand awareness and advertise	If not updated regularly, the information will be out of date and unreliable All electronic systems are prone to crashes and downtime The information may not reach the 'right' people at the 'right' time This is a less private form of communication Inexperienced staff may post inappropriate messages, or information that is difficult to recall or may rapidly go viral (spread) Staff will need to be available to respond quickly to posts from customers; this has a cost implication
Advertisement	Advertisements can be more targeted to meet the appropriate target audience Magazine advertising may have a long life and allow for 'pass on' readership	Deadlines are often months in advance, so information could be out dated by the time the advertisement is published Premium advertisements, e.g. on the TV, are extremely expensive If your advertisement is placed at the back of a magazine or newspaper it will be of little business use

2.4 How to use appropriate business formats and styles for written communication layouts

Written communication formats and styles are often referred to as output requirements. Individual businesses will have certain standards, as outlined below.

1 Image resolution – the detail that an image will hold. A higher resolution means that there will be considerably more detail in the image included in the written document.
2 Page layout – the arrangement and style applied to the content of a page of written communication. Business communication usually consists of text, images and pictures. Many businesses will have a particular 'house style' for letters, business reports and press releases. Small businesses often use the paragraph and heading settings that are available in word-processing packages.
3 Text formatting – this is the process of setting up the way that a page of text will look to the reader. The page will be adjusted by:
   a changing the font (style and size)
   b bold, italic or underlined style
   c margins
   d indents
   e columns
   f headers and footers
   g tabs.

4 Use of tables and images – when a business is presenting information that includes data, it is often most appropriate to use tables, graphs and charts. The visual impact illustrates the written points being made, and supports any analysis and judgements. The inclusion of too many or over-complicated tables and images can destroy the message and confuse the reader. If used well, tables and images will aid the readability of a business document.
5 Use of specialist software and hardware – a number of computer programs can help prepare spreadsheets, leaflets or presentations to present the information to their intended audience, e.g. Microsoft Word, Microsoft Publisher and Adobe InDesign.

2.5 The importance of corporate standards

Corporate communication that meets a business's required corporate standards is any communication that is issued by the business to any of its stakeholders.

Corporate standards are aimed at creating good impressions with everyone who sees them. They are used when producing and presenting corporate communications, such as:

● mission statements
● advertising
● packaging
● logos

- endorsements
- sponsorship.

Each business has its own corporate standards that ensure consistency and high-quality communication. They relate to things like those listed below.

- Colour schemes: to ensure a business and its communications can be easily identified, a business will have a corporate colour scheme that will be used across all business documents. For example, Sainsbury's uses orange and Marks & Spencer uses green.
- Writing guides for letters, reports and leaflets: standard letters may be sent in response to a complaint or standard enquiry. A writing guide will ensure corporate consistency and will aid quality control.
- House styles: for example, details of preferred spellings, font style, font size and paragraph layout.
- Version control: to ensure everyone using a document is certain they are using the most up-to-date version, businesses may name and label documents with a version number, e.g. v1, v2.

2.6 The importance of managing corporate profile through media activity

A business should manage its corporate profile, particularly through media activities. On television or the radio, its corporate image and profile need to be controlled and not misrepresented. Some businesses restrict the media they are willing to work with, and many train their senior staff in giving interviews and presenting themselves on TV or radio. They may also have a media spokesperson who appears on the media when there is an important announcement or issue. This attempts to ensure the business's reputation isn't damaged by a staff member saying the wrong thing.

GROUP ACTIVITY

(1 hour)

Working in small groups, choose three large national businesses. Research the corporate image that these businesses portray to their stakeholders and how it is achieved. Produce a short presentation illustrating the corporate image of each business.

KNOW IT

1 Define the term 'audience'.
2 Describe three purposes of business communication.
3 Explain the benefits of using 'face to face' communication.
4 State the advantages and disadvantages of using email for business communication.
5 Explain the importance of corporate image when producing business documents.

LO2 assessment activity

Below is a suggested assessment activity that has been directly linked to the Pass and Merit criteria in LO2 to help with assignment preparation. This is followed by top tips on how to achieve the best results.

Activity 1 Pass criteria *P4* and *P5*

You will be supplied with a range of different communications illustrating corporate standards. These could be communications from your school or college and include its website, prospectus, subject leaflets, application forms, job descriptions, letters to parents, etc. Produce your written work in report format to present to your head teacher.

P4 Based on the communication material you have been given, assess whether or not the form, style and layout is suitable for the intended audience and purpose.

P5 Using your school or college as a case study, summarise its corporate standards and corporate profile. Explain the importance of these standards and profile to your school or college.

TOP TIPS ☑

✔ The communication types you receive should be sufficient to give you appropriate opportunities to meet the requirements of P4.
✔ You should spend equal time and produce similar amounts of evidence for each of the pass criteria.

Activity 2 Merit criteria *M2*

M2 Reflect on the work you produced for P5. Explain how your school or college manages its corporate profile through its media activity.

LO3 Be able to establish a rapport with customers through non-verbal and verbal communication skills *P6 P7 M3*

GETTING STARTED

(15 minutes)

Individually, make a list of important non-verbal communication skills that you use when talking to another person. Once you have a list, rank the items in order of importance.

Communication skills are a person's ability to process, receive and send information. When communicating in a business setting, individuals need to consider a range of styles and methods that meet the communication needs of their customers. These skills should include verbal and non-verbal communication skills. By using these effectively, individuals will build positive and potentially profitable business relationships.

3.1 Non-verbal skills

Communication is much more than talking or writing. Verbal communication allows individuals to understand the **explicit** meaning of words, information or details of the message being relayed. When a person is using verbal communication, they are also conveying **implicit** messages (often unintentionally) through non-verbal behaviours like:

- facial expressions – smiling, frowning, blinking, etc.
- eye contact – this determines the level of trust between two people
- posture – how a person sits or stands (e.g. does the person fold their arms? This can be seen as aggressive or non-responsive to the message)
- para-language – tone of voice, pitch of voice or speed of talking
- individual gestures – hand gestures, head nodding or shaking, leaning forward and shrugging of shoulders
- personal space – this determines the level of intimacy between two people.

🔑 KEY TERMS

Explicit – communication that is fully and clearly expressed or explained.

Implicit – communication that implies a certain meaning but this is not expressed openly.

Non-verbal messages allow individuals to:

- match the **body language** of the person they are talking to so they are certain that the other individual is listening and focused on the conversation
- indicate interest in the conversation – for example, by smiling and nodding, and by leaning forward towards the other person
- reinforce or modify what has been said in words
- demonstrate emotions and reinforce the relationship between people
- provide feedback to the other person
- signal when a person has finished speaking – for example, making eye contact with the person expected to respond.

🔑 KEY TERM

Body language – a form of non-verbal communication in which thoughts, feelings and intentions are expressed.

We know that we pick up important information from other people by noticing these non-verbal communication cues or signals. It is very useful to develop the skill of reading these signals. As other people will read our non-verbal cues and signals, we need to be aware of the signals we give.

We also need to consider cultural differences when considering non-verbal communication. For example, in some cultures making relaxed eye contact is considered a positive trait, showing interest and warmth, whereas in others eye contact is not welcomed. In fact, choice of clothing can sometimes prevent the eyes being seen at all.

Business success means getting it right first time. The main objective as an effective communicator is to be understood.

 **PAIRS ACTIVITY**

(40 minutes)

Working in pairs, draw or find pictures that illustrate how a person's body language demonstrates the following feelings and moods:

1 upset
2 happy
3 uninterested
4 annoyed
5 nervous.

3.2 Verbal skills

Effective verbal communication relies on a number of factors, including non-verbal communication cues, listening skills and clarification. Individuals need to ensure they speak clearly, remain calm, focus on the conversations and are polite when communicating verbally with another person.

There are a number of important aspects and skills that are required when holding a verbal conversation with another person.

Tone and pace

This refers to the strength of a vocal sound made by a person in a communication or situation, and how fast they speak.

Clarifying

This is the process of ensuring that the message you have received has been understood. It allows you to gain feedback and question any points you have misunderstood.

Giving compliments, and avoiding and responding to criticism

Compliments are positive and appreciated by the other person, making them more likely to lead to successful business deals. Conversely, criticism of the other person has the potential to offend and the customer may go elsewhere. If the other person criticises you, it is professional to accept the criticism and not allow the conversation to lead to an argument. Keep calm and don't take it personally.

Opening and initiating a conversation

First impressions have a significant impact on the success of further communication. Formalities, in accordance with customs, will be expected. These may include a handshake, introduction by name, eye contact, etc. In a group situation or at a business training event, organisers may use **ice breakers** to allow all group members to get to know one another.

 **KEY TERM**

Ice breakers – activities used to introduce individuals to one another.

Questioning

Effective **questioning** can influence the conversation and, in business transactions, can mean the difference between success and failure. Questioning should be used to obtain information, check understanding, involve a person in a conversation, show interest in another individual and seek agreement. Successful conversations will use open and closed questions, where open questions allow a more in-depth conversation and closed questions tend to lead to a 'yes', 'no' or one-word response.

KEY TERM

Questioning – a method of seeking information that requires a response.

Closing a conversation

When ending a business conversation, it is good practice to briefly summarise the main points that have been discussed. The way in which a conversation is closed usually determines how it will be remembered. People will remember the non-verbal signals as well as the

Table 4.4 Communication survey

When communicating with another person and listening to them, I tend to:	Always	Frequently	Occasionally	Rarely	Never
get bored and easily distracted					
listen only to facts and ignore the rest of the information					
interrupt the other person					
ignore all non-verbal cues					
avoid eye contact					

words that were spoken. It is good practice to maintain eye contact, avoid looking at your watch or a clock, remain facing the other person (it is seen as ill mannered to turn your back), if appropriate make arrangements for a further meeting and close the conversation with a socially acceptable gesture, such as a handshake.

Addressing customers by name using appropriate convention

In a business situation, address a customer by name and demonstrate you have a working knowledge of their requirements. For example, in a formal situation, or with older customers, Mr, Mrs or Ms may be most appropriate. In less formal situations, using their first name may be acceptable but this needs to be checked with them first.

3.3 Listening skills

Research has shown that we spend 70 per cent of our time communicating with other people. Of this time, we spend:

- 16 per cent reading
- 9 per cent writing
- 30 per cent talking
- 45 per cent listening.

Listening can be seen to be the most vital part of any communication activity we take part in.

Key listening tips

- Paraphrase the message to confirm you understand.
- Repeat the message and recap to help you remember the key points.
- Understand instructions that have been given to you.

- Interpret the requirements of the tasks you have been set by asking questions if necessary.
- Probe for any missing information.
- Make suitable notes if you need to.
- Give yourself time for personal reflection.
- Seek clarification of anything you're not sure about.
- Remember the important points of the message.

PAIRS ACTIVITY

(25 minutes)

Complete the survey in Table 4.4 as honestly as possible. Once you have completed it, ask one of your peers to review your responses and give you feedback on your skills.

Active listening

Active listening is a technique in which the listener focuses on the words of the speaker and restates them to ensure the meaning is clear to both speaker and listener. Active listening is often used in situations where there are disagreements and conflicts. This approach will ease misunderstanding and improve personal relationships.

In business, listening is an important part of the communication process. In practising active listening the goal is to learn what the speaker has said.

There are five key steps in the active listening process, as follows.

1 Ensure you give your whole attention to the speaker, without any distractions.
2 Put aside your own opinions, experiences and emotions.

3 Listen with your eyes as well as your ears, to ensure you pick up any non-verbal communication cues.

4 Thank the speaker and acknowledge the contribution they have made.

5 Repeat what has been said in your own words, to confirm that your understanding is correct.

KNOW IT

1 Describe four non-verbal skills.

2 Explain the difference between implicit and explicit communication.

3 Identify five key listening skills.

4 Explain the importance of questioning.

5 Describe the term 'active listening'.

LO3 assessment activities

Below are suggested assessment activities that have been directly linked to the Pass and Merit criteria in LO4 to help with assignment preparation. These are followed by top tips on how to achieve the best results.

Activity 1 Pass criteria *P6* and *P7*

Participate in a role play, taking the role of the supervisor in a local supermarket. Your tutor or other person will act as a customer who is demanding a refund for a product they have purchased.

TOP TIPS ✔

✔ Ensure the role play gives you appropriate opportunities to demonstrate your verbal and non-verbal communication skills.

✔ Ensure someone who is not another learner acts as the customer.

✔ Each role play should last approximately three to five minutes. It would be good practice to record or video these for evidence. If this is not possible, a detailed individualised witness testimony should be provided.

✔ For P7, take the opportunity to present your response in one or more of a variety of formats, e.g. in an assignment, in a recorded discussion, as a presentation to the rest of the group.

P6 Demonstrate your non-verbal and verbal communication skills when responding to the customer complaint.

P7 Considering the role play you have completed, explain the importance of listening skills in building a rapport with customers.

Activity 2 Merit criteria *M3*

M3 Carry out a review of your non-verbal and verbal skills from the role play, suggesting improvements you would make. Consider your ability to:

● reflect on other people's comments
● confirm your understanding
● confirm understanding if there is any ambiguity
● make a relevant contribution to the conversation
● listen to others
● use and read appropriate body language
● act sensitively
● respond appropriately
● portray a professional image.

TOP TIPS ✔

✔ Take the opportunity to review your performance by getting feedback from your tutor or other group members, or by reviewing recorded evidence.

✔ Ensure you provide detailed evidence that reviews your skills, and suggest improvements for the future.

LO4 Be able to convey messages for business purposes *P8 P9 M4 D2*

GETTING STARTED 👤

(20 minutes)

In small groups, produce a mind-map of different ways in which a business can convey messages – for example, emails.

4.1 How messages can be structured to convey messages

Business information that is being conveyed to other people is usually structured in a formal manner. This may include the production of business reports, emails, notices or newsletters. Whatever the format of the message, it is the content that ensures the successful transfer of information. In general, messages are structured as follows.

- Introduction: sets out who the message is to and from, key topics to be discussed and, if appropriate, a title, heading or subject line.
- Body of message: the main content that needs to be delivered to the recipient.
- Summary: a recap of the key points.
- Conclusion: any next steps, action points, recommendations and proposals; it is the conclusion that most people refer back to when reviewing the message later.
- Invite/seek questions: invite the reader to ask questions if required, or the sender may seek questions to clarify points.
- Frequently asked questions (FAQs): this prevents stakeholders asking the same questions repeatedly and provides them with an information source.

4.2 Types of verbal and written business communications

Verbal communications

Presentations

The common fear of doing a presentation can be reduced with careful preparation. Ideally, a presentation should tell a story with a start, middle and end. The presenter is the storyteller, and needs to ensure the delivery is interesting and carefully expressed. It is often useful to think of the presentation as an extension of a one-to-one meeting. In reality, you are still speaking to individuals, it is just that there are several individuals in the room at the same time.

When preparing a presentation, here are four useful questions to ask yourself:

1 Why should or would people want to listen to me?
2 How will I know whether my presentation has been successful?
3 What resources will help me engage with the audience and tell them my 'story'?
4 What can I do so that I feel confident and prepared?

PAIRS ACTIVITY

(45 minutes)

You and your colleague work for a stationery business and you have been asked by your manager to carry out a sales presentation on the stationery you can provide for local companies. You are free to choose the range of stationery available.

Considering the four questions above, prepare a plan for presenting to local businesses.

Planned discussions

Planned discussions are usually categorised in two ways. The discussion can occur either with people that you are familiar with or with people that you do not know.

Examples of these discussions will include the following.

- One-to-one meetings when shopping for goods or services – this could be a discussion with a hairdresser or dentist that you have used for many years and are familiar with, or someone at the supermarket who you ask for product details.
- Interviews – these are often part of any formal recruitment process. A certain amount of preparation is required as you are unlikely to know the people who will be conducting the interview. Basic guidelines include:
  a ensure you know where you need to be and at what time; it is imperative to be on time
  b consider the other people you may meet – the receptionist, car park attendant, etc.
  c try to calm any nervousness through focusing on your breathing
  d see yourself as positive and welcoming when you enter the interview room
  e ensure you have prepared a list of examples of your knowledge and skills
  f prepare questions to ask the interviewer.

▲ **Figure 4.4** It is best to be well prepared for interviews

- Meeting with a colleague – you are likely to know your colleague well, so try to keep the meeting business-like. You should focus on co-operation and business objectives.
- Telephone conversations – although this is a convenient method of verbal communication, some

meaning may be lost due to a lack of non-verbal cues. Basic guidelines are:

a speak calmly and clearly to ensure you are understood

b use a warm and welcoming tone of voice

c remain polite at all times throughout the conversation

d do not eat, drink or chew when you are on the telephone

e avoid holding another conversation with someone in the same room at the same time as talking on the telephone.

● Participating in an appraisal – many organisations will ask their employees to participate in an annual appraisal. The person completing the appraisal may or may not be known to the employee. These meetings are confidential and offer one-to-one discussions and feedback. Both people need to prepare for such meetings, and to be honest and constructive in their discussions. Giving feedback to the employee involves focusing on behaviour and outcomes leading to learning and improvement. You need to listen carefully and ask for clarification if needed. You should then take time to reflect before you contest anything that may have been said.

Written communications

Although we are in an electronic age, businesses still rely on written communication as the main method of communicating with their stakeholders. There are a number of forms of written communication (Table 4.5), many of which provide a formal means of communicating with other people

Table 4.5 Types of written communication – their uses, effectiveness and alternatives

Type of written communication	Use	Effectiveness	Alternatives
Letters	Usually used for external, formal communication with customers, shareholders and other stakeholders	Keeps a clear record of the communication made and can be used in the case of a dispute	Email Face-to-face meeting Telephone conversation
Social media	Used for internal and external communication on an informal basis	Widely available, and most people currently regularly read and keep up to date with feeds May not be effective for older stakeholders	Email Notice Newsletter
Websites	Provides formal and informal information to internal and external stakeholders of a business	Very effective if user friendly and kept up to date with the information that stakeholders require.	Social media Advertisement Notice
Emails	Usually sent to internal and external stakeholders Can contain formal and informal business information	Very effective due to the speed with which they can be sent and received Can have attachments containing data and images	Letter Notice Social media
Notices	Used for internal informal information to all interested people Often more personal than business-like in structure	Stakeholders need to check the notice location regularly	Email Social media
Newsletter	Provides informal information, usually to an internal audience, but also to regular external customers Provides information on news, relevant articles and notices	Effective if produced regularly and if all stakeholders read it	Email Social media

Type of written communication	Use	Effectiveness	Alternatives
Press release	Provides formal business information to an external audience	Controls the information that a business wishes to release to the public via the press, to ensure the 'right' message is delivered	Email Social media
Promotional flyer/brief	Used to give an external audience a formal view of what a business is providing	Effective as far as the extent of the distribution network There is a limit to the number of flyers that can be produced and delivered Many people treat flyers as junk mail and do not read them	Emails Social media Press release
Report	Used for formal internal and external communication as a record of something that has been heard, observed or developed	Effective way of keeping a comprehensive record of detailed information Usually contains graphs, charts, images and appendices to support understanding	Meeting

4.3 Other considerations for conveying messages for business purposes

Businesses should proofread any messages to ensure they can be understood by their intended audience. In particular businesses should consider the following points.

Appropriate technical language

Businesses should use only those acronyms or abbreviations that will be understood by the intended audience. Technical language can be used in one-to-one emails and with specialist staff, but would be inappropriate on a promotional flyer.

According to Professor Robert Eagleson, 'Plain English is clear, straightforward expression, using only as many words as are necessary ... It is not baby talk, nor is it a simplified version of the English language. Writers of plain English let their audience concentrate on the message instead of being distracted by complicated language. They make sure that their audience understands the message easily' (source: www.plainlanguage.gov).

Use of relevant graphical information/ images to support key points

Complex information is often more easily understood and explained with the use of images. For example, in business documents, break-even graphs are frequently used to illustrate key financial data rather than detailed calculations.

Accuracy

Any business message must be accurate to ensure a business's professional reputation is not negatively affected. Accuracy of spelling, punctuation, grammar, technical terms and the quality of written communication should be checked.

Timeliness of messaging

All messages should contain relevant information and be up to date. They should give customers enough time to make a decision without being rushed.

> **KNOW IT**
> 1 Describe three key sections of business messages.
> 2 Identify three factors to take into account when using verbal communication.
> 3 State three factors to take into account when using non-verbal communication skills.
> 4 List a range of non-verbal communication skills that are vital to business success.
> 5 Describe the effectiveness of three types of non-verbal business communication.

LO4 assessment activities

Below are suggested assessment activities that have been directly linked to the Pass, Merit and Distinction criteria in LO4 to help with assignment preparation. These are followed by top tips on how to achieve the best results.

Scenario

Marionette Hotel is a small independent business that aims to offer high-quality accommodation in its 20 bedrooms, and a first-class service to families. The business has expanded over recent years and hopes to grow further.

The hotel has just built an extension that hosts a swimming pool, and a large function room that can be used for weddings, business events and other functions.

You have been employed as part of the business expansion team to work as an administrative assistant who reports to the hotel manager. The hotel manager is looking for further ways to improve the hotel. The manager is keen to involve all staff, and gain their views and opinions.

Activity 1 Pass criteria *P8* and *P9*

P8 Set up a discussion group with a small group of your peers. Chair a meeting and co-ordinate a discussion about how the hotel could be further improved.

P9 To promote staff motivation and teamwork, the hotel is going to host a social event for its employees. Compose a short notice or flyer for the staff notice board advertising the event. It should include appropriate images and all required details (venue, time, cost, contacts, dates). You are free to decide on the details of the event.

> **TOP TIPS**
> ✔ Ensure the discussion groups are planned so that all members of the group have the opportunity to speak.
> ✔ Each discussion group should last approximately three to five minutes. It would be good practice to film or record these for evidence. If this is not possible, a detailed individualised witness testimony should be provided for each learner.

Activity 2 Merit criteria *M4*

M4 Carry out a review of your own verbal and written skills as demonstrated for P8 and P9, recommending any improvements you would make. Consider your ability to:

● reflect on other people's comments
● confirm your understanding of what they have said
● clarify any ambiguity
● make a relevant contribution to the conversation
● listen to others
● use and read appropriate body language
● act sensitively
● respond appropriately
● portray a professional image
● supply all required information.

> **TOP TIPS**
> ✔ Get feedback from your tutor or other group members, or review recorded evidence.
> ✔ Ensure you provide detailed evidence that reviews your skills and suggests improvements.

Activity 3 Distinction criteria *D2*

D2 Considering the messages you conveyed in P8 and P9, and other methods of delivering business information to stakeholders, prepare a report for the hotel manager suggesting ways to adapt the structure and method of delivery of the message to ensure differing audience requirements are met. The report must include a justification of necessary adjustments that the hotel needs to consider.

> **TOP TIPS**
> ✔ Ensure you understand the requirements of a business report.
> ✔ Give practical recommendations, with examples where appropriate.

LO5 Know the constraints and issues which affect the sharing, storing and use of information for business communications *P10*

(15 minutes)

Working with a partner and using your current knowledge only, define the following terms:

1 copyright
2 patent
3 trademark.

Be prepared to share your definitions with the rest of the group.

Whenever a business produces communications for either internal or external purposes it must ensure that it appreciates the constraints and issues that affect the production, sharing, storing and use of this information.

5.1 Legal constraints

Many legal constraints affect the way businesses use information; some examples are shown in Figure 4.5.

Intellectual property rights

A business or individual should have the right type of intellectual property protection to ensure people are not able to steal or copy:

● product names
● brand names
● inventions
● product design
● any material written, made or produced.

Intellectual property protection comes in many forms, including copyright, patents and trademarks. Some protection is automatically given; other types have to be applied for.

Individuals and businesses need to decide if they own intellectual property. Someone will own intellectual property if they have:

● created it (and it is in accordance with the requirements for copyright, patent or design)
● bought it from its previous owner or creator
● a brand that could be classed as a trademark.

Intellectual property can have more than one owner, be sold or transferred as required, and can belong to people and/or businesses.

▲ **Figure 4.5** Many constraints and issues affect the sharing, storing and use of information for business communications

Copyright

Any original piece of work (for example, a piece of music, a novel, business report, photograph or piece of software) is covered by copyright. If an employee produces a piece of work for the business, the copyright owner is the business and not the employee.

Copyright is enforceable by law as it is against the law to copy or distribute copyrighted material without the owner's permission. Copyright is automatic but does not last for ever.

Data Protection Act

This provides a framework that will ensure personal information is handled appropriately. Individuals have a right to know what information is or has been held about them and how this has been used. If a business wishes to use personal information it needs to register with the information commissioner for the Data Protection Act and then ensure all of its actions comply with eight key principles. These ensure that business information about individuals is:

1 fairly and lawfully processed
2 processed for limited and necessary purposes only
3 adequate, relevant and not excessive in its content
4 accurate and up to date
5 not stored for a period that is longer than needed
6 processed in accordance with individual's rights
7 stored securely
8 not transferred without permission.

Freedom of Information Act

This act manages access to official information. It allows individuals and organisations to request information from any public authority (including local and central government departments), the policy service, the National Health Service, and schools and colleges.

Any information has to be supplied within 20 days of the request. If the information could affect national security or commercial interests, the request can be rejected.

Computer Misuse Act

The act details three main offences for which an organisation can take action against an individual or group of individuals. These are:

1 unauthorised access to any computer program or data, e.g. when a colleague uses another worker's user name and password

2 unauthorised access with the plan or intent to commit a serious crime
3 unauthorised modification or changes to computer data or contents.

Advertising Standards Authority (ASA)

The ASA handles complaints about advertising in non-broadcast media. Businesses must ensure that their advertisements meet the authority's guidelines. All advertisements must be:

- legal
- decent
- honest
- truthful.

See also Unit 5, LO2.1 (page 135) for more information about the ASA.

5.2 Ethical issues

Business ethics are moral principles which relate to acceptable and unacceptable business behaviour.

Organisation policies and codes of practice governing the use of information

Businesses usually produce a range of organisational policies and codes of practice governing the sharing, storing and use of business information. Examples are:

- use of email – for example, by instructing staff not to forward confidential information out of the business, or by using the BCC line when sending an email to several external stakeholders
- use of the internet – for example, by having an intranet or internal online system with areas that only approved people can access
- whistle blowing – where an employee raises a concern about a business practice; the concern can be identified to management within the firm or to someone outside (e.g. the press).
- staff handbooks, advising staff how they should behave while at work, including instructing them on how to deal with sensitive information
- contracts of employment outlining what staff members' roles should be.

Advertisement policies

A business will usually have clear guidance on its policy for advertising. For example, when advertising to children businesses need to ensure they are truthful and socially responsible. They need to consider the appropriateness of any images, pictures and text.

5.3 Security issues

A business needs to consider whether information will be stored electronically or manually. To ensure secure storage of all personal and business data, security issues that will surround its sharing, storage and use need to be addressed, including:

- monitoring of telephone and email communications
- confidentiality of personal data
- information storage
- backup policies and procedures

- -

L05 assessment activity

Below is a suggested assessment activity that has been directly linked to the Pass criteria in L05 to help with assignment preparation. This is followed by top tips on how to achieve the best results.

Activity 1 Pass criteria *P10*

P10 Businesses have to deal with a large volume of information, in many different forms from a wide range of sources. To ensure that a business operates effectively, it must be able to handle this information

- the increasing levels and use of information technology
- operational and business costs.

INDEPENDENT RESEARCH ACTIVITY

(45 minutes)

Read the following online article: http://tinyurl.com/h7ocd84

In pairs, discuss the content of the article and make notes that relate to LO5.3.

effectively. Prepare a factsheet for your school or college that describes the legal constraints, ethical and security issues faced by it in relation to the sharing and storing of school or college communications.

TOP TIPS

✔ Ensure you are given sufficient practical information about the school or college to allow you to complete the task.
✔ Ensure you relate theory to practice and focus on the school or college in your written work.

KNOW IT

1 Define the term 'copyright'.
2 Explain the importance of the Data Protection Act.
3 Describe the role of the Advertising Standards Authority.
4 List the three main offences listed in the Computer Misuse Act.
5 Describe the term 'intellectual property'.

Read about it

Business Information at Work, by Michael Lowe, Europa Publications, 1999
Corporate Communication, by Paul A. Argenti, Irwin McGraw-Hill, 1998
Finding and Knowing: Psychology, Information and Computers, by Claire Davies, Routledge, 2004
Web Design in a Nutshell: A Desktop Quick Reference, by Jennifer Niederst, O'Reilly, 2001

Unit 05

Marketing and market research

ABOUT THIS UNIT

Without successful marketing, customers may not be aware of products and services. Businesses strive to ensure that their products or services are sold to customers at the right price and in the right place, always ensuring that customers can access them.

This unit will enable you to understand the different marketing strategies that businesses utilise. You will gain important knowledge about the legal aspects of marketing and how these can influence the decisions that are made in business.

Businesses must research their potential markets, so this unit will also enable you to learn about both primary and secondary market research methods. You will be required to complete various forms of meaningful market research to collate results and present the findings.

LEARNING OUTCOMES

The topics, activities and suggested reading in this unit will help you to:

1 understand the role of marketing in businesses
2 know the constraints on marketing
3 be able to carry out market research for business opportunities
4 be able to validate and present market research findings.

How will I be assessed?

You will be assessed through a series of assignments and tasks set and marked by your tutor.

How will I be graded?

You will be graded using the following criteria, which are in the specification produced by OCR for the qualification.

Learning outcome	Pass	Merit	Distinction
You will:	**To achieve a Pass you must demonstrate that you have met all the pass assessment criteria**	**To achieve a Merit you must demonstrate that you have met all the pass and merit assessment criteria**	**To achieve a Distinction you must demonstrate that you have met all the pass, merit and distinction assessment criteria**
1 Understand the role of marketing in businesses	**P1** Explain the role of the marketing function in business		
	P2 Describe how carrying out market analysis can benefit a business		
	P3 Explain how businesses measure the impact of their marketing using at least two contrasting businesses	**M1** Analyse the impact of a particular marketing campaign run by a specific business	
2 Know the constraints on marketing	**P4** Describe the constraints on marketing for a specific business		
3 Be able to carry out market research for business opportunities	**P5** Select market research method, type and tools for a market research proposal and give reasons for the choice	**M2** Based on own research, assess the choice of market research method and type used, explaining their effectiveness	**D1** Justify the choice and sequence of questions used in the market research
	P6 Conduct primary and secondary research to identify business opportunities for a specific business		
4 Be able to validate and present market research findings	**P7** Assess the validity of market research findings for a specific business opportunity against its market research proposal	**M3** Based on assessment of own market research findings recommend improvements or additional market research requirements	**D2** Recommend and justify marketing decisions that the business could take
	P8 Present market research findings in an appropriate format for the data obtained and audience		

LO1 Understand the role of marketing in businesses *P1 P2 P3 M1*

(10 minutes)

Think of the last product that you purchased.

- When did you purchase the item?
- Where did you get it from – a small shop, large shop, at a retail park, online?
- Why did you purchase the product there?
- Were you persuaded by any form of advertising?
- Once you have considered all your answers, discuss them with others. What is similar and what is different?
- Why do you think this may be the case?

Feed back your thoughts and findings to the rest of the class.

1.1 Introduction to the marketing function

The marketing function

The **marketing** function is key to how a business can promote itself to its customer base. Customers may be existing (they have purchased the products or services from the business before) or potential, meaning that the customer base could expand if a sale is successful. Therefore, any business must know the **market** that it is operating in, as well as understand the needs and wants of its customers.

> ### KEY TERMS
>
> **Marketing** – the management process responsible for identifying, anticipating and satisfying customer requirements profitably (source: Chartered Institute of Marketing (CIM)).
>
> **Market** – a defined area in which consumers, businesses and organisations are involved in the manufacture, purchase and use of a specified product.

Customer needs are the problems that a customer intends to solve when they purchase a product or service.

Customer wants are different, as it is not just about gaining the product, but ensuring that the additional features are what the customer requires. For example, if you purchase a tablet computer, do you need the one with all the latest features or do you want the one

with all the latest features, which may cost more? The business from which you choose to purchase the item should ensure that it can fulfil your requirements so that you will gain customer satisfaction from the buying experience.

If customers are satisfied with the service they receive, they are more likely to return, and may recommend the business or product to friends and family. The business's customer base might therefore increase over time.

The importance of links with other functions of the business

As well as understanding customers, the marketing function must link with other functions within the business, such as production, finance and human resources because, without a joint approach, sales could be missed. If a product cannot be found by a customer (because a manufacturer has not been paid, or there were not enough materials to produce it) a customer might go to a competitor. Business reputations can easily be damaged, so all functions within a business must work together to achieve the same aims and objectives.

Setting marketing aims and objectives linked to strategic objectives

Setting marketing objectives

Up to three **marketing objectives** may be set to reach one marketing aim, so aims and objective must be achievable. Examples of marketing objectives could be:

- targeting new customers
- entering new markets, both locally and internationally
- building brand awareness.

> ### KEY TERMS
>
> **Marketing objective** – a specified and measurable goal or reason for carrying out a marketing activity.
>
> **Business objectives** – targets set by a business that detail the steps involved in achieving the overall aims of the business.

Marketing objectives should link to the wider **business objectives**, which are the overall aims and targets of the company (for example, number of sales or amount of profit). To ensure that objectives are effective, they should always be SMART (see Unit 16, LO1.1, page 276). This means the business is able to focus on where it wants to be in the future, which can then be monitored once the plans are in place to achieve the aims. This forms the essential elements of the **marketing strategy**.

Devising a marketing strategy

The business will need to decide which approach is most likely to fulfil its objectives. Some examples of marketing strategies are listed below.

- *Segmenting the market* – dividing the market (customers and potential customers) into different groups or segments by factors such as gender, age, etc.
- *Considering mass markets* – ensuring that the product can be accessed by as many customers as possible in a wide area.
- *Marketing a product to a niche market* – targeting a single segment of the market.

Analysing the market will ensure that the business's product or service is slightly different from that of its **competitors** to gain **market share**. It may be the first business to think of an idea that is original, changing the way in which consumers operate. Consider how social media and streaming sites, such as Facebook, Spotify or iTunes, changed the way people listen to music.

 KEY TERMS

Marketing strategy – how marketing messages and activities will be combined with sales objectives to contribute to a business's overall objectives.

Competitors – other businesses in the same market that provide similar products and services, and so try to gain the same customers.

Market share – the percentage of a market's total sales or revenue that a particular company contributes.

GROUP ACTIVITY

(10 minutes)

In one minute, think of ten products or services introduced over the past 30 years that have changed the way in which businesses and consumers operate and behave … Go!

Share your ideas with the group, explaining why you chose these particular products and services. Are any of your ideas the same as other people's? Why do you think this is the case?

▲ **Figure 5.1** Microwaves changed the way people cook

? **THINK ABOUT IT**

(1 hour)

Case study

Read the news story at http://tinyurl.com/pk4q7jc about a book that filters water. This product could make a significant difference in the fight against diseases spread by dirty water.

What are your thoughts about this potentially exciting finding?

Identify a suitable charity that may be interested in this new prototype by focusing on the charity's **market analysis** – this could form part of its business plan. Once this information has been researched, write an email to the charity explaining why you think the product would be a good fit for its objectives.

KEY TERM

Market analysis – marketing research that produces data about the current market, enabling a business to compete in a particular sector.

PAIRS ACTIVITY

(15 minutes)

Select a large business that has a strong product brand. Research its marketing strategy and, using this information, devise five different marketing objectives. Make up statistics if necessary, but each objective should be SMART. For example:

- to increase number of sales by x% within [time]
- to add x number of customers to email database by [date]
- to gain x% market share by [date]
- to generate x enquiries via the website within [time].

Be prepared to explain your objectives to the rest of your group.

The marketing mix

The **marketing mix** is a crucial part of a business's marketing of its products or services. Each aspect of the marketing mix must be considered carefully as if one element is wrong, this could be disastrous. For more about the marketing mix and the '4Ps', see Unit 6 (page 163).

KEY TERM

Marketing mix – a key marketing tool that allows a business to consider the product, price, place and promotion of its goods.

1.2 How businesses use market analysis

Identifying market structure

Businesses that enter an existing market aim to gain customers in order for their business to succeed. Analysing the current **market structure** will be the first step in gaining the knowledge they need.

KEY TERM

Market structure – an overview of a market's characteristics, e.g. the amount and types of competitors, the products and services these produce, the size of the market.

Number of firms

First, a business should investigate which businesses are in direct competition with it. If there are many, the business may question what makes its product or service different from the rest, but equally if there are few, the business may want to know if there have been many failures in that particular market. Remember that about 50% of businesses fail in their first two years of operation, so adequate research should ensure that this business isn't one of them.

Market share

Market share is a method by which a business can judge how it is performing against other competitors. It is normally measured as the percentage of a market's total sales or revenue to which a particular company contributes. It can be calculated as the total sales or revenue for the market, divided by the business's contribution to those sales or that revenue. If a business has a large market share then it will be dominating the market for that product or service.

INDIVIDUAL ACTIVITY

(10 minutes)

Look at the following categories and quickly note down next to each one the company or brand you consider to

have the largest market share for that product in the UK – not your personal preference!

Table 5.1 Products and brands

Product	Company/brand with biggest market share
Breakfast cereals	
Crisps	
Trainers	
Games console	
Fizzy drinks	
Smartphone	
Fast food	
Tablet	

Market size

Businesses will also look at the size of the market – for example, the number of sales by volume and the value of these sales. Measuring such data will enable the business to calculate the average number of sales that it might expect, as well as how much these sales will be worth.

Businesses have to take in to consideration the difference between how much it costs to produce a product or service and the recommended retail price (RRP, which you will sometimes see on an item). The values of manufacturing costs and retail prices are different (see Unit 13, LO2.5, page 242, for more on price setting).

Market volume

Market volume enables a business to focus on the amount of sales it made over a period of time. It can help a business to identify patterns and trends in sales, which then ensures the business can focus on where it needs to improve. Market volume statistics can be obtained both from primary sources within the business as well as externally using secondary research.

Market value

A business can determine its market value by its share price. The estimated value of shares can give a business an indication of its current market value. This can be tracked over time and then fed back to stakeholders like the board of directors, owners, managers, shareholders, employees, etc.

Other market components

Once the volume and value of sales of the business have been investigated, the business may also want to investigate other aspects of the market, such as:

- number of retail outlets stocking the product or offering the service
- potential customer numbers for the product or service
- competitors' online presence
- the most dominant products/services
- identifying market growth potential.

A really thorough investigation will produce a full picture of the current market, and the opportunities and challenges a business might face when up against its competitors.

Identifying potential market growth opportunities and recognising competitors

Competitor analysis

It is up to the customer to decide which product or service to buy into according to their own personal requirements. A business entering into a market where it has competitors needs to research them in order to compete successfully and to help with strategic planning. Some questions to ask could be:

- Who are the competitors?
- What is their competitive advantage?
- What is their market share?
- What is their online presence?
- What are their strengths?
- Where are their weaknesses?
- Who is their main customer base?

Answering these questions gives a business a real insight into the elements and gaps it may discover as a result of market analysis.

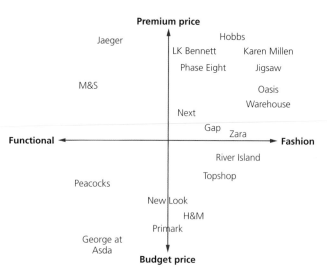

▲ **Figure 5.2** An example of market mapping

Market mapping

Market mapping is the plotting of various market conditions on a graph to identify trends and patterns between consumers and products. It can help companies locate problem areas and identify the source of problems.

Source: adapted from J. Nowacki (2002) Marketing, Philip Allan Associates

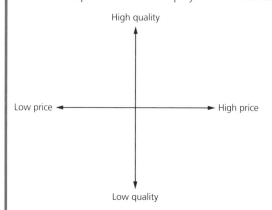
🔍 **PAIRS ACTIVITY** 👥 ⋯⋯⋯⋯⋯⋯⋯⋯

(30 minutes)

How could a new business find out what potential customers really want from a new product or service in a competitive market? Choose one of the following examples:

- a micro-brewery
- a design agency
- a prom dress maker
- a café.

Discuss your ideas in pairs, then explain your idea to the rest of the group and discuss it.

Carrying out market segmentation

When businesses want to analyse an existing market they wish to enter, they often investigate the market in different categories, known as segments. This is known as **market segmentation**.

> **KEY TERM**
>
> **Market segmentation** – splitting customers into different categories (segments) to enable the targeting of specific products or services to that particular group or category.

Demographic segmentation

This is when a business analyses the market according to economic and social variables. These could be age, gender, wealth or occupation. Businesses will use these methods to target their products at a specific demographic – for example, targeting a monthly subscription to a beauty box (parcel of designer make-up) at affluent women in their thirties.

Geographic segmentation

This is when a business investigates the market in terms of the geographical area it covers. These days the world has become much smaller because of the ease of travel. For example, in some industries it is the norm to hold meetings in different countries with international delegates, or to use Skype to hold a meeting between team members in different countries. Geographic segmentation can therefore cover any area, from a specific part of a city or town, to a region or county, to a country, or even several countries such as France, Spain and Italy together.

Behavioural segmentation

This is when a business looks at behaviour patterns and adapts its marketing to meet consumer needs. For example, data from supermarket or pharmacy loyalty cards is analysed, then the customers are segmented by what they have bought and the business sends relevant discount coupons to them for products they are likely to buy. This can be a very useful tool for planning in terms of usage rates, occasional buying, etc.

Psychographic segmentation

This is where a business divides the market into categories such as lifestyle, interests, hobbies, opinions and values. It can really help a business to determine if there is a gap within a particular market or if it is going to join a market that is more specialised.

Benefits of market segmentation for a business

There are positive and negative aspects of segmenting. The positives include the following.

- Segmentation can allow a new business to see a gap in the market. This means it could introduce something new and use the segmentation tool to target the product or service at a particular group or segment to generate sales. Equally, an existing business could develop new products to increase its market share.
- Businesses can produce products and services for each type of segment to dominate the market, meet the needs of all customers and, hopefully, retain customers.
- A business can establish a niche market so that a very specialised product or service could meet the needs of a small group of consumers.
- Marketing budgets can be spent on targeting an identified segment, rather than wasting money by taking a general approach.

One possible negative aspect of segmentation is that competitors who have a larger market share could produce a similar product and win over customers by dominating the market. Customers, however, could get frustrated that one business dominates a market and seek alternatives.

> **INDEPENDENT RESEARCH ACTIVITY**
>
> **(1 hour)**
>
> How could a new travel business specialising in adventure and extreme sport activities use market segmentation to help it succeed? Research the market thoroughly and show examples of the relevant segmentation theories discussed above.

1.3 How the impact of marketing can be measured

Once marketing methods have been put in place, how can a business measure the success and impact of its marketing? Here are some examples.

Sales and trends

If the number of units sold increases after a marketing campaign, this is a good indication that there is a link. The rate of sales can be plotted to cover different periods in order to identify trends.

Income

Businesses can also analyse the income (sales revenue) that has been generated by the increase in sales. However, this can sometimes be misleading. For example, pricing strategies such as promotion pricing (offering short-term promotions to customers to persuade them to keep buying something when the price returns to normal) may lower sales revenue and give the impression that sales have fallen.

Awareness

It is sometimes hard to know whether customer knowledge of a product, service or brand has grown. One way to measure this is via customer feedback, as this will give a clear indication of whether consumers like the product or service. These days, reviews on social media and websites influence consumers, so gaining good online feedback can really help a business, whereas negative feedback can damage a reputation.

LO1 assessment activities

Below are suggested assessment activities that have been directly linked to the Pass, Merit and Distinction criteria in LO1 to help with assignment preparation. These are followed by top tips on how to achieve the best results.

Activity 1 Pass criteria *P1*

P1 Explain the different aspects of marketing to show the assessor your application and knowledge of the marketing function, including how this can be linked to strategic marketing and your knowledge of the different stages of marketing.

Activity 2 Pass criteria *P2*

P2 Describe how carrying out market analysis can benefit a business.

Describe the different elements of market analysis in detail and link this to the benefits that completing this analysis will have on a business in the future.

Activity 3 Pass criteria *P3*

P3 Explain how businesses measure the impact of marketing using at least two contrasting businesses, such as a plc and a charity, or a sole trader and a limited company. The measures they use should differ.

Activity 4 Merit criteria *M1*

M1 Analyse the impact of a particular marketing campaign run by a specific business.

You are required to focus on only one business to fulfil the criteria. This should enable you to fully analyse the impact of the marketing methods used within that particular business.

LO2 Know the constraints on marketing *P4*

GETTING STARTED

(10 minutes)

You have purchased a product in a shop, but when you get it home you decide you don't like it. What can you do? Does the business legally have to do anything? What do you think your options are? Write down your thoughts then share them with the rest of the group.

2.1 The main elements and impacts of constraints on marketing

Constraints on marketing are the restrictions that businesses must abide by. There are several types of constraint, as described below.

Legal constraints

Some laws have been in place for many years and are updated periodically. Businesses must abide by laws or there will be consequences like fines, being taken to court, criminal sanctions such as a prison sentence or being sued by an individual using the civil court system.

An example of **legal constraints** that is particularly relevant to marketing is consumer protection; these are the laws that keep us as customers safe when we purchase or use products and services. Table 5.2 briefly details some consumer protection laws, as well as their purpose.

> ## KEY TERMS
>
> **Constraints** – restrictions that are imposed on individuals or businesses.
>
> **Legal constraints** – restrictions relating to laws that apply within the markets in which the product or service is produced and sold.

Table 5.2 Laws relevant to consumer protection

Name of law	Purpose of law
Consumer Rights Act 2015	Covers what should happen when goods are faulty, there are unfair contract terms and what should happen when a business acts anti-competitively or gives false information
Trade Descriptions Act 1968	Businesses must make sure that the products or services they sell are how they are described
Consumer Protection Act 1987	A business must ensure that customers will not be damaged by any products or services they purchase
Weights and Measures Act 1985	A business offering a product that states a particular weight on the packaging must ensure that is what consumers get when they purchase it
Consumer Credit Act 2006	Protects consumers when they purchase products using any type of credit, e.g. credit card, loan, hire purchase
Food Safety Act 1990 (updated 2009)	Businesses must make sure they store food appropriately, and cook food thoroughly so that consumers do not become ill after eating it

> ## KEY TERM
>
> **Voluntary constraints** – restrictions that are not legally required but that a business can choose to adopt – for example, to ensure best practice.

Voluntary constraints

Voluntary constraints are not legally enforceable but are there to prevent consumers being offended by marketing messages in advertising material or other communications. Examples of these include the following.

Advertising Standards Authority (ASA)

This organisation monitors the content of advertising media, including websites, posters, TV adverts, etc. The ASA website states that, 'Our ambition is to make every UK ad a responsible ad.' If consumers want to complain about a particular element of marketing because they think it is, say, misleading or dishonest, the ASA will investigate and then act upon its findings.

Advertising Codes of Practice

Codes of practice are produced for businesses to follow, but are not legally binding. They are general rules that inform organisations (including advertisers and media owners) that they should not mislead through advertising. There are specific rules about advertising children's products, alcohol, vehicles and financial products. Broadcast organisations such as Ofcom (the communications regulator in the UK) enable consumers to complain about the TV and radio sectors, as well as telephone, mobile and postal services.

Ethical constraints

Ethical constraints are when a business considers the values and beliefs relating to the products and services it is producing and, as a consequence, marketing. It is not against the law to act unethically (as long as no criminal laws are broken), but consumers are well informed and bad publicity can do substantial damage to a business's reputation. For example, businesses can lose substantial profits if consumers decide to boycott (not purchase) a product or service, and ultimately they could go out of business.

Recently it has been highlighted in the press that some charities have been targeting the elderly and vulnerable individuals to persuade them to donate. Although this approach could significantly increase their income, it is not seen as ethical.

Cultural constraints

The internet has enabled the world to seem a smaller place as we can now connect instantly with anyone. Therefore businesses need to consider **ethical and cultural constraints** such as language, religion, tradition and local customs when promoting or informing consumers about products or services. Businesses must ensure that their products or services do not offend or confuse. For example, a famous soup brand produced an advert to be shown in a country where it wanted to establish a new market. The advert showed a boy coming home from school and having a bowl of soup for dinner – nothing strange you might think, but in that country soup is eaten for breakfast not dinner! The ad was withdrawn. Many other businesses have fallen foul of language differences. Schweppes produced an advertising campaign for its famous tonic water. Unfortunately, this translated as 'toilet water'! Such errors can damage reputations and sales.

> 🔑 **KEY TERM**
>
> **Ethical and cultural constraints** – restrictions for ensuring that individuals, groups or other businesses are not adversely affected by the conduct of others.

Financial constraints

Having a specified budget makes a business investigate the most suitable marketing methods for the money available. This can restrict its options but can also be an advantage because it can force a team to think creatively about how best to utilise the finance it does have to achieve what is best for the target market. A new business competing against large, well-established businesses may want a concentrated and high-profile marketing campaign, or an existing business might want to raise its profile – but that comes at a cost.

Other examples of **financial constraints** are cash flow, the liquidity of the business, the time required (as time equals money) and the staff required to work on the marketing – the more staff required the greater the impact on costs.

> 🔑 **KEY TERM**
>
> **Financial constraints** – restrictions relating to money.

Technical constraints

The internet hosts:

- pop-up adverts on websites
- adverts appearing at the start of any downloaded media
- adverts as text messages
- email adverts.

In order for a business to compete, it will need to invest in new technology and have the required technical skills to create the necessary advertisements, while considering the legal, ethical and budgetary constraints imposed on the campaign. Technology develops fast so the skill lies in knowing how to predict what are going to be most effective methods of advertising in the future, bearing in mind that consumers themselves may have **technical restraints**, like computers that are too slow to display complex graphics in an ad.

> 🔑 **KEY TERM**
>
> **Technical constraints** – restrictions relating to technology or equipment.

Employees

Employees are a real asset to any business, but it needs the right number of staff with the right skills. If staff are too busy, or they lack marketing skills, they will act as a constraint on the business's marketing ambitions.

Broadcast codes (Ofcom)

Broadcasting codes set rules and regulations for TV and radio broadcasting. Ofcom is the body in the UK that sets the rules that protect viewers and listeners from potentially offensive and harmful broadcasts. Viewers and listeners can complain directly to Ofcom, which will then assess the complaint and decide if further investigation is required. Businesses are constrained by the need to avoid causing offence and associated inquiries.

Limitations/penalties

Limitations and penalties can be implemented by trading standards (see below) as well as for example local councils. They could penalise a business via fines if, for example, food hygiene standards are breached. In this example, if changes and improvements are not implemented, the business could be forced to close down for the safety of customers. Another example is the hours of opening for nightclubs, which could be limited if they are near a residential area.

Trading Standards

Trading Standards enforce consumer laws to keep consumers safe. Employees who work for Trading Standards within a local council represent consumers and businesses jointly to ensure that professional standards are met. Their role is to advise and to enforce laws that cover all products or services that we purchase, sell, hire or rent. They will investigate any complaints made against a business, and will ultimately prosecute traders who continue to break the law.

🔍 INDEPENDENT RESEARCH ACTIVITY

(1.5 hours)
Select three different types of constraints on marketing. Research three different businesses that have been affected by each of the constraints you have selected. Then write a blog to inform others of your findings. Ensure that you reference any articles you have used at the end of your blog.

KNOW IT

1 Name three types of constraints on marketing.
2 Describe two laws that a business must abide by and the purpose they serve.
3 What is the aim of the Advertising Standards Authority?

LO2 assessment activity

Below is a suggested assessment activity that has been directly linked to the Pass criteria in LO2 to help with assignment preparation. This is followed by top tips on how to achieve the best results.

Activity 1 Pass criteria *P4*

P4 Write a newspaper article that details the different constraints on marketing a business must consider when planning its marketing campaigns for a product or service. Describe the constraints that a medium-sized local business has encountered over the past few years and how it has learned from this experience.

TOP TIPS ☑

✔ Ensure that you choose a relevant business on which to base this activity.
✔ Use the internet to identify different articles about constraints on marketing. These will help you to gain a real understanding of the impacts of the constraints.

LO3 Be able to carry out market research for business opportunities
P5 P6 M2 D1

GETTING STARTED

(15 minutes)
● When were you last asked to complete some market research?
● What form did the market research take?
● Was it an online set of questions or someone in person asking questions?
● Where were you?
● What questions were you asked?
● Were you given any incentives to complete the research, such as getting something free of charge?

Answer these questions by yourself and then discuss your thoughts in a pair. After that, share your discussions with the rest of the group.

3.1 The purpose of market research

Introduction to market research

Market research is a method of finding out specific information about a current market in order to gain a better understanding of it, but also to find out more information to make the business grow. Businesses need to first consider what they want to find out – for example, they may want to know if they should diversify into new markets by producing products or services for a new target market. Market research may help them make that decision.

🔑 KEY TERM

Market research – collecting information about a particular market for a specific purpose.

Once a business has decided on the purpose of the research, it then needs to decide the form of market research it will use.

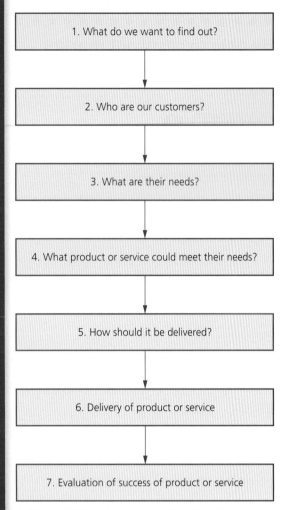

1. What do we want to find out?

2. Who are our customers?

3. What are their needs?

4. What product or service could meet their needs?

5. How should it be delivered?

6. Delivery of product or service

7. Evaluation of success of product or service

▲ **Figure 5.4** Businesses need to identify what they want their market research to find out

3.2 Methods and types of researching

The two main methods of market research that a business will use to find out specific information are:

1 primary research   **2** secondary research.

Primary research

Primary research involves a business collecting its own information (raw data) and then using this to help it plan. The most common method used is a questionnaire or survey. The results of this method may be an example of **qualitative research**, if the information is based on opinions, views and attitudes. Traditionally these were completed face to face, but they are now commonly done online – for example, being asked to feed back on a product or service that we have recently purchased. Some companies even ask for feedback on the packaging of a product they have sent out!

Questionnaires can also be sent in a text message, or presented via telephone, post, or face to face in retail shops or shopping malls. Other forms of primary research will be discussed later in this unit.

Secondary research

Secondary research is information that already exists, which has been collected and analysed by another person, business or government organisation for a given purpose. Secondary research is often classed as being either qualitative (see above) or quantitative. **Quantitative research** includes information on facts and figures, which will have almost always being analysed in some shape or form. A good example of secondary data is a census survey, which takes a snapshot of everyone's lives in the UK every ten years.

Secondary data is very useful for finding out information about a particular topic, which a business would not be able to find for itself. However, it should be assessed for reliability – for example, whether it came from a reliable source like the Office for National Statistics rather than Wikipedia.

GROUP ACTIVITY

(1 hour)

Look at the highlights of the 2011 UK census (see http://tinyurl.com/btcwo5c). What do you consider to be the ten most significant pieces of information you have found? Why is this? Present your findings and discuss with the rest of the group, explaining why you have selected these ten pieces of research. Consider how a business might use the data.

3.3 Tools used to carry out primary market research and how to use them

Other forms of primary research are detailed in Table 5.3.

Table 5.3 Tools for primary research

Tool for primary research	Explanation
Observation	Data is collected by observing: looking at something and then reporting the findings. Examples could be observing the impact of a new sales stand on customers, or a 'mystery shopper' observing staff behaviour when enquiring about a product or service
Focus group	Focus groups are used to gain a variety of different opinions within a group setting. The key element is that consumers are interviewed together. For example, a bank wants to learn if its new account will appeal to adults aged 20–30. The research would take place in a conference room after work, with the members of the group being offered a financial incentive to participate in the discussion, e.g. £50
Technology based	The increased use of social media, which includes mobile surveys and online communities, can give the organisation an understanding of needs and wants, as well as the opinions of its customers
Consumer panels	Consumers may be asked to participate in research on a number of different occasions, so a business can observe consumer behaviour and reactions to a particular products or service. This is different to a focus-group approach as the research happens over a number of different sessions
Test marketing	This type of primary research is when a business produces a product or service to try to determine how consumers will react to it nationally. They 'test' the product in a small area and then use the results to decide if they should launch the product nationwide in its current form or alter aspects using the results of the data. Businesses will test, say, consumer reactions to a product or service, the advertising, sales techniques, etc.

When the method of primary research has been selected by a business, it will then have to decide which method of sampling it will use. Sampling is the way in which a business decides who they are going to ask to complete the research, and in what form. There are a number of different sampling techniques but the two main types are **probability** sampling and non-probability sampling.

> ## 🔑 KEY TERM
> **Probability** – the likelihood of consumers completing an action, such as purchasing an item.

Probability sampling

Probability sampling is when it is likely that something will happen. There are four main methods, as follows.

1 *Random sampling* uses no single group of people, e.g. they can be of any age, gender, hair colour.
2 *Stratified sampling* divides the population into different groups. It could take the form of selecting a particular age category of people who complete the sample.
3 *Cluster sampling* divides people into different sections known as clusters, e.g. those living in a particular geographical area, and respondents are selected from that cluster. This method can be quite efficient in terms of time and money as it is limited to certain areas.
4 *Systematic sampling* is when people from a large population are chosen using the random sampling method over a fixed period of time.

Non-probability sampling

Non-probability methods of sampling do not use any random methods. These can be split into two main categories: quota and convenience.

1 *Quota sampling* is when a target number of respondents is required to meet the research needs, e.g. the business may want to survey 20,000 consumers so the research will keep going until that target is met.
2 *Convenience sampling* uses consumers who happen to be available at the time to complete the research.

In addition, *judgement sampling* is a method of sampling that is non-random and based purely upon the opinions of an expert. The results of this type of sampling can be judgemental and biased, however, so are not necessarily representative of all customers.

Qualitative and quantitative questions

Qualitative questions enable the respondent to inform you of their opinion. They can also be described as 'open ended' questions. An example would be: 'What did you like most about the last film you saw?'

Quantitative questions are the opposite because they restrict the respondent's answers. These kinds of questions can also be called closed questions.

An example would be: 'Do you like your job?' The respondent can either answer yes or no. This type of question means that the results can easily be statistically analysed by a business.

How to write and sequence questions

There are a number of different processes to consider when devising questions for a survey.

- Information: a business should be clear on the information it is seeking to discover.
- Type of survey: once the information sought is clear, the type of survey can be decided upon, e.g. online, face to face.
- Time: how long will respondents have to complete the survey? The number and complexity of questions will determine the time taken to complete the survey.
- Questions: qualitative or quantitative questions, or a mixture of both?
- Response: businesses could use predefined answers, or they could use a Likert scale. This is a psychometric measurement of opinions, beliefs or attitudes in which a respondent must agree or disagree with statements or options by ranking them, for example, from 1 to 10. The advantage to using such methods is that results are easy to understand and therefore it is easy to draw conclusions from them.
- Sequence: the order or sequence of questions is important. If a survey is long, starting with simple questions that do not require too much thought could encourage a response. It is also important that the

questions follow from one to another clearly, so flow well within the survey.

3.4 Sources for secondary market research

INDEPENDENT RESEARCH ACTIVITY
(5 minutes)

How many loyalty cards for different businesses do you think your family members have between them?

How do these cards work to benefit both consumers and the business?

Internal sources

Businesses are able to access both internal and external methods of secondary research to aid a specific purpose.

An **internal source** could be, for example, an analysis of the past five years' sales figures to help determine the highs and lows of sales during an average year. This could also be linked to a business's stock control systems, to identify which products go out of stock or need reordering regularly. If customers cannot purchase a selected product, then a rival business could win the sale.

KEY TERM

Internal source – information from within the organisation.

THINK ABOUT IT

Case study: loyalty cards

▲ **Figure 5.5** Green Shield stamps – one of the first loyalty schemes

Loyalty cards benefit both consumers and businesses. The concept started many years ago when the founder

of the Green Shield stamps loyalty scheme, Richard Tompkins, heard of a similar idea that was being used successfully in America. With Green Shield, shoppers received one stamp for every 6p they spent on shopping, which they could then use for credit in a shop that took part in the scheme, or use the stamps to order products from a catalogue. The scheme continued until 1991.

Tesco launched its very successful Clubcard in the mid-1990s and it continues today, with millions of customers collecting points each time they shop. Other successful loyalty cards are Sainsbury's Nectar Card and Boots Advantage Card.

The cards enable the user to build up points over a period of time, which can be exchanged for money-off vouchers for products or leisure activities.

A loyalty scheme enables a business to build consumer profiles – for example, by recording average monthly spend and the types of products/services bought. This in turn means that a business can target certain products at a consumer, enticing them with money-off coupons or sales promotions to get them to purchase a particular brand. Convincing them to swap permanently to a more expensive brand will in turn help profits and sales.

The system works by making consumers feel they are getting value for money and good-quality products. It looks as if loyalty cards really are here to stay.

1 Write a list of ten different loyalty card schemes, stating the name of the card and which business is associated with it.
2 Select three cards from your list and investigate how many points you get per £1 that you spend. How much do you need to spend to gain either a substantial voucher (£20) to be exchanged for money off or a free item (e.g. in a coffee shop)?
3 Consider the results you found for point 2. Do the figures surprise you in any way? Do you think that the loyalty cards are worth it? Explain your answers.

External sources

External sources of secondary research include:

- commercial sources, e.g. data provided by market research organisations
- competitors' company reports and websites
- competitors' and other company websites
- government publications such as census surveys and white papers
- trade publications such as *The Grocer*, many of which you can now subscribe to online
- the media, such as public events, press releases and newspapers.

KEY TERM

External source – information from outside of the organisation.

3.5 How to carry out market research using primary and secondary methods

Once a business has investigated the many different methods of primary and secondary research, it must consider what outcome it wants to find when completing its research. Is it that it wants to introduce a new product to the market and wants to test out if it will work? It could be a product development idea, e.g. bubblegum-flavoured yoghurt for children, and it wants consumers' opinion on the possibility of the product being produced.

3.6 Factors that influence the choice of market research methods, types and tools to be used

Having considered how the market research could be completed, a business will then need to think about the main factors that may decide which methods will be selected.

The reasons for market research

We have discussed in previous sections the importance of being clear on the information that the business is seeking to discover by completing the research using primary, secondary or both methods. Having clear aims and objectives that will form the basis of a **market research proposal** will help the team involved focus on the key areas.

KEY TERM

Market research proposal – suggesting ideas or methods to collect relevant market research material for a given purpose.

Information

Before a business attempts to complete primary research, it must be clear on what it wants to find out. This could affect the method, e.g. is a survey appropriate for the aims identified?

Availability of resources

Resources include those listed below.

- *Budget* – the allocation of finances to the research and the methods that will be used to fully meet the requirements of the market research proposal.
- The *time* allocated to complete the research from the proposal stage, development, completion, analysis and feedback stages.
- The *number and range of participants*, which will also include the type and method of sampling techniques used by the business when completing the research.
- the *location* of the research, e.g. a college, a town, a country or internationally.
- *Incentives* for taking part, e.g. money-off vouchers, some type of financial gain, a free gift or the chance of winning a prize.
- *Permission to use data* – ensuring that the information about participants has been gained without breaching confidentiality, and that their responses are quoted publicly only with their permission.

● *Reporting requirements* – how, why and when the findings will be reported, and with whom this information will be shared. Analysing quantitative results by using mean, mode and median methods, and illustrating the results using reports, graphs or charts can make the results easier to visualise. Selecting the format of presentation will depend on who will be interested in the results.

3.7 Benefits and drawbacks

Primary and secondary research both have their advantages and disadvantages. For primary research, as the business will be seeking original data, significant time will need to be allocated to devising the method of research, particularly to ensure the questionnaire is fit for purpose. There may be a cost related to paying staff to carry out the research, so if the results of the primary research do not help the business, it will be seen as a waste of both time and money. Selecting the

correct respondents helps to ensure that the results are accurate and relevant; this is why the purpose of the research must be clear.

For secondary research, spending time locating relevant information using, say, the internet (which is an excellent example of secondary research) can be expensive in terms of staff hours. Sometimes the information found may not be relevant or could have biased views and prove not to be reliable, accurate or relevant to the research. Information or research results found may be out of date and/or no longer true.

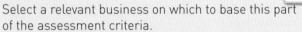

KNOW IT

1 What are the two main methods of research?
2 When is the next UK census survey due to take place?
3 What are the benefits to both consumer and business of participating in a loyalty card scheme?
4 Define the concept of a cluster sample.

LO3 assessment activities

Below are suggested assessment activities that have been directly linked to the Pass, Merit and Distinction criteria in LO3 to help with assignment preparation. These are followed by top tips on how to achieve the best results.

Activity 1 Pass criteria *P5*

P5 Identify a marketing aim you want to research and then select two or more market research methods to investigate relating to it. Explain why you have chosen these particular methods of market research.

Activity 2 Pass criteria *P6*

P6 Using the same reason for completing market research as in Activity 1, complete both primary and secondary research to identify business opportunities for a specific business. You could devise a suitable questionnaire to give to a particular sample as well as use secondary research for the same purpose. Ensure you have evidence of both types of market research.

TOP TIPS

Select a relevant business on which to base this part of the assessment criteria.
✔ You must select both primary and secondary research methods.
✔ Some form of questions, such as a survey, must be devised to justify the D1 criteria.

Activity 3 Merit criteria *M2*

M2 Once you have completed your primary and secondary research, use the results to fully assess (using means that you think are suitable) its effectiveness.

Activity 4 Distinction criteria *D1*

D1 Explain and clearly justify why the chosen types of questions were used and the order in which they were asked within your completed market research.

LO4 Be able to validate and present market research findings *P7* *P8 M3 D2*

GETTING STARTED

(10 minutes)

Look at the following scenarios and consider how you would present the results of market research that had taken place. Discuss your reasoning with a partner.

1 A local sandwich business with two equal partners asked its customers verbally if they would purchase baguettes if they were offered as an alternative to sliced-bread sandwiches. The results (yes or no) were tallied.
2 Year 12 students were asked to research what new facilities they would like to have in their social area. The results are to be fed back to the senior leadership team.
3 A small limited company that currently produces soup wanted to inform its shareholders of its plans for the next year after completing market research on diversifying its business by producing smoothies as well.

4.1 How to prepare market research findings

If the methods of research that were selected have succeeded in compiling raw **data**, the business then needs to analyse the results so that they can be used. The data is often referred to as 'raw data' until it has been processed into a form that the business will decide upon, e.g. graphs, tables, charts or diagrams. How the data is presented will depend on the type of data the business has collated.

KEY TERM

Data – information, normally in numerical form, that can be analysed to help plan a product or service going to market.

Types of visual display method

INDIVIDUAL ACTIVITY

(30 minutes)

Imagine that every year the school or college you attend completes market research that details how students and pupils travel to and from its site. The results are then sent to the county council, which requires the information for its own analysis.

Decide the following:

● the method of market research to be used
● how the information will be collated
● which specific method of displaying data will be selected.

Write down your reasoning for each point.

How to address incomplete responses

The business will need to try to consider why incomplete responses have been received and then decide how to move forward with the research. Analysing the percentage, for example, of incomplete responses will help determine if there are enough fully completed responses to draw conclusions.

Looking at the types of question that were not completed could give further insight. Was the question not clear, too long, too personal? Maybe the questionnaire took too long to complete? If incentives were offered, maybe they were not appropriate.

Table 5.4 Types of visual display method

Type of display	Advantages
Tables	A good way to display a large amount of data in a form that is easy for the user to view and reach conclusions about the results
Graphs	The user can easily view changes over a period of time, e.g. sales figures over a period of months for specific products
Charts	Bar charts and pie charts are often used display numeric details or compare products. Like graphs, they often enable the viewer to view specific information with ease. The chart must be constructed correctly with meaningful information that the user can understand and use
Histograms	These can sometimes be confused with bar charts. The main difference is that in a bar chart the height represents the value or number of products, whereas in a histogram it is the area of the bar that shows this information

The business in this situation may consider a different form of research in the future to avoid wasting time and money.

4.2 How to validate market research findings

Did the research measure what it set out to measure? When trying to validate the findings of any completed market research the business must refer back to when it started to plan its research.

● What did it want to achieve?
● What was it trying to discover?
● When planning, what methods was it going to use?
● Who or what was it going to ask?

A business may want to employ a market research specialist or business, whose role it is to analyse results and present its findings. It must assess both the **reliability** and **validity** of the findings before attempting the analysis.

KEY TERMS

Reliability – determining whether the information is consistent and therefore will aid the research.

Validity – whether the research that has been collated is accurate and genuine.

When validating the data and drawing conclusions from the information, the business may discover that further market research is required, perhaps with some minor alterations.

A review may also identify any limitations of the research. Devising the process of research is difficult, taking time and money, so a business should review the process to ensure that the results meet the requirements of the research. If they do not, then the business has the opportunity to:

● identify
● review
● redevelop
● implement the new and revised research.

Once the research is fully completed, it can then be analysed to draw conclusions in order to devise the marketing decisions the business has to make, which will be linked to the other business aims and objectives. This is a full-circle approach.

4.3 How to present the findings clearly in a format appropriate to the data obtained and audience

Once the results of the market research have been compiled using appropriate methods, they will need to be presented in a way that suits the organisation and those with whom the results will be shared. Again these could be split into two different parts: quantitative and qualitative analysis.

Quantitative analysis

Quantitative research involves questions with answers that can be collated into statistical information. For example, a questionnaire may have five short questions for respondents to answer with either yes or no, or a rating of 1–4. The business can use this information and present the findings as statistics (e.g. '40% of respondents said they would purchase this service'). The results can also be analysed using statistical analysis using the mean, mode, medium and range methods.

● *Mean:* the statistical term meaning 'average'. This is calculated by totalling all of the numbers together and then dividing by the number of results.
● *Mode:* the most frequently occurring number when viewing all of the results. It represents the largest or most frequent group of numbers within the data. These can be referred to as being the 'modal' group. Some users like to put the data into either ascending or descending order, to make the mode more obvious to the user.
● *Median:* the data is collated into numerical order and the middle value at the central point is identified. This is the median value.
● *Range:* the user will identify the lowest and the highest values in all of the data and subtract the lowest value from the highest value to determine the range of the data.

INDIVIDUAL ACTIVITY
(30 minutes)

A business with 100 employees decides to review how much they spend on lunch and speciality coffee in the office canteen, to help it plan its food budgets for the next financial year.

Table 5.5 Employee spend in canteen for statistical analysis

Amount spent per week	Number of employees
£5 or less	25
£10	35
£15	10
£20	15
£25	15

Using the data in Table 5.5, calculate the:

● mean　　　● mode　　　● median.

Think of a situation when it would be useful to calculate the range of the data.

How to present data

A business should consider things like:

● whether a formal report will be compiled using the analysis, which explains in detail all the different aspects that have been analysed along with the results
● whether this will be combined with a formal presentation
● whether the presentation will state the findings.

It will depend on the amount of results that have been analysed and the conclusions that have been drawn.

A business will need to consider its audience and plan appropriately. For example, having a presentation with endless slides of statistical information may not convey the key and relevant data to those who need to use the information.

Whether it is a report or a presentation, it should have a clear and concise structure that includes:

● an *introduction* to how and why the research was completed
● *research objectives* detailing what it was hoped would be achieved by completing the research
● *main findings* of the research, which could be illustrated using graphs, charts, etc.
● *conclusions*, which propose actions as a result of the findings
● *recommendations* for the future, including next steps.

KNOW IT

1 Write a definition of quantitative analysis.
2 What is the difference between a bar chart and a histogram?
3 A manager of a shoe shop wants to know the most popular size of children's shoe that it has sold over the past three months so that new stock can be ordered. What method of quantitative analysis should she use?
4 Why can market research sometimes limit the outcomes a business is trying to discover?
5 Explain what methods a business could use to present its market research results.

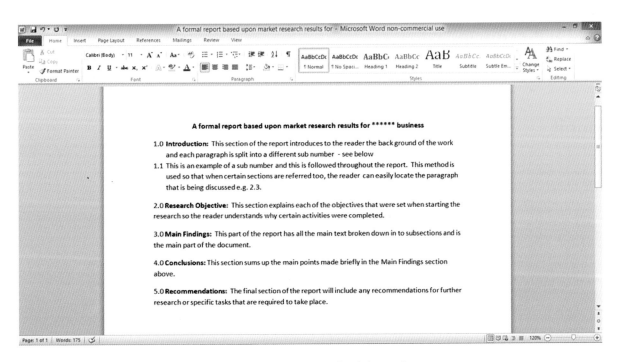

▲ **Figure 5.6** Formal reports have a set structure for presenting information

(10 minutes)

Research a UK-based market research business and its specialities. Feed back your results to the rest of the group.

LO4 assessment activities

Below are suggested assessment activities that have been directly linked to the Pass, Merit and Distinction criteria in LO4 to help with assignment preparation. These are followed by top tips on how to achieve the best results.

Activity 1 Pass criteria *P7*

P7 Using the research you completed for P6 and M2 above, assess its validity using different means, referring to the original plan you completed for the P5 criteria. Make the links between the different criteria clear, so that you can navigate around the information and see the link between the tasks from start to finish.

Activity 2 Pass criteria *P8*

P8 Present your research findings in an appropriate format for your given audience. Consider different methods, such as tables, charts, reports and presentations, and create your selected format.

Activity 3 Merit criteria *M3*

M3 Using the research you have analysed, identify whether any further research is required and, if so, write a report recommending what additional or improved research is required and for what purpose. Ensure the recommendations are clear and realistic.

Activity 4 Distinction criteria *D2*

D2 Using a suitable format, both recommend and justify the decisions that could be made as a result of completing thorough market research for a given purpose. This should be linked to the whole unit by explaining the process you went through to reach your final decisions.

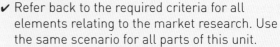

TOP TIPS
✔ Refer back to the required criteria for all elements relating to the market research. Use the same scenario for all parts of this unit.
✔ Guidance may be given on the types of market research to be completed, but all research must be meaningful and realistic.

Read about it

1 *The Times 100 Case Studies* have a variety of interesting case studies accompanied by questions to answer to further your understanding: https://www.tes.com/member/The%20Times%20100

2 *Essentials of Marketing Research* by Naresh K. Malhotra and David F. Birks, Pearson Education Limited, 2013

3 Practical information and tasks to help businesses who want to grow using marketing resources: http://tinyurl.com/jq2w9dg

Unit 06

Marketing strategy

ABOUT THIS UNIT

Marketing strategy is concerned with a business planning its marketing activities effectively to target the right customers. This unit will enable you to learn about how marketing objectives are set and the key elements, such as segmentation, the importance of brand management, the different marketing methods and marketing tools that a business will use to fulfil its marketing strategies.

The introduction of digital marketing and social media has forced businesses to engage in this now important aspect of marketing. On completing this unit you will apply the skills and knowledge learned to create a proposed marketing strategy.

LEARNING OUTCOMES

The topics, activities and suggested reading in this unit will help you to:

1 understand the purpose of marketing strategies
2 understand factors influencing marketing strategies
3 understand digital marketing
4 know what benefits branding can generate for businesses
5 be able to use business tools to propose marketing strategies.

How will I be assessed?

You will be assessed through a series of assignments and tasks set and marked by your tutor.

How will I be graded?

You will be graded using the following criteria, which are in the specification produced by OCR for the qualification.

Learning outcome	Pass	Merit	Distinction
You will:	**To achieve a Pass you must demonstrate that you have met all the pass assessment criteria**	**To achieve a Merit you must demonstrate that you have met all the pass and merit assessment criteria**	**To achieve a Distinction you must demonstrate that you have met all the pass, merit and distinction assessment criteria**
1 Understand the purpose of marketing strategies	**P1** Identify SMART marketing objectives for a specific business		
	P2 Identify a market segment for a specific business when planning a marketing strategy	**M1** Explain the importance to a specific business of market segmentation in planning a marketing strategy	
	P3 Describe marketing strategies a specific business may consider	**M2** Analyse the marketing approach taken and the marketing strategy created by a specific business to market a product	**D1** Compare two business with contrasting marketing strategies and evaluate the impact of the strategy on each business
	P4 Explain the approaches to marketing a specific business could take		
2 Understand factors influencing marketing strategies	**P5** Explain the factors influencing the marketing strategy of a specific business	**M3** Describe the impact of unforeseen changes and unexpected events on the marketing strategy of a specific business	**D2** Evaluate how a specific business has reacted to changes in the factors influencing its marketing strategy
3 Understand digital marketing	**P6** Explain why a specific business may consider developing a digital marketing strategy		
4 Know what benefits branding can generate for businesses	**P7** For a specific business, describe what they have done to create brand recognition and unique selling points, and to represent their beliefs and values		
5 Be able to use business tools to propose marketing strategies	**P8** Propose a marketing strategy for a specific business using business tools	**M4** Assess the business tools used in a marketing strategy proposal and explain how effective they were	

LO1 Understand the purpose of marketing strategies *P1 P2 P3 P4 M1 M2 D1*

GETTING STARTED

(30 minutes)

A mobile refreshment stall serving hot and cold drinks and light snacks wants to open near your school or college. In pairs discuss and devise what you think are going to be the new business's **SMART objectives**. Feed back your thoughts and findings to the rest of the class.

Consider why you think that it is important to have a clear **marketing strategy** for a new business.

KEY TERMS

SMART objectives – Specific, Measurable, Achievable, Realistic and Time-bound objectives that ensure the business focuses on the key areas within each objective stated.

Marketing strategies – methods that a business introduces to fulfil its marketing aims and objectives.

1.1 What marketing objectives might typically cover

Whether a business is well established or new to the market, planning is an important tool for moving forward successfully. Marketing objectives are a key element in successful planning, but they must be clear and, most importantly, achievable. If they cannot be achieved then this can affect overall motivation and morale in the business, which could restrict its success. Marketing objectives should take into account all the stakeholders who may want to know when specific activities are taking place, when decisions will be made or when they will be informed of such decisions.

Some examples of typical marketing objectives are described below.

To increase revenue

This would be linked to the overall aims and objectives of the business, and will often contain specific revenue targets in terms of generating sales, which can then be seen within the overall revenue.

To increase the customer base

This objective means that the business wants to increase its customer base, by reaching new customers using specific targeted marketing methods.

To increase repeat custom

Businesses will always strive to gain new customers, but retaining existing customers is equally important. Different loyalty methods can be utilised – for example, loyalty cards and discount vouchers encourage repeat business.

To introduce new products or services into the market

This could result in more revenue generated by extra sales.

To increase market share

A business will always want to gain more market share, and will compete aggressively with its competitors to achieve this overall objective

To increase brand awareness

Having a successful brand portfolio (well-known and easily recognisable products and services) enables a business to use different marketing methods for specific products aimed at the target market, to increase its market share and dominate the market. Businesses with limited brand portfolios (less recognisable products and services) cannot compete well in this situation so need to ensure that consumers are made aware of their brand.

To launch new advertising campaigns

Creating new and innovative advertising campaigns will entice or remind consumers of the products or services that a business has in its portfolio, which it is hoped will result in increased sales, customers and revenues.

To stay innovative

Businesses are always striving to invent or create new ways in which to compete in a particular market. This does not just mean launching new products, but also improving and changing existing products to meet market needs or to make use of new internal skills and technologies.

SMART objectives

Businesses should ensure that each marketing objective is SMART, to focus the team on their various elements. If objectives are clear and concise, once achieved the team will be able to see the positive impact on the business; achievements can have a real impact on the morale of the organisation, which in turn can be seen in increased production.

PAIRS ACTIVITY 👥 ·······································

(30 minutes)

The internet was invented in 1991 but didn't really become accessible to most people until 2001.

> In 2002, there were fewer than 200,000 broadband users. Four years later, there were 13 million. Now there are closer to 20 million, accounting for two-thirds of all households.

Source: http://tinyurl.com/y8puhaw

According to Ofcom:

> in 2015 80% of adults had access to broadband, browsing online for an average of 31 hours a month – this does not include work-related tasks.

Source: http://media.ofcom.org.uk/facts/

Considering the above information, discuss in pairs how businesses have had to adjust to the impact of the internet in terms of their marketing objectives. Research and consider three further examples. Discuss your findings with the rest of the group.

1.2 The role of market segmentation in planning marketing strategies is to understand the target market

By dividing potential customers into groups depending on their needs and wants

Market segmentation, as discussed in Unit 5 (page 133), divides existing and potential customers into different groups to help aid market strategies. Typically, a business may segment the market according to the following factors.

- Age: groupings will depend on the product or service – for example, cruises tend to be marketed towards retired people aged 65-plus.
- Gender: businesses produce products and services that are aimed at 'him' or 'her', but increasingly they develop products as a result of success for the other gender, to maximise sales, revenues and markets – for example, the Lynx brand is usually associated with men, but now it has created products for women, such as Lynx Attract for Her, which has a 'fruity and floral fragrance'.

- Income: in the past it could be said that only low-income groups would seek out bargains and shop in cheaper stores. However, now value for money is a concern for most people and people of all income levels shop in discount supermarkets such as Aldi and Lidl. However, certain products or services will appeal only to particular income groups, such as those with more disposable income – for example, golfing holidays will appeal to people who play golf regularly, and tend to have both the spare time and disposable income to afford the costs involved.
- Geographical area: grouping according to where the consumer lives or uses the product or service could determine if a business locates to a new outlet or moves to a particular area. It could also influence the types of products and services that are produced, and where they are marketed – for example, a ski equipment hire shop is best located at or near a ski resort.
- Buyer behaviour: businesses have adapted to consumers' demands for online selling and shopping. Our buying habits have altered considerably over the past ten years, which businesses have embraced to keep up with consumer demands. It is very rare these days for a business to not have some sort of website.

By increasing market efficiency by focusing efforts on targeting consumers with similar characteristics and needs

As well as a business considering the market segmentations, it also has to focus on how to become more market efficient, by bringing together the needs and wants of customers with similar characteristics. This means understanding where, when, how and to whom to market the product or service. By focusing on a particular target market, the business can ensure that budgets are not overspent, and that the team is focused on the main areas that have been identified by their effective market strategy.

By giving businesses commercial advantage if they attract the right customer

A **commercial advantage** is when a business increases sales over its competitors because it can create greater value through differentiation or by offering similar value at a lower price. Segmentation gives a business an understanding of what particular customers are looking for, so the marketing can emphasise what those customers see as good value.

KEY TERM

Commercial advantage – to gain an advantage over other businesses through particular marketing methods.

1.3 Different marketing strategies

Market strategies can be linked directly to the marketing tools used, to help identify the marketing methods that could be used to attract new or secure loyal customers. Different strategies can be split into the categories described below.

Market penetration

Market penetration is generally the starting point for most businesses as they can determine if it is worth continuing in the same market, producing the same products or services and targeting existing customers. It is considered to be very low risk and often does not need massive amounts of investment because it is proved to work. However, if a business becomes too comfortable in this position, other businesses can overtake them with more innovation (which is common among electronics companies), so businesses should plan strategically for all products and services in their brand portfolio.

KEY TERM

Market penetration – when a business increases the market share of a product by using different marketing strategies.

Market development

This gives a business the ability to seek new opportunities and target markets for existing products. It is a risky strategy, as new elements require investment and market research. Examples could be a local business moving to a new business premises, exploiting new regional opportunities or moving to different trading methods, such as launching an online shop.

Product development

This can be seen as quite high risk as a business will be selling new products to new but existing markets. It can be hard to persuade current customers to try something new when they are happy with the existing product, so the business will need to show confidence in its products and services. A good example is the development of Apple products over the years, including iPads and iPhones. The concept changes each time the latest products are produced. Customers will generally continue to upgrade their technology if they trust the brand.

Diversification

This is generally the highest risk out of the four main marketing strategies because the business is producing a new product or service in a new market, so this is unknown territory. A successful business may want to diversify because it recognises that this is the only way it can move forward, so it will be worth the risk – all or nothing in some ways! The business should ensure that substantial research has been completed, that there is a clear commitment by all staff and realistic budgeting. A small-scale example is a dairy farm that aims to increase its income by opening a farm animal petting zoo and playground. On page 162 you can see how this strategy is turned into a tool called an Ansoff Matrix.

Cost leadership

This method involves the business ensuring that its main strategy is to be the lowest-cost producer in its field. This requires costs to be managed effectively throughout the whole business. It is a challenging concept, but could benefit the business in the long term by keeping costs down, so that profits can be invested elsewhere in the business.

Differentiation

This is when a business decides to create its own version of a competitor's product or service. Generally, it is the product that is changed, but the business could also differentiate according to its unique selling point (USP), image, branding, technology, pricing or features. For example, a discount supermarket may sell products that look very similar to the leading brands but are much cheaper.

1.4 Approaches to marketing

When a business considers its marketing strategy, it will need to consider its approach in terms of its target market. Some businesses may want to focus on one specific product for a small target market, while other businesses may want to focus on high sales and low prices for a range of products and services. It really does depend on the business's overall approach. Five main approaches are detailed below.

Niche marketing approach

Niche means 'gap'. **Niche marketing** is when a product or service is aimed at a particular segment of the market. It can be very efficient, especially for a small business with budget restrictions, but bigger businesses have gained a large market share within a niche area. An example of niche marketing would be speciality cars – for example, Bentley or Morgan – which are designed for each customer, to satisfy their desire for a prestigious, unique car.

Mass marketing approach

Businesses use **mass marketing** for products that will appeal to all sectors of the market, focusing on high sales and low prices. As the products are produced in high volume, they can be sold at a cheaper price, which will appeal to customers. This can be an expensive strategy from a production viewpoint, but can prove to be very successful if it results in high profits. An example is Cadbury's Dairy Milk chocolate.

Product-led/product orientation approach

A **product-led/product orientation** is when a business focuses on the product it is creating before deciding on the audience. It hopes that the item will appeal because of a focus on the design and quality of the product, so the aim is to create a demand for the new product through marketing its features and benefits. This could be considered quite high risk, as not knowing your target market could result in limited sales and profits if customers do not want to buy your goods. It would then be a waste of time and investment. Electronic products like the original Walkman portable music player come under this category – nothing like it existed so there was no market for it.

Market-led/market orientation approach

A **market-led/market orientation** is more customer focused. Businesses will look in detail at research, and analyse statistics to produce a product or service that customers will purchase to fulfil their needs and wants. This could be considered to be quite low risk but, in the world of business, success is not always guaranteed as customers' needs and wants constantly change and trends come and go. For example, a pizza restaurant might identify a wish for takeaway pizzas among its customers.

Asset-led approach

An **asset-led strategy** is when a business assesses the strengths and needs of its product or service, formulating a strategy that highlights the attributes of a given product, to create a successful marketing approach. An example is Disney cruises, which are family focused and all about having fun with Disney characters on a cruise ship.

🔑 KEY TERMS

Niche marketing – targeting a product or service at a small segment of a larger market.

Mass marketing – aiming a product at all, or most, market segments.

Product-led/product orientation – when a business focuses on a product before it decides on its target market.

Market-led/market orientation – focusing on meeting the needs and wants of potential customers.

Asset-led strategy – assessing the strengths and needs of a specific market, producing the product and highlighting the product's attributes as part of a marketing campaign.

🔍 INDEPENDENT RESEARCH ACTIVITY

(30 minutes)

Consider the approaches to marketing described in Section 1.4 and, using Table 6.1, identify different products or services that come under the relevant heading. Explain why you think that the business has adopted that particular approach to marketing. Discuss your findings with the rest of the class.

For example, skiing holidays from Thompson would come under the niche marketing heading as they target people who enjoy skiing on a regular basis or who want to combine sport with a holiday. If you do not like snow, cold weather or sport, then this type of holiday would not appeal to you.

Table 6.1

Type of marketing approach	Example product/ service	Business name	Reasoning
Niche marketing			
Mass marketing			
Product-led marketing			
Market-led marketing			
Asset-led marketing			

KNOW IT

1 What does SMART stand for?
2 What is market segmentation?
3 Identify two marketing strategies that a business may introduce.
4 What are the main differences between mass and niche marketing?

LO1 assessment activities

Below are suggested assessment activities that have been directly linked to the Pass, Merit and Distinction criteria in LO1 to help with assignment preparation. These are followed by top tips on how to achieve the best results.

Activity 1 Pass criteria *P1*

P1 Write three suggested marketing objectives for a business you have identified, ensuring that each objective is SMART.

Activity 2 Pass criteria *P2*

P2 Research market segmentation and identify a potential segment for a specific business, to assist with its marketing strategy.

Activity 3 Merit criteria *M1*

M1 Explain in detail the link between market segmentation and planning a marketing strategy, referring to a specific business.

Activity 4 Pass criteria *P3*

P3 Describe the different marketing strategies that a business may consider and consequently introduce, focusing on one specific business.

Activity 5 Pass criteria *P4*

P4 Explain the approaches to marketing that a particular business could take. It must be clear which business you are referring to and why it should consider these approaches.

Activity 6 Merit criteria *M2*

M2 Investigate and analyse the different marketing approaches that a selected business may take to market a particular product. Then analyse the marketing strategy of the same business, ensuring you include a product.

Activity 7 Distinction criteria *D1*

D1 Select two contrasting businesses to give you the opportunity to complete detailed comparisons and evaluations, focusing on the impact of the implemented marketing strategies from the two businesses.

TOP TIPS

✔ Consider the nature of your chosen businesses as well as the products that they produce.
✔ You can either concentrate on a single business for Activities 1 to 6 or choose several different types of business for each activity.
✔ Ensure that you can find the relevant information to fulfil every aspect of the criteria in this section of the specification.
✔ When analysing for **M2**, ensure you separate information into components and identify their characteristics. Discuss the pros and cons of a topic or argument, and make reasoned comment.

LO2 Understand factors influencing marketing strategies *P5*

M3 D2

GETTING STARTED

(10 minutes)

Write a list of eight different factors that a business will need to consider before planning its marketing activities – for example, how many employees will work on the marketing activities.

2.1 Factors influencing marketing strategies

There are many different aspects that a business will need to consider before formulating a strategy to market its products or services. These are known as factors and generally include the following categories: resources, markets, trends, stakeholders, changes, contingency planning, stages of the product life cycle and the flexibility of the marketing mix.

Resources

There are many different aspects to resources. A resource is a business term that can be split into three main sections, as follows.

1 Human resources is concerned with the workforce, which will include skilled employees who are employed by the business.

2 Financial resources focus on the monetary aspects of the business. This includes the everyday activities such as paying wages, purchasing materials to make the products, paying bills for loans, hire purchase, etc. This can be a challenge as good financial organisation is required. Financial resources also include the future planning requirements of the business. For example, how will business expansion be financed, especially if the business does not currently have the funds? Can the business afford it? Is it a realistic goal? How risky will it be? Contingency planning will also need to be considered so that the business is prepared for unlikely events or changes.

3 Physical resources include the physical items needed for the business to run successfully. In simple terms these are its premises, facilities,

storage, equipment and stock. This will vary according to the physical requirements of the business – for example, a manufacturer may require factory facilities but a graphic design company may operate from a small office. Other physical resources are office technology, and specialist tools, machinery or equipment.

Transportation is another element of physical resources. Some businesses require transportation with special requirements, such as refrigeration to keep produce at a particular temperature. There is a real scientific approach to the storage of fruit and vegetables, to ensure that products do not spoil and reach the customer in perfect condition.

Businesses at different stages of their life cycle

Whether a business is at the start-up or maturity stage of the life cycle could determine the investments that are made. If the business is going into the decline stage, with sales falling, would potential investors or banking institutions want to invest or loan money to it?

INDIVIDUAL ACTIVITY

(45 minutes)

Watch some clips from the BBC series *Supermarket Secrets*: www.bbc.co.uk/programmes/p01wlcg6

How does the content link to your previous learning? What aspects were new? What did you find most interesting? Make notes on your findings and summarise these to the rest of the class.

Different markets

A business's current market could be identified as the 'domestic market' within the UK. A new marketing strategy may target an overseas market. **Overseas marketing** will involve considerable planning and extensive market research. If these are not addressed then it could cost the business substantially, in terms of lost revenues and investments, which could ultimately result in the business ceasing to trade at all.

> **KEY TERM**
>
> **Overseas marketing** – investing in either producing or selling products abroad.

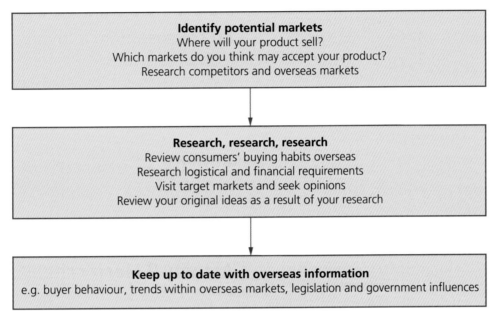

▲ **Figure 6.1** Planning to expand to an overseas market

Other markets could be business to business (B2B) and business to consumer (B2C). A definition of B2B and B2C is:

Business to business refers to business that is conducted between companies, rather than between a company and individual consumers. This is in contrast to business to consumer (B2C).

Source: www.investopedia.com/terms/b/btob.asp

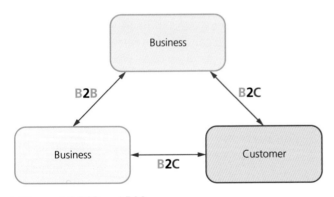

▲ **Figure 6.2** B2B and B2C

For example, a business that requires specific components to manufacture its individual products will work with another business to fulfil this process (B2B). In comparison, B2C involves businesses selling products and services directly to consumers.

Social trends

Social trends focus on what consumers are demanding at that moment – for example, food that is more natural and has been locally sourced. Customers want to know more about their food and are prepared to pay a little

extra if that information is available. Supermarkets can find it hard to compete with local farmers, who can provide such information and guarantees, which is what many customers want.

Stakeholders

Stakeholders can influence marketing. For example, if a competitor brings out a successful new product, a business may change its marketing to show why its original product is better. Customer behaviour can change too. Sometimes a product is no longer in demand – for example, for a few months in 2014 it seemed that all children in the UK and Europe were making key rings and jewellery from coloured rubber loom bands (Figure 6.3). What has happened to loom bands now?

▲ **Figure 6.3** Whatever happened to the loom band craze?

155

Flexibility of the marketing mix

The marketing mix is a key marketing tool used for a business to consider the product, price, place and promotion of its goods. It should reflect agreed marketing strategy but a business should be able to alter its elements according to customer needs and wants, new or existing competition, and also the changes in the market conditions, to continue to perform in a competitive market.

Ability to react to unforeseen changes

Unforeseen changes can affect businesses and need to be planned strategically. For example, celebrity chef Jamie Oliver has been instrumental in changing the quality of school dinners and promoting the importance of home economics. By highlighting the dangers of high levels of sugar in our diets, which is known to cause obesity and ill health, he has encouraged consumers to demand food with less sugar. Food manufacturers have had to react to this. Another example could be a sudden rise in sales for a product mentioned on TV but that later drops again.

Contingency planning

A business cannot control everything to do with its operations. Unlikely events can happen such as winter flooding, which devastates many homes and businesses. If floods were to occur again, those who were affected before will have contingency plans in place to minimise the damage.

PAIRS ACTIVITY

(30 minutes)

Identify one product that a particular business has produced over many years. This could be a popular food (e.g. a cereal or chocolate bar) or a gadget. Consider how this product has evolved and the changes that have been made to keep it competitive in the market. What are the main differences between the newer version of the product and the older product? Why do you think these changes have been made?

KNOW IT

1 Name the three main business resources.
2 What are the differences between B2B and B2C approaches?
3 What is contingency planning?

LO2 assessment activities

Below are suggested assessment activities that have been directly linked to the Pass, Merit and Distinction criteria in LO2 to help with assignment preparation. These are followed by top tips on how to achieve the best results.

Activity 1 Pass criteria *P5*

P5 Explain all the different factors that could influence an overall marketing strategy, relating every point made to a specific business. Draw a spidergram or mind-map to show these.

Activity 2 Merit criteria *M3*

M3 Describe the impact of changes and events that may directly impact upon the marketing strategy of a named business. Select a business where you can acquire such information, and perhaps use examples of changes that have happened in the past.

Activity 3 Distinction criteria *D2*

D2 Fully evaluate how a business that you have described in Activities 1 or 2 has reacted to any changes that have influenced its marketing strategy.

TOP TIPS

✔ Select businesses with products that will complement the assessment criteria.
✔ Ensure that you can gain the relevant information to fulfil all command verbs as well as the content of the specification.
✔ Remember that an analysis requires you to separate information into components and identify their characteristics, then discuss the pros and cons and make reasoned comment.

LO3 Understand digital marketing
P6

GETTING STARTED

(10 minutes)

Write a list of the digital marketing methods you have been exposed to over the past week. Compare your list to those of others in your class.

3.1 Why businesses have digital marketing strategies

The changing nature of marketing

Digital marketing is a significant development that business has had to adapt to over the past ten years. The increased reliance on technology in our everyday lives has influenced the marketing choices that are key to marketing strategy. Now messages can be received far more quickly with global 24-hour access to technology and the impact of social media. Customers can interact with business by 'liking' or recommending products and services at the touch of a button, creating a two-way interaction that was difficult when marketing took only print or broadcast form.

> ### 🔍 KEY TERM
>
> **Digital marketing** – the marketing of products or services using digital channels or media to reach consumers, e.g. email, social media.

A business's online presence can be controlled only to a certain extent. For example, it may have a website and a social media presence, but now consumers can give their opinions without any influence from the business. For example, a hotel cannot control whether it gets good reviews on the website TripAdvisor, or how many shares its Facebook posts get. A marketing video on YouTube may go viral (be watched by thousands of people) or sink without a trace. So, while digital forms of marketing may appear to be cheaper than placing a TV ad, say, it is more difficult to control and measure a digital campaign's success. Choice of platform (where the marketing appears) is therefore important.

Changes in consumer behaviour

Businesses need to focus on the constant changes in consumer behaviour, in terms of their needs and wants. We are fickle these days, changing our minds, not remaining loyal to a particular brand or business, and wanting and demanding more for our money.

The term 'digital natives' refers to those born after 1980, who may not remember a time before widespread computer and internet use. Their behaviour is likely to be different to that of older people because they have always used their digital skills and they expect to use the internet extensively for their consumer choices. For example, they may ask a question about a product or service via a business's Twitter feed rather than phoning the business. Marketing strategies need to bear this in mind, especially if the marketing team does not contain any digital natives.

To reduce costs

Businesses have embraced the explosion of digital marketing as an effective marketing method reaching as many customers as possible in the shortest amount of time. Social media posts have little financial cost, other than staff time, and sales emails can be sent via free marketing platforms. By contrast, taking out a full-page ad in a daily newspaper will cost thousands of pounds and may not be seen by as many people.

To improve reputation

Advances in mobile phone technology have enabled business to access new platforms to market their products and services, to remain ahead of competitors. This can improve a business's good reputation. However, these positive aspects can quickly turn into negative exposure. For example, if a customer has a bad experience with a business, thousands of people could hear about it within a few hours. Large businesses employ staff to monitor such feedback on websites, to try to react in an appropriate way. Sometimes the way they react to a complaint publicly expressed on, for example, social media, can turn a potentially damaging situation into a positive one.

To improve and maintain electronic customer relationship management (e-CRM)

Electronic customer relationship management (e-CRM) brings together all aspects of customer data. Businesses can also use customer information as a method of gathering data to enable them to improve their relationships – for example, by analysing customer buying habits or seeking information with regard to geographical data. Businesses should always strive to maintain and improve their e-CRM approaches to ensure that they listen to the most important aspect of business – the customers.

Increased participation in social communities and generating interest groups ('digital tribes')

Businesses have identified the importance of increased participation in social communities and generating interest groups, as an element of their marketing activities. People with similar interests gather online in specific digital communities; these are known as 'digital tribes'. Digital tribes have shared interests with regard to a particular topic, service or subject, and the community is joined for that reason. Proctor & Gamble's Savvy Circle, for example, is an online platform with a membership mainly of mothers, who are invited to discuss and complete surveys on topics relevant to their lives, such as supermarket shopping habits and use of laundry detergent. The responses are used to inform P&G's marketing activities for its many brands.

LO3 assessment activity

Below is a suggested assessment activity that has been directly linked to the Pass criteria in LO3 to help with assignment preparation. This is followed by a top tip on how to achieve the best results.

Activity 1 Pass criteria *P6*

P6 Investigate the digital marketing methods that businesses use and use this research to help you produce a detailed explanation of why a business may want to develop a digital marketing strategy.

LO4 Know what benefits branding can generate for businesses *P7*

Branding has become increasingly important. Having a strong brand can enable a business to dominate a market, enabling future products to appeal to an already loyal audience. This is very valuable as customer trust is worth so much. If a business operates in a variety of different markets, the same brand principles should be placed on every product, which will in turn reinforce the brand values associated with the business. It makes it easier to apply the brand to a variety of different markets and diversifying products.

Brands can also be a trademark, as can a logo. A trademark is normally an image that enables a business to distinguish itself. There is legislation that ensures the protection of a business's trademark so that no one else can use the distinguishing mark on their products.

For example, how many different brands of butter are there (Figure 6.4)?

▲ **Figure 6.4** Even a simple product like butter has many brands to choose from

Essentially, the product is the same apart from unsalted and salted varieties, but which type you buy will come down to personal preference. Anchor is one brand that produces butter in various forms – block butter, spreadable butter and low-fat butter – but it also produces pastry, cheese and cream. This example shows that the business has evolved over the years and entered new markets using the strength of its brand image. Businesses like Anchor and Coca-Cola constantly maintain and protect the image of their products as they recognise their value. Substantial funds are allocated to marketing, to remind consumers that the brands still need custom to maintain their dominance in their industries.

4.1 The benefits branding can generate

Brand recognition

A successful brand, as we have stated, can be a valuable asset to a business. It could enable a business to change what is essentially a lower-priced product into something that customers will be prepared to pay more for, purely because of the brand image it portrays. If the image and message are consistent, then the product with a strong brand image will be a guaranteed success. The trendy American clothing brand Hollister can charge twice as much as customers might normally pay for a T-shirt because the relaxed, carefree life portrayed by the brand is appealing to teenagers in particular.

(10 minutes)

Have you ever purchased a branded product that has broken quickly? Why did you purchase that brand? Did you consider that it could have been lower quality or did you trust the brand? What happened to the product in the end? Discuss your thoughts with your partner.

A smaller business may have a very good alternative product compared to the leading brand, but if consumers are not aware of the product or brand they may not even consider it. This demonstrates the power of brand image. For example, consider the tablet market and how this has grown over the years. The introduction of the iPad forced many businesses to try to replicate it. Now there are many different inexpensive and moderately expensive tablets trying to compete for our custom, but some people will just want to purchase the iPad.

Brands can of course be relaunched or reinvented. Sometimes the power of consumers can bring about the reintroduction of a product.

> **? THINK ABOUT IT**
>
> **Case study: Cadbury's Wispa**
>
> Cadbury's Wispa was first launched in 1981 and was popular because of its 'velvety textured' milk chocolate. It was slightly different from other chocolate bars produced at the time by Cadbury. A popular advertising campaign was launched, which featured a variety of famous celebrities, and was an instant success. The Wispa was withdrawn from the market in 2003. According to Cadbury's website, 'Wispa was discontinued in 2003 but relaunched, first temporarily in 2007 and then permanently in 2008, following pressure through social media channels to bring it back!'
>
> *Source: www.cadbury.co.uk/the-story#wispa-is-launched*

Unique selling point

The unique selling point (USP) enables a business to promote the different aspects of a product or service that stand out from other competitors, making it more distinctive. The USP of a product or service could be:

● based on differences that have been measured such as performance, strength or speed (e.g. the fastest broadband speed, the fastest-working painkiller)

- known for having a special or secret ingredient – for example, that enhances the flavour of the product (e.g. Coca-Cola's secret recipe)
- implied, which could be based upon the potential or promises from the business (e.g. mascara that seems to make your lashes longer)
- deemed to add value for customers – for example, offering an extra service for no extra cost (e.g. free postage or technical support).

Any unique selling point must be clear, truthful and distinctive, otherwise it does not fulfil the USP concept.

Alignment with customers' beliefs and values

Customer beliefs and values must be taken into consideration. If a business claims it has a USP and

it does not, then custom can be lost very quickly. Consider the advertising campaigns for Hovis bread. They are always very simple but often focus on the past, wanting us as consumers to remember when we were younger, and reminding us of the 'good old days'.

LO4 assessment activity

Below is a suggested assessment activity that has been directly linked to the Pass criteria in LO4 to help with assignment preparation. This is followed by top tips on how to achieve the best results.

Activity 1 Pass criteria *P7*

P7 For a particular business, describe what it has done to create brand recognition and unique selling points, and to represent its beliefs and values

1 Select a suitable business and research its products or service.

2 Describe how the business promotes and maintains its company or product brand.

3 Identify any USPs that complement consumers' values and beliefs.

LO5 Be able to use business tools to propose marketing strategies
P8 M4

5.1 Business tools used in developing marketing strategies

In Section 1.3, we discussed how marketing strategies are directly linked to marketing tools, enabling the business to attract new or secure loyal customers, as well as identifying if new markets could be explored to expand the business's current position.

Product portfolio analysis (the Boston Matrix)

Many businesses have a product range to maximise their sales margins and gain the most profit from their portfolio of products. A business must internally review these products to determine if they are still current and therefore worth producing. The business must not become complacent in its approach to business, and should remain informed of all areas of its products' performance.

The Boston Matrix is a tool that enables a business to:

- identify the position of each product within its portfolio
- make comparisons or judgements with regard to its current position in the market
- focus on the market share and growth of the business
- review how much the product costs and contributes to the overall business.

All these aspects focus a business, to help its future planning with regard to its marketing activities.

Figure 6.5 shows the Boston Matrix business tool.

▲ **Figure 6.5** The Boston Matrix

The business's products are placed on the matrix in relation to their market share and their rate of growth. This helps to identify which products are more valuable to the business than others. The business will have to decide what to do with the products that are not growing or having an impact on their market share.

- Star: this product has a high market share and is expanding within the market.
- Question mark: this product has a low market share in a growing market; it could be a product that is declining in this market or in competition with a new product in an expanding market.
- Cash cow: this product tends to sell well and have a good market share; however, it also has a low growth rate, so could be at the maturity stage within the product life cycle. It provides profit, which can then be reinvested into other areas of

the business, such as the development of new products and services.

- Dog: this product is not growing and doesn't have a substantial impact on the market share in the current market. If products are dogs, the business will need to decide the future of such products.

PAIRS ACTIVITY

(30 minutes)

Select one business that has a well-known portfolio of products. Using the Boston Matrix tool, place the products in areas of the matrix and then write notes to explain your justifications. Be prepared to share your findings with the rest of the group.

Ansoff's Matrix

Ansoff's Matrix (Figure 6.6) is a marketing tool that is used to determine a business's longer-term growth strategy by deciding whether to sell current or new products in existing or new markets. Depending on a business's core competencies and degree of familiarity with a product, a product can be classified under market penetration, market development, product development or product/market diversification.

▲ **Figure 6.6** Ansoff's Matrix

- Market penetration: existing products are sold into existing markets. Low risk, as the company already has the data it needs, but can be difficult to achieve if there is a lot of competition.
- Market development: existing products are sold into new markets. Moderate risk as the market is new to a business but the product is the same.
- Product development: new products are sold into existing markets. Relatively risky as a substantial

budget is needed to research, develop, produce and promote the new product, and the new product may not sell as well as existing products.

- Product/market diversification: new products are sold into new markets. The riskiest strategy as both market and product are new to a business so budgets need to be set aside for new market and product development.

The Ansoff Matrix allows comparison of different strategies in terms of level of risk. Marketing strategies can be planned depending on whether a strategy is market penetration, market development, product development or product/market diversification. However, it can be difficult to classify strategies using the matrix, e.g. Tesco developed its Hudl tablet, which would be classified as diversification. It is definitely a new product but is it targeted at a new market?

? THINK ABOUT IT

Case study: O&J Brothers

A small garage, O&J Brothers, is reviewing its current provision to a local town. It was started 35 years ago by two brothers who liked fixing cars, and moved to new premises ten years ago when the founders retired. Since then the business has expanded, taking on more employees and becoming busy and successful. The garage is well known for being reliable and reasonably priced with good customer service. It is now considering its options for the future.

Considering the Ansoff Matrix, suggest ideas that O&J Brothers could introduce for:

- new products or services
- product development
- diversification.

Explain each of your ideas. Now consider any problems with these particular strategies.

Competitive advantage (Porter's Generic Strategies)

We have already discussed the importance of businesses not becoming complacent about the products and services they produce. Remaining competitive means being fully informed and aware, making changes if required and reacting to different circumstances. It is better to be proactive than reactive. Proactive businesses are generally forward-thinking businesses that want to command a competitive edge. Michael Porter's book *Competitive Advantage: Creating and Sustaining Superior Performance* (1985), detailed his theory, which is now known as Porter's Generic Strategies. Businesses continue to use this model (Figure 6.7) in today's increasingly competitive business world.

Source of competitive advantage

▲ **Figure 6.7** Porter's Generic Strategies

- Cost leadership: a business increases it profits by reducing costs and increasing its market share. This should enable the business to charge a lower price, while still being able to retain a profit, e.g. 'value' stores like Poundland and Primark.
- Differentiation: customers purchase a particular business's goods and services rather than a competitor's because they perceive it as being better and unique in the market, e.g. many customers are willing to pay a premium for Apple phones over Android or Windows phones.
- Cost focus: a business focuses on a niche market, with an emphasis on cost. This enables a competitive advantage by being the lowest-cost operator in that segment of the market, e.g. cheaper car brands like Skoda or Hyundai.
- Differentiation focus: a business gains a competitive advantage by focusing on a niche market, with an emphasis on differentiation, e.g. high-end car brands like Ferrari or Rolls-Royce.

🔍 INDEPENDENT RESEARCH ACTIVITY

(15 minutes)

Using Porter's Generic Strategies, explain, using relevant examples, how cost leadership is a method adopted by the low-cost airline industry.

EXTENSION ACTIVITY ➡

(1 hour)

Investigate Porter's Five Forces model and consider how this could impact on the strategic marketing planning of a business.

SWOT analysis

The strengths, weaknesses, opportunities and threats to a business can focus the business on areas that may need improving and celebrating. SWOT analysis is discussed in Unit 1 (page 43).

STEEPLE analysis

STEEPLE is an acronym for:

- Social
- Technological
- Economic
- Environmental
- Political
- Legal
- Ethical.

These factors are external to a business and therefore often the business does not have control over them, yet must still react and implement the different elements into it marketing strategies.

- Social: the social implications of a given situation. The business will analyse how implementing something may impact upon people and communities. Opinions, attitudes and behaviour are considered, e.g. the growing trend towards locally sourced meat and organic vegetables.
- Technological: this can be new, existing or redeveloped technologies. Businesses must stay up to date with relevant technologies – for example, the internet has altered business models to accommodate consumer needs and demands. Businesses should be technologically aware, and understand the positive and negative impacts of new technologies.
- Economic: local, national and international economic issues can include rising inflation, trade agreements/restrictions, employment levels, importing, exporting, investments, economic growth, etc. The effect of any changes could force the business to protect itself.
- Environmental: not following regulations and legislation can lead to revoking licences, court proceedings, fines or custodial sentences. Businesses generally have their own environmental policies that detail their business's actions and philosophy to protect the environment.

- Political: local, regional and national government will create and enforce new initiatives and laws. When the UK government introduced Sunday trading hours, this had a huge impact on the shopping habits of consumers, with businesses having to consider staff contracts in terms of work hours, pay, etc. The European Union (EU) has an influence on business. For example, a law was introduced in September 2014 that banned vacuum cleaners above 1600 watts. This may be extended to hair dryers and lawn mowers, with the aim of reducing energy use to meet set targets.
- Legal: any new legislation can directly affect business. For example, the introduction of the National Living Wage in 2016 was great for employees who were not paid substantially for their work, as businesses had to pay a minimum hourly rate. There are many different business laws that any business must implement, which will include employment legislation and consumer legislation.
- Ethical: a business will consider social values to create its own ethical stance based on its values of what is right and wrong. Ethical factors vary from nation to nation, and even within a nation, and opinions cannot be changed instantly. Sometimes it can take generations for attitudes to change.

STEEPLE analysis allows a business to focus its energy on the external influences that can make it more successful. Participants must be honest, thorough, objective, decisive, think laterally and anticipate any changes. This will ensure that the business is prepared and fully informed.

The marketing mix

The marketing mix is a method used to engage and implement various marketing activities into business. It combines the aspects of product, price, place and promotion (the 4Ps) in the marketing strategy to influence overall marketing plans, which will include a business's marketing aims and objectives.

Product

This involves the item that is to be marketed by the business. Product can be an actual physical product or a service that is provided by a business. This is often referred to as the most important element of the 4Ps, as without a product the other elements are not relevant.

Great emphasis will be placed on developing a product, having clear product specifications, product strategy and product management, in order for the process to work successfully. Larger businesses often have several different brands that make up their product portfolio, emphasising their USPs when appropriate.

Price

Price is directly linked to the product as the price can determine if a sale is successful. When businesses decide upon a price, they do not just pluck a figure out of nowhere but carefully consider a number of variables.

Cost price is the amount that it costs to produce the product. This will include the costs of overheads, materials, packaging, labour, production, storage, distribution, etc.

The selling price is what consumers will be prepared to pay for the product, taking into account the business's profit margin. Businesses consider competitors' prices for similar items when pricing their own products, to remain competitive. Businesses use different pricing strategies, perhaps adjusting prices at certain times of the year to adapt to supply and demand, and ensure sales are maximised (for example, putting up prices of popular gifts before Christmas and reducing them afterwards when demand has dropped). Examples of pricing strategies are outlined in Unit 7, in Table 7.1 (page 172).

Place

Consumers should be able to buy products and services in places that suit them – at a local shop, the high street, an out-of-town retail park or on the internet. If the customer cannot get hold of the product they want, a sale will be lost as they will go elsewhere or not buy it at all, leading to a loss of revenue.

Place can be split into direct sales and indirect sales. Further information on these categories can be found in Unit 7 (page 172).

Direct sales are when the business sells products directly to the customer. This can be a cost-saving measure. Methods of direct selling include direct mail by catalogue selling, door-to-door sales such as Avon, party selling (also known as pyramid selling), such as Jamberry or Usborne Books, where if you persuade a friend to sell the product too you gain a percentage of their sales, and cold calling (telesales).

Indirect sales methods mean that a business which produces a product (the manufacturer) will use a wholesaler, retailer, agent or distributor to sell its

products to the consumer, with the intermediary taking a cut of the manufacturer's profits.

The key to place is to ensure that your customers can access the products they require when they want them.

Promotion

If customers do not know about a product they will not buy it. Businesses use promotion to attract new customers, retain existing customers, and enhance the image or profile of the business.

Advertising is the most common form of promotion, via television, radio, internet (including websites, social media, etc.), cinema, newspapers, magazines, journals and public transport. The type of advertising is determined by the budget, market, availability of the product, appropriateness and the access to the product. All must be linked to and considered as part of the business's overall aims and objectives.

Other examples of promotion are:

- sales promotions – special offers on products or services that the public is made aware of through advertising
- sponsorship of sports teams, events and television – images of footballers or rugby players with the logo of a sponsor on their shirts can been seen all over the world and gain the business the promotion that it has paid millions of pounds for
- public relations – this raises awareness of a product or service by communicating a message through the press; this could be in, say, newspaper or magazine articles and reports, the news or on the internet; PR is reliant on the press reporting the relevant information, such as the results of surveys or news of an exciting new initiative, rather than the business paying for advertising.

PAIRS ACTIVITY

(10 minutes)

Write a list of as many different methods of promotion you can think of that you have been exposed to over the past month. Think about what you have bought. This includes if you were given a paper bag or purchased a bag to carry an item home, or if you have seen advertising – when and where, etc.

Once you have completed your list, as a class place the methods of promotion into the following five categories: advertising, branding, packaging, publicity, public relations and merchandising. Discuss the findings with the group.

UNIT 6 MARKETING STRATEGY

Businesses consider the different types of promotion that will appeal to their target audience, so will have to ensure that they:

- use the right media
- have the right budget to suit the size and scale of their business
- make sure the timing is right
- consider the packaging
- emphasise the unique selling points
- use relevant sales promotions
- know the product will sell.

Therefore, promotion is very important and selecting the right method is crucial.

KNOW IT

1 What are the main elements of the marketing mix?
2 Describe Porter's Generic Strategies.
3 Explain the four main parts of Ansoff's Matrix.
4 Identify the different elements of a STEEPLE analysis.

LO5 assessment activities

Below are suggested assessment activities that have been directly linked to the Pass and Merit criteria in LO5 to help with assignment preparation. These are followed by top tips on how to achieve the best results.

Activity 1 Pass criteria *P8*

P8 Produce a marketing strategy for a particular business, using the different business tools that you have learned about while completing this unit. Your marketing strategy should look professional, using references where relevant.

Activity 2 Merit criteria *M4*

M4 Assess the business tools that you selected for your marketing strategy. Explain how effective and useful they were in helping you to create the marketing strategy.

TOP TIPS

✔ Ensure you choose a business that you can write about to fully complete all of the assessment criteria successfully.
✔ Select the business tools that are relevant to the specific business you have chosen.
✔ Remember that to assess is to offer a reasoned judgement informed by relevant facts.

Read about it

Further reading on the subject of marketing strategy:

www.marketingdonut.co.uk/marketing/marketing-strategy

http://businesscasestudies.co.uk

Competitive Advantage: Creating and Sustaining Superior Performance, by Michael Porter, The Free Press, 1985

Marketing Strategy & Competitive Positioning (5th edn), by Brigitte Nicoulaud, Graham J. Hooley and Nigel F. Piercy, Financial Times/ Prentice Hall, 2011

The New Marketing Manifesto: The 12 Rules for Building Successful Brands in the 21st Century (2nd edn), by John Grant, Texere (Business Essentials), 2000

Unit 07

Marketing campaign

ABOUT THIS UNIT

Marketing campaigns are a method used by businesses to promote and create awareness of new and existing products. The type of campaign they choose to use will depend on various elements, such as the target market and resource considerations, as well as the overall marketing campaign budget.

This unit will explain these different elements and help you to understand the decisions that a business will need to make when selecting the methods related to its marketing campaigns. You will have the opportunity to create your own marketing campaign pitch to an audience, bringing together the marketing skills and knowledge you have acquired, as well as your presentation skills.

LEARNING OUTCOMES

The topics, activities and suggested reading in this unit will help you to:

1 understand the purpose of marketing campaigns
2 understand the elements of the marketing mix
3 understand how businesses use digital marketing and the impact it has on businesses and their customers
4 understand the role of public relations (PR), advertising and digital marketing agencies in business
5 be able to plan marketing campaigns
6 be able to pitch planned marketing campaigns.

How will I be assessed?

You will be assessed through a series of assignments and tasks set and marked by your tutor.

How will I be graded?

You will be graded using the following criteria, which are in the specification produced by OCR for the qualification.

Learning outcome	Pass	Merit	Distinction
You will:	To achieve a Pass you must demonstrate that you have met all the pass assessment criteria	To achieve a Merit you must demonstrate that you have met all the pass and merit assessment criteria	To achieve a Distinction you must demonstrate that you have met all the pass, merit and distinction assessment criteria
1 Understand the purpose of marketing campaigns	**P1** Explain the purpose of a marketing campaign for a specific business, including the key factors which influenced them		
2 Understand the elements of the marketing mix	**P2** Explain how a specific business has applied the marketing mix	**M1** Compare how two contrasting businesses have applied the marketing mix	**D1** Recommend and justify improvements a specific business could make to its marketing mix
3 Understand how businesses use digital marketing and the impact it has on businesses and their customers	**P3** Describe how a specific business makes use of digital marketing	**M2** Analyse how two contrasting businesses have used social media to increase brand awareness	**D2** Evaluate the effect of digital marketing on the customers' perception of a specific business
	P4 Explain the impact of digital marketing on a specific business and its customers		
4 Understand the role of Public Relations (PR), advertising and digital marketing agencies in business	**P5** Explain the role of PR and advertising agencies in the development of a specific marketing campaign		
	P6 Explain how a specific business has used a digital marketing agency		
	P7 Explain the benefits and drawbacks of using agencies for a specific marketing campaign		
5 Be able to plan marketing campaigns	**P8** Plan a marketing campaign for a specific business's product or service	**M3** Justify the decisions made in a plan for a marketing campaign for a specific business	
6 Be able to pitch planned marketing campaigns	**P9** Prepare and deliver a pitch for a marketing campaign for a specific business's product or service, using a combination of verbal, non-verbal skills and presentation tools		
	P10 Review a pitch for a planned marketing campaign with recommendations for improvement		

LO1 Understand the purpose of marketing campaigns *P1*

GETTING STARTED

(15 minutes)

Think about the last advertisement you saw for a charity.

- Where did you see it? e.g. in a magazine, on a billboard, online.
- If there was a picture, what was it of?
- If there was text, what did it say?
- What was its message?
- Who do you think it was aimed at?
- Do you remember which charity it was for?
- Why do you remember it now?
- Would you support the charity as a result of seeing this advertisement?
- What other types of marketing have you seen for this charity?
- Do you think the marketing campaigns run by this charity are effective?

Share your answers with the rest of the class. Are there any charity adverts or marketing campaigns that you all think are particularly effective?

1.1 The purpose of marketing campaigns and key factors influencing them

Meet the objectives of a marketing campaign and the wider business

The purpose of a **marketing campaign** is to get your message out to the people that you want to hear it, by the means that you choose. The message you want to portray may depend on the product or service you are marketing. You may want to promote a specific brand image, build the profile of your business, or increase the sales and profits of a particular product or service.

> 🔑 **KEY TERM**
>
> **Marketing campaign** – a defined series of steps or activities to promote or create awareness of a new or existing product or service.

Key factors that influence marketing campaigns

There are some key factors that businesses need to consider when creating a successful marketing campaign.

Type of product or service

There are millions of products and services that we can purchase on a daily basis, but what makes one product or service better than or different to another? Unique features need to be promoted to the right people.

A business will also need to think about the how the type of products and services may influence the choice of marketing campaign. For example, informing the audience about a new service such as travel insurance will use different methods to advertising a chocolate bar.

Target audience

A business must get to know its **target audience** through research. Successful and thorough market research will enable the business to create a product or service that can then be directed or targeted at a particular type of potential customer. An audience could be a large or mass market, or a niche market. Understanding the needs and wants of customers can ensure that these are met, with the success being measured by sales of the product or service.

> 🔑 **KEY TERM**
>
> **Target audience** – the type of customers who are likely to purchase the product or service.

Stage of the product's life

The **product life cycle** is a tool in which a business can determine where a product could currently be placed on the life cycle. See Section 2.1 (page 170) for more information.

> 🔑 **KEY TERM**
>
> **Product life cycle** – a theoretical method that businesses use to focus on six main areas of a product's life: development, introduction, growth, maturity, saturation and decline.

Availability of resources

Resources can include:

- the skills of employees who are available to contribute to the campaign
- the time allocated to the campaign
- the finances that have been allocated
- the technology and materials required to create a successful marketing campaign.

Competitor activities

A business may react to a competitor's marketing campaign, to remind customers that its products are still available, just as good (if not better!) and ready to be purchased. It is, however, better to be proactive and stay ahead of competitors' activities so that it is them, not you, that has to react.

Constraints on marketing campaigns

Business need to be aware of the constraints that are placed on the way they can market their products and services, to ensure that they do not break any rules, regulations or ethical guidelines. Specific legislation and regulatory bodies protect the public from distasteful and dishonest advertising. There can also be internal constraints like limited budgets. See Unit 5 (page 135) for more information.

Full stakeholder engagement

Stakeholders play an important part in keeping the target market fully aware of the products and services the business has to offer.

It is vital that the stakeholders who are directly involved in the marketing campaign are committed and work together as a team to achieve the same aims and objectives. The team leader will co-ordinate the various elements of the marketing campaigns, allocating specific roles to individuals. Being an approachable team leader can enable the team to offer ideas and suggestions that otherwise may not have been considered, as well as promoting good team morale to get the most out of all employees.

Regular team meeting are important – not just project progress meetings for the immediate marketing team, but also facilitated meetings with relevant external stakeholders like customers and local communities.

PAIRS ACTIVITY

(45 minutes)

Identify a product or service that could be featured in a marketing campaign. It could be something that already exists, brand new, or a product or service that has been redeveloped in some form.

Write a description of the product or service, and discuss how you think it could be promoted to the target audience and who should be involved. Be prepared to share your ideas with the rest of the group.

KNOW IT

1 Write your own definition of 'marketing campaign'.
2 How can competitor activities affect a business's approach to a marketing campaign?
3 Why do constraints on marketing activities influence business?

LO1 assessment activity

Below is a suggested assessment activity that has been directly linked to the Pass criteria in LO1 to help with assignment preparation. This is followed by top tips on how to achieve the best results.

Activity 1 Pass criteria *P1*

P1 Select one business and investigate a successful marketing campaign it has recently completed. Explain the purpose of the campaign, highlighting the key factors that influenced the choices made.

TOP TIPS

✔ Select a business that you are familiar with and interested in.
✔ Ensure that you fully research the business's product or service to meet the assessment criteria.

GETTING STARTED 👤

(15 minutes)

In pairs, discuss how you would use the marketing mix (product, price, place and promotion) in order to produce and sell a variety of different pens, which will be aimed at different target groups e.g. 3–6 year olds, 7–12 year olds, teenagers, college students. Share your findings with the rest of the class.

2.1 The main elements of the marketing mix

The marketing mix combines the product, price, place and promotional elements (also known as the 4Ps) that are required within a successful marketing campaign. See also Unit 6, LO5 (page 163) for more information about the marketing mix in the context of marketing strategies.

Product

Design

To have an effective product, the design needs to fulfil the original brief that resulted from the detailed market research. The design mix is a tool that businesses can use to focus on certain aspects of potential designs (Figure 7.1).

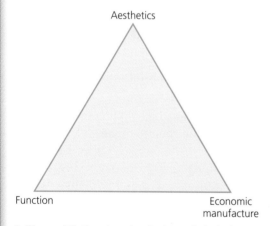

▲ **Figure 7.1** Keeping the design mix in balance

The design mix is a triangle with three main elements, as described below, which should be held in balance.

1 Function: how the item needs to operate so that the user can use it. There is no point in purchasing a clock that does not work. The business will highlight the features of the product or service as well as the unique selling points (USPs) it has to offer compared to its competitors.

2 Economic manufacture: whether the product or service is financially viable. This takes into consideration the materials that will be used to produce it, and whether alternatives are available that may reduce the costs of production or selling price. If specialist machinery is required to cut and shape the product, how will this be utilised in the future? What if there are issues with the product later on?

3 Aesthetics: how the product looks and feels. If a certain product looks better than a competitor's this can influence sales and add value to the brand. Think about a pair of trainers – we can be influenced by how they look as well as what they feel like to wear.

The product life cycle

Using this method, a business can identify the position of products or services in terms of sales over time. The product life cycle identifies several stages (or phases) at which sales figures are measured. Most sales rise soon after launch before reaching a steadier phase and eventually declining.

Some products have been around for many years and have a long life cycle – for example, Cadbury's Dairy Milk Chocolate was first produced in 1905, Kellogg's Corn Flakes were first made in 1906 and the Mini car went into production in 1959. However, these products have not remained the same during this time – food packaging and recipes change, and Minis look very different now to how they did 50 years ago.

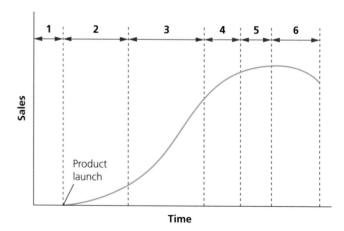

Key

1 = Development   4 = Maturity
2 = Introduction   5 = Saturation
3 = Growth   6 = Decline

▲ **Figure 7.2** The phases of the product life cycle

The phases of the product life cycle (see Figure 7.2) are as follows.

1 Development phase: the product is being prepared for launch. The team must be happy with the design, the research and testing completed, all testing checked and resulting changes to the design finalised before the product is introduced to the market.

2 Introduction phase: the product is launched into the market to be purchased. Sales are normally small to begin with but, once the product becomes more established, will start to steadily increase.

3 Growth phase: key in the life span of the product. If sales do not continue to grow at this stage and marketing strategies are tried without success, the business may decide to stop selling the product.

4 Maturity phase: profits should be maximised now because sales volumes are at their highest. The business may decide to increase its marketing to ensure that sales continue to be high, and consumers do not forget about the product and move on to something else. Remember that businesses always strive to achieve repeat custom, and want to ensure customer loyalty to particular brands or products. Businesses also may want to increase their marketing activities if the competition increases, as this could threaten sales.

5 Saturation phase: the point at which sales begin to level off – for example, because consumers do not need to buy the product again or move on to a competitor's product, which may be a modified version of the existing product. This can potentially be a difficult time, so a business needs to decide whether to continue with promotions, introduce new marketing campaigns or accept the levelling-off of sales without investing further into marketing the product.

6 Decline: sales have fallen and maybe the product's life cycle has come to an end. It may take years to get to this phase in the life cycle or just several months, depending on the product. A business must decide if the product is still relevant or viable and, if necessary, withdraw it from the market.

PAIRS ACTIVITY

(15 minutes)

Consider the following products:

● Cadbury's Wispa chocolate bar
● Nike trainers
● loom bands
● Xbox One.

Using the product life cycle diagram in Figure 7.3, place each product where you consider it should be in terms of its life cycle, focusing on sales over time. Compare your answers to those of your neighbour.

Price

Once a consumer has determined the product that they want or need, they will next consider its price. Price is the amount the customer will be charged for the product or service, taking into consideration the costs involved in producing the product and the profit margins set by the business.

Cost-plus (mark-up) pricing

The cost-plus **pricing strategy** is when a business factors into its calculations different considerations to ensure that a profit is made on each product or service sold.

● The *cost of goods* is the total cost of all the materials used to make the product, as well as non-direct costs like equipment, technology, labour costs, breakages or spoilt stock.

● The *mark-up* is expressed as a percentage and added to the cost of the product to make a profit. For example, if an item costs £2 to produce and your mark-up percentage was 50 per cent, you would add £1 to the price of your product. The mark-up is usually a percentage of the cost of the goods. This will change over time if the cost of producing the product changes.

To ensure the mark-up is large enough to maintain a good profit, the business tracks costs and adjusts prices accordingly. Customers may be aware of costs increasing for no obvious reason (for example, if they buy the product regularly or if they use online price-tracking sites for larger goods).

KEY TERM

Pricing strategies – methods a business may adopt to determine the ideal price(s) of its products and services.

Price-taking

The overall market price (the generally accepted price for a product or service) is determined by supply and demand. A price taker is a business that cannot influence the price of a product in the market, perhaps because a larger, dominant competitor (the price maker) sets the recognised market price. In this case, the price taker may not be able to sell its product or service at the desired profit margins because the price would be higher than the market price and customers reluctant to buy the product for more than they believe is necessary. For example, a farmer may want to sell her milk for a higher price than the supermarkets but cannot because the supermarkets determine the price.

Customer-based and competitor pricing

Table 7.1 Pricing strategies

Pricing strategy	Explanation
Penetration pricing	Setting the price low to break in to a market, to achieve rapid growth in market share or to encourage customers to return to a product
Price skimming	Charging high prices for a product that has little or no competition or is positioned as exclusive, e.g. a high-status brand like Rolex or new technology such as the Apple Watch
Loss leaders	Selling a product for less than it cost to produce, so that the business loses money (or, in practice, selling a product at a reduced profit margin); the idea is either that customers buy other, profitable products at the same time or that aggressive pricing is used for a short time before the business returns the price to normal, hoping that consumers will continue to purchase the product
Psychological pricing	Pricing that gives a consumer the perception of value for money, e.g. £199 instead of £200 will seem more attractive because it seems a lot cheaper than just £1 difference It could also be a core price, which seems low until additional costs are added (e.g. VAT or accessory products)
Competitor pricing	Aggressively cutting the prices of items, forcing competitors to follow suit so that they do not lose customers; this can also be called a price war; supermarkets often do this with petrol and diesel Competition law prevents competing businesses, or businesses and suppliers, agreeing to sell the same product for a set price; a business can choose to sell a product for less than the recommended retail price (RRP) but cannot sell it for more than its advertised price
Promotion pricing	Businesses will offer promotions to customers for a short period of time; the aim is to persuade customers to buy the product and continue to buy it after the promotional pricing has finished; examples include buy one, get one free (BOGOF), three for the price of two, two for £1, etc. RRP can often be displayed on items that are subsequently reduced in price, with the impact being measured by the hopefully increased sales due to customers considering they have a bargain!

A business will adopt a number of pricing strategies over a year to adapt to the supply and demand of customers.

INDEPENDENT RESEARCH ACTIVITY

(1 hour plus research time)

Select a common product that is available in several retail shops. Investigate the price of this identical product in five different businesses (e.g. a supermarket, a village store, online).

Compile a short report on your findings, detailing:

- why you chose the product
- where it was sold
- the differences in price
- why you consider the prices to be different.

Place

Place refers to the different places in which a customer can view or purchase a product or service. This part of the marketing mix must be correct as it is the final part in the decision-making process that customers have to complete in order for the sale to occur. If they have decided on the item that they want to purchase and considered the price, they then need to access the service or select the product to make the purchase.

An example is ordering online, when the delivery time will be a major consideration. For example, if the same product takes five weeks to be delivered by Business A and three days by Business B, for the same delivery price, it is clear which business customers will generally choose.

Distribution channels

Differences in delivery time may be down to the distribution channels used. These are the channels, or routes, through which a product passes when moving from manufacturer to consumer. For example, a business may choose to use a wholesaler, which buys a product in bulk from the manufacturer and sells it on in smaller quantities to retailers. The manufacturer benefits because it doesn't need to store as much stock and has sold it quickly, and the retailer benefits because the wholesaler can offer low prices or deliver several different products at once. However, the use of wholesalers is in decline because large businesses like supermarkets buy directly from manufacturers and the internet has made it easy for both retailers and customers to buy from the source.

Distribution strategies

There are three main distribution strategies that a business will consider when selecting the choice that will work for its particular products.

1 *Intensive distribution* is when a product is sold in as many outlets as possible.
2 *Selective distribution* is when only a few outlets sell the product – for example, in a particular location.
3 *Exclusive distribution* is when a product, often of a high value (e.g. a luxury car), is available through very few outlets.

Promotion

Promotion is the method(s) a business chooses to inform and persuade customers to purchase or engage in it products or services. There are many types of promotion.

PAIRS ACTIVITY 👥 ....

(30 minutes)

In pairs, discuss three very different marketing campaigns that you have seen. One should be for a product, one for a service and the third is your choice. Write some notes about:

● why this campaign appealed to you
● what the message was
● what form of promotions were used
● where you saw the material (cinema, advert on phone, internet, TV, etc.)
● if any celebrities were associated with the product or service
● any other aspects you consider to be relevant to the task.

Produce a summary to present your findings to the rest of the class.
....

Methods of promotion

Table 7.2 Methods of promotion

Method	Description
Advertising	The most popular means of promotion, taking many different forms
	It enables a business to increase the awareness of a product or service
	It informs the target market about the features of the product or service
	Advertising methods include: television, radio, the internet, digital methods, magazines, trade journals, newspapers, billboards, transportation, cinema, etc.
Sales promotion	These have increased in popularity over the years, with the traditional 'January' sales appearing to be all year around in some businesses! Includes:
	• offering discounted items such as 70% off RRP • free gifts and samples if the customer buys the product • money-off vouchers or coupons, competitions and prize draws (may not dependent on a sale but raise awareness and could encourage new sales) • special offers such as three for the price of two or BOGOF (buy one, get one free)
	It is hoped that once customers purchase an item that is part of a sales promotion, they will keep purchasing the product if and when it reverts back to its original price; these promotions can also be promoted through social media networking by 'liking' products or services
Product placement	This is when brands are featured in television programmes or films – for example, if you consider James Bond films, what car does he often drive? The gadgets he uses in the more recent films are produced by real businesses wanting to target products to a particular audience
	It has become a very competitive method of advertising because it is so effective to associate products with aspirational characters or to have them seen by millions of people on screen
Branding	(See Unit 6, page 159)
	A strong brand can enable a business to expand its current product portfolio knowing that strong brands should continue to sell, providing they invest in advertising to remind the audience that their products are still there
	Some customers associate products with various times in their lives so they can form an emotional and visual attachment to certain products, remaining loyal by purchasing a particular brand for many years.

Method	Description
Merchandising	This could involve presenting goods for sale in an attractive way, e.g. via visual displays, point-of-sale packs, demonstrations, pricing strategies, sales promotions, packaging
	It could also relate to producing branded products (e.g. pens with the company's logo) or tying products in to films and events (e.g. drinks cartons featuring cartoon characters)
Packaging	The design of packaging should be 'on brand', clearly displaying relevant logos and colours, so that consumers can easily recognise the product; some products differentiate themselves via their distinctive packaging, e.g. the retro look of Benefit Cosmetics, or the leaning Chenet wine bottle
	The packaging of products has become a real science; packaging should also stop items from being damaged, as this costs the business in terms of: • wastage rates • quality control system • reputation • repeat custom Businesses are coming under increasing pressure regarding the environmental damage excessive packaging can cause, and as a result have had to act and change their methods
Personal (face to face) selling	This is when a representative of a business visits individuals, normally at home, to sell goods, e.g. a Body Shop party representative
	If they have not agreed to it beforehand, consumers can find this approach invasive, particularly if they are not interested in the products or services, so this method of selling has received bad press over the years, however it can result in high-value sales, for example of double glazing, which is why this traditional method of selling has survived the test of time
	Talking to a salesperson in a showroom is also personal selling – it is a time-consuming use of staff so is most effective for high-value products (e.g. kitchens or cars) but even chatting to a jam producer at a farmers' market helps the customer to get to know and trust the brand, resulting in a sale
Direct marketing	This is when a business targets customers, e.g. via mail shots, emails, phone calls and text messages
	The business will hold a database containing customers' contact details and information about their previous purchases – for example, loyalty cards enable businesses to track buying habits so they can send the customer relevant vouchers or coupons
Public relations (PR)	This is raising or increasing awareness of a product or service by communicating messages through the media, e.g. via newspaper/magazine articles and reports, news, internet, social media
	PR is different from advertising because it is usually reliant on the story being picked up by the media rather than paying for adverting space
Sponsorship	Sponsorship of events, sports teams or television programmes enables businesses to display their logos and messages on elements like team kits or programmes, which can be seen by the audience attending the event or watching television
	Sponsorship can enhance the image of a business, increase sales of the products that are associated with the sponsorship activities, as well as create a positive image for the business

PAIRS ACTIVITY

(30 minutes)

1 Individually, think of five different products and write down the advertising slogans or messages associated with them that you see either on the television in advertisements or in magazine adverts – for example, 'How do you eat yours?' (Cadbury's Creme Egg).

2 Give the slogans to your neighbour and see if they can identify each product.

3 Now find five different company logos and give them to another person to see if they can identify the businesses.

Discuss the main points raised from completing these tasks.

LO2 assessment activities

Below are suggested assessment activities that have been directly linked to the Pass, Merit and Distinction criteria in LO2 to help with assignment preparation. These are followed by top tips on how to achieve the best results.

Activity 1 Pass criteria *P2*

P2 Select a suitable business, and explain and describe how it has applied the marketing mix to promote its products or service.

Activity 2 Merit criteria *M1*

M1 Select two contrasting businesses (for example, they sell completely different products or services, or hold different values). Explain and compare how these businesses have applied the marketing mix to their business. What is the same? What is different?

Activity 3 Distinction criteria *D1*

D1 Identify one business that has used the marketing mix for the products or services it produces, and recommend and justify improvements it could make to the marketing mix to move the business forward.

LO3 Understand how businesses use digital marketing and the impact it has on businesses and their customers *P3 P4 M2 D2*

3.1 How businesses use digital marketing

Digital tools and techniques

Digital marketing is the process of promoting products and services using electronic media, particularly the internet. Channels include apps, podcasts, text messaging, instant messaging, digital TV and radio channels, social marketing via social media, streaming and video ads, electronic billboards, search engine marketing, emails and web banners.

Digital media is so pervasive that consumers have access to information any time and any place they want it, an ever growing source of entertainment, news, shopping and social interaction.

Digital marketing means that consumers expect companies to know them, send personalised, relevant communications, and provide offers tailored to their needs and preferences. A huge advantage of digital marketing is the ability to track consumer behaviour in real time, e.g. via cookies on websites.

Social media

The impact of social media on our everyday lives has increased dramatically. It enables social interaction between friends, relatives, peers or groups with common interests. As well as social networks like Facebook, Twitter and Instagram, social media includes blogs, forums and review websites.

Although businesses tend to have a social media presence (such as a Twitter feed or a blog), they cannot control much of what is said about them online. Now consumers are exposed not just to what a company says about its brand, but also to what the media, friends, relatives and others are saying – and often people are more likely to believe them than the business.

Social media can both be a positive and negative aspect of marketing. Good comments can result in more sales, but negative comments can have the opposite effect, leading to lost income. Achieving a happy medium is vital. Quickly reacting to complaints and showing good customer service can be one way of repairing damage to a reputation.

Email marketing

A business may email customers directly to inform them about products or services that it wants to promote in some form, to generate enquiries and sales.

The customer must have provided their email address voluntarily, and should be able to unsubscribe at any time.

Affiliate marketing

This is receiving a cut of sales created for another company – for example, by referring customers from an email or website to buy products from that company online. A book blog may link the novels it reviews to

Amazon, and the blog owner gets a percentage cut of any sales made.

Aggregators marketing/comparison websites

Comparison websites enable the user to view a variety of different products, and compare and filter the prices, features, offers and other categories. Customers tend to use these websites when investigating car, home and house insurance, gas and electricity, and other household-related expenses.

Aggregators provide information, which is then placed on the comparison websites for users to view. There are many price comparison websites and some, like Martin Lewis's Cheap Energy Club, raise interest in consumer rights and try to ensure that customers get the best prices.

Search engine marketing (SEM)

Users of the internet will use a search engine to find specific information. SEM involves a business paying for advertisements to appear on search engine results pages, linking to the company's website. The ads appear when a particular keyword or phrase is used – for example, an ad for dining room furniture may appear among the results for 'oak dining table'. The business pays for its ad if the customer clicks on it; this is known as pay-per-click (PPC).

There is quite an art to getting the ad correct, so that it appears in front of the target customers.

Search, rank and relevance

Search engine optimisation (SEO)

This is the attempt to be ranked high in a list of search engine results. Most users don't look beyond the first page of search results, so there is a lot of competition to ensure websites are featured as near to the top of the page as possible. Search engines like Google don't tend to explicitly state how they rank websites, but useful, up-to-date web content and relevant keywords help. Appearing on search results is a free method of advertising, but businesses can spend a lot of time and money optimising their websites to be placed ahead of their competitors in search results.

Customer feedback

Digital marketing methods mean that users can feed back their experiences of the business and its products or services in a variety of different forms, which can be used to improve their experiences. Some examples are listed below.

- Net Promoter Score (NPS): a customer loyalty metric based on the question 'How likely is it that you would recommend our business (or product/service) to someone you know?' Customers respond on a scale from 0 (very unlikely) to 10 (very likely). Once the results have been compiled, the percentage of 0–6 scores is subtracted from the percentage of 9–10 scores to get the NPS. The higher the score, the more enthusiastic the customers.
- Customer experience (CX): this is the perception of a brand after the customer has interacted with it. In digital terms, it can be the ease of using a website or the level of online customer service.
- Customer satisfaction score (CSAT): this measures a customer's satisfaction with a service that they have recently experienced by asking them to answer a series of short questions. It is normally stated as a percentage, with 100 per cent being the most satisfied and 0 per cent the least. Most businesses want to achieve 80 per cent plus. Some businesses contact customers who appear to be dissatisfied as a result of completing the survey, to try to discover more information and react appropriately to the complaints.

Measurement methods

Businesses can use a variety of different means to measure the impact of digital marketing. These might include:

- levels of customer satisfaction using some of the methods discussed above
- sales generated as a result of a digital marketing campaign
- comparisons and analysis between competitors
- enquiries and brand recognition resulting from the marketing campaign
- the return on investment of initiatives such as PPC
- the percentage of income generated from returning customers, which could have been identified as one of a business's key performance indicators (KPIs).

3.2 The impact of digital marketing on businesses and consumers

Since digital marketing has grown in popularity, businesses have viewed it as an integral part of their marketing plans, as the impact it has on both business and consumers has been considerable. Table 7.3 highlights some key points.

Table 7.3 The impact of digital marketing

Method	How digital marketing has an impact
Market segmentation	Influences different touchpoints for target markets – methods can be altered easily according to the segmentation, so a range of communication methods can be used to spread the word among several market segments, e.g. targeting college students to promote a new drinks brand
4Ps	Enables the tailoring of the 4Ps to reflect opportunities created by digital marketing, e.g. capture a wider audience via, for example, online purchasing
Messages	A variety of different messages can be sent directly to targeted users of digital channels, e.g. emails about 24/48-hour flash sales, sales promotions or offers; the business can determine the frequency and personalisation of the information, however the messages have to be managed so users do not become overloaded, feel the communication is intrusive and opt out
Access	Many customers access a variety of digital marketing methods every day by checking their mobiles, various email accounts, social media and so on; customers who are not confident with IT will have limited access to this information, so a business will need to ensure that maximum coverage is viewed by its customers and suitable provision made to help non-confident IT users
Reputation	Social media can be a positive form of advertising for a business when things are going well but, if things go wrong, it can have direct consequences for its reputation; customers can review products and services by leaving both positive and negative feedback – this has become a method of marketing in its own right, but businesses do not have control over what the public comments on; comments cannot always be 'taken down' as soon as they are written, and doing this may appear to be ignoring the problem in any case
Costs	Digital marketing methods are often free, or at least lower cost than print or broadcast advertising, however innovative ideas can be expensive and staying ahead of the competition is key; investing in specialist skills or software may increase marketing efficiency and ultimately profit margins
Consumer behaviour	Business have recognised and reacted to recent changes in consumer behaviour, e.g. online shopping; being online provides a 24/7 global audience so information (e.g. stock levels) must stay current and accurate; customers must be able to access the information and goods or services even when there is a high demand (e.g. when tickets for a popular band are released); seasonal shopping is less predictable as, for example, customers may want to buy summer wear in a British winter if they are going to Australia for Christmas
Control management	Customers are aware of how that they can influence a business; this can be shown with demands for 'retro' products, from confectionery to nostalgic toys, e.g. Cadbury reintroduced its Wispa chocolate bar, which originated from the 1980s; equally, a business will try to manage and control the flow of online comments so that it is aware and can take action if appropriate – messages can go 'viral' very quickly, which can create problems for a business

LO3 Assessment activities

Below are suggested assessment activities that have been directly linked to the Pass, Merit and Distinction criteria in LO3 to help with assignment preparation. These are followed by top tips on how to achieve the best results.

Activity 1 Pass criteria *P3*

P3 Write a description of how a business uses digital marketing to create awareness of the business.

Activity 1 Merit criteria *M2*

M2 Complete a detailed analysis that investigates how two contrasting businesses have used social media to ensure that their brands, products or services are more visible.

Activity 3 Pass criteria *P4*

P4 Selecting one business, explain how digital marketing has impacted upon the business and its customers.

Activity 4 Distinction criteria *D2*

D2 Select a business and evaluate the effect that digital marketing has had on how customers perceive the business, by carrying out your own research.

TOP TIPS ✔

- ✔ Ensure that the businesses you select fully complement the assessment criteria.
- ✔ When considering the impact of digital marketing, consider how it influenced customers to take actions such as visiting the website, or buying the product or service.

LO4 Understand the role of public relations (PR), advertising and digital marketing agencies in business *P5* *P6 P7*

GETTING STARTED

(10 minutes)

Look at Figure 7.3.

▲ **Figure 7.3** Why do some films have big launch parties?

Film companies often have a launch event to celebrate a film being released. This is a form of PR.

- Why do such events happen?
- What activities do film companies carry out to ensure maximum media coverage?

Write a list and compare it with your neighbour's.

Public relations is a discipline that looks after reputation, with the aim of earning understanding and support, and influencing opinion and behaviour. It is the planned and sustained effort to establish and maintain goodwill and mutual understanding between an organisation and its publics (source: Chartered Institute of Public Relations).

🔑 **KEY TERM**

Public relations – methods used to communicate a business's messages, to maintain its reputation and to build relationships with stakeholders.

Businesses often need to bring in external expertise to handle specialist areas like PR, advertising and digital marketing agencies.

4.1 The role of public relations (PR) agencies in business

Many companies bring in PR expertise to fulfil various promotional criteria.

To promote, protect and enhance businesses using positive messages via media

Successful PR can promote and enhance the business profile as well as protect the message that a business is trying to portray. Messages placed in the media via PR look more natural than advertising and are more likely to be trusted. The content can be anything from a press release about a new product to the results of a survey (e.g. a bed manufacturer might commission a survey about the public's sleep habits and relate the results to its beds).

Event planning

Events like exhibitions and seminars are also a form of PR, as the business is positioned as an authority in the subject of the event. For example, a computer software company might hold a conference for users of its accounting software, enabling customers to share their views and be exposed to new products and services. The objective is to enhance the business's reputation as an expert in its field, and to increase customer loyalty and, ultimately, sales. Specialist event hire agencies are often brought in to plan and run this sort of event.

Media training

Sometimes a senior member of staff needs to address and respond to reporters and journalists who want to know about an event or incident. As such situations can be stressful and intense, PR experts give senior employees specialist training in dealing with a variety of different people who require the information but want to ask their own questions. The senior employee has to respond appropriately and professionally, using a pre-agreed message.

Spokesperson duties

Sometimes someone needs to comment on behalf of a business – for example, as a reaction to a situation within the business (for example, a product recall or the appointment of a new CEO). A PR specialist will choose suitable wording and be able to answer questions from the media in an appropriate way.

? THINK ABOUT IT

Case study: Glastonbury Festival

The world-famous Glastonbury Festival started in 1970, when it ran over two days with 1,500 people attending at a cost of £1 each, which included free milk from Pilton Farm, which the music festival's founder Michael Eavis owned and ran. In 1971 the festival was free to the 12,000 who attended. Music, dance, poetry and theatre were included, as well as performers such as David Bowie, Joan Baez and Fairport Convention.

The next festival did not happen until 1978 and only as a result of travellers who came from Stonehenge thinking that a festival was taking place at Glastonbury. The event was free as it was not planned, but 500 people still had fun!

In 1979, the festival became a three-day event with a focus on children by the Children's World charity, which still happens today. 12,000 people attended with tickets costing £5.

However, the organisers lost a considerable amount of money, so the event did not run the next year. The festival has continued successfully most years since 1981, now attracting more than 155,000 people paying £228 each.

1 Research the PR methods the Glastonbury Festival has used over the years.
2 What are the advantages of these PR methods to the Glastonbury Festival? Explain your findings.

4.2 The role of advertising agencies in business

Advertising agencies may be brought in at a cost to the business, but they should be an efficient investment because they are skilled in targeting particular customer groups. The role of the advertising agency is to:

- have an understanding of the business that is using its services
- have up-to-date knowledge and expertise in current types of advertising
- provide suitable creative ideas for advertising campaigns, including the choices of media to be utilised and message to be created

- provide relevant designs using graphic design tools, which can be used as part of the advertising
- write scripts for advertisements and promotion campaigns (if required)
- recommend and plan campaigns, giving detailed timelines and expectations
- analyse and report back on the results of advertising campaigns.

4.3 The role of digital marketing agencies in business

A digital marketing agency is slightly different from an advertising agency, as it is contracted to focus on digital marketing only. This is a highly specialist area that is becoming increasingly time consuming to maintain. Often, digital agencies contain many skillsets, from account managers to digital copywriters, designers and social media experts.

A digital marketing agency will be contracted to do one of more of the following:

- manage a business's website by keeping it up to date and current; it will advise and recommend changes to ensure it stays current, appears in search engines and is easy for customers to use
- write blogs and other useful online content

- implement digital techniques to boost traffic and maintain online visibility
- monitor and manage the business's social media activity, or recommend why it could benefit the business if it currently does not partake in social media
- provide knowledge of target groups, and the channels or platforms the business could reach by using particular digital methods
- use the latest technology to target customers in digital marketing campaigns
- plan, create and send promotional emails
- work with other marketing agencies contracted by the business to ensure campaigns are consistent across all channels.

PAIRS ACTIVITY

(30 minutes)

Choose and research a digital marketing agency to discover the businesses it works with and the products and services it has helped to promote. Report your findings back to the class.

4.4 Benefits and drawbacks of using agencies

Table 7.4 outlines the benefits and drawback of businesses using advertising and/or digital marketing agencies.

Table 7.4 Benefits and drawbacks of using marketing agencies

Benefits	Drawbacks
The business will have access to specialists, and their knowledge and creativity	There will be a fixed or variable cost, depending on the service, and the duration of this service, that the business requires
The agency provides an independent view on the business, which can be a benefit as a 'fresh approach' can often help a business	The agency's knowledge of products or services may be variable, so the business will need to ensure that it has as much information as the agency needs to provide a suitable service for the area in which the business operates
The agency will have access to detailed demographic information that could be invaluable to a business.	The agency may prioritise other clients who have larger contracts, making response times variable
The agency provides specialist skills that may not be available in-house, and reduces the time taken in-house to carry out campaigns	The business loses a certain amount of control over its marketing activities, and may spend considerable time briefing agencies and attending meetings with them

KNOW IT

1 How can PR help a business?
2 Why may a 'spokesperson' be employed by a business?
3 Why may a business require the skills of a digital advertising agency?

4 Outline the main differences between an advertising agency and a digital marketing agency.

LO4 assessment activities

Below are suggested assessment activities that have been directly linked to the Pass criteria in LO4 to help with assignment preparation. These are followed by top tips on how to achieve the best results.

Activity 1 Pass criteria *P5*

P5 Using a new business, or one that you have researched for previous questions, identify a marketing campaign, and explain how PR and advertising agencies have been directly involved in it.

Activity 2 Pass criteria *P6*

P6 Explain how a digital marketing agency has been directly involved in the digital marketing for a specific business.

Activity 3 Pass criteria *P7*

P7 Explain and describe the benefits and drawbacks of using both a digital marketing agency and an advertising agency for a specific marketing campaign. These benefits and drawbacks must be applied to the real examples you have given.

TOP TIPS
- ✔ Make sure you describe a specific marketing campaign.
- ✔ Ensure that the marketing campaigns and businesses you select fully complement the assessment criteria.
- ✔ Research the digital marketing agencies and advertising agencies that the businesses use, so you are more aware of their specialities. You could do this by going to an agency's website and finding its list of clients.

LO5 Be able to plan marketing campaigns *P8 M3*

 GETTING STARTED

(10 minutes)

A new business wants to plan a marketing campaign. Write down a list of the key points it should consider when planning this campaign.

5.1 How to plan a marketing campaign

From the market stallholder selling fresh fruit and vegetables to the large global organisation, all businesses will promote themselves in some way. The basis for devising a marketing campaign will be different for each business. An example of a local cheese producer is used here to illustrate the approaches.

There are three main stages when planning a marketing campaign; these include the following.

Rationale for a marketing campaign

The first stage involves the business considering the following factors.

- The *marketing aims*, which detail the main reasons for the campaign, such as informing a specific target audience about changes to a product. The local cheese maker could decide to promote a new flavour of cheese and/or promote the business in general.

- The *marketing objectives* of the marketing campaign, which should ideally be SMART, and informative and persuasive to the target market. This includes the metrics that will be used, e.g. the number of clicks from a link in an email, the number of new subscribers to a web service or the percentage increase of sales via a website.

- The *available resources* such as the allocated budget, time frames, the location and the option of contracting an agency to facilitate the campaign. The local cheese maker may want to investigate attending local and national 'excellence' events, farmers' markets and/or food shows, to generate an interest in the brand.

- The *unique selling point (USP)* of the product or service that is to be featured in the marketing campaign – what makes it special? The cheese maker will want to make it clear to its target market what is different about its cheeses, e.g. locally produced or organic.

- Clarification of *target market*, as well as the segment within the marketing campaign to ensure that the product or service is relevant to them and the marketing channels used are appropriate.

All these considerations will need to be justified. A business may put together a detailed report to present to management, which could then consider the various options. In this situation, an **executive summary** would include the main justifications for the campaign, including measurable outcomes.

> ## KEY TERM
>
> **Executive summary** – a section at the start of a large business document that briefly summarises the main points made within the main report, to ensure that readers get an insight into the content (a summary) of the document without having to read it all immediately.

Decisions to be made for a marketing campaign

The second stage will involve important decisions relating to the following points.

- Identifying appropriate marketing techniques by considering the most appropriate marketing mix, timescales involved, etc.
- Choice of effective channels, taking into consideration how a particular channel will help the business reach its main aims and objectives, devised and linking to the first stage of this process. The local cheese maker could use taste testing at events as an effective channel to help aid the marketing campaign. It may (with permission) film customers trying the cheese with positive reactions and show the videos on YouTube or its own website.
- The content to portray through the key messages, ensuring they are clear, interesting and easy to adapt if required.
- The style that will be adopted throughout the campaign and, if successful, in the future – for example, recognition of a brand by creating a consistent visual identity via the logo, colours, font, style, phrases and key words or tone of voice.

> ## INDEPENDENT RESEARCH ACTIVITY
>
> **(1 hour)**
>
> Plan a small marketing campaign for the local cheese maker taking into account the rationale and decisions that they business should make in order for the campaign to be successful. Be prepared to justify all the decisions you make.

How to monitor a marketing campaign

The third and final stage is monitoring and analysing the impact that the campaign has had. This could be by measuring:

- consumer reaction and involvement, e.g. level of response on social media, use of hashtags, number of clickthroughs from emails, proportional increase in website traffic, number of customer enquiries, level of new customers, level of returning customers
- financial data, e.g. return on investment, proportional increase in sales, profits before and after the marketing campaign.

> ## KNOW IT
>
> 1 Describe the three main stages of planning a successful marketing campaign.
> 2 Why may a business choose to monitor its marketing campaign?

LO5 assessment activities

Below are suggested assessment activities that have been directly linked to the Pass and Merit criteria in LO5 to help with assignment preparation. These are followed by top tips on how to achieve the best results.

Activity 1 Pass criteria *P8*

P8 Select a product or service from a specific business and plan a successful marketing campaign that clearly considers all the various elements of a marketing campaign.

Activity 2 Merit criteria *M3*

M3 Provide clear justifications of the various elements detailed in your suggested marketing campaign for the previous question.

> ## TOP TIPS
>
> ✔ Ensure that you investigate a variety of different marketing campaigns to ensure that you have good knowledge that can be explained and shown in your work.
> ✔ Ensure that the marketing campaigns that are selected fully complement the assessment criteria.
> ✔ Investigate a variety of different businesses that provide a mixture of both products and services so that you can identify any differences between the campaigns.

L06 Be able to pitch planned marketing campaigns *P9 P10*

GETTING STARTED

(15 minutes)

Individually, you have one minute to think of an existing product.

Now change that existing product slightly. It could be the flavour of a chocolate bar, the colour of the stripe on a trainer, the away kit of a football team, the features on a game or app.

Write down the changes, then plan and deliver a one-minute pitch to your neighbour based on your new and improved product. Will they want it? Would they invest in it? It's up to you!

Review your ideas and feed back to the rest of the class.

6.1 How to deliver a pitch for a marketing campaign

Before a marketing campaign, information often needs to be 'pitched' to an audience, such as the client or a senior manager. Relevant points of the campaign would be selected, such as its potential costs, aims, objectives, channels, duration of campaign and target audience.

How to adapt a campaign pitch for different audiences

The audience for the pitch could be internal to the business (for example, managers who need to be convinced that the campaign is a good idea) or external (for example, the design company that will create the artwork for the campaign). A pitch needs to be altered and adapted according to the audience – a finance director wouldn't necessarily be interested in the colours that will be used, but designers would need to know this information rather than the overall cost of the campaign.

The skills required to deliver a pitch

▲ **Figure 7.4** Could you deliver a pitch for a marketing campaign?

Delivering a pitch requires specialist skills if it is to be effective and, as a consequence, it does not suit everyone. Those involved in the pitch should have good verbal and non-verbal communication skills, as well as a variety of different aids to pitch effectively to an audience.

- *Verbal communication skills* are the words chosen, how a person projects their voice, the tone and clarity of what they are saying, and the volume and pace of their communication method. Verbal skills also include how a person responds to questions. Do they remain professional or appear agitated? How do they react if they are unsure of the answer? Do they freeze? Do they blush with embarrassment?
- *Non-verbal communication skills* are the body language that we display through gestures, the eye contact that we may or may not give, as well as the facial expressions that we cannot always hide. Non-verbal communication skills can give the audience additional visual information.
- *Visual aids* are crucial, e.g. presentation software, handouts and memory aids. Consideration must be given to the preparation and notes required to design the correct aids for the pitch. It might even be appropriate to show examples of the product, the campaign design or creative ideas from similar campaigns (acknowledging the source). If specialist technology is required, ensure contingency plans are in place – for example, if such technology were to fail.

6.2 How to review a pitch for a marketing campaign

The outcomes of the pitch can be reviewed – for example, by noting how the audience reacts during and after the pitch, or how effectively the messages were portrayed. Pitching to an audience is a pressurised role. Consider the people who take part in TV shows like *Dragon's Den*. The pitch they deliver can result in an investment, but equally can result in nothing.

A business will need to gather feedback from the audience, which can be completed by several means:

- instant verbal feedback
- feedback in the form of written or online questionnaires
- reviewing the orders that may be taken as a result of the pitch
- the level of interest generated
- subsequent enquiries
- interpretation of the messages given from the pitch via a question-and-answer session
- increased or decreased profit margins.

The team may decide also to identify any improvements to the pitch so that, if subsequent pitches are required in future, the messages can be altered and changed to make the pitch better and fit for purpose. These may focus on:

- the way in which the messages were presented
- a simpler format
- bolder statements being used.

INDIVIDUAL ACTIVITY

(1 hour)

1 Watch some clips of candidates from the BBC One show *The Apprentice* pitching products and services.
2 Write a list of both positive and negative aspects of each pitch.
3 Using this information, formulate some advice that could be given to someone who is about to pitch to an audience.

KNOW IT

1 Write a definition of non-verbal communication skills.
2 What skills are required to deliver a successful pitch?
3 What could be the consequences for a business of a positive pitch?
4 What could be the consequences for a business of a negative pitch?

LO6 assessment activities

Below are suggested assessment activities that have been directly linked to the Pass criteria in LO6 to help with assignment preparation. These are followed by top tips on how to achieve the best results.

Activity 1 Pass criteria *P9*

P9 Select a business that produces a product or service. Prepare and deliver a pitch to a given audience, ensuring that a variety of verbal, non-verbal and presentation aids are used within your pitch for a specific marketing campaign.

Activity 2 Pass criteria *P10*

P10 Complete a review of a pitch that you have either witnessed or participated in for a marketing campaign, offering some constructive recommendations in order for the pitch to be improved.

From feedback about your own pitch (for P9), write a short report detailing how you can improve your pitch.

TOP TIPS

- ✔ Ensure that suitable businesses with specific products or services fully complement the requirements of the assessment criteria.
- ✔ Make sure that any recommendations for improvements are achievable.

Read about it

Marketing Communications, by John Egan, Sage, 2014

Marketing: The Business Mindset You Need to Grow Your Business, Increase Sales, Make More Money and Expand Your Brand, by John Robert, Createspace, 2014

Online Marketing Strategy: How to Get the Best Results in Your Marketing Campaigns (e-book), by Jose Vergara, 2015

The Best Digital Marketing Campaigns in the World: Mastering the Art of Customer Engagement, by Damian Ryan and Calvin Jones, Kogan Page, 2011

The Best Digital Marketing Campaigns in the World II, by Damian Ryan, Kogan Page, 2014

Useful websites

Watchdog: www.bbc.co.uk/programmes/p00zkz1k/clips

Which?: www.which.co.uk

Accounting concepts

ABOUT THIS UNIT

All businesses require accurate bookkeeping records to ensure they meet the requirements of stakeholders. This unit is intended to give you vital skills and knowledge of maintaining business records, using books of original entry and double-entry bookkeeping; this will enable you to progress to the other units in the accounting pathway.

This unit will give you an introduction to the foundations of business accounting. It will help you to gain essential skills in, and knowledge of, the purposes of accounting, and the accounting procedures used to produce final accounts. You will consider the reasons for keeping accurate financial records, and the importance of updating cash books and preparing bank reconciliation statements.

The aim is to prepare you for work, in areas of business and accounting that will require accurate recording of financial transactions. The unit will ensure you are familiar with the basic requirements of International Accounting Standards (IASs).

LEARNING OUTCOMES

The topics, activities and suggested reading in this unit will help you to:

1 understand why businesses keep accurate accounting records
2 be able to use the accounting equation
3 be able to prepare the principal documents in business transactions
4 be able to use basic double-entry bookkeeping to prepare a trial balance
5 be able to reconcile a cash book with a bank statement

How will I be assessed?

You will be assessed through a series of assignments and tasks set and marked by your tutor.

How will I be graded?

You will be graded using the following criteria, which are in the specification produced by OCR for the qualification.

Learning outcome	Pass	Merit	Distinction
You will:	**To achieve a Pass you must demonstrate that you have met all the pass assessment criteria**	**To achieve a Merit you must demonstrate that you have met all the pass and merit assessment criteria**	**To achieve a Distinction you must demonstrate that you have met all the pass, merit and distinction assessment criteria**
1 Understand why businesses keep accurate accounting records	**P1** Explain the reasons for keeping accounting records in business organisations		
	P2 Describe the accounting record requirements of at least three different stakeholders for a specific organisation	**M1** Explain how the failure to keep accurate accounting records could impact on stakeholders with reference to a specific business	**D1** Assess how a specific business applies an accounting concept or policy to their accounting records
2 Be able to use the accounting equation	**P3** Calculate the value of assets, liabilities and capital from given data		
3 Be able to prepare the principal documents in business transactions	**P4** Prepare principal source documents for given business transactions	**M2** Compare the accounting procedures for cash and trade discounts	**D2** Evaluate the use of cash and trade discounts in more than one business organisation
	P5 Produce a three-column cash book from given financial information		
4 Be able to use basic double-entry bookkeeping to prepare a trial balance	**P6** Explain the need for subdivisions of the ledger		
	P7 Explain the difference between capital and revenue items of expenditure and income	**M3** Analyse the effect of the incorrect placement of capital and revenue items of income and expenditure	
	P8 Prepare ledger accounts and accompanying trail balances for business transactions		
5 Be able to reconcile a cash book with a bank statement	**P9** Update a completed cash book from given data		
	P10 Produce a bank reconciliation statement		
	P11 Describe payment methods for business transactions		
	P12 Explain the purpose of a bank statement and the need for a bank reconciliation statement		

LO1 Understand why businesses keep accurate accounting records

P1 P2 M1 D1

(10 minutes)

Working in pairs, write a definition of the word 'accounting'. Be prepared to share your definition with the rest of the group.

1.1 Purposes of accounting

What is accounting?

The American Accounting Association defines accounting as:

> the process of identifying, measuring, recording and communicating the required information relating to the economic events of an organisation to the interested users of such information.

Source: American Accounting Association, *A Statement of Basic Accounting Theory* (Evanston, IL: American Accounting Association, 1966), p. 1

Accounting affects all people in their personal lives, as well as large businesses. One good example is that students going away to university must learn to budget. This is a form of accounting.

Accounting involves:

- the recording of data, e.g. all goods bought and sold
- classifying and summarising the data that is collected
- communicating the information to various people.

All businesses have an obligation to keep financial records and prepare accounts each year. The **accounting cycle** (Figure 11.1) is the collective process of recording and processing the accounting events of a business. The process will be continually repeated, hence the term accounting cycle.

KEY TERM

Accounting cycle – the process of recording and processing the accounting events within a business.

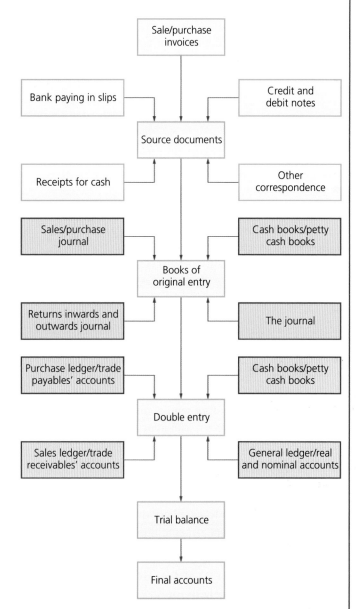

▲ **Figure 11.1** The accounting cycle

To record transactions

The successful operation and running of a business requires accurate and up-to-date business records. The owner or the finance department (depending on the size) of the business is required to record all of the money coming into the business and all of the money that is paid out of the business.

Transactions will be recorded by completing:

- source documents – an original record that contains the details of all transactions entered in the accounting system, e.g. invoices, paying-in slips, receipts

- double-entry accounts – a system of bookkeeping for which every transaction has one debit entry and one credit entry (see LO4, page 198)
- ledgers – a book or collection of accounting/financial information.

If the business does not keep these records, it is likely that it will:

- forget to chase payments from customers
- be charged interest/fees for late payments to suppliers
- have poor cash flow management.

If the business has insufficient records of its transactions, it will be extremely difficult for it to produce financial statements, and then monitor, manage and measure their performance.

Businesses record transactions for a number of reasons:

- to provide a permanent record of all financial transactions from which financial accounts and management reports can be prepared
- to provide a means of controlling business assets and ensure there is sufficient information for decisions to be made
- to comply with statutory regulations and requirements, provide the government with information used in economic planning, and act as the basis for tax authorities to calculate business tax
- to provide owners who are not directly involved in the business with appropriate financial information
- to give information to suppliers and loan providers when businesses are seeking financial help.

To monitor, manage and measure business performance, and make appropriate decisions

Businesses will update their records on a regular basis. Depending on the number of transactions this could be daily, weekly or monthly. By checking these records, owners and managers are able to assess how the business is performing in relation to sales and expenses, and will be able to review its bank balance. Most businesses will prepare **forecasts** and budgets to monitor business performance. Corrective action can be implemented if necessary to manage the performance of the business. Reviewing up-to-date forecasts and budgets will allow owners and managers to make appropriate business decisions and set targets for the business as a whole.

KEY TERM

Forecast – a financial prediction or estimate.

At the end of a financial period – usually monthly, six-monthly or annually – a business will want to measure its performance. Businesses can use a range of different measures, including:

- liquidity – a business's ability to meet its short-term debts
- profitability – a business's ability to earn profit from all of its business activities
- efficiency – this measures the productivity of a business's assets.

Once a business has measured and reviewed its business performance, the management and owners will be able to make appropriate financial and operational decisions.

To provide information and communicate information internally and externally

Businesses require **financial information** in a format that is readable, understandable and useable to anyone who has a need to access it.

KEY TERM

Financial information – data and monetary information about an individual or business, e.g. account balances, credit card numbers, loan transactions.

In businesses, there are a wide range of stakeholders who require access to financial data. These will include employees, who require their salary and income tax details, a manager assessing sales income data or a shareholder who is deciding whether a business is a sound investment.

A public limited company has a legal duty to present its year-end accounts in a set format, distribute them to all shareholders and file a publicly available copy with Companies House.

PAIRS ACTIVITY

(30 minutes)

Consider the following list of stakeholders. For each stakeholder group, decide whether they are an internal or external stakeholder to a business.

Stakeholder groups:

- managers
- employees
- owners
- shareholders
- potential investors
- customers
- lenders
- suppliers.

Talk about the financial information that each group of stakeholders will be interested in. For example: government – external stakeholder – will be interested in profitability, tax liabilities and financial growth information for economic data.

1.2 Accounting requirements of various types of business organisations

Different types of businesses (see Unit 1, page 2) require different accounting processes and documents, as shown in Table 11.1.

Table 11.1 The accounting requirements of different types of business organisations

Type of business	Number of owners	Control	Examples	Accounting requirements
Sole trader	1	The sole trader	Plumbers Decorators Newsagents Builders	Income statement Statement of financial position
Partnership	2–20, except in the case of accountants and solicitors	The partners	Solicitors Architects Surveyors Estate agents Doctors' surgeries	Income statement **Appropriation account** Statement of financial position **Current accounts** **Capital accounts** – fluctuating or fixed
Private limited company	1–50	Shareholder(s)	Wide range of businesses in all sectors – primary, secondary and tertiary	Income statement Statement of financial position
Public limited company	2+	Shareholders	Tesco British Airways Nike Nokia Microsoft BP	**Annual report** that includes: • general corporate information • accounting policies • income statement • statement of financial position • statement of cash flows • notes to the financial statements • chairperson's and directors' reports • auditor's report
Third-sector organisations	No owners	Trustees	Charities Clubs Societies Associations	**Receipts and payments account** Income and expenditure account Bar/refreshments, etc. trading account Statement of financial position

---

🔑 KEY TERMS

Appropriation account – shows the distribution of net profit.

Capital and current accounts – used by partnerships, to record individual partners' day-to-day transactions and finance invested.

Annual report – a comprehensive report of a company's activities throughout the last year.

Receipts and payments account – a summarised cash book for a specific period, prepared by non-profit organisations at the year end.

1.3 Accounting concepts and policies

The financial accounts of a business should reflect a 'true and fair' view of its financial position. To ensure this occurs, accountants apply a series of rules known as accounting concepts.

There are two approaches when preparing any financial reports:

1 objectivity – using recognised methods and calculations that everyone in the accounting and business world will agree with

2 subjectivity – using your own methods even if no one else in the industry recognises or agrees to them.

Fundamental accounting concepts

These are the main accounting concepts that are used by all accountants when preparing business accounts (see Table 11.2).

Table 11.2 Fundamental accounting concepts

Concept	Explanation
Going concern	The assumption that a business will continue to trade in the foreseeable future
Consistency	This requires accountants, when faced with choice between different accounting techniques, not to change policies without good reason Examples include the valuation of inventory and the choice of depreciation method
Prudence	To recognise revenue or profit only when they are achieved When applying the concept of prudence, accountants usually look for the worst-case scenarios In applying the concept, profits will not be overstated and losses will be provided for as soon as they are recognised
Accruals/ matching	This determines when transactions should be entered into the accounts The concept ensures that revenues are matched to expenses in a particular accounting period Income and expenses are entered into the final accounts as they are earned or incurred, not when the money is received

Generally accepted concepts

These concepts are used and applied by most accountants when preparing business accounts (Table 11.3).

Table 11.3 General accounting concepts

Concept	Explanation
Materiality	Accountants should not spend time trying to accurately record items that are immaterial (not important)
Historical cost	A business asset should be recorded in the financial accounts at the cost when it was purchased, not its current value, because it is rare that two people will agree on the current value of an asset One problem of historical cost is that it ignores any increases in value due to inflation
Money measurement	This concept states that only transactions that can be expressed in monetary terms should be recorded in a business's accounts Items that cannot be valued in this way include the attitude of local residents to business plans, skills of a workforce and management competency
Realisation	Revenue should be recognised when the exchange of goods or services takes place Revenue (income) should not be inflated by sales that have not yet happened
Business entity	The financial affairs of a business should be completely separate from those of the owner
Dual aspect	Every transaction has two effects on accounts: one debit and one credit

GROUP ACTIVITY

(30 minutes)

Working in small groups, consider each of the scenarios (1–5) listed below and identify the accounting concept that applies from this list:

- business entity
- money measurement
- materiality
- going concern
- consistency.

Give a brief explanation of why it is being applied.

Scenarios

1 Mr Ahmed, who owns a small textile retail shop, has taken goods originally costing £500 from the shop for his own personal use.
2 Dora Delivery Services has good industrial relations and would like to record this in the final accounts at a value of £20,000.
3 Maclean Solicitors has purchased two doormats costing £5 each. They are expected to last for a number of years and the business thinks it should record them under **non-current assets** in the final accounts.
4 Prior to completing the final accounts for the local butcher's shop, the accountant has asked the owner, Mr Smith, to prove that his business is likely to continue for many years to come.
5 Mrs Failsworth, who owns a local garage, would like to change the depreciation method she uses for petrol pumps. The change of method will increase her net profit.

KEY TERM

Non-current assets – items acquired for use within the business that are likely to be used for a considerable amount of time (usually more than 12 months), e.g. motor vehicles, premises, machinery.

KNOW IT

1 Define the term 'accounting'.
2 State three purposes of accounting.
3 Name the four fundamental accounting concepts.
4 Define the prudence concept.
5 Explain the difference between 'subjectivity' and 'objectivity'.

LO1 assessment activities

Below are suggested assessment activities that have been directly linked to the Pass, Merit and Distinction criteria in LO1 to help with assignment preparation. These are followed by top tips on how to achieve the best results.

Activity 1 Pass criteria *P1* and *P2*

P1 P2 For the purpose of this activity you are working as an accounts administrator for BFC Accounting. You have been asked to prepare an information booklet that can be distributed to new customers who are unfamiliar with accounting processes and procedures. You can choose any format, style or presentation to produce the resource. However, it must include the following content:

- an explanation of why business organisations keep accounting records
- using a local supermarket as your case study example, provide a description of the accounting record requirements of the following stakeholders: employees, customers, bank.

TOP TIPS
✔ Check with your tutor that your choice of supermarket is suitable.
✔ Ensure the business choice gives you appropriate opportunities to meet the requirements of P2.
✔ Spend equal time and produce similar amounts of evidence for each of the pass criteria.

Activity 2 Merit criteria *M1* (in addition to *P1* and *P2*)

M1 Produce an additional page for your information booklet using your choice of supermarket. Explain how the failure to keep accounting records could impact on the supermarket's stakeholders.

TOP TIPS
✔ Ensure you focus on both the business and its stakeholders.
✔ Ensure you provide detailed evidence that meets the command verb 'explain'.

Activity 3 Distinction criteria *D1* (in addition to *P1 P2* and *M1*)

D1 Produce an additional page for your information booklet using your choice of supermarket as the case study. Assess how the supermarket you have studied applies the accounting concept of consistency to its accounting records.

TOP TIPS
✔ Ensure you understand the accounting concept of 'consistency'.
✔ If publicly available, it would be advisable to download a copy of the financial report.
✔ Give practical recommendations, with examples where appropriate.

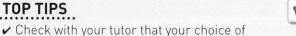

LO2 Be able to use the accounting equation *P3*

GETTING STARTED

(10 minutes)

Working individually, search on the internet for the formula for the accounting equation. Rearrange the formula into all of its different formats.

2.1 Principle of the accounting equation

The accounting equation recognises that the assets owned by the business are always equal to the claims against the business. It can be written like this:

Assets = Capital + Liabilities

For example, the total of all of the assets in a business (premises, equipment, cash, etc.) must total the amount of money invested by the owner (known as **capital** or **equity**) and any money that is owed to trade payables or loan providers (mortgage, loans etc.).

The statement of financial position is a formal way of showing the accounting equation. It simply lists all the assets that are owned by an organisation and all the **liabilities** that are owed by the organisation.

🔑 KEY TERMS

Capital/equity – how much a business is worth. It represents how much the owner(s) have invested in the business.

Liabilities – the debts owed by an organisation.

2.2 Calculations using the accounting equation

(10 minutes)

Using the accounting equation (Assets = Capital + Liabilities), complete Table 11.4. You will need to rearrange the formula to complete all of the sections.

Table 11.4

Non-current assets (£)	Current assets (£)	Amounts falling due after one year (£)	Amounts falling due within one year (£)	Capital/equity (£)
70,000	16,000	20,000	8,000	
	24,000	20,000	4,000	60,000
20,000	3,000	0	8,000	
55,000	9,000	15,000		45,000
30,000		20,000	10,000	15,000

(20 minutes)

1 Classify the following items as either assets or liabilities:

- office machinery
- trade receivables
- bank loan
- cash in hand
- delivery vehicles
- premises
- cash at bank
- motor vehicles
- inventory of goods
- trade payables
- bank overdraft
- fixtures and fittings.

2 Define the following terms, giving practical examples where appropriate:

a non-current assets
b current assets
c liabilities – amounts falling due after one year
d liabilities – amounts falling due within one year
e capital/equity.

3 Complete Table 11.5 by using the accounting equation.

Table 11.5

	Assets	Liabilities	Capital
	£	£	£
(i)	15,500	2,800	
(ii)	38,000	5,900	
(iii)	19,800		15,500
(iv)	18,600		17,450
(v)		7,300	29,200

4 Complete Table 11.6 by using the accounting equation.

Table 11.6

	Non-current assets	Current assets	Amounts falling due after one year	Amounts falling due within one year	Capital/equity
	£	£	£	£	£
(i)	80,000	26,000	10,000	18,000	
(ii)		34,000	20,000	6,000	70,000
(iii)	25,000	6,000	2,000	8,000	
(iv)	45,000	19,000	5,000		45,000
(v)	25,000		10,000	5,000	25,000

5 Simon is opening a new business. He has purchased a delivery van for £3,000, a retail shop for £50,000 and a stock of goods for £2,000. Simon was unable to pay for all of the stock and owes the supplier £700. A friend, Ahmed, has lent Simon £5,000. After all of these transactions, Simon has £500 cash in hand and £1,500 cash in the bank. Using the accounting equation, calculate the opening capital of Simon's business.

LO2 assessment activity

Below is a suggested assessment activity that has been directly linked to the Pass criteria in LO2 to help with assignment preparation. This is followed by top tips on how to achieve the best results.

Activity 1 Pass criteria *P3*

You will need to be confident in using the accounting equation to calculate assets, liabilities and capital/equity.

P3 Using the accounting equation, complete the following numerical task.

Ibrahim launched a new retail business on 1 April. Before opening, Ibrahim bought:

- fixtures and fittings £2,000
- motor van £3,500
- stock of good £5,000

Ibrahim paid in full for the fixtures and fittings and motor van, however he still owes £1,500 for some of the goods.

Jessica lent Ibrahim £3,000 for a non-slip floor covering for the shop.

After all of these transactions, Ibrahim has £2,800 cash in the bank and £100 cash in hand.

1 Calculate Ibrahim's total assets.
2 Calculate Ibrahim's total liabilities.
3 Using the accounting equation, calculate the opening capital of Ibrahim's business.

> **TOP TIPS**
> ✔ You can use a calculator, but should write down all workings.
> ✔ Practise a range of questions using the accounting equation prior to attempting the assessment task.

LO3 Be able to prepare the principal documents in business transactions *P4 P5 M2 D2*

> **GETTING STARTED**
>
> **(15 minutes)**
>
> Working in a small group, produce a spider diagram identifying as many source documents as you can in five minutes. Share your ideas with another group.

3.1 Purpose and completion of the principal source documents in business transactions

Source documents are original records that contain the details to verify the financial transactions that are entered into the internal accounting system of a business. They provide evidence that a financial transaction has taken place.

> **KEY TERMS**
>
> **Source document** – a document or form designed to provide details of a business transaction.
> **Day books/journals** – account books from which financial transactions are transferred to the ledgers.

A business requires source documents:

- to provide evidence that transactions have happened
- to record business transactions and complete **day books/journals**, ledgers, etc.
- to trace the movement of goods, e.g. goods purchased from suppliers
- to prepare the final accounts and calculate profitability
- to calculate tax liabilities
- for auditing purposes.

Principal source documents

- Sales invoice – records the details of goods and services sold and the amount owing by the customer. The customer is given the original copy and the business keeps a duplicate copy.
- Purchase invoice – records the details of the goods/services purchased and the amount owing to the supplier.
- Credit note – used by a supplier for goods returned or to correct an overcharge in an invoice. A debit note would be issued in the case of an undercharge in an invoice.
- Statement of account – issued by suppliers, shows all transactions between the supplier and the customer over a period of time.
- Cheque – records the amount paid on a particular numbered cheque to the payee. The business will retain the cheque stub for its records.

- Receipt – acknowledges money received from customers or paid to suppliers.
- Petty cash voucher – acts as evidence of small cash payments to another person or business.
- Bank statement – summarises the cash movement through the business bank account.
- Payroll records – verify payments made to employees (wages and salaries); may include timesheets for workers.
- Credit sales – sales in which payment will be made some time in the future, either in small regular payments or as a single lump sum. The buyer owns the goods being sold from the time the arrangement is made.

Source documents usually relate to a particular business activity, as shown in Table 11.7.

Table 11.7 Examples of how source documents relate to different activities

Business activity	Source document
Cash sales	Cash receipt Cash register records (till rolls) Bank statement Bank deposit slip
Cash purchases	Cheque stub ATM receipt Bank statement Payroll records (if wages are paid in cash)
Petty cash payments	Petty cash voucher Cash receipts
Credit sales	Sales invoice Business debit note
Credit purchases	Purchase invoice Statement of account Supplier debit note Credit card statement
Purchase returns	Supplier credit note
Sales returns	Business credit note

3.2 Purpose, effect and recording of cash and trade discounts

Cash discounts

Cash discounts may be offered by a business for early payment by a customer. Usually a business gives 30 days' credit, with an incentive to pay earlier. Payment does not necessarily have to be in cash, but could be by bank transfer or cheque. Cash discounts are recorded in the ledger accounts. In order to record cash discounts allowed and cash discounts received, a business will need to produce a three-column **cash book** rather than

a two-column cash book. In an income statement, a discount allowed is recorded as an expense and a discount received as an additional income.

> **🔑 KEY TERMS**
>
> **Cash discount** – a reduction in the amount owing to a supplier when the customer pays the amount owing before the due date.
>
> **Cash book** – a book in which receipts and payments are recorded.
>
> **Trade discount** – a reduction in price charged by suppliers when a trade customer buys in bulk.

Trade discounts

Trade discounts are allowed by one business to another. A lower price is offered compared to the price charged to the general public. Trade discounts are not shown in the ledger accounts (the net price is recorded), represent a deduction from the list price and can be shown in the journal.

3.3 Purpose and preparation of day books and journals

The financial information from the source documents is transferred into books of prime entry. These books record certain types of transaction before they become part of the double-entry bookkeeping system (see page 198). The most commonly used books of prime entry are shown in Table 11.8.

Table 11.8 Books of prime entry and their purpose

Book of prime entry	Transaction type recorded
Sales day book	Credit sales
Purchases day book	Credit purchases
Returns outwards day book	Returns of goods sold on credit
Returns inwards day book	Returns of goods bought on credit
Two-column cash book	All bank transactions
Three-column cash book	All bank transactions with discounts
Petty cash book	Small cash transactions
General journal	All transactions not recorded in any other book

The totals of the transactions from the books of prime entry are recorded in double-entry format in the accounting ledgers of a business.

Sales day book

A sales day book is produced from the duplicate copies of sales invoices and debit notes that a business has sent to its customers. Only credit sales are recorded in the sales day book – cash sales are recorded in the cash book. The headings used in a sales day book are shown in Table 11.9.

Table 11.9 Headings in a sales day book

Date	Narrative	Invoice number	Total amount

Purchase day book

A purchase day book is produced from the sales invoice received by a business from the supplier of the goods on credit. The headings used in a purchase day book are shown in Table 11.10.

Table 11.10 Headings in a purchase day book

Date	Narrative	Invoice number	Total amount

Returns outwards day book

A returns outwards day book (also known as a purchases returns day book) records any goods that a business has returned to the supplier. The information to complete the day book is found on the credit note that the business will have received. The headings used in a returns outwards day book are shown in Table 11.11.

Table 11.11 Headings in a returns outwards day book

Date	Narrative	Credit note number	Total amount

Returns inwards day book

A returns inwards day book (also known as a sales returns day book) records all of the goods that have been returned by customers. The information to complete the day book is found on the credit note sent to each customer. The headings used in a returns inwards day book are shown in Table 11.12.

Table 11.12 Headings in a returns inwards day book

Date	Narrative	Credit note number	Total amount

General journal

During the day-to-day running of a business, not all financial transactions can be categorised for the day books. A business uses a general journal to record all transactions that cannot be recorded in its other day books. Items that typically appear in the general journal include:

1 the purchase and sale of non-current assets (e.g. motor vehicles, fixtures and fittings)
2 drawings (money taken out of the business by the owner(s))
3 additional capital put into the business by the owner(s)
4 accounting adjustments.

The headings used in a general journal are shown in Table 11.13.

Table 11.13 Headings in a general journal

Date	Narrative	Debit	Credit

INDIVIDUAL ACTIVITY

(15 minutes)

Amina sells perfumes from a retail shop in the south of England. Listed below are three of her recent business transactions.

1 Amina sold perfume to a customer for £30 cash.
2 Amina purchased a range of perfumes for £900 from her credit supplier.
3 Amina returned perfume, costing £250, which she had bought for resale, to her credit supplier.

Identify the source document and book of prime entry that would be used for each of the three transactions.

3.4 How to record cash and petty cash transactions

Preparation of three-column cash books, petty cash books and reconciliation of imprest systems

A cash book is the cash ledger account and bank ledger account of a business combined into one ledger account. A three-column cash book has discount, cash and bank columns.

Three-column cash book example

Table 11.14 Extract from a three-column cash book

Date	Narrative	Discount	Cash	Bank	Date	Narrative	Discount	Cash	Bank
		£	£	£			£	£	£
1 Jan	Bal b/d		200	3,000	3 Jan	Insurance		250	
5 Jan	I Kay	7		273	5 Jan	Rent			350
7 Jan	Sales			250	6 Jan	Rates			400
8 Jan	H Iqbal		430		7 Jan	Wages			280
					8 Jan	F Smith	23		437
Any money received is entered on the left-hand side of the cash book, known technically as the debit side of the account					Any money paid out is entered on the right-hand side of the cash book, known as the credit side of the account				

It is possible to have a closing balance that is a debit balance for the cash account and a credit balance for the bank account. It is impossible for a business to have a credit balance for the cash account (no business has a negative amount of cash). A credit balance for the bank account implies that the business is using an overdraft facility at the bank.

Cash discounts are recorded in a three-column cash book. Two types of cash discount are recorded in the ledger accounts:

1 **discounts allowed** are allowances given to a customer when they settle accounts within a specified time; they are entered on the debit side of the cash book
2 **discounts received** are the benefits received from suppliers when the business pays its bills within a specified time; they are entered on the credit side of the cash book.

> 🔑 **KEY TERMS**
>
> **Discount allowed** – a discount a business offers to a customer when it settles its bills promptly.
>
> **Discount received** – a discount a customer receives from a supplier for settling their bills promptly.

Petty cash book

Many businesses keep a separate cash book and **petty cash** book. The petty cash book is used for transactions that involve only small amounts of money. Examples of petty cash transactions include:

● petrol costs
● postage
● stationery
● refreshments
● bus fares.

> 🔑 **KEY TERM**
>
> **Petty cash** – a small amount of cash held in a business to purchase minor items (e.g. stationery, coffee) reducing the need to write a cheque or pay on credit.

Businesses prefer not to enter these small transactions in the cash book as they 'clutter up' the financial details. They usually ask a junior member of staff to take responsibility for the petty cash book, allowing more senior accounting staff to deal with the main cash book. The monthly totals from a petty cash book are transferred into the main cash book.

The member of staff who is responsible for the petty cash will hold a 'float'. This is an amount of money (cash) that is given to the person responsible at the start of the month (or other accounting period). This 'float' is used to pay employees small amounts of money when they have incurred an expenditure on behalf of the business. In most cases the employee needs to fill in a petty cash voucher and provide a receipt or other documentary evidence.

Petty cash vouchers will include:

● details of the expenditure
● amount spent (including VAT)
● signature of the employee claiming the money
● signature of the person authorising the payment
● petty cash voucher number for referencing details.

For most businesses there is a petty cash limit – for any claim over the limit a more senior accounts manager will have to authorise the transaction, and the money may be paid by cheque or direct into a bank account rather than in cash.

Imprest system

At the beginning of a month (or other suitable time period), the petty cashier is given a set amount of money known as the float. During the month (or other time period) the petty cashier will pay expenses out of this money in accordance with the business policies.

At the end of the period, the amount of money that has been spent will be added up and reconciled with the petty cash vouchers. This means that there must be vouchers for all of the money that has been handed out by the petty cashier. The petty cashier will then ask the cashier for further money to reimburse the float and return it to the original amount at the start of the month, known as the **imprest** amount.

> **KEY TERM**
>
> **Imprest system** – a form of financial accounting system, most commonly used in the petty cash system.

Example of the Imprest system

Date	Details	£
December 1	Float received from the cashier	200.00
December 31	Amount spent during the month	130.00
December 31	Balance of cash in hand	70.00
January 1	Amount of money received from cashier to restore the float to original amount	130.00
January 1	Cash at start of January, i.e. Imprest amount	200.00

Petty cash book format

An example of a petty cash book format is given in Table 11.15. These categories will vary depending on the type of business.

Table 11.15 Sample headings from a petty cash book

Receipts	Reference	Date	Details	Voucher no.	Total	Travel	Stationery	Cleaning	Postage

---

KNOW IT

1 Name five source documents.
2 Explain the difference between cash and trade discounts.
3 Explain the difference between a cash book and a petty cash book.
4 Describe the use of an imprest system.
5 Name three books of prime entry.

LO3 assessment activities

Below are suggested assessment activities that have been directly linked to the Pass, Merit and Distinction criteria in LO3 to help with assignment preparation. These are followed by top tips on how to achieve the best results.

Activity 1 Pass criteria *P4*

P4 For the purpose of this criteria, you are to use your school or college as the business case study. The school or college is planning to purchase a range of stationery from a retailer of your choice.

Design and complete an order form for your school or college to send to the stationery retailer. Based on the details of the order form, design and prepare the sales invoice that the retailer will return to your school or college with the goods.

Following the delivery of the stationery, you are unhappy with one of the items. Prepare the credit note that the retailer would return to your school or college.

Activity 2 Pass criteria *P5*

P5 Thomas runs a small retail outlet selling a range of stationery items to businesses and local individuals. He has provided the details in Table 11.16 about his financial transactions for the month of April.

Table 11.16 Thomas's transactions in April

Date	Transactions
April 1	Balances brought forward from the month of March: Cash £115 Bank £390
April 2	Thomas paid trade payables by cheque: £540 to P John £120 to T Makda – this total is before receiving a 5% discount
April 9	Thomas made cash sales of £699
April 16	Thomas paid £500 cash into the business bank account
April 17	Thomas received a number of cheques from his customers; in all cases the customer had been allowed a 2.5% discount W Wall £264 L Oakdale £360 C Ahmed £120
April 18	Thomas made cash purchases of £78
April 20	Thomas paid his landlord rent by cheque £560
April 21	Thomas withdrew £200 cash from the business bank account for his own use
April 25	Thomas received commission by cheque of £64

Using the information above for the month of April, produce a three-column cash book.

The cash book should be balanced off at the end of the month.

TOP TIPS

✔ You can choose whether to hand-write or type up your accounting documents.
✔ You should practise a range of questions prior to attempting the assessment task.
✔ You can refer to the documents in this unit to assist with the layout of financial documents.

Activity 3 Merit criteria *M2*

M2 Thomas has asked for your help. Compose an email to him that compares the accounting procedures for cash and trade discounts.

TOP TIP

✔ If possible, send your email in appropriate business style to your assessor or tutor.

Activity 4 Distinction criteria *D2*

D2 Choose two local business organisations that offer customers cash and trade discounts. Evaluate the use of these discounts in the two businesses.

TOP TIPS

✔ Your tutor should confirm your choice of businesses.
✔ It may be good practice for the tutor to select two businesses and arrange a trip or speaker to prepare the learners to complete the task.

LO4 Be able to use basic double-entry bookkeeping to prepare a trial balance *P6 P7 P8 M3*

GETTING STARTED

(15 minutes)

Thinking about a luxury restaurant, similar to the one in Figure 11.3, make a list of all of the types of income and expenditure that such a business may incur.

▲ **Figure 11.2** What might be the income and expenditure of a restaurant like this?

4.1 Double-entry bookkeeping

Double-entry bookkeeping has been used for hundreds of years. It has substantial benefits as it allows accountants to assess the accuracy of accounting records.

🔑 KEY TERM

Double-entry bookkeeping – records based on the assumption that every financial business transaction has opposite effects on two different accounts: one debit and one credit.

For every transaction recorded in the books there are two entries – one is a decrease and one is an increase. It is from here that the term double-entry bookkeeping is derived.

Remember, double-entry bookkeeping is much easier to explain in practice than in theory.

Consider the purchase of a car (see Figure 11.3).

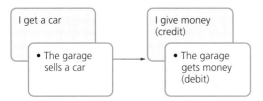

▲ **Figure 11.3** Buying a car involves debits and credits

Irrespective of whether you are completing the accounts of the garage selling the car or the person buying the car, there are two parts to every transaction.

These transactions are then transferred to a double-entry accounting system.

Preparing ledger accounts

Dr.	Name of account				Cr.
Date	Narrative	£	Date	Narrative	£

▲ **Figure 11.4** Format for a 'T' account (or ledger account)

Table 11.17 Should you record the transaction as a credit or debit?

ACCOUNTS	TO RECORD	ENTRY IN THE ACCOUNT
ASSETS	INCREASE	Debit
	DECREASE	Credit
LIABILITIES	INCREASE	Credit
	DECREASE	Debit
CAPITAL	INCREASE	Credit
	DECREASE	Debit

Assets example

When a business buys a second-hand motor vehicle for £500 in cash, two things have happened:

1 the amount of the business's motor vehicle account has *increased* by £500 (Figure 11.5)
2 the amount of cash in the business's cash account has *decreased* by £500 (Figure 11.6).

Dr.	Motor vehicle				Cr.
Date	Narrative	£	Date	Narrative	£
	Cash				
		500			

▲ **Figure 11.5**

Dr.	Cash				Cr.
Date	Narrative	£	Date	Narrative	£
				Motor vehicle	
					500

▲ **Figure 11.6**

Liabilities example

When a business buys equipment for £1,000 on credit from Berry Ltd, two things have happened:

1 the amount of the business's equipment account has *increased* by £1,000 (Figure 11.7)
2 the amount owed to Berry Ltd (a liability) has *increased* by £1,000 (Figure 11.8).

Capital example

When a business owner starts their business with £15,000 in cash, two things will have happened:

1 the amount of cash in the business's cash account has *increased* by £15,000 (Figure 11.9)
2 the amount of the business's capital (owed back to the owner has *increased* by £15,000 (Figure 11.10).

Dr.		Equipment				Cr.
Date	Narrative	£	Date	Narrative	£
	Berry Ltd				
		1,000			

▲ Figure 11.7

Dr.		Cash				Cr.
Date	Narrative	£	Date	Narrative	£
	Capital				
		15,000			

▲ Figure 11.9

Dr.		Berry Ltd				Cr.
Date	Narrative	£	Date	Narrative	£
				Equipment	
					1,000

▲ Figure 11.8

Dr.		Capital				Cr.
Date	Narrative	£	Date	Narrative	£
				Cash	
					15,000

▲ Figure 11.10

(30 minutes)

Using the above examples as a template, complete the double-entry accounts for the following transactions.

- The owner started their business with £20,000 in cash.
- The business bought a motor car for £5,800 in cash.
- The business bought office furniture for £2,000 on credit from H Grey.
- The owner introduced £5,000 extra cash as capital into the business.
- The business bought fixtures and fittings for £10,000 on credit from P Iqbal.

Balancing ledger accounts, making transfers and interpreting account balances

This requires you to follow the steps listed below.

1 Add up both sides to find out their total.
2 Place the highest total in the sum boxes on both sides level with each other.
3 Deduct the smaller total from the larger total to find the balance. There is usually a shortfall.
4 Now enter the balance on the side with the smallest total and call it 'bal c/d'.
5 Now enter the balance on the line below the totals on the opposite side and call this 'bal b/d'.

Balancing accounts example

Taking the combined accounts we used in the earlier example, we can practise balancing accounts.

Look at the accounts in Figure 11.11.

When interpreting these balances, all of the items will be transferred to the statement of financial position (as indicated by the words 'Balance c/d'). If the item were to be transferred to the income statement, the words 'Balance c/d' would be replaced with 'Income statement' or 'Profit/loss'.

For the purposes of this unit, you will need to consider only transfers to the statement of financial position.

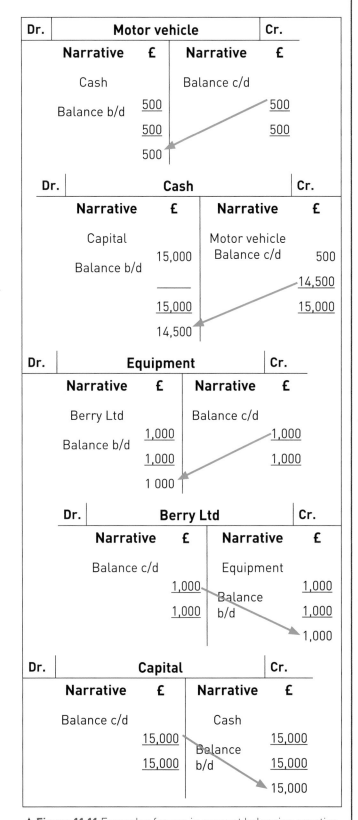

▲ **Figure 11.11** Examples for use in account balancing practice

The meanings of the transactions depicted in Figure 11.11 are explained in Table 11.18.

Table 11.18 Meaning of the transactions in Figure 11.11

Account	Balance	Meaning
Motor vehicle	£500 debit	The business owns motor vehicles that originally cost £500; these are categorised as non-current assets
Cash	£14,500 debit	The business has £14,500 cash in hand; this is a current asset
Equipment	£1,000 debit	The business owns items of equipment that originally cost £1,000; these are categorised as non-current assets
Berry Ltd	£1,000 credit	The business owes Berry Ltd £1,000; this will be categorised as part of the business liabilities (amounts falling due within one year)
Capital	£15,000 credit	The business owner has introduced or invested a total of £15,000; this is categorised as capital or equity

PAIRS ACTIVITY

(20 minutes)

Using the ledger accounts you prepared for the previous activity, balance the accounts you have prepared and interpret the balances.

4.2 To recognise the division of the ledger

As we have already learned, businesses keep separate books for different types of business transactions. These are known as day books, cash book, petty cash book and the general journal.

At the end of a period of time (day, week, month, etc.), the transactions in these books are totalled, and then transferred, or posted, from the books of prime entry into the ledgers using double-entry bookkeeping. A ledger is a collection of accounts that are of a similar type.

Traditionally, the business ledger was a leather-bound book that was split into three sections (subdivisions), as follows.

1 The *sales ledger* contains all of the business's customers' accounts. The ledger records the details of sales made and how much money is owed by the customer.

2 The *purchases ledger* contains all of the business's suppliers' accounts. The ledger records the details of purchases made and how much money is owed to the supplier.

All of the accounts in the sales and purchases ledgers are personal accounts and are given the names of the customers and suppliers.

3 The *nominal (general) ledger* contains impersonal accounts (e.g. rent, heat and light, wages and salaries, bank charges) and real accounts (e.g. premises, machinery, fixtures and fittings).

Today, very few businesses use leather-bound books, instead ledgers are completed and stored electronically.

4.3 Classification and treatment

Of expenditure and income

It is important to distinguish between capital and revenue items in order to determine which statement they will appear in.

- Capital items appear in the statement of financial position.
- Revenue items appear in the income statement.

Capital expenditure is money spent on acquiring, improving and adding value to non-current assets. This expenditure is usually a one-off payment. Capital expenditure is recorded in the statement of financial position under non-current assets.

Revenue expenditure is money spent on the day-to-day running of a business organisation. This expenditure is usually in the form of expenses and payments that have the potential to be repeated throughout the year. Revenue expenditure is recorded in the income statement under expenses.

KEY TERMS

Capital expenditure – business spending on non-current assets.

Revenue expenditure – business spending on regular or day-to-day items.

Table 11.19 shows some examples.

Table 11.19 Examples of the differences between capital and revenue expenditure

Example	Capital expenditure	Revenue expenditure
Motor vehicle	Purchase cost Delivery cost (to the business) Modifications to the motor vehicle Painting of the business logo onto the motor vehicle	Road tax Insurance Fuel Servicing Repairs Drivers' wages
Machinery	Purchase cost Delivery cost (to the factory) Installation Testing Initial staff training	Insurance Fuel/power Servicing Maintenance Repairs Replacement of worn-out parts Operating costs including wages

Of capital income and revenue income

Capital income is money that is raised by a business in order to purchase non-current assets. The assets purchased will be used to run the business and will not be resold. Examples of these assets include premises, plant and equipment, motor vehicles and office equipment.

Capital income is obtained by businesses from (for example):

- owners or partners in the case of a sole trader or partnership
- the issue and selling of shares in the case of private or public limited companies
- a loan
- a property mortgage.

> ### 🔑 KEY TERMS
>
> **Capital income** – money invested either in the initial setting up of the business or for the purchase of non-current assets.
>
> **Revenue income** – money that comes in to a business from its day-to-day operations.

Revenue income is money that is earned by a business in the process of carrying out its main operating activities. This income usually comes from (for example):

- the manufacture and sale of goods
- the reselling of goods that were bought with the purpose of resale, e.g. by supermarkets

- extraction and sale of raw material, e.g. mining or farming
- provision of services, e.g. dentists, solicitors and accountants.

INDIVIDUAL ACTIVITY

(20 minutes)

Categorise each of the 15 items below as one of the following: capital income, capital expenditure, revenue income, revenue expenditure.

1 Electricity
2 Capital invested by sole trader
3 Commission received
4 Rent received
5 Wages
6 Sales income
7 Money received from sale of shares
8 Legal costs involved with the purchase of a new factory
9 Loan received
10 Factory painting
11 Purchase of a vehicle
12 Extension to a factory
13 Further capital invested by partners
14 Cost of posting goods to customers
15 Purchase of stationery

4.4 To prepare a trial balance from balances in a ledger account at a given date

A **trial balance** is a statement of all debits and credits from a business's double-entry accounts. Any discrepancy in the totals will indicate an error in the bookkeeping process.

> ### 🔑 KEY TERM
>
> **Trial balance** – a statement of all debits and credits from a business's double-entry accounts.

Total debit entries = Total credit entries

The figures used to prepare the trial balance are the closing balances from the ledger accounts prepared by the business (see the example in Figure 11.12). Following the construction of the trial balance, the totals will be transferred to the income statement and statement of financial position.

	Debit	Credit
	£	£
Motor vehicle	500	
Cash	14,500	
Equipment	1,000	
Berry Ltd		1,000
Capital		15,000
	16,000	16,000

▲ **Figure 11.12** Example trial balance based on ledger accounts from the previous example

LO4 assessment activities

Below are suggested assessment activities that have been directly linked to the Pass and Merit criteria in LO4 to help with assignment preparation. These are followed by top tips on how to achieve the best results.

Activity 1 Pass criteria *P6* and *P7*

P6 P7 Brenda has set up a new retail business that incurs both capital and revenue expenditure, and maintains double-entry accounts. She has requested accounting advice and information from you. Prepare an information booklet or leaflet that:

● explains the need for subdivisions of the ledger
● explains, giving one example of each, the difference between capital and revenue expenditure and income.

Activity 2 Pass criteria *P8*

E Wing has provided the following financial information:

● she started her business with £30,000 in cash
● the business bought a motor van for £7,800 in cash
● the business bought shop fixtures for £5,000 on credit from S Singh

LO5 Be able to reconcile a cash book with a bank statement *P9 P10 P11 P12*

GETTING STARTED

(10 minutes)

Working in pairs, make a list of all of the items you are likely to see on a bank statement.

(20 minutes)

Using the ledger accounts you prepared for the previous activity, prepare a trial balance based on the closing balances.

KNOW IT

1 Explain the difference between capital and revenue expenditure.
2 Give five examples of revenue expenditure.
3 Explain the use of a sales ledger.
4 Describe the use of a trial balance.
5 Explain the concept of dual aspect.

● E Wing introduced £5,000 extra cash as capital into the business
● the business bought office equipment for £3,500 on credit from Ismail Supplies.

P8 Using the information provided above, prepare ledger accounts and accompanying trial balances for business transactions.

TOP TIPS

✔ Use either a manual or computerised method to prepare your accounting documents.
✔ Practise a range of questions prior to attempting the assessment task.

Activity 3 Merit criteria *M3*

M3 Advise E Wing on the effect of the incorrect placement of capital and revenue items of income and expenditure. Your analysis should include practical examples to illustrate your written work.

TOP TIP

✔ Try to use a range of evidence types to complete the task, e.g. a business report, a discussion with your assessor or tutor, or a presentation.

5.1 Methods of payment and receipt of money

There are many ways to pay and receive money – some are physical and others are electronic (Table 11.20).

Table 11.20 Methods of payment and receipt of money

Method	Description	Advantages	Disadvantages
Cash	Notes and coins.	Payment and receipt is immediate Ideal and convenient for small purchases Can be reused for other transactions instantly	Has to be counted Can be stolen so has to be stored securely
Cheques	A paper-based form of payment that is due to be phased out in the UK The cheque is a promise to pay the amount stated; it has to be presented to a bank to obtain payment; this usually takes three working days – known as the time taken for the cheque to 'clear'	Safer than cash More secure for larger amounts of money	It has to be taken to a bank, which can be inconvenient Takes time for the money to be available The cheque could be returned if there are insufficient funds available Errors in writing the cheque will result in it being refused by the bank
Debit card	A card issued by a bank and connected to a current account When a customer hands over a debit card, the receiver will either process the card 'contactless' or via 'chip and pin'; contactless cards have a financial spending limit for each transaction – this amount varies depending on the card provider; chip and pin cards do not have a spending limit The amount will be transferred to the receiver's bank account within three days	A business is guaranteed the payment due Customers can use a debit card for telephone and internet purchases as well as in shops More secure than cash	Takes time for the money to be available The bank will charge a fee to the business for using the service There is a danger of fraud
Credit card	A significant difference to a debit card is that the money does not come out of a current account and the account holder is borrowing the money Interest will be charged on outstanding balances	Offers protection from fraud Cash-back and reward schemes are available A business is guaranteed the payment due Customers can use a credit card for remote purchases	Takes time for the money to be available The bank will charge a fee to the business for using the service High interest rates mean that they are expensive if debts are not paid off
Electronic methods: CHAPS Faster Payments mobile payment	CHAPS guarantees same-day payment to another account as long as the request is made by 2 pm on a working day There is no limit to the amount of money that can be sent, however there will be a charge to send the money Faster Payments are electronic payments made in less than two hours between two bank accounts Mobile banking allows individuals to make mobile payments via their smartphone or cellular devise	Fewer security issues as no cash changes hands Bank statements record all of these transactions Mobile payments are very convenient	Banks require notice before releasing potentially large sums of money, e.g. for a house purchase Due to its electronic nature the contents need to be checked carefully before processing; errors can be very costly
BACS, including direct debit	An electronic system to make payments from one bank account to another Its main use is for direct debits and direct credit from businesses; they usually take three working days to clear The money is transferred automatically from one account to another; the business requiring payment has to request payment from the customer's bank account Used for paying regular bills that vary in amounts, e.g. mortgage, gas, electricity, TV licence	A business is guaranteed the payment due Businesses are able to change the amount and due date Customers do not have to remember to pay bills on a certain day Customers do not need to write and post cheques	The money will still be taken even if there is no money in the bank account; this may incur charges and interest costs Customers may fail to accurately budget by forgetting to check prices, and increases in utility costs or mortgage interest
Standing order	Money is transferred automatically from one account to another The customer instructs their bank to make regular payments to another account – the amount must be the same each time	Customers do not have to remember to pay bills on a certain day. Customers do not need to write and post cheques.	If there is insufficient money in the bank account, the standing order will not be paid Customers may forget to cancel a standing order and end up paying for products and services they neither want nor receive

5.2 How to update the cash book

When a business receives its monthly **bank statement**, a cashier is required to tick off the items that appear in the cash book and on the bank statement. Any items that are unticked on the bank statement need to be placed in the cash book (bank columns) to update the business cash book.

> 🔑 **KEY TERM**
>
> **Bank statement** – a record of the balance in a bank account, and the amounts that have been paid into the account and withdrawn from it.

5.3 The need for bank reconciliation statements

A bank reconciliation statement is a report that seeks to match the balance in the cash book and the balance on the bank statement. The word reconciliation in this case means to explain the difference between the two documents.

The purpose of a bank reconciliation statement is to:

● check the accuracy of the bookkeeping in the cash book
● assist in the identification of fraud
● help to detect errors on the bank statement
● aid the business in controlling its cash flow
● highlight any **dishonoured cheques** (cheques that have been submitted to the bank for payment but for some reason the bank has refused to pay them).

> 🔑 **KEY TERM**
>
> **Dishonoured cheque** – a cheque that a bank will not pay because there is not enough money in the account.

Businesses need to reconcile their cash book with the final balance on their bank statement.

There are a number of reasons why the two balances may not agree. These include:

● timing differences, for example the time it takes for a cheque or bank deposit to clear
● omissions from the cash book – these will include standing orders, direct debits, bank charges, etc.
● errors either in the cash book or on the bank statement
● dishonoured cheques – this could be due to a shortage of funds in the account from which the money was to be drawn.

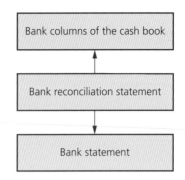

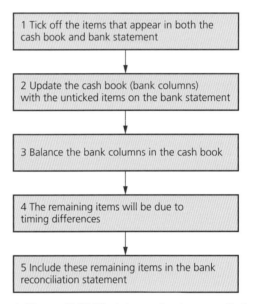

▲ **Figure 11.13** What does a bank reconciliation statement relate to?

5.4 How to prepare a bank reconciliation statement

Format of a bank reconciliation statement

Figure 11.14 shows the format of a bank reconciliation statement.

Bank reconciliation statement as at xxx

	£
Balance at bank as per cash book	x
Add unpresented cheques	<u>x</u>
Less uncleared deposits	<u>x</u>
Balance as per bank statement	<u>x</u>

▲ **Figure 11.14** Format of a bank reconciliation statement

5.5 The use and purpose of a bank statement

Bank statements list all of the transactions that have gone in to and come out of an account. They can be printed or viewed online. Banks will produce bank statements for their customers for many reasons, including:

- giving the customer a permanent record of their financial transactions
- providing information for regulatory tax authorities of loan/mortgage providers
- allowing a customer to check their direct debit and standing order payments

- checking the account for fraud or theft
- identification of bank charges and interest payments.

KNOW IT

1 Describe the use of a bank statement.
2 Explain the difference between a credit card and a debit card.
3 State three reasons why the balance in a cash book may not match the bank statement balance.
4 Explain the need for bank reconciliation statements.
5 Discuss the difference between a standing order and a direct debit.

LO5 assessment activities

Below are suggested assessment activities that have been directly linked to the Pass criteria in LO5 to help with assignment preparation. These are followed by top tips on how to achieve the best results.

Activity 1 Pass criteria *P9* and *P10*

Figures 11.15 and 11.16 show extracts from the cash book and bank statement of Miffy Book Store.

Dr		£			Cr £
August 1	Balance b/d	54	August 8	P Horton	182
August 8	C Sherlock	94	August 21	D Bruna	35
August 14	J Wilson	113	August 28	D Waterworth	74
August 27	S Patel	265	August 31	Balance c/d	235
		526			526

▲ **Figure 11.15** Cash book extract

Date		Dr	Cr	Balance
August 1	Balance b/d			54
August 11	C Sherlock		94	148
August 12	P Horton	182		(34)
August 16	Bank charges	45		(79)
August 18	J Wilson		113	34
August 24	D Bruna	35		(1)
August 29	Credit transfer: ABC Ltd		55	54

▲ **Figure 11.16** Bank statement extract

P9 Update the cash book from the data given.

P10 Prepare a bank reconciliation statement.

Activity 2 Pass criteria
P11 **and** *P12*

P11 P12 You are required to prepare a business report that contains the following:

- a description of the payment methods that are used for business transactions.
- an explanation of the purpose of a bank statement and why businesses need to prepare a bank reconciliation statement.

TOP TIPS
....
- ✔ You can use either a manual or computerised method of preparation for the accounting documents.
- ✔ Practise a range of questions prior to attempting the assessment task.

Read about it

Business Accounting Volume 1 (10th edn), by Frank Wood and Alan Sangster, FT Prentice Hall, 2005

Business Accounting, Rob Jones, Causeway Press, 2004

Business Accounts (3rd edn), David Cox, Osborne Books, 2004

Unit 12

Financial accounting

LEARNING OUTCOMES

The topics, activities and suggested reading in this unit will help you to:

1 understand the impact of legislation, concepts and principles on accounting processes
2 understand the reporting requirements of private limited companies and public limited companies
3 be able to prepare final accounts for sole traders
4 use ratios to assess the performance of businesses.

How will I be assessed?

You will be assessed through a series of assignments and tasks set and marked by your tutor.

How will I be graded?

You will be graded using the following criteria, which are in the specification produced by OCR for the qualification.

Learning outcome	Pass	Merit	Distinction
You will:	To achieve a Pass you must demonstrate that you have met all the pass assessment criteria	To achieve a Merit you must demonstrate that you have met all the pass and merit assessment criteria	To achieve a Distinction you must demonstrate that you have met all the pass, merit and distinction assessment criteria
1 Understand the impact of legislation, concepts and principles on accounting processes	**P1** Explain how legislation affects an organisation's accounting processes		
	P2 Describe how accounting concepts and principles are applied in financial statements		
2 Understand the reporting requirements of private limited companies and public limited companies	**P3** Describe the main elements of a public limited company's annual report and a private limited company's accounts		
	P4 Explain how the content of public limited companies' reports are used by different stakeholder groups	**M1** Analyse the benefits and limitations to different stakeholder groups of the content of publicly available reports	
	P5 Explain the roles and responsibilities of directors and auditors with regard to company accounts		
	P6 Describe the key differences between the: • internal final accounts and • publicly available final accounts for a limited company	**M2** Compare the content and layout of the final accounts of a sole trader or partnership with those of a private limited or public limited company	
3 Be able to prepare final accounts for sole traders	**P7** Explain the purpose of an income statement and a statement of financial position		
	P8 Prepare an income statement and statement of financial position for a sole trader including relevant adjustments		
4 Use ratios to assess the performance of businesses	**P9** Use ratios to measure the performance of a business	**M3** Analyse the liquidity, profitability and efficiency of a business organisation	**D1** Evaluate the financial performance of a business organisation
			D2 Evaluate the usefulness of ratio analysis when assessing the performance of a business organisation

LO1 Understand the impact of legislation, concepts and principles on accounting processes *P1 P2*

(10 minutes)

Working in small groups, make a list of accounting and finance **legislation** that affects business organisations. Be prepared to share your ideas with the rest of the class.

> **KEY TERM**
>
> **Legislation** – a law or set of laws that a government has suggested and that have been made official by Parliament. Once approved, individuals and business organisations are bound to abide by the content.

1.1 Relevant legislation

Companies Act

The Companies Act is an Act of Parliament that forms the main source of company law in the United Kingdom. The act provides a comprehensive code of practice for all aspects of company operation. In particular, it comments on:

- different categories of company
- company formation
- constitutional documents – articles and memorandum of association
- company name and registered office
- director's duties
- company secretaries
- share capital
- debentures (a type of loan for businesses)
- shareholder communication, including annual general meetings
- accounts and reports
- auditor's liability
- filing of accounts
- mergers and takeovers
- registrar of companies
- offences under the Companies Act.

Partnership Act

The Partnership Act governs the rights and duties of individuals running a business in partnership with one another. According to the act, a partnership is defined as 'the relation which subsists between persons carrying on a business with a view of profit' (source: www.legislation.gov.uk).

It is advisable to produce a partnership agreement that suits all of the needs and requirements of the specific partnership. If a partnership does not have a formal partnership agreement, or it fails to cover an area of dispute, then the content of the Partnership Act applies. The following conditions would apply:

- all profits and losses are to be shared equally
- partners will receive 5 per cent interest on loans made to the partnership
- no interest on drawings is charged to partners
- no interest on capital is payable to partners
- no salaries are to be paid to partners
- see Unit 1 (page 4) for more on partnerships.

Charities Act

The Charities Act sets out the regulatory framework in which charities operate. It lays out the conditions bodies must meet to obtain or maintain charitable status. For the purposes of the law in the United Kingdom, a charitable organisation has to demonstrate that it operates solely to serve the public interest and promote one or more of a range of causes. These include prevention or relief of poverty, and development or advancement of education, religion, arts, sport, etc.

(20 minutes)

Working in pairs, choose one charity in the United Kingdom.

Thinking about the Charities Act, explain how the charity of your choice meets its requirements.

See the following websites for background information:

http://tinyurl.com/nx5fegp

http://tinyurl.com/gmgqpxc

1.2 Impact of relevant legislation on different forms of business ownership

Table 12.1 Impact of the Companies Act, Partnership Act and Charities Act on different types of business

	Sole traders	Partnerships	Private limited companies	Public limited companies	Third-sector organisations, e.g. clubs, societies, charities
Legislation	No legal requirements	Subject to the Partnership Act	Subject to the Companies Act	Subject to the Companies Act	Subject to the Companies Act and, if appropriate, the Charities Act
Legal prescriptions	None	No formal requirements Often create an agreement between the partners	Memorandum of Incorporation is required when setting up	Memorandum of Incorporation is required when setting up	Memorandum of Incorporation is required when setting up
Ownership	One owner who owns and manages the business	Two or more partners who own and manage the business	Shareholders – family and friends	Shareholders – publicly available	No owners – operate under the guidance of 'trustees'
Formation documents	No requirements	Partnership agreement	Memorandum of Incorporation	Memorandum of Incorporation	Memorandum of Incorporation
Registration requirements	No registration required, although the owner (in their own right) will need to register with HMRC for tax purposes	No registration required, although the partners (in their own right) will need to register with HMRC for tax purposes	Register with Companies House	Register with Companies House	Register with the Charity Commission if the charity is based in England or Wales and has more than £5,000 income per year If the charity is a charitable incorporated organisation (CIO) it must register whatever its income
Acquisition of capital	Contributed by the owner	Contributed or loaned by the partners	The company is allowed to make a share offer to family and friends only	The company is allowed to make a share offer to the general public	Dependent on government and private-sector funding
Availability of financial information	Available only to the owner	Available only to the partners	Available only to current and prospective shareholders	Freely available to the general public	Freely available to members and other interested parties
Payments to owners	All profits are paid to the owner	All profits are paid to the partners in the agreed sharing ratio	Profit distributed in the form of dividends to shareholders in accordance with their shareholder status	Profit distributed in the form of dividends to shareholders in accordance with their shareholder status	No part of the income should be paid to members
Financial statement requirements	Optional	Optional	Compulsory annual financial reports	Compulsory annual financial reports	Compulsory annual financial statements
Audit requirements	Optional	Optional	May be eligible for audit exemption	Compulsory audit by qualified auditor	Voluntarily audited or independently reviewed
Filing requirements of financial statements	None	None	Companies House	Companies House	Depending on certain criteria, financial statements may need to be filed with the Charity Commission

1.3 Accounting concepts

Accounting concepts are rules of accounting that have to be followed by businesses when preparing their accounts and financial statements. As covered in Unit 11 (pages 189-90), there are four fundamental accounting concepts:

1 accruals/matching
2 consistency
3 going concern
4 prudence.

In addition, businesses will apply a number of other concepts when producing financial documents. These include:

● materiality
● money measurement
● historical cost
● realisation
● dual aspect
● business entity.

INDIVIDUAL ACTIVITY

(50 minutes)

Revisit Unit 11 (page 189) and revise the topic on accounting concepts. Prepare a set of flash cards that can be used for future reference. These should include definitions of the following concepts:

● prudence
● consistency
● going concern
● materiality
● matching.

1.4 Accounting principles

Accounting principles are the rules or guidelines that businesses must follow when reporting financial information to stakeholders.

Relevance

Relevance means that any financial accounting information produced by a business must meet the needs of the users and have an impact on the decisions they are looking to make. The business needs to ensure that there is a need for the information that it is producing. Irrelevant information should be eliminated from the financial accounting information.

Reliability

Businesses must ensure that any information they release is accurate, and shows a true and fair view of their financial conditions and operating records.

The concept of true and fair view does not mean 'absolute' truth about all business financial affairs. Any financial statements are the result of a management team's judgements and estimates. It is usually accepted that, by complying with the accounting principles, a business has shown a true and fair view.

Comparability

Comparability is vital to the usability of accounting information. Any business accounting information will be comparable with previous period's data when accounting standards, policies and procedures are consistent from one financial period to another. To allow comparison between different businesses, there needs to be consistent use of accounting standards, policies and procedures. The introduction of the International Accounting Standards (ISAs) has aided comparability around the world.

Understandability

Understandability refers to financial information that is understandable by individuals with a reasonable background knowledge and understanding of business issues.

For financial information to be understandable it needs to be concise, fully complete and clear in its presentation. Complex information should still be presented. However, it must be presented in an orderly rather than random fashion.

INDIVIDUAL ACTIVITY

(30 minutes)

Fill in the gaps below using the appropriate accounting concept or principle. The same term can be used more than once.

1 When a business believes that a number of its trade receivables may not pay their debts, it should record all possible losses in its financial accounts. This is an example of the .... concept.
2 The idea that a business is separate to its owner is best defined by the .... concept.
3 Everything that a business owns is also owed to someone else. This is explained by the .... concept.

4 If an accounts clerk buys an accounting book in which to record petty cash transactions, the clerk should not record the accounting book as a non-current asset, due to the .... concept.

5 The .... concept states that if the FIFO (first in first out) method of inventory valuation is used in one year, then it should be used in the following year.

6 An accountant is interested only in the total value of an owner's drawings, not how the owner spent the money, because of the .... concept.

7 The management of the local manufacturing company is incompetent. The accountant is not able to record this in the accounts of the company due to the .... concept.

1.5 The application of accounting concepts and principles to financial statements

Valuation of non-current assets

Non-current assets are those of material value that are:

- of long life, and
- to be used in the business, and
- not bought with the main purpose of resale.

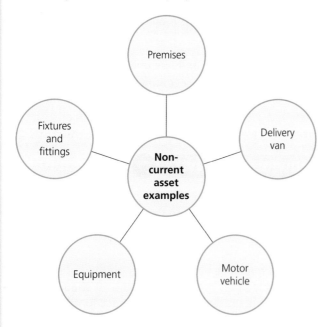

▲ **Figure 12.1** Examples of non-current assets

In accordance with the historical cost concept, non-current assets are to be recorded in the financial accounts at the cost for which they were purchased. Businesses can provide for depreciation on these assets.

Depreciation

Depreciation is the cost of a non-current asset consumed over its lifetime. This means that part of the cost of the non-current asset will be transferred to the expenses in the income statement every year until all of the cost of the asset has been transferred. This is an application of the matching concept.

International Accounting Standard 16 (IAS 16 – Property, Plant and Equipment) details the accounting procedures for non-current assets and the provision of depreciation:

> The objective of IAS 16 is to prescribe the accounting treatment for property, plant, and equipment. The principal issues are the recognition of assets, the determination of their carrying amounts, and the depreciation charges and impairment losses to be recognised in relation to them.

Source: www.iasplus.com/en-gb/standards/ias/ias16

There are several causes of depreciation, as follows.

- Physical deterioration:
  - wear and tear
  - erosion
  - rust, rot and decay.
- Economic factors:
  - obsolescence – assets becoming out of date
  - inadequacy.
- Time factors: some intangible assets have a finite life span, e.g. goodwill.
- Depletion.

Amortisation is a term that can be used instead of depreciation when assets are used up because of the time factor. It is used for intangible non-current assets (those that do not have a physical existence) – for example, leasehold property and goodwill.

Remember that premises and buildings will be depreciated however freehold land should not be depreciated.

Appreciation is the term given to an increase in value of a non-current asset. The normal accounting practice is to ignore any appreciation. To account for appreciation would contravene the historical cost and prudence concepts. There are two exceptions to this rule: partnerships and limited companies.

GROUP ACTIVITY

(15 minutes)

Working in small groups, discuss the following question:

Is depreciation a movement of cash?

Be ready to feed back your ideas to the rest of the class.

▲ **Figure 12.2** Words associated with 'depreciation'

There are a number of concepts that relate to the application of depreciation. These include:

● historical cost – states all non-current assets should be shown in the accounts at their original cost
● prudence – states that businesses should not overstate the value of their assets
● consistency – states that, once a depreciation method is chosen, the policy should not be changed without a valid reason.

Straight line method of depreciation

Straight line depreciation is the simplest method of calculating depreciation. It spreads the cost of a non-current asset equally over its useful life. This means that the depreciation expense is the same every year. It is used for assets that are used equally throughout their life – for example, equipment.

Straight line depreciation is calculated using the following formula.

Annual straight line depreciation = $\dfrac{\text{Cost} - \text{Disposal value}}{\text{Number of years owned}}$

Reducing balance method of depreciation

This is used by businesses for non-current assets that are likely to experience a high usage in the early years of the asset's life – for example, motor vehicles.

The annual depreciation is based on a percentage of the asset's net book value, which is calculated as follows:

Net book value = Original asset cost – Accumulated depreciation

Valuation of inventory

Inventory comprises a number of components, as follows.

● Raw materials: the items a business uses to produce other goods, e.g. flour and yeast for the production of bread.
● Work-in-progress: items being produced that are part completed, e.g. when a car is on a production line and has yet to be completed.
● Finished goods: goods that a business has manufactured and are fully complete; the business has the intention of selling these on to a customer.
● Goods for resale: goods that a business buys with the intention of selling them on to a customer, e.g. a supermarket buys lemonade, fish fingers and rice.
● Consumables: items that a business purchases to use within the business, e.g. cleaning materials, stationery.

Many businesses are now trying to reduce the amount of inventory they hold by using a just-in-time (JIT) system (see Unit 3, page 98). When deciding how much inventory it should hold, a business must balance the costs of holding inventory against the benefits.

The costs include:

● warehousing and storage
● insurance
● risk of theft or going out of date
● financial cost of tying up funds in inventory (opportunity cost).

The benefits of holding inventory include the:

- ability to meet customer demand immediately
- ability to maintain continuous production
- avoidance of having to reorder at short notice (at unfavourable prices or on timescales suppliers cannot meet)
- avoidance of having to reorder frequently, thereby avoiding administration costs.

Example valuation of inventory

Inventory is valued at the lower of cost and net realisable value.

Cost is defined as the cost of the item plus any expenses incurred in bringing the product to its present location and condition.

Net realisable value (NRV) is the estimated resale value of the inventory, less any selling or distribution costs.

An example valuation of inventory is shown in Table 12.2.

Table 12.2 Example valuation of inventory

Inventory group	Cost	NRV	Valuation
	£	£	£
Tents	4,500	8,000	4,500
Sleeping bags	6,500	6,800	6,500
Clothing	4,800	6,100	4,800
Footwear	2,500	1,900	1,900
Cooking equipment	2,900	3,000	2,900
Miscellaneous	6,900	9,900	6,900
Total	28,100	35,700	27,500

INDIVIDUAL ACTIVITY

(20 minutes)

Complete Table 12.3 to show the inventory valuation of a local pet shop.

Table 12.3 Fill in the gaps to produce a valuation of inventory

Inventory group	Cost	NRV	Valuation
	£	£	£
Leads and collars	2,000	2,500	
Rabbit hutches	1,200	1,000	
Water dishes	600	750	
Fish tanks	3,500	3,000	
Pet food	2,000	1,300	
Pet toys	1,500	1,900	
Total			

Valuation of inventory methods

1 FIFO (first in first out) – this method (Figure 12.3) assumes that inventory will be used or sold in the order in which it was bought. Any leftover inventory will be the items purchased most recently.

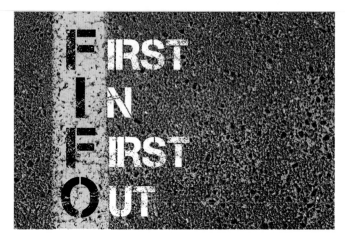

▲ **Figure 12.3** The first in first out inventory method is standard in many stockrooms and warehouses

2 LIFO (last in first out) – this method uses the newest inventory first. Any leftover inventory will be the items that were purchased earliest. This method leads to out-of-date prices and therefore goes against accounting principles.
3 AVCO (average weighted cost) – this method calculates the average cost of all inventory that has been purchased.

The FIFO and AVCO methods both meet the accounting regulations and can be used in the production of final accounts. Although the LIFO method is well known, it is not generally accepted in the production of accounting statements. The value of a business's inventory appears in both the income statement and the statement of financial position of that business.

Matching concept (accruals and prepayments)

The matching concept states that revenues and expenses are to be matched to the same accounting period.

Expenses

An accrual is an amount due in an accounting period that remains unpaid at the end of that period –for example, a utility bill (gas, electricity, etc.).

A prepayment is a payment made in advance of the accounting period to which it relates – for example, insurance.

Accruals of expenses are added to the relevant expense in the income statement and included in the 'amounts falling due within one year' in the statement of financial position.

Prepayments of expenses are deducted from the relevant expense in the income statement and included in the current assets in the statement of financial position.

Income

Deferred/prepaid income is income received in advance of the period to which it relates – for example rent received.

Accrued income is income due in the period but not yet received – for example, rent receivable

Prepayments of income are deducted from the relevant additional income in the income statement and included in the 'amounts falling due within one year' in the statement of financial position.

Accruals of income are added to the relevant additional income in the income statement and included in the current assets in the statement of financial position.

Bad debts

Many businesses will allow customers to buy now and pay later; these sales are known as credit sales. There is, however, a risk that customers may never pay for the goods they have purchased. This is classed as a normal business risk so bad debts will be included as a business expense in the income statement for the period.

Provision for doubtful debts

If a trade receivable that owes money to a business has the potential to not pay the debt due, then this is a doubtful debt. Doubtful debts are not definitely irrecoverable; there is still the potential that the trade receivable will pay the money owed. Once it has been proven that the debt will not be paid then the doubtful debt becomes a bad debt. The concept of prudence requires a business to account for the potential loss. Businesses can identify specific trade receivables that are unlikely to pay and include them in the accounts as a specific provision for doubtful debts, or they can estimate an overall total and include the details in a general provision for doubtful debts.

KNOW IT

1 Name three accounting concepts.
2 Define the materiality concept.
3 Explain what is meant by depreciation.
4 Name two methods of calculating depreciation.
5 Explain the difference between FIFO and LIFO.

LO1 assessment activity

Below is a suggested assessment activity that has been directly linked to the Pass criteria in LO1 to help with assignment preparation. This is followed by top tips on how to achieve the best results.

Activity 1 Pass criteria *P1* and *P2*

P1 P2 For the purpose of this activity, you are working as an accounts assistant for a financial accounting firm. A customer, Mr Sparkle, has requested information and guidance. Prepare an email to Mr Sparkle that includes:

● an explanation of how legislation affects an organisation's accounting processes
● a description of how accounting concepts and principles are applied in financial statements.

TOP TIPS

✔ Ensure you focus on the command verbs in each task.
✔ You should spend equal time and produce similar amounts of evidence for each of the pass criteria.

LO2 Understand the reporting requirements of private limited companies and public limited companies *P3 P4 P5 P6 M1 M2*

GETTING STARTED

(15 minutes)

Working in pairs, choose a public limited company. Download its annual report and make a list of its contents. Give a brief description of each of the items.

2.1 The main elements of private limited companies' annual accounts

Private limited companies do not have to follow the same legal requirements that public limited companies need to meet. Generally, private limited companies will produce the following financial statements.

● *Income statement*: this measures a company's performance over a period of time, usually one year. The income statement compares the income of the company against the cost of sales for the same period, thereby calculating gross profit. The company will then deduct the expenses incurred in earning this revenue, to calculate the net profit for the period.

● *Statement of financial position*: a snapshot of the company's assets and liabilities on a particular day in the financial year, usually the final day of the financial year.

2.2 The main elements of public limited companies' annual reports

Table 12.4 Elements in a plc's annual report

Element	Definition
General corporate information	This section of the annual report provides a general overview of the company; it allows readers to infer information on corporate strategies, company objectives and market analysis
Accounting policies	The company has a legal obligation to disclose the accounting policies that have been used in the preparation of the annual report; these will include depreciation methods, inventory valuation and doubtful debt policies
Income statement	This is a historical record of the trading of the company over a specific period of time; it calculates the profit figure for the year Unlike the income statement of a sole trader, a company will produce an appropriate account; this is included after the net profit has been calculated; the term appropriation refers to how the profit will be divided up; a limited company has its own legal identity and is therefore liable to pay corporation tax on its profits The income statement serves a number of purposes, including: • providing information to shareholders on how the company has performed • enabling shareholders to calculate the potential and guaranteed return on an investment • ensuring the company meets its legal requirements • identifying whether the profit earned by the company is sustainable over time; this highlights the profit quality • allowing comparisons with similar companies • providing evidence and support for loan applications
Statement of financial position	This shows the financial position of the company on a given date There are three main components: 1 assets 2 liabilities 3 capital and reserves The main difference between the statements of a sole trader and those of a limited company comes in the capital section; the company's share capital is kept separate and is not adjusted by any of the profits retained within the company The statement illustrates the accounting equation studied in Unit 11 (page 191) The statement of financial position allows users to assess the security of their capital/equity invested in the company; in particular, they can review: • liquidity risk • financial risk • credit risk • business risk
Statement of cash flows	This is a summary of cash inflows and cash outflows over the most recent accounting period; it focuses on the liquidity of the company and the changes in the cash flow over the most recent period; it allows the company to: • meet its legal requirements • highlight liquidity problems • highlight profits that are of 'high quality' or 'poor quality' – those that are or are not sustainable • assess the link between one statement of financial position and the next • examine changes in the capital structure of the company

cont. ⟶

Element	Definition
Notes to the financial statements	These will provide a considerable amount of detailed information to support the figures that are included in income statement, statement of financial position and statement of cash flows
Chairperson's and directors' reports	These will include a review of company performance, discuss corporate governance and include details of directors' pay
Auditor's report	This is a statement from the company's auditors expressing their opinion on whether the accounts produced by the company show a true and fair view of the financial performance and position of the company at that time.

Public limited company – income statement format

Income statement for the year ended ....

	£	£
Turnover		x
Cost of sales		(x)
Gross profit		x
Selling and distribution expenses	x	
Administration expenses	x	
Finance costs	x	
		x
Profit on ordinary activities		**x**
Other operating income		x
Profit on ordinary activities before tax and interest		x
Interest payable		x
Profit on ordinary activities before tax		x
Corporation tax		x
Profit after tax		x
Profit and loss b/f		x
		x
Dividends	x	
General reserve (transfer)	x	x
Retained profit		**x**

▲ **Figure 12.4** Example income statement format

Public limited company – statement of financial position format

Statement of financial position as at ………………..

NON-CURRENT ASSETS

	£	£
Land and buildings		X
Office equipment		X
Delivery vehicles		X
		X

CURRENT ASSETS

Inventory	X	
Trade receivables	X	
Accrued income	X	
Prepaid expenses	X	
Bank	X	
Cash	X	
	X	

Amounts falling due in less than one year

Trade payables	X	
Accrued expenses	X	
Prepaid income	X	
Dividends	X	
Taxation	X	
Bank overdraft	X	
	X	

Working capital		X
Total assets less current liabilities		X

Amounts falling due in more than one year

Long-term loan	X	
		X
Net assets		**X**

Capital and reserves

Share capital		X
Revaluation reserve		X
Share premium		X
General reserve		X
Profit and loss		X
		X

▲ **Figure 12.5** Example statement of financial position

(90 minutes)

Using the following link, download two consecutive annual reports for the Lego Group: http://tinyurl.com/heewlxj

Review the two annual reports and prepare a short report on the financial position of the Lego Group. You should conclude your report by stating whether you think the group has improved over this period of time.

2.3 The way in which publicly available reports are used by different stakeholder groups

Stakeholders are individuals, groups or organisations that have a particular interest in a business enterprise.

Internal stakeholders are those who work directly within a business organisation.

- *Employees* will want to ensure that they will get paid for the work they have completed and will review the annual information to check the business is likely to continue to ensure their job security.
- Like employees, *managers* will want to ensure they receive their wage or salary and have job security. They will also review the financial performance of the business organisation, so they can compare the performance over time and against other similar business organisations.
- *Directors* will want to ensure that the business is going to continue for the foreseeable future and is a going concern. The directors will calculate and review the profitability and liquidity of the business organisation.

External stakeholders do not work directly within a business organisation. They are, however, affected by the decisions that the business organisation will make.

- *Shareholders* will review business data and annual reports to ensure the business is profitable. They will want to ensure their investment is continuing to grow and that share price increases. They will review the dividends that have been received in the past and are likely to be received in the future.
- *Potential investors* will want to review potential profitability, assess the risk to their potential investment and consider any return in the form of dividends they may receive.
- *Suppliers* are interested in knowing that the business is able to pay for the goods that it has purchased. The supplier will use the information to assess the credit status and risk profile of the business requesting credit.

- *Customers* can review information to ensure they are charged the right price for goods and services, and price strategies to ensure they are not overcharged and that discounts have been applied appropriately. By reviewing the information, a business will aim to reinforce its reputation so customers will continue to purchase from it in the future.
- *Lenders* will need to ensure that the business is able to repay the initial amount and interest charged on loans on time. The lender will use the financial information and reports to assess creditworthiness and the risk they will incur by lending any money.
- *Government* will want to ensure that all business organisations pay the tax they owe. It is a legal requirement for businesses to pay HMRC throughout the financial year.
- *Analysts* will review all the data and compare it with that of other firms. Their reviews will predict future performance, and may be used to offer advice to the government on interest rates and inflation, etc.

2.4 The roles and responsibilities of directors and auditors with regard to company accounts

Directors

Directors are responsible for the preparation of a company's annual report and accounts in accordance with the applicable law and regulations. Under company law, directors have a duty to prepare financial statements for each financial year that give a true and fair view of the affairs of the company. Directors have a role to:

- select and consistently apply accounting policies
- make reasonable and prudent judgement and estimates
- state and ensure the financial statement complies with all relevant accounting standards.

The directors are responsible for ensuring the company keeps proper accounting records that disclose accurate information, and for the safeguarding of the company's assets. They need to take reasonable steps to prevent and detect fraud. The 'Business overview' section of an annual report and accounts will state the name and function of every director.

Auditors

An external, independent auditor is employed to offer an opinion on a company's financial statements, in particular whether these show a 'true and fair' view of the financial affairs. An external audit increases the degree of confidence that stakeholders can place on the accounting records.

The auditor will gather information and evidence that is required to gain reassurance that the financial information is accurate. They may complete observations and practical tests, and compare and confirm information.

The most important auditing duties include:

- questioning management and other employees to understand the company; in particular, they will ask about company operations, financial reporting and any known fraud or errors
- understanding and evaluating internal control systems
- observing a physical inventory stock take
- confirming the balances of accounts receivable and accounts payable
- investigating differences or variances in account balances.

An auditor may offer objective advice on improving financial reporting and internal control.

It is vital that an external auditor remains independent from the company – not part of management and not

responsible for the financial statements, which belong to and are the responsibility of the company; the auditor only offers an opinion on their validity.

An auditor is not able to:

- authorise or complete any transactions on behalf of the company
- prepare or change any source documents
- hire or terminate the employment of an employee
- report to the board of directors on behalf of the company management
- sign tax returns for the company
- approve invoices for payment
- maintain company assets
- design or maintain internal controls or financial management systems
- supervise the company's employees.

2.5 The key differences between internal final accounts and the publicly available final accounts of a limited company

Table 12.5 Internal versus publicly available final accounts of a limited company

	Internal final accounts	Publicly available final accounts
Purpose	To provide management with ongoing information on which to make decisions The accounts should allow management to make decisions on: - inventory levels - cost of expenses - sales - liquidity - profitability, etc. Management will look at variances over time, and plan to make improvements and changes as needed	To provide information to a wide range of stakeholders who have an interest in a particular company The accounts will allow each stakeholder group to make informed decisions
Content	Companies are free to choose the exact content, but it usually includes: - income statement and appropriation account - statement of financial position - statement of cash flows Management may produce other management accounting data for internal use, for example: - cash flow forecasts - break-even analysis (see Unit 13, LO2) - standard costing	In accordance with the regulations, publicly available accounts will include: - general corporate information - accounting policies - income statement (including appropriation account) - statement of financial position - statement of cash flows - notes to the final statements - chairperson's report - director's report - auditor's report
Structure and format	Companies are free to choose a structure and format that meets their needs; for internal use, companies will include information and data that would be damaging if a competitor received this information – for example, for internal use detailed sales figures may be included, whereas a total would be included in publicly available accounts	Companies House provides guidance on the format of the final accounts; publicly available accounts must meet the regulations and requirements that are set out; there are complex instructions for different types and sizes of business organisations that legally have to publish their accounts

KNOW IT

1 Identify the main elements of a public limited company's annual report.
2 Explain the role of an auditor.
3 Name three internal stakeholders.
4 Discuss how an investor may use a public limited company's annual report.
5 Explain the difference between the internal accounts and the publicly available final accounts of a limited company.

● ●

LO2 assessment activities

Below are suggested assessment activities that have been directly linked to the Pass and Merit criteria in LO2 to help with assignment preparation. These are followed by top tips on how to achieve the best results.

Scenario

For the purpose of this assignment you are working as an accounting trainee for a firm of chartered financial accountants.

Activity 1 Pass criteria *P3 P4 P5 P6*

The accounting firm provides information sheets to provide support and guidance to its clients. You have been asked to produce the following three information sheets that will be available to all clients.

1 **P3 P6** Internal final accounts and publicly available accounts and reports. This information sheet should:
  • describe the main elements of a public limited company's annual report and a private limited company's accounts; you could include practical examples, internet links or examples to enhance your descriptions
  • describe the key differences between internal final accounts and publicly available final accounts for a limited company.
2 **P4** Users of public limited companies' reports. This information sheet should explain how the content of public limited companies' reports are used by different stakeholder groups. It would be advisable to choose a range of internal and external stakeholder groups.
3 **P5** Directors and auditors. This information sheet should explain the roles and responsibilities of directors and auditors with regard to company accounts.

TOP TIPS

✔ You should spend an equal amount of time on each of the pass criteria.
✔ You should ensure your information sheet is easy to read and can be understood by non-accountants.
✔ You can use any layout or design you feel is appropriate.

Activity 2 Merit criteria *M1* and *M2*

M1 M2 Prepare a presentation that is appropriate to be delivered to accounting clients, with accompanying speaker notes. Your presentation needs to include the following:

● an analysis of the benefits and limitations to different stakeholder groups of the content of publicly available reports
● a comparison of the content and layout of the final accounts of a sole trader with those of a public limited company.

TOP TIPS

✔ You should spend an equal amount of time on each of the merit criteria.
✔ You will not be required to present your presentation, but need to ensure it is suitable for the intended audience.
✔ You can use any layout or design you feel is appropriate.
✔ You need to make sure you meet the command verbs for each criteria.
✔ It may be appropriate for you to complete your assignment for P6 and P7 before completing this work. You would then be able to compare the accounts you have produced for a sole trader with those of your chosen public limited company.
✔ You are free to choose any sole trader and public limited company; it would be sensible to check your choice with your tutor.

LO3 Be able to prepare final accounts for sole traders *P7 P8*

GETTING STARTED

(20 minutes)

Review the work you covered on final accounts in Unit 1 (page 23) and Unit 11 (page 187).

Working in small groups, consider what items might be included in the final accounts of a local restaurant. Complete Table 12.6 with examples that would be included in the relevant categories.

Table 12.6 Items in the final accounts of a restaurant

Expenses	Non-current assets	Current assets	Amounts falling due within one year
Electricity	Premises		

3.1 Preparation of final accounts for a sole trader from a trial balance

From a completed trial balance and closing inventory information, it is possible to prepare the final accounts for a business organisation. There is sufficient information to produce an income statement and statement of financial position.

Table 12.7 Income statement versus statement of financial position

	Income statement	Statement of financial position
Purpose	To show whether a sole trader has made a profit or loss during the financial year As the owner has contributed all of the capital to start up and operate the business, they want to ensure they are receiving an appropriate level of return in the form of profit	To give the owner an overview of the business's financial position; it highlights to the owner what the company owns and owes
Use	Both allow the owner (sole trader) to evaluate the business's current financial position and make appropriate changes to their business practices Sole traders will provide these statements to lenders to enhance an application for a loan or mortgage	

PAIRS ACTIVITY

(30 minutes)

Barrie runs Mountain Sports and Golf Shop in central Scotland. He is a sole trader and has prepared the trial balance shown in Figure 12.6 as at 31 December.

	Dr. £	Cr. £
Opening inventory at 1 January	18,160	
Sales		92,340
Purchases	69,185	
Sales returns	420	
Advertising	1,570	
Discounts received		640
Wages and salaries	10,240	
Rates	3,015	
Internet	624	
Telephone	216	
Insurance	405	
Sundry expenses	318	
Premises	20,000	
Trade receivables	14,320	
Trade payables		8,160
Fixtures and fittings	2,850	
Cash at bank	2,970	
Cash in hand	115	
Drawings	7,620	
Capital/equity		50,888
	152,028	152,028

▲ **Figure 12.6** Mountain Sports and Golf Shop trial balance

224

Closing inventory at 31 December was £22,390.

Using the formats on pages 219 and 220, we are able to place the information in Figure 12.6 into the final accounts. Every item in the trial balance can be used only once, but the closing inventory (as it appears as additional information) needs to be used twice.

It may be helpful for you to annotate your trial balance to indicate where you are going to place each item. For example, sales – income statement, premises – statement of financial position, etc.

Opening inventory at 1 January (Income statement)	18,160	
Sales (Income statement)		92,340
Purchases (Income statement)	69,185	
Sales returns (Income statement)	420	
Advertising (Income statement – expenses)	1,570	
Discounts received (Income statement – additional income)		640
Wages and salaries (Income statement – expenses)	10,240	
Rates (Income statement – expenses)	3,015	
Internet (Income statement – expenses)		
Telephone (Income statement – expenses)	624	
Insurance (Income statement – expenses)	216	
Sundry expenses (Income statement – expenses)	405	
Premises (Statement of financial position – non-current assets)	318	
Trade receivables (Statement of financial position – current assets)	20,000	
Trade payables (Statement of financial position – amounts falling due in less than 1 year)	14,320	
Fixtures and fittings (Statement of financial position – non-current assets)		8,160
Cash at bank (Statement of financial position – current assets)	2,850	
Cash in hand (Statement of financial position – current assets)	2,970	
Drawings (Statement of financial position)	115	
Capital/Equity (Statement of financial position)	7,620	
Closing inventory at 31 December was £22,390 (Income statement AND Statement of financial position)		50,888

Once you have decided where to place each item, you are ready to prepare your final accounts. Ensure you accurately title each of the statements that you produce.

Income statement

Figure 12.7 shows Mountain Sports and Golf Shop's income statement for the year ending 31 December.

Mountain Sports and Golf Shop
Income statement for the year ending 31 December

	£	£	£
Sales		92,340	
Less returns inwards		420	
Net sales			91,920
Less cost of goods sold			
Opening inventory	18,160		
Purchases	69,185		
		87,345	
Less closing inventory		22,390	
Cost of sales			64,955
Gross profit			**26,965**
Additional income			
Discount received		640	640
			27,605
Less expenses			
Advertising		1,570	
Wages and salaries		10,240	
Rates		3,015	
Insurance		405	
Telephone		216	
Internet		624	
Sundry expenses		318	
			16,388
Net profit			**11,217**

▲ Figure 12.7 Mountain Sports and Golf Shop income statement for year ending 31 December

Statement of financial position

Again using the example of Mountain Sports and Golf Shop, Figure 12.8 shows its statement of financial position.

Mountain Sports and Golf Shop
Statement of financial position as at 31 December

FIXED ASSETS	Cost	Depreciation	Net book value
	£	£	£
Premises	20,000	0	20,000
Fixtures and fittings	2,850	0	2,850
	22,850	0	22,850
CURRENT ASSETS			
Inventory		22,390	
Trade receivables	14,320		
Less provision for doubtful debts	0	14,320	
Bank		2,970	
Cash		115	
		39,795	
Creditors falling due in less than one year			
Trade payables		8,160	
		8,160	
Working capital			31,635
Total assets less current liabilities			54,485
Net assets			54,485
Financed by:			
Capital			50,888
Net profit (from the Income statement)			11,217
Less drawings			7620
			54,485

▲ **Figure 12.8** Mountain Sports and Golf Shop statement of financial position

3.2 Adjustments to the final accounts for a sole trader

Sole traders will usually have adjustments that need to be made to their final accounts. These adjustments will include:

- inventory valuation
- depreciation of non-current assets
- bad debts
- provision for doubtful debts
- accruals
- prepayments.

PAIRS ACTIVITY

(30 minutes)

Using Figures 12.9 and 12.10, below, adjust the final accounts you prepared in the previous example, to take account of the following items.

1 Premises should be depreciated using a straight line method at a rate of 2 per cent per annum.
2 Fixtures and fittings should be depreciated using a straight line method at a rate of 20 per cent per annum.
3 Rates include a prepayment of £1,000.
4 Discounts received of £500 are outstanding.
5 Telephone expenses of £300 are outstanding.
6 One debt of £750 is to be written off as a bad debt.

Mountain Sports and Golf Shop
Income statement for the year ending 31 December

	£	£	£
Sales		92,340	
Less returns inwards		420	
Net sales			91,920
Less cost of goods sold			
Opening inventory	18,160		
Purchases	69,185		
		87,345	
Less closing inventory		22,390	
Cost of sales			64,955
Gross profit			26,965
Additional income			
Discount received (640 + 500) (d)		1,140	1,140
			28,105
Less expenses			
Advertising		1,570	
Wages and salaries		10,240	
Rates (3,015 - 1,000) (c)		2,015	
Insurance		405	
Telephone (216 + 300) (e)		516	
Internet		624	
Sundry expenses		318	
Premises depreciation (20,000 x 2%) (a)		400	
Fixtures and fittings depreciation (2,850 x 20%) (b)		570	
Bad debts (f)		750	
			17,408
Net profit			**10,697**

▲ Figure 12.9

Mountain Sports and Golf Shop
Statement of financial position as at 31 December

FIXED ASSETS	Cost	Depreciation		Net book value
	£	£		£
Premises	20,000	400	(a)	19,600
Fixtures and fittings	2,850	570	(b)	2,280
	22,850	970		21,880
CURRENT ASSETS				
Inventory		22,390		
Trade receivables (14,320 - 750) (f)	13,570			
Less provision for doubtful debts	0	13,570		
Prepayment of rates (c)		1,000		
Accrual of discounts received (d)		500		
Bank		2,970		
Cash		115		
		40,545		
Creditors falling due in less than one year				
Trade payables		8,160		
Accrual of telephone expenses (e)		300		
		8,460		
Working capital				32,085
Total assets less current liabilities				53,965
Net assets				**53,965**
Financed by:				
Capital				50,888
Net profit (from the Income statement)				10,697
Less drawings				7,620
				53,965

▲ Figure 12.10

(90 minutes)

Using Figure 12.11, prepare an income statement and statement of financial position for Jamina, who runs a sole-trader dress shop. She has supplied the following trial balance and additional information at her financial year end, 30 April.

Jamina Dress Shop
Trial balance as at 30 April

	Dr.	Cr.
	£	£
Sales		17,665
Purchases	12,332	
Capital		55,000
Trade receivables	4,353	
Trade payables		3,477
Cash at bank	2,101	
Cash in hand	90	
Premises	35,000	
Fixtures and fittings	7,450	
Motor vehicle	8,700	
Wages	1,900	
Motor expenses	461	
Drawings	2,500	
Telephone and internet	500	
Insurance	755	
	76,142	76,142

▲ Figure 12.11

Additional information

1 Closing inventory is valued at £5,600.
2 Premises should be depreciated using the straight line method at a rate of 2 per cent per annum.
3 Fixtures and fittings and motor vehicles should be depreciated using the straight line method at a rate of 10 per cent per annum.
4 Telephone and internet expenses include a prepayment of £200.
5 Insurance of £500 is outstanding.
6 One debt of £300 is to be written off as a bad debt.

KNOW IT

1 Explain what is meant by prepayments and accruals.
2 Define the term 'closing inventory.'
3 Explain the difference between a bad debt and a provision for doubtful debts.
4 Explain the purpose of a statement of financial position.
5 List five expenses that would be included in an income statement.

LO3 assessment activities P7 and P8

Below are suggested assessment activities that have been directly linked to the Pass criteria in LO3 to help with assignment preparation. These are followed by a top tip on how to achieve the best results.

Activity 1 Pass criteria P7

P7 Produce an information poster to inform students about final accounts, which explains the purpose of an income statement and a statement of financial position.

Activity 2 Pass criteria P8

P8 Using Figure 12.12, prepare an income statement and statement of financial position.

Use the trial balance and additional information supplied by Alexander, who runs a sole-trader music business, operating online and via a market stall.

Alexander's financial year runs to 31 December.

Additional information at 31 December

1 Closing inventory is valued at £17,230.
2 The motor vehicle and stall fittings should be depreciated using the straight line method at a rate of 20 per cent per annum.
3 Rent of £300 is outstanding.
4 Discounts received of £250 are outstanding.
5 One debt of £2,500 is to be written off as a bad debt.

TOP TIPS

✔ You can use either a manual or computerised method to prepare the income statement and statement of financial position.

Alexander Music
Trial balance as at 31 December

	Dr. £	Cr. £
Capital		30,955
Drawings	8,420	
Cash at bank	3,115	
Cash in hand	295	
Trade receivables	12,300	
Trade payables		9,370
Opening inventory	23,910	
Motor vehicle	4,100	
Stall fittings	6,250	
Sales		130,900
Purchases	92,100	
Returns inwards	550	
Mobile telephone	215	
Discounts received		307
Postage costs	309	
Motor expenses	1,630	
Rent of market stall	2,970	
Internet	405	
Wages	12,810	
Stationery	492	
Administration costs	1,377	
Sundry expenses	284	
	171,532	**171,532**

▲ Figure 12.12

LO4 Use ratios to assess the performance of businesses *P9 M3 D1 D2*

GETTING STARTED

(15 minutes)

Working in pairs, prepare a spider diagram of reasons why individuals or groups would need to assess the performance of a business organisation.

4.1 & 4.2 Using ratios and their usefulness when assessing the performance of a business

Purpose of ratios

The purpose of accounting is to convey financial information to interested parties. Absolute numbers in isolation are meaningless. A profit of £10,000 could

be excellent, satisfactory or poor depending on the business organisation that is being reviewed. It is in these circumstances when ratios are used.

There are a number of considerations when assessing performance of a business.

1 Figures need to be related to other figures (ratios) to put them into perspective.
2 Trends in the same business over a number of years will show whether it is progressing or deteriorating.
3 Results of one business may be compared with the results of another business (inter-firm comparison) to see if it is performing as well as it should be. This is appropriate only if:
   • they are in the same line of business (for example, two fish and chip shops)
   • the structures of the business are similar (for example, two sole traders, not a public limited company and a sole trader).

Limitations of ratio analysis

When assessing the performance of a business using ratio analysis, remember that this has a number of limitations.

1 Ratios show only the results of carrying on business. They do not indicate the causes of poor ratios. Further investigation is required.
2 The accuracy of the ratio depends upon the quality of the information from which it is calculated. The required information is not always disclosed in accounting statements and account headings may be misleading.
3 Ratios can be used only to compare 'like with like'.
4 Ratios tend to ignore the time factor in seasonal businesses.
5 They can be misleading if accounts are not adjusted for inflation. For ratios to be meaningful, comparisons have to be made:
   • inter-firm
   • against a benchmark or industry standard
   • from year to year.

Users and uses of ratio analysis

Table 12.8 Who uses ratio analysis?

User	Use
Management	To analyse past results To plan for the future (budget) To control their business
Investors	To compare investment opportunities
Banks and lenders	To assess the creditworthiness of the firm
Financial analysts	To inform: • the financial press • trade associations • trade unions
Government	To compile national statistics

GROUP ACTIVITY

(30 minutes)

Working in small groups, choose a supermarket in your area. Identify three user groups that would be interested in the ratio analysis the supermarket would complete. Produce a table that identifies the groups and states the use they would make of ratio analysis.

Profitability ratios

Profitability ratios are usually calculated before liquidity ratios as the income statement is usually constructed before the statement of financial position.

Gross profit mark-up

$$\frac{\text{Gross profit} \times 100}{\text{Cost of sales}}$$

Gross profit mark-up is the amount of profit that is added to the cost price of goods or services to cover expenses and ultimately make a profit. For example, goods that cost £200 to purchase, which are being sold at 50 per cent mark-up would have a selling price of £300.

Gross profit margin

$$\frac{\text{Gross profit} \times 100}{\text{Sales (Revenue)}}$$

This expresses the gross profit as a percentage of sales. It should be similar from one year to the next within the same business, but will vary between organisations in different sectors – for example, gross profit margin on jewellery is considerably higher than that on food. A significant change from one year to the next, particularly a fall, requires investigation into the buying and selling prices.

Gross profit percentage and net profit percentage need to be considered in context. For example, a supermarket may have a lower gross profit percentage than a small corner shop but, because of the supermarket's much higher turnover, the amount of profit will be much higher. Whatever the type of business, gross profit – both as an amount and as a percentage – needs to be sufficient to cover the expenses of the business and then make an acceptable return on capital.

Net profit margin

$$\frac{\text{Net profit} \times 100}{\text{Sales (Revenue)}}$$

As with gross profit margin, net profit margin is expressed as a percentage and should be similar from year to year for the same business; it should also be comparable with other businesses in the same line of business. Net profit percentages should ideally increase every year, indicating that the profit and loss account expenses are being kept under control. Any significant fall should be investigated to see if it has been caused by:

● a fall in gross profit percentage, and/or
● an increase in one particular expense, e.g. wages and salaries, advertising.

Return on capital employed

$$\frac{\text{Net profit before tax and interest} \times 100}{\text{Long-term capital employed}}$$

This expresses the profit of a business in relation to the owner's capital (i.e. the capital that the owner(s) have invested in the business). It is normally compared with other forms of investment such as a building society or bank account. A person running a business is investing a sum of money in that business, and the profit is the return on that investment. However, it should be noted that the risks in running a business are considerably greater than depositing the money with a building society or bank, and an additional return is needed to allow for the extra risk.

Liquidity ratios

Liquidity ratios include the current ratio and the acid test ratio.

Current ratio

$$\frac{\text{Current assets}}{\text{Current liabilities (amounts falling due within one year)}}$$

The current ratio uses figures from the balance sheet and measures the relationship between current assets and current liabilities. Although there is no ideal current ratio, an acceptable ratio is about 2:1, i.e. £2 of current assets to every £1 of current liabilities. However, a business in the retail trade may be able to work with a lower ratio, e.g. 1.5:1 or even less, because it deals mainly in sales for cash and so does not have a large figure for trade receivables. A current ratio can be too high; if it is above 3:1 an investigation of the make-up of current assets and current liabilities is needed – for example, the business may have too much inventory, too many trade receivables or too much cash at the bank, or even too few trade payables.

Acid test (quick) ratio

$$\frac{\text{Current assets} - \text{Closing inventory}}{\text{Current liabilities (amounts falling due within one year)}}$$

The acid test ratio uses the current assets and current liabilities from the balance sheet but omits inventory. This is because inventory is the most illiquid (i.e. not easily turned into cash) current asset it has to be sold, turned into trade receivables and then the cash has to be collected from the trade receivables. Therefore, this ratio provides a direct comparison between trade receivables and cash/bank and short-term liabilities. The balance between liquid assets and current liabilities should ideally be about 1:1, i.e. £1 of liquid assets to

each £1 of current liabilities. At this ratio a business is expected to be able to pay its current liabilities from its liquid assets. A figure below 1:1, e.g. 0.75:1, indicates that the business would have difficulty in meeting pressing demands from trade payables. However, as with the current ratio, some businesses are able to operate with a lower acid test ratio than others.

Efficiency ratios

Efficiency ratios include inventory turnover, trade receivables collection period and trade payables payment days.

Inventory turnover

$$\frac{\text{Cost of sales}}{\text{Average inventory}}$$

Inventory turnover is the number of times inventory is changed during a year. The figure depends on the type of goods sold. For example, a market trader selling fresh flowers who sells out every day will have an inventory turnover of 365 times per year. By contrast, a jewellery shop – because it may hold large inventory of jewellery – will have a much slower inventory turnover, perhaps four or five times per year. Nevertheless, inventory turnover must not be too long as it may become out of date and obsolete. A business that is improving in efficiency will have a quicker inventory turnover comparing one year with the previous one, or with the inventory turnover of similar businesses. A business must also remember the costs of storing inventory when considering its inventory turnover. An inventory turnover of 12 times a year means that about 30 days' inventory is held. Note that inventory turnover can be calculated only by a business that buys and sells goods, not by a business that provides a service.

Trade receivables collection period

$$\frac{\text{Trade receivables} \times 365}{\text{Credit sales}}$$

This ratio determines how long it takes, on average, for a trade receivable to pay a business the amount of money that it owes – how long it takes a business to collect the money owed by a trade receivable. The figure is calculated as a number of days. A collection period of 90 days implies that it takes on average three months for a trade receivable to settle its account.

Businesses that are having cash flow issues will try to reduce their collection period to ensure they have sufficient money to pay their debts when they become due.

Collection periods will vary depending on the type of business being considered. In particular, they will depend on:

- the nature of the goods being sold
- the price of the goods
- whether the business trades mainly wholesale (business to business) or retail (business to customer).

Wholesale businesses tend to have longer collection periods than retail businesses. Many businesses – for example, sandwich shops – are unlikely to have a collection period, as customers will pay for the goods when they are purchased.

Businesses will offer different collection periods depending on the:

- size of the customer's business
- discount already offered
- credit risk of the customer.

Trade payables payment days

$$\frac{\text{Trade payables} \times 365}{\text{Credit purchases}}$$

This ratio determines how long it takes, on average, for a trade payable to pay a business the amount of money that it owes. The figure is calculated as a number of days. A payment period of 60 days would imply that a business takes, on average, two months to settle the accounts of any goods bought on credit. In general, businesses aim to have a longer trade payables payment period than trade receivables collection period. This ensures they will have received sufficient money from their trade receivables to be able to pay their trade payables.

Gearing ratio

$$\frac{\text{Non-current liabilities} \times 100}{\text{Capital employed}}$$

The gearing ratio highlights the capital structure of business organisation. It shows the proportion of debt finance a business has, relative to the amount of capital or equity invested by an owner or shareholder.

In general, the higher the level of gearing, the greater the risks to the business. This is because the repayment and interest charges due on debts have to be paid. They are not optional, unlike the payment of dividends to shareholders or profit to a sole trader.

INDIVIDUAL ACTIVITY

(60 minutes)

Using the following link, download the latest annual report and accounts for Sainsbury's plc: http://tinyurl.com/zq3yfk2

Choose five ratios that would be appropriate to make an assessment of Sainsbury's performance. For the last two years, calculate the ratios you have chosen.

Prepare a short report that assesses the performance of Sainsbury's over this period.

KNOW IT

1 What is the difference between the current ratio and the acid test ratio?
2 Explain how a business can measure its profitability.
3 Discuss what is meant by gearing.
4 List five users of ratios.
5 Explain how a business uses efficiency ratios.

LO4 assessment activities

Below are suggested assessment activities that have been directly linked to the Pass, Merit and Distinction criteria in LO4 to help with assignment preparation. These are followed by top tips on how to achieve the best results.

Activity 1 Pass criteria *P9*

For this task, you will require the final accounts you prepared for **P8**.

P9 Calculate a range of appropriate ratios to measure the performance of Alexander Music.

TOP TIPS

✔ Practise a range of questions prior to attempting the assessment task.

Activity 2 Merit criteria *M3*

M3 Based on your final accounts for **P8** and your ratio calculations for **P9**, analyse the liquidity, profitability and efficiency of Alexander Music.

> ### TOP TIPS
>
> ✔ You should choose a suitable format in which to complete this task, e.g. a business report, discussion with the assessor or tutor, presentation.

Activity 3 Distinction criteria *D1* and *D2*

D1 Based on your final accounts for **P8**, your ratio calculations for **P9** and your analysis for **M3**, evaluate the financial performance of Alexander Music. You should make recommendations for improvement.

D2 Evaluate the usefulness of ratio analysis when assessing the performance of Alexander Music.

> ### TOP TIPS
>
> ✔ You should choose a suitable format in which to complete these tasks, e.g. business report, discussion with the assessor or tutor, presentation.
> ✔ When evaluating the usefulness of ratio analysis, review the weaknesses of ratio analysis in assessing business performance.

Read about it

Business Accounting Volume 1 (10th edn), by Frank Wood and Alan Sangster, FT Prentice Hall, 2005

Business Accounting, by Rob Jones, Causeway Press, 2004

Business Accounts (3rd edn), by David Cox, Osborne Books, 2004

Unit 13

Management accounting

LEARNING OUTCOMES

The topics, activities and suggested reading in this unit will help you to:

1 understand business costs and pricing methods used by businesses
2 be able to use break-even analysis
3 be able to use budgets using budgetary techniques
4 be able to calculate capital investment appraisals
5 be able to prepare and use cash flow forecasts.

How will I be assessed?

You will be assessed through a series of assignments and tasks set and marked by your tutor.

How will I be graded?

You will be graded using the following criteria, which are in the specification produced by OCR for the qualification.

Learning Outcome	Pass	Merit	Distinction
You will:	To achieve a Pass you must demonstrate that you have met all the pass assessment criteria	To achieve a Merit you must demonstrate that you have met all the pass and merit assessment criteria	To achieve a Distinction you must demonstrate that you have met all the pass, merit and distinction assessment criteria
1 Understand business costs and pricing methods used by businesses	**P1** Describe types of cost incurred and pricing methods used by a specific organisation		
	P2 Explain the impact of pricing policies on production and costs for a specific business		
2 Be able to use break-even analysis	**P3** Calculate break-even from organisational costing information	**M1** Assess the implications of changes in costs and revenue on break even	
	P4 Prepare and use a break-even chart for decision making		
	P5 Explain the strengths and weaknesses of break-even analysis		
3 Be able to use budgets and budgetary techniques	**P6** Prepare a budget for a specific business using budgetary techniques		
	P7 Calculate variances for a specific business based on budget and actual figures	**M2** Analyse variances based on budget and actual figures and identify likely causes for the variances	**D1** Recommend and justify actions a business should take based on variances
4 Be able to calculate capital investment appraisals	**P8** Explain the advantages and disadvantages of capital investment appraisal techniques for a specific business decision		
	P9 Calculate a capital investment appraisal for a specific business decision		
	P10 Interpret an organisation's capital investment appraisal results and recommend a decision		
5 Be able to prepare and use cash flow forecasts	**P11** Prepare a 12-month cash flow forecast including cash and credit sales and purchases for a specific business	**M3** Analyse the cash flow position identified in a 12-month cash flow forecast for a specific business	**D2** Recommend and justify the actions a specific business might take in order to improve its cash flow position
	P12 Describe how a specific business could improve its cash flow position		

LO1 Understand business costs and pricing methods used by businesses *P1 P2*

GETTING STARTED

(10 minutes)

Working in small groups, make a list of the costs that are likely to be incurred by your school or college. Be prepared to share your ideas with the rest of the class.

1.1 Definitions and examples of business costs

Table 13.1 Types of costs

Costs	Definition	Examples
Fixed costs	Costs that remain unchanged as the output level of a business changes It does not matter what level of output a business produces, fixed costs will remain the same	Rent Salaries Interest on loans Advertising Insurance Depreciation
Indirect costs/ overheads	Costs that cannot be linked with the output of any particular product They are related to the level of output of the firm but not in a direct manner and not for any one product For example, the cost of powering a machine will be related to the level of output but not to a particular product	Depreciation Insurance Supervisors' salaries Head office expenses Power
Variable costs	Any cost that varies directly with the level of output; varying directly means that the total variable cost will be dependent on the level of output – if output doubles, then the variable cost would double; if it halves, the variable costs would halve; if output is zero, no variable costs are incurred	Wages Heating Lighting Factory labour Raw materials and components Packaging costs Royalties
Direct costs	Similar to a variable cost in that it compares the cost with the level of output; however, a direct cost is any cost that is directly related to the output level of a particular product It is a more appropriate classification for a firm that makes more than one type of product For example, a firm may produce a table from one type of wood and a chair from another type of wood; both types of wood are classified as direct costs as they are directly related to the level of output of a particular product, not to the level of output in general	Direct labour Direct materials Royalties
Semi-variable costs	In reality, nearly all costs would not easily be classified into either fixed or variable; most will fall somewhere between the two classifications; we can classify these costs as semi-variable costs	Most bills for the telephone, gas and electricity will consist of a standing charge that is fixed and a variable element that depends on the usage

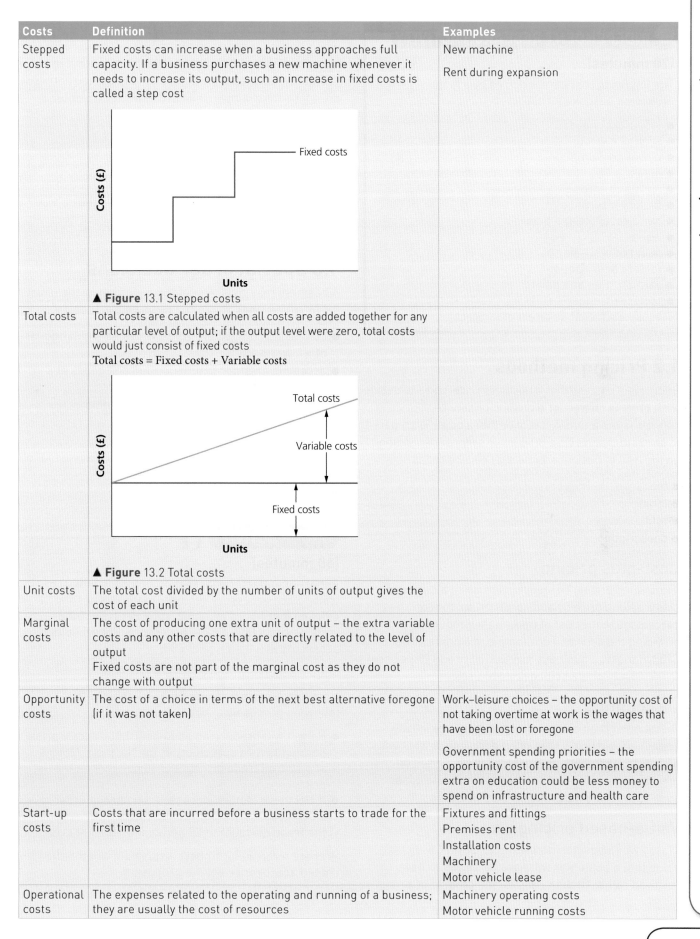

Costs	Definition	Examples
Stepped costs	Fixed costs can increase when a business approaches full capacity. If a business purchases a new machine whenever it needs to increase its output, such an increase in fixed costs is called a step cost ▲ **Figure** 13.1 Stepped costs	New machine Rent during expansion
Total costs	Total costs are calculated when all costs are added together for any particular level of output; if the output level were zero, total costs would just consist of fixed costs Total costs = Fixed costs + Variable costs ▲ **Figure** 13.2 Total costs	
Unit costs	The total cost divided by the number of units of output gives the cost of each unit	
Marginal costs	The cost of producing one extra unit of output – the extra variable costs and any other costs that are directly related to the level of output Fixed costs are not part of the marginal cost as they do not change with output	
Opportunity costs	The cost of a choice in terms of the next best alternative foregone (if it was not taken)	Work–leisure choices – the opportunity cost of not taking overtime at work is the wages that have been lost or foregone Government spending priorities – the opportunity cost of the government spending extra on education could be less money to spend on infrastructure and health care
Start-up costs	Costs that are incurred before a business starts to trade for the first time	Fixtures and fittings Premises rent Installation costs Machinery Motor vehicle lease
Operational costs	The expenses related to the operating and running of a business; they are usually the cost of resources	Machinery operating costs Motor vehicle running costs

INDEPENDENT RESEARCH ACTIVITY

(20 minutes)

The following costs are incurred by a factory producing bespoke furniture:

- labourers' wages
- synthetic wood
- power consumption
- glass
- nails and screws
- factory insurance
- handles, locks and hinges
- wood
- supervisors' salaries
- factory depreciation
- varnish, glue and paints
- factory manager's salary.

Classify each cost as direct or indirect.

1.2 Pricing methods

Pricing is a process that a business undertakes to decide what price to charge for a product or service. A price is defined as the amount of money that a buyer is prepared to pay in exchange for a product or service. Depending on the type of business, price may also be called:

- fee
- fare
- rent
- subscription.

Cost-plus pricing

A cost-plus pricing strategy occurs when a business sets a selling price by adding a fixed amount or percentage to the cost of making the product or providing the service. For example, if a product costs £100 to make, a business may decide to add 25 per cent to the cost to give a selling price of £125.

Discounting

Discounting is an approach where items are initially priced unrealistically then offered for sale at what will appear to customers as a reduced price. This is often used by large retail stores when selling white goods such as washing machines and dishwashers.

Value-based pricing

This is when businesses set prices primarily on the value that a customer will have perceived to have received rather than the cost of the product or prices

charged in the past. This approach is usually used when there is a shortage of product – for example, ice creams or cold drinks at an outdoor festival in hot weather – or when a product is an add-on to another product – for example, ink cartridges for a printer.

Competitive pricing

Most businesses operate in a competitive environment. To ensure they are able to compete, businesses will set their prices in accordance with the prices charged by their competitors. This is often the case in the service industry – for example, hairdressers in a local area will tend to charge similar prices.

1.3 Special order decisions

A business may consider selling goods below the usual selling price. These circumstances will include:

- combating competitors who are selling similar goods at a lower price
- accepting an order to produce and sell goods at a special price
- maintaining production in difficult trading conditions so that a skilled workforce will remain in employment
- assisting in the disposal or sale of obsolescent (out of date) or perishable goods
- promoting a new product.

GROUP ACTIVITY

(60 minutes)

Robert manufactures accessories for the motor trade. Each accessory requires materials costing £25 and four hours of labour at £9 per hour. Other variable costs total £6 per accessory. Robert sells the accessory at a list price of £80.

Robert's monthly fixed costs are £33,000.

Northern Motors has approached Robert with the following proposals.

- Robert will produce an additional 1,000 accessories per month as a special order for Northern Motors at a special trade discount of 10 per cent on the list price.
- If Northern Motors increases the special order to 2,000 accessories per month, Robert will increase the trade discount to 20 per cent on the list price.

Prepare a report for Robert, explaining whether he should accept or reject the proposals.

1.4 Impact of pricing policies on production and costs

Price is an important part of the marketing mix and directly influences a business's profits by generating revenue rather than affecting costs. Businesses often differentiate their products and services based on price. For example, does a higher price lead to better quality or does a lower price mean better value or lower quality?

The price that a business sets needs to be consistent with other items in the marketing mix. A high-priced product needs to have features and benefits which mean that all customers feel justified in paying the higher price.

The main reason for setting the right price for a product is to generate the level of sales that will allow the organisation to meet its objectives. These objectives often include:

- maximising profits
- maintaining or increasing market share
- entering new markets
- increasing sales volume
- getting new products in a new market.

KNOW IT

1 Name three variable costs.
2 Define the term opportunity cost.
3 Sketch a graph that illustrates stepped costs.
4 Explain how businesses will decide whether to accept a special order decision.
5 Explain the impact of pricing policies on production and costs.

LO1 assessment activity

Below is a suggested assessment activity that has been directly linked to the Pass criteria in LO1 to help with assignment preparation. This is followed by top tips on how to achieve the best results.

Activity 1 Pass criteria *P1* and *P2*

P1 P2 Choose a business as a case study for this activity. You should be familiar with the business and know its products or services.

Prepare a short report, including practical examples throughout. The report needs to include:

- a description of the types of costs incurred by the business you have chosen

- a description of the pricing methods used by the business you have chosen
- an explanation of the impact of the pricing policies of your chosen business on its production and costs.

TOP TIPS
✔ You should check with your tutor that the business you have chosen is suitable for the assignment.
✔ Ensure you focus on the command verbs in each task.
✔ You should spend equal time and produce similar amounts of evidence for each of the pass criteria.

LO2 Be able to use break-even analysis *P3 P4 P5* *M1*

GETTING STARTED

(20 minutes)

Review the work you completed in Unit 1 and for LO1 of this unit. Prepare a glossary of costing key terms.

2.1 Calculations

Contribution per unit and total contribution

Contribution is the amount remaining after variable costs have been deducted from sales revenue. Contribution is not the same as profit since when we reach a figure for contribution we have deducted only variable costs, not fixed costs.

Contribution is the amount of money that is remaining from the selling price, after variable costs have been deducted, which can be used to pay fixed costs and eventually become profit.

Contribution per unit = Selling price per unit − Variable costs per unit

Total contribution = Total sales revenue − Total variable costs

Total revenue

Revenue is the money earned from selling the output (products or services). It is based on both the level of output and the selling price of this output.

Total revenue = selling price × output level

Break-even point by use of formulae

Most businesses will want to maximise their profits but being profitable is not always possible. New businesses, small businesses and businesses facing an economic slowdown may find that they cannot generate profits at all. In this case, it may be more realistic for them to aim to break even.

The break-even point is the level of sales where total costs equal total revenue, therefore there is no profit or loss.

Break-even assumptions

A number of assumptions are made when calculating the break-even point for a business. These include:

● all output is sold
● there is no inventory of goods remaining unsold
● the business makes only one type of product
● all costs are classified as either fixed costs or variable costs – there are no semi-variable costs.

Break-even formula

$$\frac{\text{Break-even point}}{\text{(measured in units of output)}} = \frac{\text{Total fixed costs}}{\text{Contribution per unit}}$$

Margin of safety

If a business is generating a profit, its output level will be higher than the break-even output level. The margin of safety measures how far output can fall before the business begins to make a loss. It is measured by the number of units of output between the current level of production and the break-even level of production.

Margin of safety (in units) = Actual output in units − Break-even output in units

Profit model – calculation of profit/loss

Selling price per unit − variable costs per unit

= contribution per unit × number of units

= total contribution − fixed costs

= profit/loss

PAIRS ACTIVITY

(30 minutes)

Look at the data given in Table 13.2.

Table 13.2

		£ per unit
Direct materials		7
Direct labour		
Other variable costs	2	
Fixed costs		10
Selling price	30	
Number of units produced and sold 50,000		

Now, calculate the following.

1 Contribution per unit

Contribution per unit = Selling price per unit − Variable costs per unit

Contribution per unit = 30 − (7 + 3 + 2)

Contribution per unit = 30 − 12

Contribution per unit = ?

2 Total revenue

Total revenue = Selling price × Number of units sold

Total revenue = £30 × 50,000 units

Total revenue = ?

3 Total contribution

Total contribution = Total sales revenue − Total variable costs

Total contribution = 1,500,000 − (£12 × 50,000 units)

Total contribution = 1,500,000 − 600,000

Total contribution = ?

4 Break even in units

$$\text{Break-even point (units)} \atop \text{(measured in units of output)} = \frac{\text{Total fixed costs}}{\text{Contribution per unit}}$$

$$\text{Break-even point (units)} = \frac{(10 \times 50,000)}{18}$$

$$\text{Break-even point (units)} = \frac{500,000}{18}$$

Break-even point (units) = ? (to the nearest unit)

5 Break even in £s

Break even in £s = Break even in units × Selling price

Break even in £s = 27,778 units × £20

Break even in £s = ?

6 Margin of safety

Margin of safety (in units) = Actual output in units – Break-even output in units

Margin of safety (in units) = 50,000 – 27,778

Margin of safety (in units) = ? units

7 Profit/loss

	£
Selling price per unit	30
– variable costs per unit	12
= contribution per unit	18
× number of units	50,000
= total contribution	900,000
– fixed costs	500,000
= profit/loss	**?**

Table 13.3 Figures for business calculations

Business	A	B	C	D	E
	£ per unit	£ per unit	£ per unit	£ per unit	£ per unit
Direct materials	5	7	15	30	3
Direct labour	2	9	4	8	5
Other variable costs	1	2	2	4	1
Fixed costs	4	6	8	16	3
Profit	5	7	10	20	4
Selling price	20	32	40	75	18
Number of units produced and sold	10,000	25,000	20,000	40,000	15,000

Contribution/sales ratio

The contribution/sales ratio is used when several products are being manufactured and sold by a business. The ratio is also used when a business has produced a marginal costing statement. From the contribution/sales ratio it is possible for accountants to calculate the break-even point.

$$\text{Contribution/sales ratio} = \frac{\text{Contribution}}{\text{Sales}}$$

2.2 Producing graphs

Break-even graphs

The break-even point can be calculated by drawing a graph which shows fixed costs, total costs and total revenue. The graph will illustrate how each of these change with the level of output. The point at which the total cost and total revenue lines cross is the break-even point.

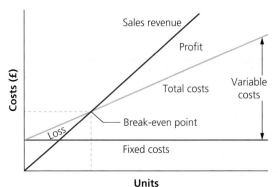

▲ **Figure 13.3** Example of a break-even graph

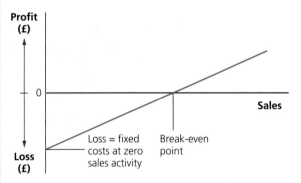

(30 minutes)

The financial information in Table 13.4 is given for the production and sales of Snuffies, a pet toy. The financial data is based on an output of 2,000 Snuffies.

Table 13.4 Production and sales data for Snuffies

Cost per Snuffie	£
Raw materials	9
Components	1
Direct labour	5
Royalties	2
Fixed costs	3
Selling price	25

Produce a break-even graph for Snuffies to show the break-even point in units.

Contribution to sales (profit/volume) graphs

▲ **Figure 13.4** An example of a sales profit/volume graph

2.3 & 2.4 Analysis and use of break-even data and contribution to sales graphs

Businesses use break-even data and contribution to sales graphs to:

● estimate how many goods or services need to be sold to make an acceptable profit

● analyse the level of costs that they are able to manage – for example, an airline may calculate that if fuel increases above a certain price then it will not be able to survive

● calculate the price they should charge for their goods or services

● assess how changes in revenue will affect their profits and break-even point

● review how increases in costs will affect their profits and break-even point.

When analysing and using break-even data and contribution to sales graphs, it is vital to consider the advantages and limitations of the analysis (see Table 13.5).

Table 13.5 Advantages and limitations of using break-even data and contribution to sales graphs

Advantages	Limitations
Graphical representation allows businesses to provide financial data that has a visual impact; this is important for non-finance specialists	Data is based on estimates so it is uncertain
Businesses are able to consider 'what if' scenarios and predict likely outcomes	Fixed costs do not necessarily remain constant – stepped costs are not used in this analysis
Calculation of the margin of safety will provide a risk assessment of how far sales can fall before a business will make a loss	Many businesses sell more than one product – break-even analysis assumes only one product is made
	Most businesses hold inventories and have unsold production – break-even analysis assumes all production is sold
	Break-even analysis applies only when selling prices remain constant; this is not usually the case, with inflation and selling prices changing frequently
	Break-even analysis assumes that all costs are fixed or variable – in reality there are semi-variable costs such as telephone, gas, electricity, etc.
	Break-even analysis assumes that all financial relationships are linear; this means that all lines on the break-even graph will be straight – due to economies of scale (e.g. bulk buying), this is not always the case

2.5 How to use break-even analysis to make business decisions

Break-even analysis can be used to make business decisions in the following ways.

Make or buy

Businesses may choose to manufacture their own products for various reasons:

- the product is unique, is not produced by anybody else and there is a demand for it
- the business wants to supply its own brand of a particular product
- the business does not want to be dependent on outside suppliers who may be unreliable regarding delivery and price
- the business believes it can manufacture its products cheaper than it can buy them from outside
- the key consideration when deciding whether to 'make or buy' is whether a business has spare capacity.

If a business has spare production capacity it has more than enough capacity to make the products required, therefore:

- the production resources will remain idle
- fixed costs will still need to be paid but are irrelevant in the decision as the business won't need to pay any extra fixed costs
- a business need only consider the variable costs of making the products compared to the purchase cost of buying in the products.

Decision:

- if the buying price is less than the variable costs of making – BUY
- if the buying price is greater than the variable costs of making – MAKE

If a business has no spare production capacity the business will need to acquire more space or cease making another product in order to create the required space. Stopping making another product to free up capacity causes the business to lose money in the form of lost contribution. The business needs to compare the contribution lost plus any extra costs of making the product with the purchase price of buying the product.

Decision:

- if the relevant costs of making are greater than the purchase price – BUY
- if the relevant costs of making are less than the purchase price – MAKE

Acceptance of additional work

As with a 'make or buy' decision, a business needs to assess whether it has sufficient capacity to accept any additional work. The same considerations and decisions would apply as for a 'make or buy' decision.

Acceptance of special orders

See Section 1.3 (page 238).

Discontinuing a product or service based on contribution

A business decides to discontinue a product or service when its contribution is lower than other products or becomes negative. This would occur when the variable costs of production increase or the selling price reduces. Before discontinuing a product or service, a business must ensure that this will not affect the sales of other products. For example, a business would need to continue producing a mobile phone charger if it still produced the mobile phone.

Price setting

Businesses will use break-even analysis, and in particular contribution and profit calculations, to work out the best selling price to charge for a product. In many cases it is possible to increase profit by reducing the selling price of an item but increasing the number of sales made.

GROUP ACTIVITY

(1 hour)

Lang Ltd manufactures decorative lamps. Each lamp requires materials costing £8 and two hours of labour at £6 an hour. The lamps are sold at £25 each and current output is 400 lamps per week. Fixed costs are £700 per week.

If the company reduced the selling price of each lamp to £23, then it is estimated that sales would rise to 600 lamps per week. No further resources would be required to make 600 lamps per week.

A further reduction in selling price to £22 would increase sales to 1,100 lamps per week. An increase in production to 1,100 lamps per week would require extra resources and therefore add 15 per cent to fixed costs.

Working in groups, discuss the selling price that Lang Ltd should charge for the lamps in order to make the most profit. Include both financial and non-financial factors in your solution. Be prepared to share your solution with the rest of the class.

'What if' scenarios

This analysis evaluates the expected return or value of a proposed change in business activity. Businesses will create various scenarios that may occur and then review the potential outcomes prior to making a management decision. For example, a business may calculate the break-even point for a particular product, changing the variables (fixed costs, variable costs, selling price) to review the effect on the break-even output.

Optimum use of scarce resources

A scarce resource (also known as a limiting factor) is something that limits a business's activities. This may be the level of sales that can be achieved – for example, there is a limit to the number of Christmas trees that are wanted in March. Alternatively, it may be a shortage of resource that prevents a business from reaching its sales potential. Scarce or limiting factors include:

- supply of skilled labour
- supply of raw materials
- factory space
- machine availability
- finance available
- capacity of the plant or factory.

When a business has a scarce resource that is limiting production, it needs to take a number of steps to decide which products it should produce.

- Step 1: Determine the limiting factor and how much is available – for example, how many labour hours are available for the next year.

- Step 2: Rank the options using contribution earned per unit of the scarce resource. Based on the amount of the limiting factor needed to make each product, the business needs to decide which product will make the most contribution for the resource being used – for example, some products require less labour than others and may therefore make a higher contribution.
- Step 3: Based on the solution to step 2, the business should allocate the resources available and make the most profitable product mix.

KNOW IT

1 Define break even.
2 State the break-even formula.
3 Explain what is meant by margin of safety.
4 Identify the strengths and weaknesses of break-even analysis.
5 Sketch a contribution to sales (profit/volume) graph.

LO2 assessment activities

Below are suggested assessment activities that have been directly linked to the Pass and Merit criteria in LO2 to help with assignment preparation. These are followed by top tips on how to achieve the best results.

▲ **Figure 13.5** Prepare accounting data for Nutcracker Sweets

For the purpose of this assignment you are on work experience in the accounting department at Nutcracker Sweets, a sweet and chocolate manufacturer.

The management accountant has asked you to prepare some management accounting data to help decide whether the business should introduce a new range of luxury lollipops.

The estimated information in Table 13.6 has been given to you relating to the new lollipops.

Table 13.6 Nutcracker Sweets data

Data per lollipop	£
Direct materials	0.30
Direct labour	0.50
Direct expenses	0.25
Fixed costs	0.20
Selling price	2.00

The data is based on a production output of 500 lollipops.

Activity 1 Pass criteria *P3* and *P4*

P3 Calculate the number of lollipops that Nutcracker Sweets requires to break even.

P4 Prepare a break-even chart for the new lollipops. Based on your break-even chart, state the margin of safety and profit/loss that Nutcracker Sweets would make if it were to produce and sell the estimated 500 lollipops.

Activity 2 Pass criteria *P5*

P5 Prepare a presentation for the management accountant. The presentation is for delivery to the board of directors. It needs to explain the strengths and weaknesses of break-even analysis.

TOP TIPS
- ✔ You should spend an equal amount of time on each of the criteria.
- ✔ For P3 and P4, you should show all workings.
- ✔ For P4, you can choose to produce your chart using computer software or on a piece of graph paper. You need to ensure that your chart is clearly labelled.
- ✔ You should ensure your presentation is easy to read and can be understood by non-accountants.
- ✔ For P5 you can use any layout or design you feel is appropriate.

Activity 3 Merit criteria *M1*

M1 Prepare a report that assesses the implications of the following changes to the break-even point for the new lollipops. You should consider each change individually – the changes are independent of one another. You should discuss financial and non-financial factors:

- increase in direct materials
- decrease in direct labour
- increase in direct expenses
- decrease in fixed costs
- increase in selling price.

TOP TIPS
- ✔ Your report should include calculations to support your assessment.
- ✔ You can use any layout or design you feel is appropriate.
- ✔ Make sure you meet the command verb.

LO3 Be able to calculate budgets using budgetary techniques *P6 P7 M2 D1*

GETTING STARTED

(15 minutes)

Working in pairs, answer the following questions.

1 What is a budget?
2 Name three examples of budgets that businesses prepare.
3 State five purposes of budgets.

3.1 How and why businesses prepare and revise budgets

Definition of a budget

A budget is a financial plan for a specific period of time. Budgets can be prepared for any activity that involves controllable costs of variable revenues. Large businesses may produce departmental budgets that are then combined into a master budget that covers all of the business operations. Businesses may approach budgeting in a number of ways.

- Objective budget: this simply states the business objectives so a member of staff is aware of what they are working towards.
- Investment budget: this assesses the viability of a long-term investment project; it may be combined with capital investment appraisal.
- Zero-based budget: this ignores all previous predictions and data; every item in the budget will require clear justification.
- Fixed budget: all figures are absolute – there can be no variation in the data included in the budget; in a fixed budget all figures must be adhered to by the employees.
- Flexible budget: this allows a certain level of variation; the budget includes a contingency, with acceptable upper and lower limits included throughout.

Purposes of budgets

A number of purposes of budgeting have been identified by management accountants. These include those listed below.

- Planning: the process of preparing a budget ensures managers are required to draw up action plans. This often acts as a form of contingency planning. This planning will allow businesses to allocate the resources they have in the organisation.
- Co-ordination: budgeting will allow businesses to co-ordinate the activities of all departments within the organisation. Senior managers will produce an overall plan from the departmental budgets.
- Control: budgets allow businesses to control financial affairs and evaluate organisational performance. This control is in the form of variance analysis (page 247).
- Communication: budget targets will be communicated between employees and managers.
- Motivation: by taking part in the budgeting process, employees will feel empowered, increasing their motivation levels.
- Performance monitoring and evaluation: businesses often use budgeted data to compare actual performance against these predictions. Managers will evaluate business performance based on these comparisons.

 GROUP ACTIVITY

(60 minutes)

Working in small groups, choose a business in your local area. Using the following list of budget purposes, prepare a list of practical examples of the purposes based on the business you have chosen:

1 use of budgets for short-term target setting
2 monitoring business performance
3 control measures
4 motivation to achieve performance levels
5 monitoring the relationship between costs and revenues at different activity levels
6 to aid communication with senior management.

3.2 How to prepare different types of budget

Businesses follow a budgeting process when preparing their budget. The steps involved usually include:

1 establishing the aims and objectives of the business
2 setting the budgeted figures for production, marketing and finance
3 preparing individual departmental budgets
4 establishing processes for monitoring budgets
5 reviewing any variances that occur between actual and predicted figures
6 using previous experience and knowledge to set the following period's budget.

Budget examples

Businesses prepare a number of different budgets in different formats.

Sales budgets

These show forecast unit sales values, as in Table 13.7.

Table 13.7 Example of a sales budget

	January	February	March	April	May	June
	£	£	£	£	£	£
Product 1	500	300	400	700	300	500
Product 2	1,000	700	600	300	600	900
Product 3	500	300	400	700	300	500
Total	2,000	1,300	1,400	1,700	1,200	1,900

Production budgets

These show forecast unit production, as in Table 13.8.

Table 13.8 Example of a production budget

	January	February	March	April	May	June
Product 1 (units)	500	300	400	700	300	500
Product 2 (units)	1,000	600	800	1,400	600	1,000

Purchases budgets

These show forecast spend on goods, as in Table 13.9.

Table 13.9 Example of a purchases budget

	January	February	March	April	May	June
	£	£	£	£	£	£
Purchases of goods	5,000	6,000	9,000	10,000	15,000	12,000

Trade receivables (debtors) budgets

These show what is forecast to be owed to the company, as in Table 13.10.

Table 13.10 Example of a trade receivables budget

	January	February	March	April	May	June
	£	£	£	£	£	£
Opening balance	0	500	1,500	2,000	2,500	2,500
Sales	1,000	2,000	3,000	2,500	3,000	2,500
	1,000	**2,500**	**4,500**	**4,500**	**5,500**	**5,000**
Less receipts	500	1,000	2,500	2,000	3,000	2,000
Closing balance	500	1,500	2,000	2,500	2,500	3,000

Trade payables (creditors) budgets

These show forecast payments to creditors and the amount outstanding at the end of each month, as in Table 13.11.

Table 13.11 Example of a trade payables budget

	January	February	March	April	May	June
	£	£	£	£	£	£
Opening balance	0	500	500	1,000	1,500	1,500
Purchases	1,000	2,000	3,000	2,500	3,000	2,500
	1,000	**2,500**	**3,500**	**3,500**	**4,500**	**4,000**
Less payments	500	2,000	2,500	2,000	3,000	2,000
Closing balance	500	500	1,000	1,500	1,500	2,000

Cash budgets

A cash budget has the same format as a cash flow forecast. This format is shown on page 253.

3.3 & 3.4 Calculation, interpretation and use of variances to inform decision making

The most vital part of any budget analysis is the controlling and monitoring completed by management. Budgets are monitored using variance analysis. This is a method used to compare budgeted and actual figures of business organisation.

A standard cost is a planned cost of production usually expressed as the cost of producing one unit. Standard costing is a management technique where standard costs are compared with actual costs. The difference between standards and actual costs is known as a variance.

Variance = Actual level – Budgeted level

Variances will be either *favourable* (when the actual results are better than predicted) or *adverse* (when the actual results are worse than predicted). Variance analysis is used to examine the differences.

When actual costs are significantly different from standard costs, it means that the production process is not going to plan. As a result, management can take corrective action. Standard costing is a means of controlling production by establishing planned outcomes. Standards must have the effect of motivating staff in order to work towards achieving standards.

Adverse variances will:

- reduce profit below the predicted levels
- incur actual costs higher than predicted costs.

Favourable variances will:

- increase sales above the predicted levels
- decrease costs to a level below the predicted levels.

KNOW IT

1 Explain the use of a departmental budget.
2 State three purposes of the budgeting process.
3 List five types of budget.

4 Explain the difference between a fixed and flexible budget.
5 What is the difference between a favourable and an adverse variance?

LO3 assessment activities

Below are suggested assessment activities that have been directly linked to the Pass, Merit and Distinction criteria in LO3 to help with assignment preparation. These are followed by top tips on how to achieve the best results.

Activity 1 Pass criteria *P6*

West End Motors produces a single oil filter for use in petrol engines. Each oil filter can be sold for £16. The costs of producing each oil filter are:

● direct materials £8.60
● direct labour £3.40.

On 1 May, there was an opening inventory of 270 oil filters.

Predicted oil filter sales are:

● May 2,700
● June 2,800
● July 2,900
● August 3,500

Each month's closing inventory is to be maintained at 10 per cent of the following month's sales.

P6 Prepare a production budget for West End Motors, for each of the three months to 31 July.

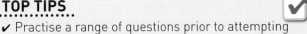

TOP TIPS

✔ Practise a range of questions prior to attempting the assessment task.

Activity 2 Pass, Merit and Distinction criteria *P7 M2* **and** *D1*

West End Motors has provided budgeted and actual sales and profit figures for the first three months of the year.

Table 13.12 West End Motors financial data

	January	February	March
Budgeted oil filter sales	2,700 units	3,000 units	2,900 units
Actual oil filter sales	2,900 units	2,800 units	3,000 units
Budgeted profit	£1,300	£1,500	£1,750
Actual profit	£1,100	£1,600	£1,950

P7 Using the data provided, calculate any variances that are appropriate to allow West End Motors to review its budget predictions.

M2 Analyse the variances calculated in P7. Identify the likely causes for the variances.

D1 Recommend and justify actions that West End Motors should take based on your calculations and analysis in P7 and M2.

TOP TIPS

✔ Practise a range of questions prior to attempting the assessment task for P7.
✔ Choose a suitable format in which to complete the M2 and D1 tasks, e.g. business report, discussion with the assessor or tutor, presentation.

LO4 Be able to calculate capital investment appraisals *P8 P9 P10*

(10 minutes)

Working in pairs, produce a list of capital projects that businesses may undertake – for example, the purchase of a new production line.

4.1 & 4.5 Capital investment appraisal methods, calculations and interpretation

Investment refers to the purchase of capital goods to use within a business. They are often used to produce other goods to sell on to a consumer. Investment can be autonomous (replacing worn-out or out-of-date assets) or induced (investment is required due to expansion or business growth).

Reasons that businesses will need to invest include:

- replacing out-of-date equipment
- replacing worn-out machinery
- business expansion or growth
- availability of new technologies
- reacting to competitors' actions in the market.

Investment appraisal is used to review potential capital investment projects. The appraisal will estimate the potential return of each project so an informed decision can be made. A number of methods can be used, but you need to focus on the three main ones:

1 payback
2 accounting rate of return (ARR)
3 net present value (NPV).

Payback

The payback method works out how long it takes for a project to repay the initial investment. When comparing projects, the one with shortest payback period (i.e. the project that returns the initial capital cost of the investment first) should be chosen.

For example, Edinburgh Ltd is planning to expand and is choosing between two projects:

1 Project A – costs £100,000, with an annual return of £25,000 for five years
2 Project B – costs £250,000, with an annual return of £100,000 for four years.

Accounting rate of return

This method allows the calculation of a percentage rate of return for investment projects. The percentages of different projects can easily be compared and a judgement made as to whether a project is viable. Businesses and investors often compare the accounting rate of return (ARR) with the percentage rate that can be gained by investing the capital in a bank or building society account. For example, an ARR of 5 per cent may be seen as a low return considering the risk that is involved.

Payback calculation

Table 13.13 Based on the payback period, Project B should be chosen

Project A			Project B		
Year	Net cash flow	Cumulative cash flow	Year	Net cash flow	Cumulative cash flow
0	-100,000	-100,000	0	-250,000	-250,000
1	25,000	-75,000	1	100,000	-150,000
2	25,000	-50,000	2	100,000	-50,000
3	25,000	-25,000	3	100,000	50,000
4	25,000	0	4	100,000	150,000
5	25,000	25,000	5		
Payback period		4 years	Payback period		2 years and 6 months

Note: Year 0 is the current time when the initial outlay will be paid.

Accounting rate of return (%)

$$= \frac{\text{Average annual return (profit)} \times 100}{\text{Initial outlay}}$$

To calculate the accounting rate of return for Project A and Project B for Edinburgh Ltd using the data in Table 13.13:

Project A

Accounting rate of return (%)

$$= \frac{[(125,000 - 100,000)/5 \text{ years}] \times 100}{100,000}$$

Accounting rate of return (%) = 5%

Project B

Accounting rate of return (%)

$$= \frac{[(400,000 - 250,000)/4 \text{ years}] \times 100}{250,000}$$

Accounting rate of return (%) = 15%

Based on the accounting rate of return, Project B should be chosen.

Net present value

The net present value (NPV) method of investment appraisal involves discounted cash flows and considers the time value of money. The principle is that money today is worth more than it will be in the future. For example, at a discount rate of 10 per cent, £1 today is likely to be worth approximately 91p in one year's time and 83p in two years' time. Businesses are free to choose an appropriate percentage – this is often based on the current interest rates so comparisons can be made. Due to the complicated calculations required to work out these discounted figures, tables of discount factors are available.

Discounting exists for two main reasons.

1 Risk: money in the future is uncertain – it is difficult to predict what money will be worth in a number of years' time.
2 Opportunity cost: businesses need to decide what they are foregoing (missing out on) before taking on

an investment project. In most cases the business will be losing out on interest in a bank account.

We can calculate the NPV for Project A and Project B for Edinburgh Ltd using the data in Table 13.13. Edinburgh Ltd has decided to use a discount factor of 10 per cent, as shown in Table 13.14.

Table 13.14 Extract from present value table of £1 @10%

Year	10%
0	1
1	0.909
2	0.826
3	0.751
4	0.683
5	0.621

Table 13.15 NPV for Project A

Year	Net cash flow	Discount factor	Discounted cash flow
0	-100,000	1	-100,000
1	25,000	0.909	22,725
2	25,000	0.826	20,650
3	25,000	0.751	18,775
4	25,000	0.683	17,075
5	25,000	0.621	15,525
Net present value for Project A			-£5,250

Table 13.16 NPV for Project B

Year	Net cash flow	Discount factor	Discounted cash flow
0	-250,000	1	-250,000
1	100,000	0.909	90,900
2	100,000	0.826	82,600
3	100,000	0.751	75,100
4	100,000	0.683	68,300
Net present value for Project B			£66,900

Based on the net present value, Project B should be chosen – it is predicted to have a considerably higher net present value than Project A.

Based on all of the investment appraisal methods, Edinburgh Ltd should proceed with Project B.

🔍 INDEPENDENT RESEARCH ACTIVITY

(1 hour)

Bach Ltd produces windows and doors for luxury homes. It is assessing the viability of two projects to enable the company to expand:

1 Project 1 – costs £300,000, with an annual return of £80,000 for five years
2 Project 2 – costs £550,000, with an annual return of £150,000 for four years.

Table 13.17 Extract from present value table of £1 @10%

Year	10%
0	1
1	0.909
2	0.826
3	0.751
4	0.683
5	0.621

For each project, calculate:

1 payback period
2 accounting rate of return (ARR)
3 net present value (NPV).

4.2 Advantages and disadvantages of capital investment appraisal methods

4.3 & 4.4 External and qualitative factors which affect investment decisions

In addition to considering numerical data, businesses need to consider external and qualitative issues before making a final investment decision.

They will need to assess whether in the current economic climate they should take the risk of investing their money in capital projects or whether it is more effective to save the money or use it for other purposes – for example, employing staff.

To make these decisions, businesses will review current economic data, including:

- inflation rates
- interest rates
- exchange rates
- employment rates.

In addition to economic factors, businesses need to consider non-financial factors that will affect a capital decision made. For example, if a project involves replacing staff with machinery, a business will need to review the impact on staff morale and motivation. If morale and motivation decrease, then overall productivity and efficiency will decrease. This decision will affect the relationship a business has with its stakeholders. Employees will be unhappy and customers who have heard about the employees may stop purchasing goods from the business.

Table 13.18 Advantages and disadvantages of capital investment appraisal methods

	Advantages	Disadvantanges
Payback	Easy to calculate Easy to understand Appropriate for businesses with cash flow issues Payback emphasises the speed of return on an investment – this is particularly important in rapidly changing markets	Ignores the time value of money Ignores all money received after payback of the original outlay Assesses short-term considerations only The timing of cash flows is ignored Overall project profitability is not considered
Accounting rate of return (ARR)	Shows the profitability of an investment project The percentage accounting rate of return provides easy comparisons across a range of projects	More difficult and time consuming to calculate than payback Ignores inflation Ignores the time value of money
Net present value (NPV)	Considers the time value of money A positive return would imply a project is worth completing	Time consuming Difficult to understand for non-accountants Based on the business's arbitrary choice of interest rate.

Businesses need to review any legal requirements and industry standards – for example, lone working policies and guidelines, minimum wage payments or health and safety standards that need to be met. All of these factors involve considerable costs, which need to be considered when making an investment decision.

GROUP ACTIVITY

(45 minutes)

Working in small groups, consider a nuclear power station in the UK. The business owners are planning to expand to provide additional power supplies to the national grid. This will considerably increase profits. Discuss the non-financial factors that need to be considered before a decision can be made. Be ready to share your ideas with the rest of the class.

KNOW IT

1 What is investment?
2 Name three methods of capital investment appraisal.
3 Explain the advantages and disadvantages of payback, accounting rate of return and net present value.
4 Why is 'discounting' important?
5 Give three examples of external and qualitative factors that affect investment decisions.

L04 assessment activity

Below is a suggested assessment activity that has been directly linked to the Pass criteria in L04 to help with assignment preparation. This is followed by top tips on how to achieve the best results.

Activity 1 Pass criteria *P8 P9* **and** *P10*

Snowman Ltd produces and sells winter supplies (winter tyres, de-icer, etc.) to other businesses and to the general public. It is considering expanding overseas. This would involve considerable capital investment. It is considering the viability of two capital projects:

1 Project 1 – costs £500,000, with an annual return of £120,000 for five years
2 Project 2 – costs £750,000, with an annual return of £200,000 for four years.

Table 13.19 Extract from present value table of £1 @10%

Year	10%
0	1
1	0.909
2	0.826
3	0.751
4	0.683
5	0.621

P8 Prepare a presentation with accompanying speaker notes that explain to the managers the advantages and disadvantages of:

● payback
● accounting rate of return (ARR)
● net present value (NPV).

P9 For each project, calculate:

● payback period
● accounting rate of return (ARR)
● net present value (NPV).

P10 Prepare a management report that interprets your solutions to the calculations in P9. In the conclusion, you need to recommend a decision to Snowman Ltd.

TOP TIPS

✔ Practise a range of questions prior to attempting the assessment tasks for P9 and P10.
✔ For P10, you should include financial and non-financial factors in your description.

LO5 Be able to prepare and use cash flow forecasts *P11 P12 M3 D2*

GETTING STARTED 👤 ....

(15 minutes)

Working in small groups, consider the cash inflows and cash outflows that would be involved in the operations of a car manufacturer. Complete Table 13.20 with practical examples of inflows and outflows.

Table 13.20 Inflows and outflows of a car manufacturer

Cash inflow	Cash outflow

5.1 The structure of a cash flow forecast

Maintaining adequate cash flow is vital to success. It is important to prepare a cash flow forecast as part of business planning. This is an estimate of the likely cash inflows and outflows over a period of time. Existing businesses will use historic data to prepare the forecast, whereas new or start-up businesses will use market research information to construct the cash flow forecast as part of the business plan.

Businesses can choose an appropriate timescale for which to complete their cash flow forecast, usually a 12-month period; however, for a specific project, this could be reduced.

Businesses need to consider any 'credit periods' that have been offered or taken – for example, accounting for credit sales and credit purchases by recording the receipts and payments in the month when the cash will be received and paid.

A cash flow forecast has three main sections, as follows.

1 Cash inflows – money received, for example:
   a sales income – cash and credit sales
   b income from investments
   c capital from the owner
   d bank loan
   e mortgage
   f rent received
   g commission received
   h one-off receipts, e.g. the sale of an unused non-current asset.
2 Cash outflows – money paid out, for example:
   a salaries and wages
   b raw materials
   c purchase of capital equipment, fixtures and fittings, etc.
   d cash and credit purchases.
3 Balances – the opening and closing balances each month.

Table 13.21 shows an example cash flow forecast for a start-up business organisation.

Table 13.21 Example cash flow forecast

	January	February	March	April
	£	£	£	£
Cash inflows				
Capital	10,000			
Cash sales		5,000	15,000	20,000
Credit sales		3,000	9,000	12,000
Loan	20,000			
Total cash inflows	**30,000**	**8,000**	**24,000**	**32,000**
Cash outflows				
Cash purchases	2,000	3,000	3,000	4,000
Credit purchases	5,000	4,000	4,000	6,000
Equipment purchase	25,000	0	0	0
Salaries and wages	2,000	2,000	2,000	2,000
General expenses	3,000	3,000	3,000	3,000
Value added tax	0	0	3,000	0
Total cash outflows	**37,000**	**12,000**	**15,000**	**15,000**
Opening balance	0	(4,000)	9,000	17,000
Net cash flow	(7,000)	(7,000)	(11,000)	(2,000)
Closing balance	**(7,000)**	**(11,000)**	**(2,000)**	**15,000**

(60 minutes)

Think about what you may like to do when you complete your studies. Prepare a cash flow forecast for your personal budget, either for your first year at university or your first year at work.

You could consider including the following items in your cash flow forecast:

- student loan
- part-time job
- rent of a flat
- television licence
- mobile phone contract.

5.2 How to improve cash flow management

Businesses can improve their cash flow in a number of ways. These include those described below.

Increasing cash inflows

1 By chasing trade receivables – businesses need to focus on ensuring that these debtors pay the money owed.
2 By reducing the trade credit period offered to trade receivables. This will ensure that businesses will receive the money owed for goods and services as quickly as possible.
3 By reducing the potential for bad debts – all potential credit customers should have their credit history reviewed to reduce the risk.

Decreasing cash outflows

1 By delaying paying trade payables until trade receivables have settled their accounts.
2 By attempting to secure the best trade credit terms. Agreeing to pay trade payables over a longer period of time will reduce cash flow issues.

LO5 assessment activities

Below are suggested assessment activities that have been directly linked to the Pass, Merit and Distinction criteria in LO5 to help with assignment preparation. These are followed by top tips on how to achieve the best results.

3 By reducing wages and salaries – businesses may need to release non-essential employees, reduce the amount of overtime offered or reduce wage rates of all staff. This may be an unpopular decision and may demotivate the workforce.
4 By delaying purchasing any non-current assets – for example, machinery or motor vehicles. Businesses with cash flow issues should manage with their existing assets and delay any unnecessary purchases.

Additional sources of finance

In order to help cash flow problems, businesses may choose to seek additional sources of finance. These will increase the amount of cash coming into the business; however, many need to be repaid with interest. Additional sources of finance will include:

- loan
- overdraft
- hire purchase
- sale and lease-back
- leasing.

(30 minutes)

Working in small groups, review the sources of finance studied in earlier units. Prepare a mind-map of sources of finance that could assist businesses with a cash flow problem. Include definitions for each of the sources.

KNOW IT

1 Explain the purpose of a cash flow forecast.
2 Name three cash inflows and three cash outflows.
3 List the components of a cash flow forecast.
4 Explain how to improve cash flow management.
5 List five additional sources of finance available to businesses.

Activity 1 Pass criteria *P11* and *P12*

▲ **Figure 13.6** Help Jonathan manage the cash flow for his party business

P11 P12 Your friend Jonathan operates a mobile business running children's parties. He has asked for your help with his cash flow management. Jonathan has provided the following information relating to his business:

- opening balance (1 April) – cash in bank is £650
- predicted income from parties and associated purchases (shown in Table 13.22)
- income from parties is received in stages – 20 per cent on the day of the party and 80 per cent one month later
- all associated purchases are paid for one month in arrears
- Jonathan rents musical equipment for £1,500 per annum, paid in quarterly instalments in January, April, July and October
- Jonathan leases a motor van to travel to all of the parties; he pays £150 per month.

1 Prepare a 12-month cash flow forecast, starting on 1 April, for Jonathan.
2 Describe how Jonathan could improve his cash flow position.

TOP TIPS

✔ Practise a range of questions prior to attempting the assessment task.
✔ For P10, you should include financial and non-financial factors in your description.

Activity 2 Merit criteria *M3*

M3 Analyse the cash flow position identified in the cash flow forecast you have prepared for Jonathan.

TOP TIPS

✔ Choose a suitable format, e.g. business report, discussion with the assessor or tutor, presentation.

Activity 3 Distinction criteria *D2*

D2 Recommend and justify the actions, Jonathan could take in order to improve his cash flow position.

TOP TIPS

✔ You should choose a suitable format in which to complete the D2 tasks, e.g. business report, discussion with the assessor or tutor, presentation.

Table 13.22 Predicted income for Jonathan's business

	Income from parties £	Associated purchases £		Income from parties £	Associated purchases £
February	640	630	November	480	300
March	680	480	December	1,500	940
April	500	400	January	610	550
May	550	500	February	640	630
June	610	550	March	680	480
July	640	630	April	1,100	780
August	680	480	May	1,300	550
September	700	700	June	1,500	940
October	540	300	July	950	480

Read about it

Business Accounting, by Rob Jones, Causeway Press, 2004

Business Accounting Volume 1 (10th edn), by Frank Wood and Alan Sangster, FT Prentice Hall, 2005

Business Accounts (3rd edn), by David Cox, Osborne Books, 2004

Unit 15

Change management

ABOUT THIS UNIT

Business change happens constantly, for many reasons, and businesses must be aware of potential and existing changes and developments, on a local and global scale. They must adjust their processes, products or services to take change into account, in order to remain competitive.

Change can have both positive and negative impacts on stakeholders. In this unit, you will learn about the importance of managing change by examining barriers to change and how these can be removed. You will also investigate the different approaches to managing change, and the advantages and disadvantages of each approach.

You will learn about the importance of managers gaining the commitment of their team members. This may involve managing resistance to change, both during and after implementation.

You will develop your ability to interpret quantitative and qualitative data to establish effective change management. You will learn that you need to be able to support the implementation of change to ensure that the organisational objectives of change are met.

LEARNING OUTCOMES

The topics, activities and suggested reading in this unit will help you to:

1 understand the drivers of change
2 understand the key aspects of theories of change management
3 be able to to plan for change, manage change and overcome barriers
4 be able to the impacts of change on businesses and stakeholders
5 be able to how data is used to monitor change management in businesses.

How will I be assessed?

This unit will be externally assessed via a test set and marked by OCR.

How will I be graded?

This unit will be externally assessed via a test set and marked by OCR.

LO1 Understand the drivers of change

GETTING STARTED 👤

(10 minutes)

Using Table 15.1, classify the following examples into the different drivers of change.

1 a manufacturing business has decided to locate its new factory in Eastern Europe
2 more and more male workers are preferring to work part-time to spend more time with their children
3 mobile payments are becoming more widely used as a method of payment
4 there is an increasing awareness among consumers about food miles
5 the UK government introduced changes to the law on workplace pensions
6 the UK inflation rate fell below zero in 2015.

Table 15.1 Drivers for change

Drivers for change	Example
Developments in technology	
Market changes	
Changes in legislation	
Changes in the workforce	
Changes in the economy	
Internal changes	

1.1 The drivers of change

Drivers of change are causes of change in a business. They can come from within a business or its external environment.

Developments in technology

How developments in technology can impact or cause change in a business has been discussed in some depth in Units 1 and 14. The introduction of robotics in production methods and computerisation of stock control systems, enabling 'just in time' processes, have no doubt improved efficiency, but the impact on the workforce cannot be ignored. Automation inevitably brings about job losses, and the employees that remain need training to use the new machinery.

Technology has caused major changes in the way products can be promoted. Social media is now widely used to create awareness of a business's products, but do employees have the skills and knowledge to fully exploit these digital methods to their advantage? Facebook, Twitter and Instagram are new and different approaches to marketing and, when used effectively, allow a business to target its customers like never before, at a fraction of the price of traditional above- and below-the-line advertising.

With three out of four UK adults owning a smartphone, mobile advertising is another development that is expected to grow rapidly. Businesses need to keep up with this new technology and exploit its advantages fully.

Electronic channels of distribution such as e-commerce have revolutionised how goods reach consumers. However, employees need to be trained to use new technology to operate e-commerce as new hardware and software become available. It is essential for e-commerce businesses to put in place an effective way of distributing orders so that deliveries are made on time. With this new way of operation come new investment needs in equipment, machinery and skilled staff.

Market changes

Information on lifestyle changes allows businesses to spot opportunities and threats. It has become trendy among the younger generation to lead a healthier lifestyle as one in four in the 16–30 age group claim that they do not drink alcohol, compared with one in seven of those aged 60 and above.

Special diets, such as veganism and vegetarianism, have become more popular, together with increased participation in activities such as yoga, meditation, jogging and cycling. Businesses in the restaurant, sports and leisure industries must adapt their products and services to these changes. They should also make changes to their marketing strategies, focusing on a healthier lifestyle.

Perhaps one of the most accurate indicators of our changing spending habits is reflected in the 'basket of goods' used to measure inflation (Figure 15.1).

Basket of goods 2015

What's in and what's out?*

This is a sample of everyday items used to measure changes in the prices of goods and services, as well as helping to calculate consumer price inflation. It's grown from around 150 items in 1947 to over 700 this year.

IN

Games consoles online subscription
Represents the explosion in all forms of online gaming

Streaming music subscription
This expanding technology is over-taking traditional media

E-cigarettes
Used by smokers as a cigarette alternative or quitting aid

Protein powder
Consumed by increasing numbers of gym-goers

Sweet potato
Currently popular in the nation's kitchens

Headphones
Often bought by gamers, or as upgrades to the free pairs bundled with smartphones

Craft beer/ale
Speciality beers and ales are currently extremely fashionable

Mobile phone accessories
The market for chargers, covers, external speakers etc is booming

Some goods removed this year include yoghurt drinks – which have faded in popularity – and sat navs, partly owing to smartphone apps and also because many new cars have built-in units.

OUT

*This infographic only represents a selection of the 13 ins and 8 outs for 2015

www.ons.gov.uk
Source: Consumer Price Inflation basket of goods and services, 2015

Office for National Statistics

▲ **Figure 15.1** Can business in all sectors choose to ignore these recent changes?

In a recent survey on ethics and sustainability, 25 per cent of respondents said that the businesses they work for practise sustainability in their operations, while 48 per cent said that sustainability is embedded in the activities of most departments. Sustainability has become top priority for most businesses and sustainable innovations are expected to grow in response to changes in consumer attitude in this area.

▲ **Figure 15.2** Does it pay to be good? by Remi Trudel and June Cotte. Sloane Review: Winter 2009, January 08, 2009. Used with permission.

Figure 15.2 makes interesting reading for businesses that are weighing up the advantages and disadvantages of ethical practices – they clearly pay, as the results show.

Competition has a huge impact on a business, especially when it comes to homogenous products. In 2015, business news was dominated by job losses at a steel plant called Caparo Industries. The main reason for its closure was the company's inability to compete with steel imported from China. Businesses now find themselves having to compete on a global scale so, unless changes are made to become more lean and efficient, it would be impossible for businesses in the developed world to compete with cheaper labour and lower running costs in emerging countries.

Changes in legislation

New legislation on employment is constantly being introduced as the way we work changes. For example, the law says that employees have the right to apply to work flexible hours (having a different start and finish time from the standard hours), or to work from home, and employers must consider their application in a reasonable manner. Employers can be taken to an employment tribunal if they fail to do so.

Concerns have been raised about **zero-hours contracts**, which have been gaining popularity among UK businesses, especially those employing more than 250 workers. Employers need to keep up to date with developments in this area, as well as the increase in the minimum wage and maternity/paternity pay, to avoid disputes and fines.

> **🔑 KEY TERM**
>
> **Zero-hours contract** – an agreement to hire an employee on varying numbers of hours, with no guarantee of work.

Changes to health and safety legislation also need to be considered. The Construction (Design and Management) Regulations 2015 were amended to ensure workers' safety on construction sites. A principal designer must now be appointed to plan, co-ordinate, manage and ensure that risks are minimised or removed through design work.

In terms of environmental legislation, the Energy Savings Opportunity Scheme (ESOS) has been made compulsory for a large number of organisations in the UK. They need to know how to comply because the Environment Agency can now charge a fixed penalty of up to £5,000 for any business that is not compliant, plus an additional £500 for each working day until it is compliant.

Changes in the workforce

Demographic issues are also relevant. According to research carried out by the Office of National Statistics (ONS), the number of workers in the 50–64 age group has increased in the last 15 years, particularly women, and the percentage of workers aged 65 and over has doubled in the past decade. This is primarily due to the raising of the retirement age as well as people living longer.

Implications of this change for employers include adapting the working conditions and arrangements to suit older workers; training opportunities need to be designed specifically for this demographic, particularly in IT.

Workers have the right to request flexible working, for example if they have childcare or other caring responsibilities. This would have an impact on the hours they work, which may be shorter or with different start and end times to colleagues.

Depending on the nature of a business, different skills are required at different levels. Demand for managers, professionals and other people to work in the care and leisure industries is likely to rise in the future. Advancements made in ICT will definitely lead to an increased demand for ICT skills. Technological advancement will also lead to an increase in working from home, so employers will need a workforce that can plan and organise their own work independently.

Government initiatives aim to improve the quality of state schools by improving the skills levels and qualifications of school leavers so that employers can look forward to a bigger pool of skilled labour. The government's plan to increase apprenticeships by three million by 2020 will also help ensure that the future workforce has the skills required by employers in the UK.

Changes in the economy

Inflation has been well below the UK government's target in the past few years, which is generally good news for most businesses. However, deflation in the form of falling prices of food and fuel could lead to lower economic growth. Some people believe that deflation will lead to a decrease in consumer spending, but the evidence in Spain suggests that consumers spend more due to cheaper prices. Whatever the impact, businesses need to be prepared for the changes this economic factor might bring.

Unemployment affects consumers' ability to spend and this will have a direct impact on a business's potential sales. In an economic cycle of boom and bust there will be winners and losers. During an economic boom, unemployment is low, and consumer confidence and spending are high, so most businesses will experience an increase in sales and profit.

It is in a recession that businesses need to adapt to lower consumer spending through cutting prices, reducing production volume to survive. In the recession following the credit crunch in 2007, value retailers such as Poundland, Aldi and Lidl saw an increase in sales and market share as consumers switched to products sold at lower prices. There is evidence that this spending behaviour took hold and became a habit as consumers continued to hunt for bargains even when the economy had recovered.

Changes in taxation including income tax and VAT will cause changes in consumer spending. Corporation tax decreases will lead to an increase in retained profit, which businesses could use to expand.

Internal changes

The austerity measures put in place by the UK government in 2010 have put budgetary pressures or restrictions on various government departments. With less money to spend, they have had to change the way they work and encourage savings in their workforce. This also has a knock-on effect on their suppliers, which might not be getting the same level of work from government departments so have to make budgetary restrictions of their own.

A change in mission, corporate aims and objectives as a result of a change in strategic direction will change the culture, values and ways in which a business operates. The increased pressure on businesses to operate ethically and sustainably by consumers and governments will also cause a change in corporate aims and objectives.

A business may bring in new methods and channels of distribution, for example by starting to sell goods online that had previously been sold in a shop. This will require a change to processes.

Restructuring how a business is organised can be brought about by many changes – for example, an expansion that requires more human resources to form different project teams through matrix management (see Unit 1, Section 3.1, page 14), or a direct response to increase efficiency by delayering from a hierarchical to a flat structure. It could also be due to a change in culture brought about by a new CEO who believes in a different style of leadership; employee empowerment would increase with a more democratic leader.

Restructuring could be confined to certain functional areas only (e.g. marketing, finance, human resources, production) for reasons such as the introduction of new technology. For example, social media has revolutionised how businesses market their products so new roles and responsibilities, usually in the marketing function, have to be created accordingly. New software and hardware to improve the accuracy of financial records could mean new IT technicians are required in the finance or support functions. The introduction of robotics in the production function usually leads to fewer workers being needed.

KNOW IT

1 Explain how a just-in-time production method works.
2 Describe two examples of ethical practices that a business in the manufacturing industry could adopt.
3 Analyse possible impacts of a zero-hours contract on an employee.
4 Explain the economic cycle.
5 Outline two reasons why a business might consider changing its organisational structure.

LO1 assessment activities

You will find suggested activities for this section combined with the LO2 assessment activities on page 264.

Understand the key aspects of theories of change management

 GETTING STARTED

(30 minutes)

There are many theories about change management but three in particular are often used by businesses to help prepare for change and to see it through.

Go online to find out about the McKinsey 7-S model, Kotter's 8-Step Process for Leading Change and Lewis's Change Management Theory.

Write a brief summary of each of the theories.

2.1 Theories of change management

The McKinsey 7-S model

The McKinsey 7-S model (Figure 15.3) is a framework that can be used to determine how likely an organisation is to achieve its aims and objectives. The model looks at seven internal elements of an organisation to see how well aligned they are. It is based on the belief that these elements are all interrelated: changing one element will affect the alignment, which means other elements might need to be changed to achieve the desired outcome. It can be applied to organisations of all sizes, even teams and projects. The seven 'Ss' can be classified as hard or soft.

▶ **Figure 15.3** The McKinsey 7-S model

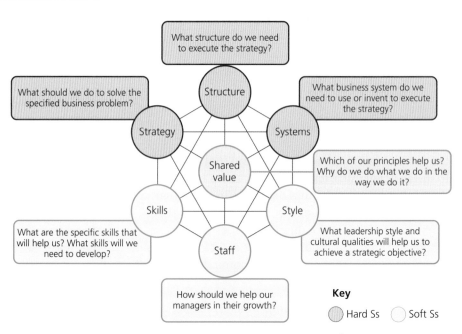

Source: adapted by permission of Aleksey Savkin, BSC Designer, www.bscdesigner.com/7-s-framework.htm.

Hard Ss can be controlled by management and they are easy to identify:

● strategy – the long-term plan designed to gain competitive advantage
● structure – the organisational structure and the chain of command
● systems – processes and procedures followed in decision making and in carrying out daily activities.

Soft Ss are less clearly defined and more difficult to control:

● skills – capabilities and competences of a workforce
● staff – the type and number of staff needed to achieve a planned strategy, including how they will be recruited, trained, motivated and rewarded
● style – management style that exists in an organisation, e.g. democratic, autocratic
● shared value – this is the foundation of an organisation, its vision and values that guide how employees behave and how the business is run.

How can the model be used?

The model is used to help identify what needs to be realigned to improve performance. This is based on the premise that the seven Ss need to support one another to achieve the shared value and be co-ordinated. This can be done by looking at the seven Ss that currently exist and asking the following questions.

● Is the shared value consistent with the hard Ss? If it is not, what needs to change?
● Examine the hard Ss. Do they support one another? If not, what needs to change?
● Look at the soft Ss to see whether they support the hard Ss. If not, what needs to change?

The next steps are as follows.

● Adjust and align the Ss, analyse the impact of the adjustments on the elements and the alignment. Readjust and realign if need be until a balance is achieved. This could be a lengthy process of fine-tuning.
● Maintaining alignment (and performance) during other types of change. To maintain alignment, the steps described above need to be repeated on a regular basis, bearing in mind that, when an element is adjusted, there will be an impact on the alignment of all the Ss with one another. The process should focus on whether the Ss will ensure the achievement of the set goal.

How the model can be used to understand how organisational elements (Ss) are interrelated

This can be achieved by studying the impact on the other elements of changing an element. For example:

● How will a change in the structure of an organisation from hierarchy to flat affect the leadership style?
● What is needed in terms of staff and skills to achieve the shared value?

To find out how the elements are interrelated, you will need to study how they work together and how they are co-ordinated – to achieve one element, what do you need in terms of the other elements?

How the model can be used to implement change

This can be done by:

● analysing the current situation (Point A) by assessing how the elements are aligned
● analysing how the elements should be aligned to achieve the proposed situation (Point B)
● identifying gaps and inconsistencies between Point A and Point B; start with the shared value – is there a difference between A and B? Will the existing elements enable the new strategy to be achieved, e.g. are there enough employees with the right skills? Do the elements need to be realigned to achieve the new objective?

Change can be implemented by finding answers to these questions through fine-tuning the alignment of the elements until the desired balance is achieved to reach Point B.

Kotter's 8-Step Process for Leading Change

In this model, change is a campaign to persuade all stakeholders that it will be a success. The eight steps are described in Table 15.2.

Table 15.2 Kotter's 8-Step Process for Leading Change

Step	How the model can be used to deliver change
1 Urgency	Create a compelling reason that change is needed
	For change to happen, 75 per cent of management needs to agree that it is necessary
	Convince people by creating a scenario to show what could be gained if change is achieved; get support from stakeholders (e.g. customers and shareholders) to strengthen your argument
2 Coalition	Get the leaders brought in
	Form a strong team from key personnel within the organisation; influential people from different departments at different levels could be recruited to form a coalition
3 Vision and plan	Create a vision that is clear and easy to understand
	It should be precise and paint a picture of how you want to see the organisation in the future; a strategic plan should accompany this vision
4 Communicate	Communicate the vision relentlessly to all stakeholders involved
	Whenever possible, embed it in the daily activities of the business; it should be regular and repeated frequently to get the vision across to employees at all levels
	Questions and uncertainties should be dealt with openly and honestly
5 Remove obstacles	Address systems, people and processes to identify barriers and obstacles to change
	Who or what is preventing or slowing down the change process and what can be done to overcome the problem(s)?
	Appoint change leaders to implement the change, and reward people who have made the change
6 Create wins	Create and celebrate wins
	Create short-term targets that are realistic and achievable, with the aim of winning people over
	When targets are achieved, celebrate this and reward people who achieved them; this motivates people towards the change that has been planned
7 Build on change	Use wins to build the case to extend the change
	Build on the success that has been achieved so far
	Analyse strengths and weaknesses, identify areas for improvement
	New change champions can be appointed to support the coalition, and new targets set to help progression towards the change
8 Embed to culture	Make it a necessity for the organisation
	The change achieved so far needs to be incorporated into the core values of an organisation to make it permanent; this can be achieved through showing evidence of change in daily activities and in every aspect of an organisation
	Every effort should be made to ensure that change is supported by all stakeholders through celebrating and rewarding success regularly so that it is not forgotten

Lewin's Change Management Theory

Lewin's three-stage model can be described using the process of changing the shape of a block of ice. You need to unfreeze it (stage 1) to change it into water (stage 2). The water can then be refrozen (stage 3) to any shape you want (Figure 15.4).

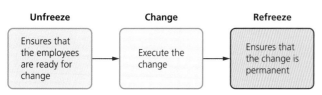

▲ **Figure 15.4** Lewin's Change Management Theory

Unfreeze

This is the preparation stage for change. This can be done by challenging the core value of an organisation, convincing stakeholders that things cannot carry on as they are. It can be the most difficult and stressful stage out of the three as it involves changing the existing culture, processes and procedures that might have been in place since the organisation was established. Stakeholders can be persuaded via data such as declining sales revenue and profit, weakening customer base and market share, as well as consequences if change is not put in place. There will be resistors to change as people generally stay away from the unfamiliar; there will be fear of the adverse consequences of change, and mistrust that it is only for the good of a few at the top of the hierarchy.

Change

Change can take place only when stakeholders are convinced that it is necessary and that it will benefit them in some way. It might take a long time to get from unfreeze to change, people need to get used to new ideas, new ways of doing things and, ultimately, they need to embrace the change and contribute proactively to bring it about. Communication is very important at this stage as stakeholders need to know exactly what is happening in order to dispel mistrust and uncertainty.

Refreeze

This can begin when stakeholders have embraced the new ideas and changes that are taking place. It is vital at this stage to internalise the change and incorporate it into the core values of an organisation. It should be evident in day-to-day activities and used all the time.

The refreeze stage is successful when employees feel confident and comfortable with the new way of doing things. Successes should be rewarded and celebrated to reinforce that change was necessary and that it also paves the way for future changes.

How Lewin's theory can be used to deliver change

Start by persuading stakeholders that change is needed. Once this is achieved, encourage stakeholders to participate in the change and make sure there is an effective communication system to inform people of what is taking place. Change needs to be internalised and incorporated into an organisation's main culture to become the norm – part of the value system.

INDIVIDUAL ACTIVITY

(20 minutes)

Follow this link to read about change management in the real business world: http://tinyurl.com/p4zguyj

Can you see any evidence of the application of the theories and models for managing change that you have just learned about?

KNOW IT

1 Explain the hard and soft elements in the McKinsey 7-S model.
2 How can the 7-S model be used to identify what needs to be realigned to improve performance?
3 How can the 7-S model be used to understand that organisational elements are interrelated?
4 Describe Kotter's 8-Step Process for Leading Change.
5 Explain how Lewin's Change Management Theory can be used to deliver change.

LO3 Be able to plan for change, manage change and overcome barriers

GETTING STARTED

(15 minutes)

Imagine that a recent survey at your school or college found that most students are in favour of a later start to the school day. You are on the school council and you have decided to start a campaign to persuade your school that it is a good idea. Identify the barriers to change or obstacles you are likely to come across.

3.1 Ways to plan and manage change

Whether or not models are used, certain steps will help to manage the change process, as discussed below.

Consult with key stakeholders

This initial stage is crucial – get it right and the change can be managed more smoothly, it will take less time and is more likely to succeed.

Key stakeholders could include internal ones such as the managers and employees who are likely to be at the forefront of implementing the change, as well as external stakeholders such as shareholders, customers and the local community if the change will have an impact on them.

To consult is to seek information and advice, so key stakeholders should be approached to gauge their opinions on the change strategy, to increase the likelihood that the final change plan will be acceptable to them. This process can reassure them that they are being listened to.

Set clear aims and objectives for the change

It is at this stage that the direction and end goal of the change are defined. It also determines the scope of change, which is how significant the change is going to be and how many key stakeholders it is going to impact. Aims and objectives set need to be clear so that everybody involved knows exactly what needs to be done to achieve the change. This should have both a reassuring and motivating effect if the targets set are precise and easy to understand, and are followed.

Identify resource requirements

Depending on the scope of the change, relevant resources such as personnel numbers and skills, physical resources such as IT systems, equipment, machinery, land and buildings need to be identified. Once the requirements for these resources have been determined, funding needs to be put in place for their procurement in time for the change.

Evaluate stakeholder feedback

Evaluating stakeholder feedback from discussions and formal meetings allows management to fine-tune the elements of the plan to ensure its success. This will again provide proof that management has listened to its stakeholders and embraced their feedback. The plan for change is finalised at this stage and ready for implementation.

Assign a project group

The scope of the change will determine the size of the project group required to implement the change. When assigning a project group, the management team needs to consider the skills, knowledge and experience required – it is usually a multidisciplinary team with specialists from different functional areas. It might be necessary to recruit and select from outside the business or provide training to current staff, whichever is more practical and cheaper within the time constraints. The project could also be outsourced to a specialist organisation if management believes this is the better way to achieve the desired outcome.

Appoint project champions or change leaders

Project champions or change leaders are appointed to take charge of communication, select employees for training, review progress on a regular basis, supply resources and remove barriers. Project champions are usually business managers at a senior level with experience of managing change. They have a clear idea of the status quo and the direction in which the organisation should be heading. They also play a crucial role in marketing the project to various stakeholders, often through removing barriers to change (see the next section).

Proactive versus reactive approach

A proactive approach requires management to anticipate change before it is necessary. This approach enables management to be prepared for change, or even to profit from it. A reactive approach is when change is implemented after something has happened. For example, in the past Nike had been criticised for having poor labour records in its supply chain; the company is now taking a proactive approach towards the issue by training factory managers in the Far East on human resource management so that they can implement environmental, health and safety practices. This initiative was introduced not because it is a legal requirement but because it is now part of Nike's CSR policy. By taking a proactive stance Nike has gained credibility as a responsible employer. If the company had adopted a reactive approach it would still be operating under the shadow of its poor labour records.

Communicate the plan, vision and urgency for change

This is an essential part at the beginning of the change management process. Stakeholders need to know what the plan for change is, they need to know the vision – the end result – and why change is necessary and imminent.

Engage in dialogue with stakeholders

During the implementation process, stakeholders have to be reminded constantly of why, how and where the change is leading. Regular discussion opportunities and formal meetings should be organised for management to listen to concerns, answer questions on the impact change will bring and to allay fears of adverse consequences. This, if carried out with sensitivity and openness, should ensure smooth delivery of change and gain stakeholder support as they feel part of the process.

Effective leadership

Appointing managers with the right skills and competencies will increase the likelihood of successful change management. A strong leader is required to ensure that change takes place. They need to have a clear vision of the future and be able to communicate this vision to stakeholders. This requires good communication skills. To gain support, a good leader needs to be able to listen to and consider other people's opinions. They obviously also need to be able to plan, organise and problem solve throughout the change process.

Develop strategies for knowledge/ skills gaps

After identifying knowledge or skills gaps in the workforce, plans need to be put in place to remove them. This could be achieved through training existing staff or recruiting new staff with the knowledge in question. Consulting outside agencies or appointing a 'change champion' who is knowledgeable could remove this barrier.

Monitor progress against the plan

A plan needs to be used continually to monitor the change process. It should contain targets to measure progress so that remedial action can be put in place if the change is lagging behind. A plan is a working document, which means it can be adjusted in face of obstacles as part of the monitoring process.

Sell the positive benefits of change

This should not just take place at the beginning of the process – stakeholders need to be reminded constantly during the process of how they could gain from the change. This constant reminder not only reinforces the reason for change, it could also help to remove barriers to change.

Invest in training initiatives

This is crucial if the change concerns new working practices, or it could be the introduction of modern technology in the day-to-day operations of a business. Employees need to be empowered with the skills and knowledge they need to embrace change. Training programmes increase their confidence, which in turn will lead to a greater motivation for change.

3.2 Possible barriers to change

Table 15.3 Possible barriers to change

Lack of employee engagement	This is often a result of inadequate or ineffective communication; if employees are not clear about the reason for change, the impact of change and the way change can be achieved, then they are not likely to support the new idea
	Key stakeholders need to be consulted by managers, e.g. employees, owners or shareholders, customers and suppliers; without an open and honest dialogue, stakeholders are unlikely to embrace and support the change
Lack of agreement on the need for change	Sometimes it can be as fundamental as a lack of agreement between management and employees on the need for change; this barrier should be removed as soon as possible through persuasion (as in Lewin's model) and also through creating a vision of the future when change has taken place (as suggested by Kotter's model)
	Change cannot take place without an agreement on the need for change as employees are key contributors to the process and they need to be in agreement with management
Economic implications	Implications such as loss of jobs, lower pay or loss of bonuses can create resistance; management needs to take into account the importance of these hygiene factors and, where possible, allay fears that these scenarios will take place
Stakeholder habits are often well established and difficult to change	Over the years, businesses develop their own ways of communication, adopt different leadership styles, use different IT systems, establish different ways of delegating authority to suit their perceived culture and values; these are usually so deeply anchored in a business's shared value that they are difficult to change
	Change may take a long time to achieve and stakeholders need to be persuaded that new ways of doing things are vital to the survival of a business, creating a sense of urgency as in Kotter's model
Stakeholder inertia	This refers to the unwillingness to do anything or try anything new, when stakeholders prefer to stick with what has always happened; this could be due to a lack of clear vision or objectives brought about by poor leadership
	For example, Kodak, despite inventing the first digital camera, could not resist the inertia to continue with its then highly profitable film division; its failure to take the riskier option at the time of developing digital technology caused its downfall
Stakeholder fear	This can include fear of the unknown – for example, employees could be wondering what is going to happen to their job, their working conditions and the way they are treated
	Fear of having to learn new skills due to the introduction of new technology, and new procedures could cause anxiety and uncertainty
Existing power structures	The existing leadership team could be adopting a power culture, where decisions are made at the top of the hierarchy because management feels that it knows best
	Reasons for decision made are not shared and employees are not expected to contribute to the decision-making process
	If the reason for change is not shared, an atmosphere of uncertainty and mistrust leads to resistance to change

Resistance from work groups	Resistance from groups like trade unions is often a result of the uncertainty that change might bring to job security, pay and general working conditions; the power of trade unions to harness support cannot be underestimated, as was seen in the case of the 200 Hovis workers who, in 2013, went on a ten-day strike against zero-hours contracts and the use of agency staff
	Constant dialogue with trade unions is a prerequisite for a successful change management
Failure of previous change initiatives	This can provide indicators to employees that future change programmes will not succeed either
	This negative expectation is likely to lead to low motivation for change among employees
Poor leadership	Leaders and managers must carry stakeholders along in their passionate vision for why the change must take place and paint a clear picture of how it will lead to improvements. If this message is not communicated, and stakeholders are not made aware of clear objectives, the change may not be successful.

KNOW IT

1 Describe the steps that you need to take to plan change.
2 What is the main purpose of appointing a project champion?
3 Describe five barriers to change.
4 Explain how trade unions can prevent change.
5 Explain how change can be managed.

LO4 Be able to assess the impacts of change on businesses and stakeholders

GETTING STARTED

(10 minutes)
Imagine that you have been successful in persuading your head teacher to start the school day at 10 am but lessons will finish at 5 pm. What impact would this have on:

● your parents, who both work 9 to 5
● your teachers
● your fellow students.

4.1 The possible impacts of change on businesses

Product life cycle

Businesses with a product portfolio aim to keep a range of products at various stages of their life cycle. Products at the end of their life cycle may be withdrawn earlier than planned due to a change in corporate policy, a decision to allocate resources to a new product

or an emergency forcing the product to be dropped to minimise adverse consequences for the business.

For example, the Apple iPod has come to the end of its life cycle, and a decision may be made to withdraw it from the market altogether if Apple decides to invest all its resources in a new invention. Various strategies have been introduced to increase the appeal of the iPod but the successes were short-lived, as shown in Figure 15.5.

As Apple focuses on the development of its iPhone and iPad, the iPod will become a casualty of Apple's own innovation.

Research and development

When designing and developing a new product or service, a budget needs to be set aside for research and development. A business needs to find the best way of producing a product or providing a service. Prototypes need to be produced and tested, and strengths and weaknesses analysed and improved on. New materials could be needed, and new equipment and machinery installed to improve the end product. It can be a costly, time-consuming process that requires a lot of expertise to get right.

Training

As discussed earlier, training is essential in change management to empower employees and the project team with the skills and capabilities to bring about the change. Training comes with a cost and it must be planned carefully so that it is appropriate, necessary and not duplicated. If budgets are tight, management might explore the possibility of training key personnel only, who then disseminate the skills and knowledge to team members. When assessing training needs, a skills gap analysis needs to be carried out to identify who needs training, how many need to be trained and what they need to be trained in.

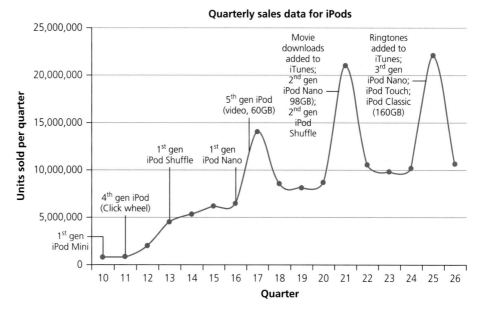

▶ **Figure 15.5** The life cycle of Apple's iPod

Recruitment and selection

This is an option if internal training is either not viable or the skills gap is too wide to be bridged. The benefits of recruiting from outside a business include the availability of new ideas and new practices, an essential element for change. However, recruitment and selection can be an expensive and time-consuming process, so the impact on productivity and profitability has to be taken into account.

Cost and profit implications

Change is costly for the reasons already discussed. As costs increase, profits decrease. As profit is a key performance indicator (KPI) of a business, costs must be managed so that they do not get out of control.

New opportunities

Change provides new opportunities. A business that has decided to sell only fair trade products may be able to build stronger customer loyalty, which may pave the way for new products to be introduced to its target market more easily. Costa Coffee's decision to expand to China may open up new opportunities that are not available in the UK. Its joint venture with prominent Chinese companies would benefit the company beyond the provision of capital. With a better understanding of the language, culture and buying habits of Chinese customers, Costa would find other opportunities to expand its product range in the future.

Different physical resource needs

Change often requires new or different physical resources such as premises, machinery and equipment. For example, the decision to automate production will mean large investments in machinery, training and maintenance. As physical resources often come at a high cost, these need to be identified carefully in terms of the need for and scope of the change.

4.2 Possible impacts of change on stakeholder groups

Owners

Even if they are passionate about the need for the change, owners still risk negative outcomes, such as a reduce return on investment in the short or long term or a fall in share prices as investors become nervous about the uncertainty. On a smaller level, the owners' personal objectives may be affected – for example, they may have to revise their financial targets or even accept a less favourable work–life balance while the change is put in place.

Managers

Managers and supervisors may struggle to convince their teams of the need for change. They need to strongly buy in to the vision in order to communicate down the hierarchy. Employees who are directly affected by the change, for example by being put at risk of redundancy, may become difficult to manage or go off sick, so that everyday tasks cannot be completed effectively. Taking ownership of the change objectives should help managers.

Employees

The possible financial impact on employees in terms of pay, redundancies and loss of benefits has been discussed earlier in this unit. Non-financial impacts, such as loss of status due to restructuring and redeployment, can affect employee morale and motivation. Retraining can be stressful for some employees who dislike doing things in different ways. A change in the culture could mean a new work ethos that employees are not familiar with. Working conditions can change – for example, a change in shift patterns can affect an employee's work–life balance. All these factors can impact on morale, leading to low productivity, absenteeism and labour turnover.

Customers

Businesses plan change with the aim of having a positive impact on customers; this is usually evident in new products with better design and function. There was a lot of speculation about the specification of the new iPhone 7 before it launched. Would it have a better screen resolution, bigger storage and wireless charging?

However, change can also have less desirable impacts such as those caused by obsolescence of products. With the demise of the video tape and video player, some consumers find that they have lost years of images and films because they are now unable to play the tapes. A similar concern is often raised about our current digital images and films. Will we lose these precious records when the technology we are using now becomes obsolete?

A business could decide to improve its customer service and after-sales policy to provide longer guarantees on its products. New procedures could be put in place to simplify the complaints process for customers. These changes would have a positive impact on customers.

Local residents

People living near the business may not share its enthusiasm for change, especially if it takes the form of a new factory, an extension or increased deliveries. They may be concerned about increased noise, congestion, pollution, resulting in protests, letters to the local press, withdrawal of goodwill, and objections to planning permission.

Suppliers

The impact on suppliers may be more or less orders from the business and revised contract terms and conditions, for example regarding how long payment or delivery takes.

There are bound to be winners and losers among suppliers as a result of change. When General Mills announced that it would reduce the greenhouse emissions in its agricultural supply chain the implication was clear for its suppliers – either improve greenhouse emission rates or lose a major customer. For smaller suppliers, this can be a costly process that they cannot afford. However, suppliers who are able to adopt a more sustainable agricultural practice would benefit from orders from a multinational such as General Mills.

***

KNOW IT

1. Using an example, explain how change can impact on the life cycle of a product.
2. How can the research and development department contribute to change?
3. Describe three ways employees may be affected by change.
4. Describe three ways customers of a business may be affected by change.
5. Analyse likely impacts of change on the employees of a business you have researched.

***

LO5 Be able to use data to monitor change management in businesses

GETTING STARTED

(10 minutes)

Imagine that your school day now starts at 10 am. How would you measure the impact of this change on stakeholders like you, your classmates, your teachers and your parents?

5.1 The different types of data used to monitor the change management process

Quantitative data for monitoring and evaluating change management

Figure 15.6 shows how key performance indicators (KPIs) can be used to measure a business's performance.

KPIs must be quantifiable and must be chosen according to a business's aims and objectives – for example, they can be used to measure how successfully a change strategy has been implemented. Different functional areas will have different KPIs, as shown in Table 15.4.

As no two businesses are the same, the KPIs that best measure a business's performance would be different. Most of the KPIs listed in Table 15.4 have been covered in detail in Unit 1, LO8 (see page 44).

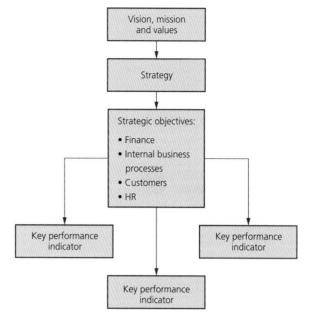

▲ **Figure 15.6** Where do KPIs come from?

Source: www.exploreHR.org

Table 15.4 Examples of KPIs in different functions

Functional area	KPI
Production	Total output level, capacity utilisation, labour productivity, waste level
Finance	Profit, costs, cash flow, break even, ratio analysis
Human resources	Labour turnover, absenteeism, punctuality
Sales	Sales revenue, market share

Qualitative data for monitoring and evaluating change management

Qualitative data are non-quantifiable and therefore more difficult to analyse. These could include the following.

- Customer survey or feedback: how satisfied were they with the product/service? Do they think it represents value for money? Are they happy with their shopping experience? What do they think about the after-sales services?
- Employee feedback: how well do they perceive the change that has been implemented? What benefits/drawbacks have they experienced as a result of the change? How has the business benefited from the change strategy?
- Media coverage on how a business has changed, how the change has been managed and how stakeholders have been impacted is important as a measure of success: positive media coverage will benefit a business in terms of improving reputation and its revenue and profit.

All the data discussed above should be used to measure a business's performance in change management using aims and objectives set at the beginning of the process.

This important process can be demonstrated by using Marks & Spencer's Plan A, the company's CSR policy, launched in 2007. Table 15.5 lists Marks & Spencer's achievements in 2015.

Table 15.5 M&S: measuring success against objectives

Objectives	Achievements
Involve all our customers in Plan A	One million M&S customers raised more than £2.2 million for Oxfam Saved 4 million items of unwanted clothes from going to landfill
Making Plan A how we do business	Improved energy efficiency by more than 10 per cent in our stores Reduced packaging by 16 per cent without compromising quality Reduced number of food carrier bags given out by 400 million each year
Extending our social and environmental commitments across the 5 pillars	Purchased GreenPalm Certificates for all palm oil used in M&S products

Source: http://corporate.marksandspencer.com

These achievements should be measured against the objectives to see how much progress has been made. It is evident that there is still some way to go for Marks & Spencer to fully achieve its objectives, but the success in its CSR policy can be seen in the improvement to its reputation as a leading sustainable retailer, setting the standards for others to follow.

INDIVIDUAL ACTIVITY

(20 minutes)

Follow this link to read about Amey's award-winning change management strategy: http://tinyurl.com/j7zrko2

Identify the key strengths of the change management process and explain how this helps Amey to achieve its change strategy.

5.2 The need for continual monitoring of the change management process against the original objectives and plan

To make sure the process is on track or identify any issues

This is the main purpose of monitoring – to ensure that the change strategy is moving in the right direction within the timescale allowed. It is necessary to ask questions such as:

- Are objectives being achieved or not?
- Will the final goals be reached given the progress made so far?
- Are there enough resources to enable the change to be carried out?

If targets have been achieved, then it is important to reward and celebrate. If not, problems and issues need to be identified and obstacles removed.

To identify improvements to the original objectives and plan

A plan should be treated as a working document that evolves and improves during change management. It is necessary to ask questions such as:

- Should the deadlines be changed?
- Are the objectives still realistic?
- Should priorities be changed?

These are all relevant in identifying improvements to the original plan.

Improvements to the original objectives and plan could be brought about by changes in internal and external factors such as a downturn in the economy, the loss of key personnel responsible for the change management, or unexpected events such as natural disasters. The most important issue to bear in mind is knowing why improvements are necessary.

To identify how well the managers are managing the change

This could be done by comparing the progress made against the objectives set for these managers. This process offers the opportunity to reward and celebrate achievements, which is important to encourage and motivate managers towards the end goal. It also allows barriers to change to be identified and removed.

To identify when the change management process is complete

It is important to know when to stop using the original objectives and plan as a measuring tool. To identify when change is complete, the aims must be clear and objectives SMART. A clear vision of success must be created at the outset to indicate to stakeholders what it looks like. Both quantitative and qualitative data should be used as indicators for completion as well as for evaluation. Once it is decided that the change is complete, the strengths and weaknesses of the process should be evaluated to inform areas for improvement in preparation for future projects.

> **KNOW IT**
>
> 1 What is the difference between quantitative and qualitative data?
> 2 Using an example, explain what key performance indicators could be.
> 3 Analyse the likely impacts of high absenteeism on a business you have researched.
> 4 Outline three examples of qualitative data.
> 5 Explain why there is a need to monitor change management continually.

Assessment practice questions

Below are some practice questions for you to try. Use the information provided below to answer the following questions.

Resource 1

Gemma's Gourmet Pizzas operates 10 takeaway outlets in trendy parts of London. Prompted by a slowdown in sales due to a change in consumer trend for healthy eating, Gemma, the managing director, has decided that the company should respond to this change for the long-term survival of the business.

An initial change management meeting has taken place. Below is a summary of the main contributions and thoughts of those who attended this meeting.

Table 15.6 Team thoughts about producing healthy pizzas

Name	Job role	Verbal contribution	Unexpressed thought
Gemma	Managing Director	Heathy pizzas are the future for our company. We must respond to consumer trend and, if we get it right, it will enable us to charge premium prices whilst satisfying customer needs.	None
Chris	Human Resources Manager	I suggest that our chefs should have a say in designing the new recipes. They are all professionally trained and could advise us on how to make the new ingredients work.	I hope that the chefs will embrace the new idea. Some will need more convincing than others that change in necessary, especially those who have been cooking pizzas for a number of years.
Imran	Marketing Manager	The first thing we need to do is to find out exactly what our customers want. We could carry out a survey amongst our existing customers since the future of our business depends on what they want to eat.	This is not going to be as straightforward as it seems. I wonder how much time I will be allowed for this mammoth task!
Tom	Finance Manager	I think it's a good idea. The company's revenue has been in decline for the last two years so change is definitely needed. However, we do need to make sure that the new recipes do not push up costs.	None
Lu	Supply Chain Manager	This might mean that we will need to source new suppliers if our existing ones do not stock what we need. If we can't find local suppliers it means looking further afield, compromising on food miles.	This is going to be a lengthy process and we might lose a few reliable suppliers.
Beth	Product Development Manager	We will need to come up with new recipes to incorporate healthy ingredients as well as putting down on salt and sugar.	This is not going to be easy. Heathy food tends to taste bland. I am certainly not one for compromising on cheese and pepperoni!

1. Refer to Resource 1.
   a. Outline the driver of change at Gemma's Gourmet Pizzas. [3]
   b. Analyse three likely barriers to change at Gemma's Gourmet Pizzas. Which one of these three barriers is likely to have the greatest impact on Gemma's Gourmet Pizzas if it is not managed successfully? Give reasons for your choice. [16]
   c. Using Kotter's 8-Step Process for Leading Change, produce a plan of action showing how Gemma's Gourmet Pizzas should manage the change. Justify your plan of action. [16]

Resource 2

It has now been over a year since the healthy pizzas have been introduced. Gemma, the managing director, is monitoring the change management process. A summary of the most recent quantitative and qualitative data is given below.

Table 15. Key Performance Indicators (KPIs) of Gemma's Gourmet Pizzas

Indicator	2015	2016
Annual sales	£2.1m	£2.5m
Average customer spend	£30.00	£35.00
Gross profit margin	85%	65%

Feedback from a customer survey

- The new pizzas are great! I can now have pizzas four times a week rather than two.
- I am not impressed! The new pizzas taste like cardboard; bring back the real thing!
- Pizzas are considered 'junk' food. You cannot disguise it with healthy claims.
- I like the new pizzas in general but wish there were more cheese at times.
- They are a bit pricy! I mean £20 for a 10-inch supposedly healthy pizza is more than the cost of an average main in a restaurant.

2. Refer to Resource 2.
   a. Identify and explain likely impacts of the change on Gemma's Gourmet Pizzas'
      i   customers [2]
      ii suppliers [2]
      iii chefs. [2]
   b. Analyse the qualitative and quantitative data shown in Resource 2. Evaluate how well the managers at Gemma's Gourmet Pizzas are managing the change. Justify your answer. [16]

Unit **16**

Principles of project management

ABOUT THIS UNIT

A business's projects can be on a small scale, like a desk move, or large and complicated, like the construction of a shopping centre. Whatever its scope, the project will consist of tasks and activities leading towards a defined result.

Planning and ongoing monitoring are key to the success of a project. In this unit, you will find out about the different stages of project management and the role of a project manager. You will learn about the external and internal factors that can influence the success of a project, and how to identify and prevent potential issues. You'll also understand why the components of a project plan are important not just at the start of the project but throughout its life cycle.

LEARNING OUTCOMES

The topics, activities and suggested reading in this unit will help you to:

1 understand the stages of project management
2 understand the skills project managers need to have
3 understand how and why projects are monitored and factors that influence a project
4 be able to prepare project plans.

How will I be assessed?

You will be assessed through a series of assignments and tasks set and marked by your tutor.

How will I be graded?

You will be graded using the following criteria, which are in the specification produced by OCR for the qualification.

Learning outcome	Pass	Merit	Distinction
You will:	To achieve a Pass you must demonstrate that you have met all the pass assessment criteria	To achieve a Merit you must demonstrate that you have met all the pass and merit assessment criteria	To achieve a Distinction you must demonstrate that you have met all the pass, merit and distinction assessment criteria
1 Understand the stages of project management	**P1** Explain the stages of project management used in a specific business project		
2 Understand the skills project managers need to have	**P2** Explain the skillset a project manager needs to have and why		
3 Understand how and why projects are monitored and factors that influence a project	**P3** Explain how the factors that influence or present a risk to a specific project are monitored	**M1** Analyse the factors that influence, and the factors that present a risk to, a specific project and explain the potential impact(s) on the project	**D1** Evaluate the effectiveness of the methods used for monitoring a specific project
4 Be able to prepare project plans	**P4** Prepare a project plan for a specific project	**M2** Explain how the risks to a specific project could be mitigated	**D2** Evaluate the impact on a specific project if contingencies have to be implemented
	P5 Justify the choice of the project plan tool(s) used		

• •

LO1 Understand the stages of project management *P1*

GETTING STARTED

(15 minutes)

In pairs, draw a flow chart showing the stages of **project management** using the phrases provided below, and explain why you have arranged them in that particular order.

- project planning
- project closure and post-implementation review
- project initiation
- project direction.

> 🔑 **KEY TERM**
>
> **Project management** – the process of planning, organising, monitoring and applying resources to achieve an end goal.

1.1 The stages of project management

Project initiation

When a **project** first begins to be planned, several elements need to be considered.

The first step is to define aims and objectives with an end goal, as this sets the direction for the project. A project should also have a clearly defined purpose that explains the reasons why it is happening, so that the people involved are motivated to complete the tasks they have been assigned.

KEY TERM

Project – a set task or series of tasks to be completed. A project is temporary because it has defined beginning and end times. The outcome of a project is the end product, result or goal that the project is planned to achieve. Projects can take place in and across various departments, e.g. filling a skills gap in human resources, researching and developing a new product, constructing a new building, installing a new IT system.

The scope of a project defines the boundaries that determine what work needs to be completed in the lifetime of a project. The deliverables define the scope of a project. They refer to the tangible or intangible items produced as a result of a project (e.g. a document, a piece of software or a training programme). These can be for internal or external customers.

Key targets and deadlines can be established by setting SMART objectives (see Unit 6, page 149, and page 283 of this unit) to pave the way for the final aim to be achieved. Smart objectives are small steps that allow progress to be achieved and measured.

A feasibility study is an assessment of a project's practicality, validity, costs and benefits. It helps answer the important question of whether the project should go ahead and, if so, what are the best ways of carrying it out? Investigating a project in this way also helps to define the scope so that time and money are not wasted on carrying out unnecessary activities.

A project proposal gives structure to a project. It can be used as a communication tool, a tool for organising resources and as a contract between two parties so that everybody knows exactly what they can expect to see as an end result. As shown in Figure 16.1, it is written in a very clear and concise manner.

▶ **Figure 16.1** An example of a project proposal

Proposal outline

Project proposal

Project details
Project name: Young Enterprise
Project manager: D Wainwright
Project start date: 5 September 2015
Project end date: 30 May 2016

Project description
To recruit a group of at least six Year 12 students to set up and run a Young Enterprise company in the academic year September 2015 to May 2016

Project objectives
- To promote enterprise to students in Year 12
- To provide opportunities for students to set up and run a real business
- To develop students' employability skills, e.g. organisation, time management, decision making, negotiation, communication, presentation
- To develop students' confidence in serving members of the public

Project cost

Registration fee:	£750
Staffing:	£500
Travelling:	£100
Total:	£1,350

Benefits
Students will have a hands-on experience of what is entailed in running a real business. This will enhance their understanding of the challenges that businesses face on a day-to-day basis; it will also help students studying Business with their coursework and exams.
Students will have a rare opportunity to interact with the general public, as well as present their concepts and ideas to panels of judges. This has been found to greatly increase students' confidence.
The project will also promote Business Studies within the school and help with the recruitment of A-level Business groups in future. The success of the Young Enterprise company will raise the profile of the school within the local community as well as nationally.

A business case (Figure 16.2) records the reasons for starting a project. It contains a cost–benefit study, as well as details of the potential impacts on stakeholders of the project. Its main purpose is to present a well-written argument to convince a decision maker of the importance of initiating a project.

▲ **Figure 16.2** Elements of a project business case

Defining project controls such as time, cost and quality strategies is important as a tool for monitoring the progress of a project once it is initiated. Project controls provide the project team with the data for continuous analysis and assessment of a project, to ensure that it is managed effectively.

Having a clearly defined communication strategy is crucial to the successful completion of a project. It explains to the project team how communication will support them in achieving the project aim. It sets out the objectives of communication, the channels of communication that will be used, what is to be communicated and to whom, and the timescale involved.

Project planning

When the project initiation stage is complete, a project plan can be produced. This should cover key areas such as resource requirements, to include human, physical and financial resources, quality targets and control methods as well as a risk plan. This is covered in detail in LO4, below (page 285).

Project direction for the execution and implementation stage

Managing the project controls defined in the initiation stage is vital when the project is under way. The **project manager** needs to continually monitor the four key controls of time, cost, quality and risk (Figure 16.3) to ensure the smooth running of the project. These controls should be checked against those stated in the project plan to ensure targets are met.

> 🔑 **KEY TERM**
>
> **Project manager** – the person in charge of initiating, planning, executing and monitoring activities scheduled to achieve a planned outcome.

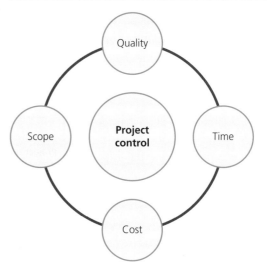

▲ **Figure 16.3** It is important to balance time, cost, quality and risk

Reporting project status using the communication strategy that has been defined is important for all stakeholders involved so that they know whether the project is progressing as planned. A project status report should contain, first, the overall 'health' of the project, identifying any problems currently encountered, as well as foreseeable ones in the future. It should contain milestones, which are targets that have been achieved and are scheduled to be achieved. This allows the progress to be measured. Lastly, a project status report should contain brief descriptions of issues encountered so far so that management can decide whether to step in or not.

Managing risk is the proactive process of trying to minimise the potential negative consequences brought about by undesirable events. Risks can be internal and external. Internal sources of risk include the availability of funds, human resources, and infrastructure such as hardware and software. These risks are more manageable than external risks as they are, to a considerable degree, within the control of the business. External risks such as changes in economic factors, natural disasters and actions of suppliers are far less predictable and outside a business's control.

Risks identified in the project planning stage should be monitored for their chances of occurrence, and reprioritised if necessary. Resources required for minimising the negative impacts of risks should be made available and deployed when risks are encountered throughout the lifetime of a project. Risk management should also involve avoiding risks if possible, or even turning these threats into opportunities to improve the end result.

Managing communications involves getting the right information to the right people at the right time. This could be achieved using the communication strategy devised at the project initiation stage. Crucial information to be managed at this stage includes reporting on the status of the project, notifying key stakeholders of issues encountered or feedback from stakeholders on their perception of the progress made so far.

Project closure and post-implementation review

At the end of a project, reviews should be carried out on the following aspects.

- The extent to which aims and objectives have been met. This can be done by comparing what has actually been achieved with the aims and objectives set at the beginning of a project. This could be measured in terms of the benefits and rewards achieved, as well as whether these have been delivered within the timescale and budget constraints. Depending on the nature of the project, assessing whether the needs and requirements of internal and external customers have been met is also an important benchmark with which to measure the success of a project.
- Lessons learned at the planning and implementation stages: strengths and weaknesses should be identified to see where improvements can be made in terms of resource availability and communication systems, as well as training of personnel to bridge a skills gap identified in the process. This will prepare a business for the next project, increasing the chances of success.

> ### KNOW IT
> 1 Why is it important to have SMART objectives?
> 2 Why is it important to draw up a project proposal?
> 3 What is a communication strategy?
> 4 Explain what it means to adopt a proactive approach to managing risk.
> 5 Explain two ways of measuring the extent to which aims and objectives have been met.

• •

L01 assessment activity

Below is a suggested assessment activity that has been directly linked to the Pass criteria in L01 to help with assignment preparation. This is followed by top tips on how to achieve the best results.

Activity 1 Pass criteria *P1*

P1 Choose a project that interests you, from your work placement or a business you have investigated. Explain how the project is managed, i.e. project initiation, project planning, project direction for the execution and implementation stage, project closure and post-implementation review.

TOP TIPS
✔ Ensure the key stages of project management are described using examples from the business project you have chosen.
✔ The project that you choose does not have to be a very big and complicated one – projects could range from installing a new piece of software to relocating a factory overseas.

LO2 Understand the skills project managers need to have *P2*

GETTING STARTED 👤 · · · · · · · · · · · · · · ·

(10 minutes)

Table 16.1 lists the skills a project manager needs to have. For each one, give an example or a situation in which a project manager can demonstrate it.

Table 16.1 Project management skills

Skill	Example
Communication	
Team building	
Planning	
Conflict management	
Time management	
Negotiation	
Problem solving	
Influencing	
Leadership	
Critical thinking	
Business case writing	
Risk management	
Cost control	

2.1 The skills project managers need

Communication

A good project manager needs to be able to communicate effectively, both verbally and in writing, using appropriate style and language in different situations. They need to be aware of the different communication channels available, such as email, Skype and Facebook, as well as the strengths and weaknesses of each method, so that they can choose the most effective one for different purposes.

A good communicator also needs to be able to listen to different points of view and respond accordingly. This is especially important when dealing with a problem as, without a thorough understanding of a situation from different perspectives, the project manager will not be able to deal with it effectively.

Team building

A project team needs to have a common purpose. By listening to team members the project manager will be able to respond to and resolve different issues that might exist. Team rapport can then be built by finding common ground so that team members can get on well together and work more effectively. Motivating team members by reminding them of the purpose and benefits of the project, how well they are doing, and rewarding them for their achievements all help to bind people together. A project manager needs to be able to build a team that works well together to complete a project successfully.

Planning

Planning skills such as scheduling what work needs to be done by whom and by when are important if the project is to remain on track. The availability of different resources needs to be planned carefully to reduce waste and keep within budget. Changes to the original plan are inevitable in the course of a project and the manager needs to be able to plan for these changes, which could involve reprioritising of resources so that the project delivers the expected outcomes and benefits.

Conflict management

This could involve effectively resolving disagreements between team members or stakeholders. Resources are often limited and constrained by the budgets set, so a good project manager should have the skills for allocating resources according to needs and requirements. Priority should be given to tasks that, if incomplete, will have the greatest negative impact on the success of the project. Managing disagreements between people can be very demanding, and a good project manager should be able to adopt different styles as shown in Figure 16.4, according to different situations and personalities involved. Sometimes the project manager can prevent disagreements escalating by recognising and acting on difficulties early.

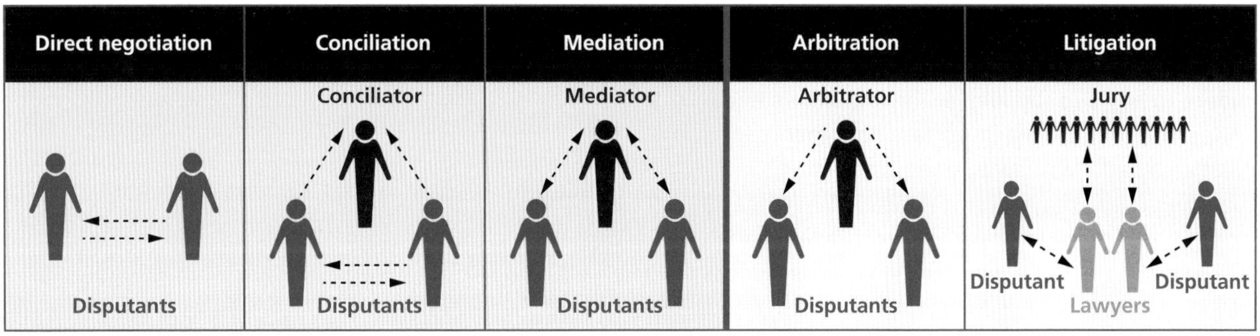

Direct negotiation	Conciliation	Mediation	Arbitration	Litigation
	Conciliator	Mediator	Arbitrator	Jury
Disputants	Disputants	Disputants	Disputants	Disputant Lawyers Disputant

▲ **Figure 16.4** There are many ways to manage conflict. Source: www.partnersglobal.org

Time management

Good time-management skills ensure that deadlines are not missed. However, the project manager should have a thorough understanding of the processes involved before setting the deadline for each task. It is counter-productive to set unrealistic deadlines that are unachievable. Time management also involves measuring progress against the schedule to see whether everything is on track. Identifying tasks that are expected to be delayed enables the project manager to reallocate resources to ensure that they are completed on time; this is especially important for tasks on the critical path (see Unit 3, page 96, and later in this unit, page 286).

Negotiation

Negotiation skills are important when dealing with conflict, as well as in securing maximum rewards or benefits for the project. Negotiation is a bargaining process with the goal of achieving a solution and, in the context of project management, arriving at a solution that maximises the chances of success as well as the rewards of a project. The project manager needs to be persuasive and firm in a negotiation process to achieve the best outcome, and also know the boundary that must not be crossed to achieve the goal.

Problem solving

Problem-solving skills are essential, as problems are usually encountered throughout a project. The first stage involves defining and identifying the problem, as the project manager needs to be able to describe the problem clearly. When they know what problem they are facing, the next stage is to find alternative solutions to overcome it. This is the process of analysing the strengths and weaknesses of each alternative to arrive at the one that would best solve the problem in terms

of minimising costs, maximising reward or minimising damage. When a solution is chosen it needs to be implemented and evaluated at the end of the process to identify areas for improvement.

Influencing

Good project managers need to be able to influence team members and stakeholders by having a clear view of what they want and then persuading others to buy into the idea. This could be done through constant reminders of the end benefits, or by emphasising how team members or stakeholders could benefit personally from the end result.

Leadership

A good project manager needs to have a vision of what they want to achieve and how it can be achieved. The quality of a good leader encompasses all the skills we have discussed so far: planning, team building, time management, conflict management, problem solving, decision making, etc. The ability to delegate effectively comes from a thorough understanding of the strengths and weaknesses of each team member. Delegation motivates team members and gets the job done. However, a good leader also needs to lead by example in the hope that team members will copy their behaviour and share the same attitude to work.

Critical thinking

Critical thinking involves the ability to weigh up the advantages and disadvantages of different alternatives to arrive at the best solution to a problem. The project manager needs to be able to structure and present the arguments for and against an issue clearly and succinctly, using qualitative and quantitative data to back up a point of view. Information gathered should be analysed and synthesised before a reasoned judgement is reached.

Business case writing

Business case writing skills are important to persuade stakeholders to buy into the idea at the initiation stage. It is perhaps one of the most important documents in a project as a badly written business case might mean that the project may never go ahead. A business case needs to be written logically in a persuasive way, explaining what needs to be done and why, to persuade stakeholders that action is needed. The document needs to be written in such a way as to attract commitment from stakeholders financially and non-financially, so that an action can be agreed on and implemented.

Risk management

This starts with the identification of risks. A risk register can be used to list all the risks identified in order of their likelihood of occurrence, as well as the amount of potential damage they could cause. A good project manager needs to know when to reclassify risks as needing immediate action during the course of a project. Contingency planning needs to take place to counteract the adverse consequences of risks if they take place; this is a proactive approach to risk management. When planning the project, risks must be taken into account when estimating the costs and resources needed.

Cost control

The purpose of cost control is to make sure that the project does not require more money than is budgeted.

A project manager needs to be familiar with financial planning tools such as cash-flow forecasts and variance analyses to ensure that a project is within budget. Identifying areas of overspend using variance analyses helps a manager to put corrective actions in place where financial targets have been missed. A cash-flow forecast can be used to see where costs can be cut so that a project is completed within the budget agreed.

 INDIVIDUAL ACTIVITY

(20 minutes)

Follow this link to read about successful project management approaches: http://tinyurl.com/haol3hp

Using the information from the link, identify and describe the skills that a project manager needs.

 KNOW IT

1 What does a good communicator need to be able to do?
2 Why is it important to manage conflict between stakeholders?
3 Describe the four stages of problem solving.
4 What is critical thinking?
5 Explain two ways in which a project manager can control costs.

LO2 assessment activity

Below is a suggested assessment activity that has been directly linked to the Pass criteria in LO2 to help with assignment preparation. This is followed by top tips on how to achieve the best results.

Activity 1 Pass criteria *P2*

P2 Design a questionnaire to find out the skills that a project manager needs to demonstrate. You could interview the manager or owner of your work placement or people occupying a senior position in your school/college. From your findings, explain why a project manager should have those skills.

TOP TIPS

✔ When you choose your interviewees, make sure each one is a leader in the organisation they work for.
✔ Your questionnaire should cover all the skills listed in the specification. Do not leave it to your interviewees to tell you what skills a leader needs.
✔ Interview the people you have chosen; remember to ask them to describe at least one example of a time/situation when they have had to demonstrate each skill.
✔ When explaining why it is important for a project manager to demonstrate each skill, use the examples you have been given in your interviews.
✔ You could present your findings as a PowerPoint presentation.

LO3 Understand how and why projects are monitored and factors that influence a project *P3 M1 D1*

GETTING STARTED

(10 minutes)

Explain the difference between the internal and external factors that could influence a project, and give an example for each.

3.1 How and why projects are monitored

Using methods of monitoring a project and reasons for monitoring

The progress of projects can be monitored using a number of different methods. Some or all may be appropriate for different projects.

Budget variance analysis

This is a quantitative method used to identify areas of overspend by comparing the actual amount of money spent with the budgeted amount. Reasons for why the variance occurs can then be investigated and corrective actions taken. Variances can also turn out to be favourable, which on the one hand should be celebrated but, on the other, could mean that the budget was over-generous and should be adjusted in the future. Budget variance analysis can be a very effective cost control tool if the budget was set properly in the first place. Quantitative analyses of this nature ensure that the project remains viable, which is an important assessment of whether it will achieve a positive outcome. Cost is a very important criterion for judging viability.

Quality management

This is a continuous process that starts at the project initiation stage and ends only when the project aim has been achieved. At every stage during project execution, the project manager needs to monitor the quality of product or services produced as well as the way the project is executed. The key question to ask is, 'Will the end user or project sponsor be satisfied with the product or service?'

The purpose of quality management is to identify issues and problems as soon as possible, to minimise the impact of any potential damage. This is known as prevention, which is less costly than trying to correct the mistake later on. The concept of continuous improvement is important, and the way the process worked could be analysed at the end of a project. Evaluating strengths and weaknesses and identifying areas for improvement can help increase the rate of success of future projects.

Risks and decisions logs

These are very useful tools for monitoring all the activities and decisions that have been made during a project. A risks log is a document showing issues and problems identified at the project planning stage, together with the probability of them occurring and the impact they would have on the project. It should also show the name of the person responsible for monitoring and mitigating the risks, with review dates clearly stated. A decisions log is a record of all the decisions made in the lifetime of a project, showing when the decisions were made and by whom. These logs may identify possible solutions to problems encountered, and could be presented in meetings to assess how well the project has been managed.

Regular reporting

This is crucial if the whole project team, as well as stakeholders, are to be informed of the progress of a project. Using the communication strategy drawn up in the project initiation stage will ensure that the project team knows who to report to, what to report and by when. These reports could be used to delegate tasks to team members, encouraging them to develop and use their skills. On the other hand, a task can be escalated up an organisation's hierarchy because the current responsibility holder might not have the skill or knowledge to make the right decision or execute a particular task to the standard required.

Comparison of actual versus planned progress

This is another simple monitoring tool that should be used on a regular basis. This process enables a project manager to report the progress against the plan, as well as to identify any issues or problems. Potential slippages (late delivery of elements of the project) can also be identified so that solutions can be found to ensure that these do not present a huge problem further down the line. A project manager would check that there are no discrepancies between actual and planned progress. If actual progress is found to be slower than planned, the causes for the delay should be investigated and actions put in place to get the project back on track. This could be achieved with additional resources or finding alternative ways of executing the plan.

Reasons for monitoring projects include:

- data collected during monitoring can be used to assess progress
- helps to ensure that projects are carried out as planned
- allows members of the project team to share information and experiences
- mistakes or weaknesses identified could be highlighted, and areas for improvement drawn up
- to reassure stakeholders involved that the project team is in control of various aspects of the project.

3.2 Factors that influence a project and which need monitoring

Internal

An organisation's aims and objectives would have a direct influence on a project's nature and outcome. For example, a business that is aiming to reduce its carbon footprint is unlikely to invest in a project relating to fossil fuel. A project's aims and objectives should be aligned with those set for the whole business, and should be designed to support and drive the business towards the direction it is heading. They should also be clearly defined; the use of SMART objectives is recommended so that all stakeholders involved can use them as a yardstick with which to measure progress.

Resources available will have a definite influence on the scope and nature of a project. For example, automating a production line would require a large amount of funds, so a shortage of capital might lead to a business introducing partial automation instead. To introduce a new IT system, a business would need to make sure that there is expertise within the workforce, or look for other options. A shortage of resources such as materials and equipment could result, due to poor planning and co-ordination. The consequence of this is likely to be a delay to the completion of the whole project, especially if the activities delayed are on the critical path.

Procedures and policies such as corporate social responsibility (CSR) dictate the kind of project a business would plan for. Projects should reflect a business's vision and the image it wants to portray to its stakeholders. For example, Marks & Spencer's Plan A project aims – to achieve efficiency and environmental and ethical excellence in its operations – are very much in line with what the company wants to achieve: to be the most ethical retailer.

External

Using Plan A as an example again, Marks & Spencer will need to find suppliers that can provide clothing made in an ecological factory or homeware made using recycled materials, to implement the project. A restaurant planning to introduce modern technology such as a point-of-sale system will need to hire contractors with that specialism to implement it successfully. Without the availability of specialist suppliers and contractors, some projects remain just a plan.

External sources of finance such as bank loans, debentures and hire purchase might be needed to fund a project. If a business cannot access these sources of finance the project might not be implemented. Inflation rates need to be monitored closely as an increase will mean higher costs for materials, fuel, salaries, etc., which would make a project less viable. Exchange rates also need to be monitored if a business imports resources from abroad. A weaker pound (being able to buy less for each pound) will mean higher costs.

Laws and regulations will impact on the implementation of a project, so they need to be monitored closely. For example, planning permission is needed if the project involves changing the use of premises from one category to another, e.g. changing a shop into a residential home. Planning permission is also required if a farmer wishes to change the use of a piece of agricultural land to a non-agricultural activity such as a campsite. Planning rules have been relaxed for warehouses and industrial buildings, but it is good practice to check with the local authority to see whether planning permission is needed before work is started. The project manager needs to keep up to date with changes in employment law, such as an increase in the minimum wage, the introduction of the living wage, paternity and maternity leave and pay, etc., so as to avoid breaking the law. Changes in the Health and Safety at Work Act, such as the simplification of the Construction Regulations, revisions to ISO 14001, and an increase in fines for infringement of health and safety, can all be relevant to a project, so need to be monitored closely.

Other factors that present a risk to the success of the project

Poor leadership by failing to communicate, for example, can lead to poor co-ordination of activities. A good project manager needs to be able to communicate with internal and external stakeholders to inform, to discuss and to negotiate the best options for a project. Without good leadership a project is unlikely to achieve its end goal.

Poor planning can lead to slow progress as activities are not co-ordinated. Risks and decisions logs need to be updated regularly to monitor progress. Poor contingency plans could lead to delays in the supply chain that could directly impact on the completion date of a project.

Failing to manage change is another risk factor. As discussed earlier in this unit the project plan is a working document and a project manager should be able to adapt it according to what is required. Changes often occur during the lifetime of a project and the project manager needs to exercise a certain degree of flexibility in response to change. Change can also be a result of changes in external factors, which are outside of a business's control.

Poor project reporting could be a result of a poorly designed communication strategy at the initiation stage or stakeholders involved are not clear about how it works. This impedes the progress of a project as, without a good communication framework, team members cannot co-ordinate their activities. Reporting of problems that have been encountered and the corrective actions taken should take place regularly if the project is to be monitored effectively.

Other factors could be the objective(s) of project not being clearly defined (see Section 4.1) and a lack of resources (see Section 3.2).

KNOW IT

1 Explain how budget variance analysis could be used to monitor a project.
2 Explain why quality management should be a continuous process.
3 Describe the information you expect to see in a risks and decisions log.
4 Explain how changes in the Health and Safety at Work Act could affect a construction company.
5 Identify and explain two causes of change that might have an impact on the success of businesses such as Dyson introducing a new product.

LO3 assessment activities

Below are suggested assessment activities that have been directly linked to the Pass, Merit and Distinction criteria in LO3 to help with assignment preparation. These are followed by top tips on how to achieve the best results.

Activity 1 Pass criteria *P3*

P3 Explain how the project you chose for P1 can be monitored using budget variance analysis, quality management, risks and decisions logs, regular reporting, and comparison of actual versus planned progress.

Activity 2 Merit criteria *M1*

M1 Analyse the likelihood of the factors discussed in Section 3.2 affecting your chosen project. For each factor, explain the potential impact(s) on the project you have chosen.

Activity 3 Distinction criteria *D1*

D1 Focus on the method(s) your chosen project used for monitoring purposes. You should discuss the strengths and weaknesses of the method(s) used and write a conclusion on how useful the method(s) chosen is/are for monitoring the project you chose for P1. Suggest a better method if appropriate.

TOP TIPS

✔ For P3 you need to show understanding of how each method stated in Section 3.1 can be used to monitor the project you have chosen, using examples where possible.
✔ D1 is a development of P3, so you are advised to do the relevant activities together. Focus on how the methods for monitoring projects are useful to the project manager.
✔ For M1, use examples from the project you have chosen to demonstrate your understanding of how each factor in Section 3.2 can impact on the project, e.g. deadline not met, aims and objectives not achieved, end result not satisfactory, loss of revenue.

4.1 The components of a project plan

Project vision

In this section of the project plan, you need to describe what the project is all about. The key outcomes should be stated clearly, together with the deliverables, so that the readers know what they can expect to see at the end of the project. Very often a project has various aims and objectives, so these should be prioritised so that the reader is clear which are more important than others.

The target audience, such as the **project stakeholders** and their needs, should be clearly stated. This should further clarify the vision of the project, as the readers will be able to see how stakeholder needs can be met by the outcomes of the project. The aim is to persuade the reader to agree with the rationale of the project.

> ### KEY TERM
>
> **Project stakeholders** – anybody who has an interest in a project. They could be internal or external to a business, e.g. client, customers (internal and external) or users, project manager, team members, suppliers, consultants, project sponsors and contractors. They might gain from a successful project or they might have an influence on how projects are completed.

Aims should be stated clearly and prioritised. These show the goals that the project is planned to achieve and set the direction for the whole project team. SMART objectives are small targets that should be set to move the project towards the end goals. These objectives can act as a motivating tool for team members as well as useful tools for measuring success.

Resource requirements

This section is where the required resources are listed. It helps the project manager to organise what is needed in advance so that physical resources, such as materials, equipment, machinery, tools and software, are available when needed. Skilful management of resources enables a project to be run smoothly and within budget.

Human resource requirements should also be stated clearly, such as how many people are needed in the project management team, as well as the support staff, so that planning to supply these team skills can start without delay. An organisational chart can be used to illustrate each person's role and responsibilities as well as the project manager's own role. This information also helps to establish authority and lines of communication, and prevents both gaps in delivery and duplication of activities by different people.

Project schedule

A project schedule is like an action plan that shows all the activities and tasks that need to be carried out and by whom, with their respective timeframes. The timeframes should state the start date of each activity, the expected end date and the duration, which is how long you expect the activity to take. In addition, it is useful to have milestones, which are key dates for important events – for example, project team members would want to know when they are expected to finish a prototype. Milestones can also be used to measure progress and are an indicator of whether a project is going to finish on time. As shown in Figure 16.5, milestones are usually marked using a diamond shape on a Gantt chart.

Milestones mark the dependencies; these are activities that cannot begin before certain other activities have been completed. Dependencies show the relationship between activities; some activities can be carried out together, while others cannot finish before another is complete. These can be shown on a critical path diagram (see Unit 3, page 96).

A project schedule should also contain information on the resources required for each activity, so that these can be organised and planned for well in advance to avoid delays.

Budget and costings

This should be a comprehensive list of all resources required (materials, equipment, machinery, venues) with their respective costs, as well as any salaries and

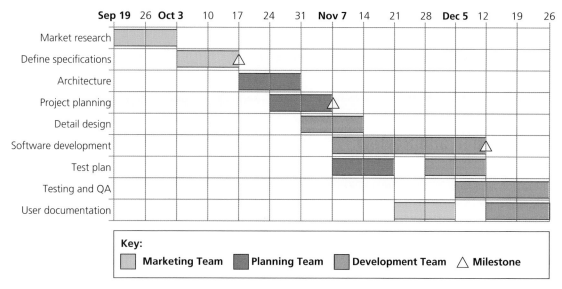

▲ **Figure 16.5** Milestones are easy to spot on a Gantt chart

consultancy fees you expect to pay during the project. This document shows the total cost required for the project so that sources of funds can be obtained. It also serves as a cost-controlling tool. Variance analyses can then be carried out at the end of the project to identify areas of over/underspend – very useful when evaluating the outcome of the project.

Contingency plan

A list of 'plan Bs' should be drawn up against each risk identified using the risk register. Team members should be able to follow the actions described in a contingency plan to counteract the damage caused by a risk occurring, so these should be written in a clear and concise way. In addition, a contingency plan should allow extra time and budget for the risks identified to ensure that resources are available when responding to the risks.

Communication plan

This is crucial for establishing clear lines of communication so that project team members know who to report to. The frequency and subject of reports should be stated so that stakeholders can be informed of progress on a regular basis, especially when a milestone is achieved. It is useful to state the method of communication recommended (e.g. email, phone, meeting) so that people can be prepared for meetings if necessary. It also serves as a reminder for people to check their emails or voicemail.

Methods for monitoring

Methods for monitoring a project, as discussed in Section 3.1, are based on the nature and scope of a project. The project team should be aware of the value of these monitoring tools and not see them as a way of judging their performance, rather as a tool for identifying problem areas for corrective actions to be taken.

Methods for evaluation

Feedback from project stakeholders could be obtained through surveys or observation. Questions on how well they think the project has been managed and whether their needs have been met can be analysed to see whether the aims and objectives of a project have been met. Similar projects can be studied to compare the quality of execution as well as the outcomes. Focus groups and interviews can be organised to obtain qualitative information on how the stakeholders involved view the process, the end results, whether the project has delivered what it promised to do in the first place and the most important question of whether stakeholders have benefited from the project outcomes and, if so, to what extent.

Feedback should not only take place at the end of a project. Information should be gathered at every key stage of a project. For example:

- at the project initiation stage, to establish how well the case for carrying out the project has been presented
- at the project planning stage, to see how extensive and comprehensive the plans are and how well they have been communicated to the project team
- at the project direction stage to find out how well the project has been executed and monitored.

4.2 Project management tools

In this learning outcome you have to demonstrate that you can use project management tools such as critical path analysis (CPA) and Gantt charts, which were discussed in Unit 3 (see page 96). Other tools that you might consider using are described below.

Program Evaluation and Review Technique

Program Evaluation and Review Technique (PERT) is a project planning tool similar to a CPA. A diagram can be used to show how tasks are scheduled, the dependencies and the order in which they should be carried out. Each task is represented in a rectangle with the time it is expected to take. However, it is somewhat pessimistic in its approach to the time taken to complete various tasks within a project.

The technique estimates the shortest (optimistic) time and the longest (pessimistic) time to complete a given task. To calculate the estimate duration of a project (for inclusion in the diagram) it weights the likely times by a factor of 4.

The formula used for estimated duration of a project is:

$$\frac{\text{Optimistic time} + (4 \times \text{Likely time}) + \text{Pessimistic time}}{6}$$

By applying this formula it is more likely to gain a realistic time for a given project rather than, as is often the case, an optimistic time given at the tendering or planning stage. This data is then shown in diagrammatic form.

Software packages

Computer software has been developed by various companies for managing projects, one of the most popular being Microsoft Project. These packages allow a business to manage a project from start to finish and the project team can have an input in the process. The software can carry out scheduling by working out the order in which tasks should be carried out, together with resource requirements. In addition, the software can be used for cost control and budget management, and can produce documents that allow collaboration and communication to take place regularly.

Flow diagram

A flow diagram can be used to illustrate a project plan more clearly. It allows the project to be broken down into small tasks, which can then be put in order of execution. It helps the planner to think in detail and logically sequence the tasks for implementation. A flow diagram (like the one in Figure 16.7) provides a clear overview of the whole project, showing stages where review might be necessary by creating a loop.

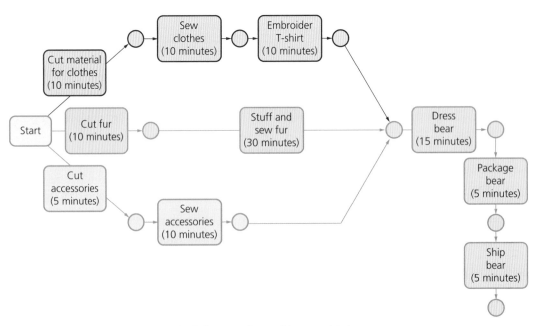

▲ **Figure 16.6** An example of a PERT diagram for making a teddy bear

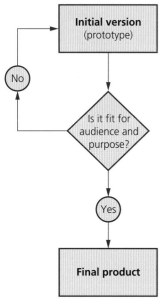

▲ **Figure 16.7** An example of a project planning flow diagram

LO4 assessment activities

Below are suggested assessment activities that have been directly linked to the Pass, Merit and Distinction criteria in LO4 to help with assignment preparation. These are followed by top tips on how to achieve the best results.

Activity 1 Pass criteria *P4*

P4 Choose a fundraising project, a Young Enterprise business start-up or any small project that you could carry out within your school or college. Produce a project plan for your chosen project.

Activity 2 Pass criteria *P5*

P5 Choose at least one project plan tool listed in Section 4.2 and explain why it has been chosen for your project.

Activity 3 Merit criteria *M2*

M2 Create a risk register for your chosen project. For each risk identified, produce a contingency plan and explain how it can mitigate the risk.

Activity 4 Distinction criteria *D2*

D2 Build on the contingency plans you outlined for **M2** and discuss the impact(s) on your chosen project if these 'plan Bs' have to be carried out.

TOP TIPS ✔

- ✔ For P4, you must ensure that all the bullet points in Section 4.1 are covered.
- ✔ For P5, explain the advantages of the project-planning tool you have chosen, giving examples of how the tool could help you plan, execute and monitor your project more effectively.
- ✔ For M2, refer to risk management in Section 2.1. Start by identifying the risks you might encounter while carrying out the project and put them in order of likelihood of occurrence. Explain actions that could be taken (contingency plan) to mitigate the risks identified should these occur.
- ✔ For D2, the focus is on the potential impact(s) on your chosen project of carrying out the contingency plans outlined for M2.

Unit 17

Responsible business practices

LEARNING OUTCOMES

The topics, activities and suggested reading in this chapter will help you to:

1 understand how businesses operate responsibly
2 understand the importance of adopting responsible business practices
3 be able to review the impact of responsible business practices on different stakeholders
4 understand the difficulties and potential conflicts businesses face when implementing responsible business practice(s).

How will I be assessed?

How will I be graded?

You will be graded using the following criteria, which are in the specification produced by OCR for the qualification.

Learning outcome	Pass	Merit	Distinction
You will:	To achieve a Pass you must demonstrate that you have met all the pass assessment criteria	To achieve a Merit you must demonstrate that you have met all the pass and merit assessment criteria	To achieve a Distinction you must demonstrate that you have met all the pass, merit and distinction assessment criteria
1 Understand how businesses operate responsibly	**P1** Explain how and why a specific organisation operates responsibly		
2 Understand the importance of adopting responsible business practices	**P2** Explain why a specific business has adopted responsible business practices	**M1** Assess the processes a specific business went through to select which responsible business practices to implement	**D1** Justify the choice of responsible business practices that a specific business has implemented
	P3 Describe the consequences for a specific business of failing to operate responsibly		
3 Be able to review the impact of responsible business practices on different stakeholders	**P4** Review the responsible business practices of a specific business to determine if these meet the needs of its stakeholders		
4 Understand the difficulties and potential conflicts businesses face when implementing responsible business practice(s)	**P5** Explain the difficulties that a specific business may face in implementing responsible business practice(s)		
	P6 Explain the impact of conflicts of interest that a specific business has faced or might face when implementing responsible business practices	**M2** Explain how a specific business reached a compromise when dealing with conflicting stakeholder needs	**D2** Evaluate the success or failure of the compromise that a specific business has reached when dealing with conflicting stakeholder needs

LO1 Understand how businesses operate responsibly *P1*

GETTING STARTED

(20 minutes)

As a group, list what you think a business should do if it is operating responsibly. One person could write the ideas on the whiteboard.

How many stakeholder groups are included in your list? How would each stakeholder group be affected if a business did not operate responsibly?

PAIRS ACTIVITY

(10 minutes)

Discuss:

● what you think are the differences between legal responsibilities and **ethical values**?
● is legislation necessary or should a business behave ethically anyway?

CLASSROOM DISCUSSION

(10 minutes)

Feed back your ideas to the class.

1.1 Why businesses operate responsibly

? THINK ABOUT IT

Vodaphone

Everyone we deal with – from our customers, partners, suppliers and employees, to governments, regulators and NGOs – rightly expects us to act responsibly and with integrity at all times. The trust of our customers and other stakeholders is essential to Vodafone and critical to the value of our brand. To maintain that trust, we must ensure we always conduct our business in a responsible, transparent and ethical manner.

Source: www.vodafone.com/content/sustainabilityreport/2015/index/operating-responsibly.html

As a class, discuss what you think are the benefits to Vodaphone of operating responsibly.

To comply with legislation and regulations

Some degree of legislation is necessary to ensure that businesses act in an ethical manner. Much as it is hoped that businesses would choose to act ethically, there will always be those who may not do so voluntarily. Legislation and regulations, such as the Consumer Protection from Unfair Trading Regulations, aim to protect stakeholders from unethical behaviour. Businesses must therefore comply with this legislation or risk prosecution.

PAIRS ACTIVITY

(20 minutes)

1 Research the following examples of legislation and regulations:
   ● Consumer Protection from Unfair Trading Regulations
   ● Consumer Rights Act
   ● Equality Act
   ● Environmental Protection Act
   ● Health and Safety at Work Act
   ● Working Time Regulations.
2 Write a brief summary of what each example states that businesses should/should not do to ensure that they are operating ethically.

To comply with the principles of corporate governance

Corporate governance involves setting the strategic aims and values that an organisation will follow by balancing the interests of different stakeholders including owners, managers, customers, suppliers, the government and the local community. Businesses that operate responsibly should recognise that stakeholders may have conflicting interests but should try to reach an acceptable comprise.

🔑 KEY TERMS

Ethical values – principles that an individual chooses to live by or a business chooses to operate by, such as honesty, fairness and responsibility. For example, 'We put our customers first everyday' and 'We care for our colleagues everyday' (George clothing).

Corporate governance – the concept that businesses should follow rules and principles that balance the interests of stakeholders. In a limited company the directors are responsible for the governance of the company, i.e. ensuring that principles are followed.

For example, the shareholders in a business may focus on increasing profit, but if this means paying workers low wages then is the business operating responsibly? The shareholders may argue that as long as the national **living wage** is being paid then this is acceptable, whereas workers may feel that they are not being paid a fair wage for the role.

Similarly, in 2012 Starbucks was criticised in the media for minimising the amount of tax it had to pay in the UK. Although this did not contravene any legislation, it could be argued that it did not operate responsibly and that the principles of corporate governance were not complied with.

To address environmental issues

Environmental issues are controlled by legislation such as the Environmental Protection Act. However, businesses aiming to operate responsibly will try to minimise the environmental impact of their business as far as possible, even if this goes beyond the requirements of relevant legislation.

KEY TERMS

Living wage – the minimum level of income needed by workers to meet their basic needs.

? THINK ABOUT IT

DPD, the parcel delivery company

As a responsible company, we are committed to ensuring that environmental management is a key priority. As delivery experts, our aim is to make a positive impact through what we do each and every day.

On an ongoing basis, we will:

- Prevent or minimise pollution and reduce the impact of our vehicle fleet on the environment,
- Consider our impact on the environment when embarking on new activities and projects.
- Reduce the impact of our current operations.
- Use recyclable and reusable materials wherever possible.
- Develop targets to enable the continual improvement of the company's environmental performance.
- Comply with applicable environmental, legal and other requirements.

Source: www.dpd.co.uk/pdf/environmentalpolicy.pdf

As a class, discuss which of DPD's stakeholders will be affected by its environmental policy. These could be positive or negative impacts.

To promote sustainability

We are more aware than previous generations of the need to ensure that businesses consider the economic, environmental and social impact of their operations, e.g. resources used today should be renewed and still available, wherever possible, for future generations. A business that operates responsibly will therefore consider **sustainability** within its day-to-day operations.

? THINK ABOUT IT

Tata Steel

Sustainability drives everything we do. To us, this is about addressing the big challenges we all face today. It is about how we can ensure a high quality of life, for all, both now and for generations to come. This means we need to balance economic prosperity and social equality with looking after the one planet on which we live.

We define sustainability as an enduring and balanced approach to economic activity, environmental responsibility and societal benefit. Our goal, therefore, is to make a positive contribution to society and to sustain the communities in which we operate, through the value we create, the employment we provide, and through the social value of the products that we develop and manufacture.

Source: www.tatasteeleurope.com/en/sustainability/sustainability-challenges

It is commendable that Tata Steel has a sustainability policy – however, do you think that its customers will choose their steel supplier based on sustainability or will other factors be more important? Discuss this as a class.

To avoid accusations of corruption

No organisation wants to be accused of **corruption** as this will adversely affect its reputation. By operating responsibly, a business is reducing the likelihood of being the subject of such accusations.

KEY TERM

Sustainability – considering the economic, environmental and social impact of business operations, e.g. by using the resources that we need now but trying to ensure that there will still be sufficient remaining for future generations.

Corruption – using power for individual gain, e.g. a buyer for a supermarket chain accepting bribes from a supplier to stock its product in the stores.

For example, the corruption scandal experienced by football's international governing body, Fifa, in 2015 will undermine the confidence and trust of football fans for many years to come, even though those accused are no longer employed by the organisation.

Fair trade employers

A fair trade employer promotes fair trade within the workplace, e.g. providing fair trade coffee in meetings. These fair trade products are the result of organisations in developed countries, such as the UK, paying producers in developing countries, such as Ethiopia, fair prices.

A fair trade employer will also stipulate that suppliers should not use child labour within their factories and that all workers should be provided with good working conditions. Similarly, if the employer produces its own products then it will ensure that its own workers are treated fairly and that all relevant legislation is adhered to.

Provide fair working conditions

In the UK there is legislation in place that requires businesses to operate responsibly by providing fair working conditions. This includes the Workplace (Health, Safety and Welfare) Regulations, which state that employers must provide adequate ventilation, heating and lighting in the workplace, and the Equality Act, which states that businesses must pay the same wage or salary to a woman and a man doing equal work in the same employment.

Professional bodies' codes of conduct

Professional bodies such as the Royal Institute for Chartered Surveyors (RICS) aim to maintain the reputation of the profession they represent. If one member is found to be operating or acting irresponsibly this could have repercussions for the reputation of all members of that profession. Each professional body therefore has a **code of conduct** members must abide by.

KEY TERM

Code of conduct – a set of guidelines outlining rules and responsibilities.

INDEPENDENT RESEARCH ACTIVITY

(10 minutes)

Research one of the professional bodies listed below to discover what its code of conduct requires members to do/not to do:

- Association of British Travel Agents (ABTA)
- Chartered Institute of Plumbing and Heating Engineering (code of professional standards)
- College of Policing (code of ethics)
- Royal Institution of Chartered Surveyors (RICS; ethics and professional standards).

GROUP ACTIVITY

(15 minutes)

Join with other students who have researched the same professional body to produce a factsheet that summarises your findings.

These factsheets for a range of professional bodies can then be referred to by all students within the class.

1.2 How businesses operate responsibly

GROUP ACTIVITY

(45 minutes)

1 In a small group, investigate the ways in which one of the businesses listed below operates responsibly:
  - Apple, Inc.
  - Asda Ltd
  - British Airways
  - Jaguar Land Rover
  - Next plc.
2 Produce a short presentation that introduces your chosen business and summarises your findings.
3 Present your findings to your peers.

Human resources

Pay a fair/living wage

A national living wage for over-25s in the UK was announced in the 2015 budget. The aim is to ensure a wage that is high enough for workers to have a normal standard of living, i.e. be able to afford necessities such as food and paying household bills. To be paid a fair or living wage in return for providing labour is therefore something that workers expect. In the UK, any business that does not pay a living wage is contravening legislation. If workers believe that they are not being paid a fair wage then they are likely to be demotivated and productivity may fall.

Good working conditions

The provision of good working conditions, such as a safe and comfortable environment and the provision of adequate rest breaks, is governed in the UK by legislation. The absence of good working conditions may demotivate workers as they may feel that their employer does not value their safety and/or their contribution to the business.

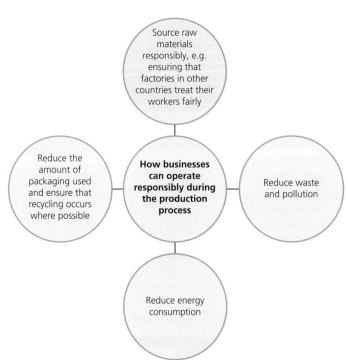

▲ **Figure 17.1** How businesses can operate responsibly during the production process

Production

Finance

If any organisation is to operate responsibly it is important that it apply ethical accounting methods. Any financial information provided by an organisation should be accurate and reliable; this includes a sole trader submitting accounts for the purpose of calculating tax liabilities or a public limited company publishing accounts that will influence whether an individual chooses to invest their savings into

the business. Ethical accounting methods are also necessary to prevent fraudulent activities and to gain public trust.

Window dressing is an example of an accounting method that, although not illegal, could be described as unethical. This involves a business manipulating its accounts to give a better impression of its financial position – for example, assigning intangible assets such as customer loyalty a high value on the balance sheet may suggest that the business is in a better financial position than it actually is.

Marketing

Take into consideration what is in the best interests of society

Businesses aim to satisfy consumer needs and wants, but they also need to consider the long-term effects that doing so may have on society. For example, developing new packaging made from recyclable materials may still allow a business to meet customer wants but with less potential impact on the environment. This may also give the business a unique selling point.

Similarly, promotional activities, such as Sainsbury's Active Kids voucher scheme, encourage customers to shop with the business to gain the vouchers, but also benefit the wider community, in this example by providing sports equipment for schools and local teams. With the level of obesity among children rising, such a scheme is in the best interests of society.

Reinforce social and ethical values

Within their marketing, businesses may choose to reinforce social and cultural values. For example, British Airways produced a TV advertisement prior to the London 2012 Olympics showing patriotic spirit and encouraging citizens to support Team GB, as well as promoting the airline.

In addition, businesses may choose to support charities and use this in the promotion of their brand. For example in 2015, Marks & Spencer launched its Sparks Card. Customers select a charity from a list chosen by Marks & Spencer when registering their card. Every time a purchase is made and their card is scanned at the checkout, Marks & Spencer donates 1p to the chosen charity. The benefits of the scheme can be promoted as part of a marketing campaign.

However, an alternative viewpoint is that some marketing and advertising does not reinforce **social values** as it encourages the desire for material possessions. We are shown images of people who are happy and content because they own or use a certain product. This creates a desire to own the product and marketers strive to create this desire in an attempt to increase sales. It could be argued that such businesses are not operating responsibly from a social value and/or ethical point of view. For example, promoting a new sports car that has poor fuel economy may lead to an increase in car sales but with an adverse impact on the environment. However, by creating a demand for the product or service, they are contributing towards the success of the business, which in turn provides job security and income for members of society.

> ## 🔑 KEY TERM
>
> **Social values** – values that impact on the way society behaves, such as individuality, respect and equality.

Pricing strategies

Warren Buffett, the US billionaire, said, 'The single most important decision in evaluating a business is pricing power. If you've got the power to raise prices without losing business to a competitor, you've got a very good business.'

Source: www.bloomberg.com/news/articles/2011-02-18/ buffett-says-pricing-power-more-important-than-good- management

This may be beneficial for the financial success of a business, but it could be argued that it is not necessarily operating responsibly.

Businesses that have a monopoly on a product, e.g. a pharmaceutical company that owns the patent for a life-saving drug, need to make a decision as to whether to set the price high and make high profits from sales, or to operate more responsibly and choose a pricing strategy that is likely to result in the drug being available to more people.

The FAIRTRADE Mark was first introduced in the UK in the 1990s. At that time fair trade products were priced higher than similar non-fair trade products, which meant that consumers had to make a decision about whether to act ethically and pay the higher price or buy the better-value option. Today

many mainstream products display the FAIRTRADE Mark, such as Cadbury's Dairy Milk and Morrisons' own-label coffee; the pricing strategy used is no longer to inflate the price as these companies would experience falling sales if they did not price their products competitively. Products displaying the FAIRTRADE Mark must meet international fair trade standards, which are set by the international certification body Fairtrade International.

▲ **Figure 17.2** The FAIRTRADE Mark can be seen on many types of packaging, in supermarkets and elsewhere

Businesses may also use promotional offers such as buy one get one free, which encourage wastage. Customers may be enticed to buy two of a product but in reality will only use one of them, especially if it is a

> ## 🔑 KEY TERM
>
> **Ethics** – moral judgements about what is right and what is wrong.

> ## ❓ THINK ABOUT IT
>
> The link below is to an article in the *Guardian* (10 December 2015): 'Brands up their game in ethical advertising':
>
> www.theguardian.com/media-network/2015/dec/10/ unethical-advertising-outdated-trend-feelgood- marketing
>
> The articles states: 'Consumers around the world are saying loud and clear that a brand's social purpose is among the factors that influence purchase decisions.' Do you agree with this statement?

perishable item, e.g. packs of fruit. The **ethics** of this offer could be questioned as product wastage increases.

Local community

Consider the impact on the local environment

If businesses are operating responsibly, they should consider any impacts their operations may have on the local community and take action to minimise them. For example, if supermarket delivery lorries have to drive through residential areas to reach a store then delivering during daytime only will reduce any noise disturbance. Similarly, a factory should take all precautions possible to reduce the risk of polluting the local environment.

Support for local charities

Many businesses, both large and small, support local charities. For example, Yorkshire Building Society donated £25,000 to local areas and local communities affected by the Boxing Day 2015 floods.

Sponsorship/charity involvement

Many businesses choose to sponsor events or involve themselves in charity work. This not only benefits society but also provides an opportunity for employees to participate in work for good causes. For example, the 2016 London Marathon was sponsored by Virgin Money. The event was renamed the Virgin Money London Marathon and the Virgin Money logo appeared on promotional materials. This provided Virgin Money with the opportunity to familiarise consumers with its brand while also supporting a range of good causes and charities.

On a smaller scale, the Hull-based Sewell Group provides salaried staff with up to two days' paid leave a year to volunteer with local charities and groups as part of their personal development.

> **KNOW IT**
> 1 Describe the difference between legal and ethical responsibilities.
> 2 State two ways in which the Working Time Regulations require a business to operate responsibly.
> 3 Describe the role of professional bodies in ensuring that businesses operate responsibly.
> 4 Explain two ways in which a business can choose to operate responsibly.

●●●●●●●●●●●●●●●●●●●●●●●●●●

LO1 assessment activities

Below are suggested assessment activities that have been directly linked to the Pass criteria in LO1 to help with assignment preparation. These are followed by top tips on how to achieve the best results.

Activity 1 Pass criteria *P1*

Investigate a specific organisation to gather information about how and why this business chooses to operate responsibly.

> **TOP TIPS**
> ✔ If you use secondary research, make sure that you have sufficient information about 'why' the organisation operates responsibly, to enable you to complete this section of the activity.

Activity 2 Pass criteria *P1*

Produce a presentation. Your presentation should be divided into two sections as follows.

● Section 1: an explanation of how your chosen organisation operates responsibly.
● Section 2: an explanation of why your chosen organisation operates responsibly.

> **TOP TIPS**
> ✔ Make sure that your explanation is applied to the chosen organisation throughout your presentation.

●●●●●●●●●●●●●●●●●●●●●●●●●●

LO2 Understand the importance of adopting responsible business practices *P2 P3 M1 D1*

(**GETTING STARTED**) 👤 ·······························

(5 minutes)

Individually, consider the scenarios below. Are they 'right' or 'wrong'? Make sure you can justify your answer.

1 Your window cleaner offers you a lower price if you pay cash.
2 Your employer has banned workers from accessing social media in the workplace.
3 You need some paper for your printer at home so you take a pack from work.

As a class, discuss your ideas.

2.1 Different stakeholder groups and their different needs for a business to adopt responsible business practices

Employees

Security of employment

Employees should be provided with greater employment security if a business adopts responsible business practices. One reason for this is that a business with a good reputation is likely to gain customers and sales, resulting in the need for employees to continue the operation of the business.

Good working conditions

Good working conditions will not only help to motivate employees but will also ensure that relevant legislation is being met.

Owners

Figure 17.3 shows some examples of how business owners can benefit from responsible business practices.

Good rate of pay

Again, a good rate of pay will help to motivate employees, improve the quality of the product/service provided, and help the business to attract skilled and experience staff when required.

Customers

Good-quality products

Customers expect good-quality products that meet their needs. Adopting responsible business practices helps to maintain the quality of products and services, in part due to having motivated employees, while also ensuring that any materials are ethically sourced.

Choice of products

Customers expect to have a choice of products available to them. Some consumers will choose which products to buy based on ethical concerns, whereas others will be more concerned about the price of a product, e.g. eggs from caged hens are priced lower than those from free-range hens.

If growing numbers of consumers are concerned about whether a business has been operating responsibly, this should encourage more businesses to operate in this way. As a result, there should be a greater choice of ethical products available to consumers. This increase in competition may also help to lower the prices of such products.

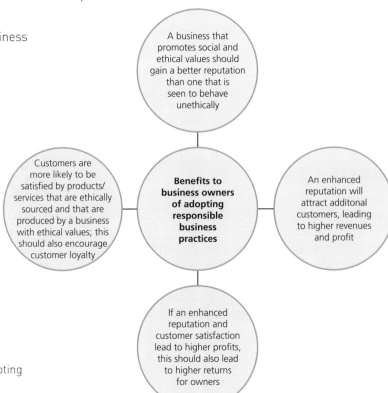

▶ **Figure 17.3** Benefits to business owners of adopting responsible business practices

Low prices

Customers generally want low prices although, depending on the product/service, their perception of value for money will also be important. For example, if a tin of beans has a very low price but the taste is not acceptable, most customers will not continue to buy this product because it does not represent value for money.

Adopting responsible business practices helps to keep prices low(er) for customers. This may be because productivity and efficiency are improved, and therefore a business can pass any cost savings on to customers, or because it is not taking advantage of monopoly power to charge high prices to make high profits.

Suppliers

Regular orders

Suppliers rely on their customers, i.e. other businesses, to order and purchase products/services to generate revenue. If orders are received regularly then this helps suppliers to forecast potential sales as well as plan production requirements. A business that operates responsibly, and as such has loyal customers who buy frequently, will be able to provide regular orders to its suppliers.

Being paid on time

Paying suppliers on time is an example of responsible business practice. Suppliers, particularly if they are a small business, will rely on payments from customers to provide the cash flow they need to operate on a day-to-day basis. If payments are delayed, this may cause liquidity problems.

Sustainable resources

Sustainability is a topic addressed regularly in the media and as such many businesses today have a sustainability policy. As a result, materials from sustainable sources are required to maintain a business's reputation and to meet the objectives set out in this policy. Suppliers must be in a position to meets these needs.

For example, the University of Exeter published a 2015/6 Sustainable Food Policy: www.exeter.ac.uk/media/universityofexeter/campusservices/sustainability/pdf/2015_Sustainable_Food_Policy.pdf

Competitors

Share of market

A business that operates responsibly and therefore has a good reputation may find that its market share increases due to customers choosing to purchase its products/services. If this happens then competitors will need to decide whether to adopt such practices, if they do not already, in an attempt to maintain their market share.

Innovative products/services

If a business is innovative and designs a product or packaging that is ethically or socially better than alternatives offered by competitors, e.g. sustainable packaging or a product that uses significantly less energy, then this will provide the business with a unique selling point.

However, if all businesses within a market are operating responsibly, then a business is unable to promote this as a unique selling point. Instead it must establish a different factor that it can promote and so hopefully attract customers to buy its products/services rather than those of a competitor. One such method is to create innovative new products/services.

Local community

Clean environment

The local community will want their local environment to be clean and free from pollution as far as possible. A business that adopts responsible business practices should meet all relevant legislation, such as the Environmental Protection Act, as well as having policies in place to minimise any risk to the environment. Employees will also play a part in ensuring that the local environment is clean, e.g. not dropping litter as they walk to work or not dropping cigarette butts if they smoke outside the business's premises.

Opportunities for employment

Local communities often rely on large businesses within their area for employment. A successful business, which operates responsibly, is likely to create greater opportunities for employment within the local area. Businesses may also choose to promote staff from within the business rather than recruit new employees nationally for a senior job vacancy.

For example, the City of London Corporation works with local businesses to help them recruit new employees from the local vicinity and also to raise the aspirations of the workforce in these areas.

Pressure groups

Protect the interests of different groups

Pressure groups are set up by individuals who have a common concern or objective. This could be products being tested on animals or a business moving production abroad where labour is cheaper. Pressure groups will campaign publicly in an attempt to change behaviours, e.g. to make a business rethink the decision to move production abroad or influence the government to intervene to discourage this.

🔑 **KEY TERM**

Pressure group – a group made up of individuals with a common concern or objective. They join together in an attempt to influence decision making by business organisations or the government.

A business that adopts responsible business practices and considers the needs and preferences of different groups is less likely to experience concerns from pressure groups, which in turn should reduce the likelihood of negative publicity within the media.

2.2 Reasons for adopting responsible business practices

To meet the needs of different stakeholder groups

▲ **Figure 17.4** Meeting the needs of different stakeholder groups

To meet business needs

There is a range of potential benefits for a business adopting responsible business practices. In turn, these may help the business to meet its needs, i.e. its aims and objectives. These might include those listed below.

- **To improve their reputation:** a business can enhance its reputation with existing customers and the general public, e.g. by promoting the support it gives to local charities.
- **To have better public relations:** the public relations (PR) function within a business will promote positive aspects of business's behaviour, e.g. in April 2016, Tesco announced that it planned to invest £6 million over the next two years to help support British agriculture.
- **To improve recruitment prospects:** if a business is seen to operate responsibly then it should find it easier to attract skilled and experienced candidates to apply for vacant job roles. This is because it will be seen to care for its workers, e.g. by providing good working conditions and fair pay.
- **To increase sales:** a business that has a good reputation and where staff are motivated should see an increase in its sales. This is because many customers will be attracted to a business that demonstrates good ethical values and also because motivated employees are likely to provide better customer service.

🔑 **KEY TERMS**

Public relations (PR) – the relationship between a business, the general public and other organisations. The PR function within a business is responsible for maintaining a positive relationship and minimising the impact of any poor publicity.

Business profile – a summary of a business; what it does, who it is and what its values are.

- **To increase productivity:** if a business provides good working conditions for employees then they are more likely to be motivated in their work and pay greater attention to detail. This should result in an increase in productivity. Being able to attract and recruit experienced and skilled staff should also have a positive impact on productivity. In addition, if the business increases sales and revenue, this may provide it with the finance required to invest in new technology, which again would help to increase productivity.

- **To improve the business profile:** this is a summary of the business – what it does, who it is and what its values are. Being seen to operate responsibly and including this within the business profile is a valuable marketing tool.
- **To improve efficiency:** a business whose staff are motivated is likely to have less wastage and/or dissatisfied customers due to errors and poor quality than a business that has demotivated staff who do not pay attention to detail. Similarly, if suppliers have a good relationship with a business then deliveries of raw materials and so on are more likely to be reliable and therefore available when the business needs them.
- **To improve customer satisfaction:** this can be related to both internal and external customers. The internal customers of a business, i.e. the employees, will be happier if the business operates responsibly, providing good working conditions, fair pay and so on. The satisfaction of some external customers may also be improved by operating responsibly. For example, if customers are concerned about whether products are ethically sourced, ensuring this is the case will improve the satisfaction of these customers.

2.3 The consequences of a business failing to operate responsibly

PAIRS ACTIVITY

(10 minutes)

Read this article from the *Guardian* (June 2013): www.theguardian.com/world/2013/jun/23/rana-plaza-factory-disaster-bangladesh-primark

Discuss what you think the potential consequences could have been for Primark.

Loss of customer confidence/loyalty

If it becomes public knowledge that a business is not operating responsibly, it could experience a loss of customer confidence, which in turn could result in loyal customers no longer purchasing from that business.

For example, in 2012 Nokia had to apologise for a Lumia smartphone advertisement that showed video footage allegedly filmed using the new phone. However, the footage had actually been filmed using different equipment. Customer confidence in Nokia would have been affected and potential customers would question any other claims made by the company about its smartphones.

Poor reputation

If failure to operate responsibly is reported in the media then the business is likely to acquire a poor reputation. This may be failing to treat workers appropriately, failing to protect the environment or, as in Nokia's case, trying to suggest that products are better than they actually are. This may then have the knock-on effect of losing customers, who may be attracted to a competitor with a better reputation.

Reduced competitiveness

A business that either uses ethical behaviour as a unique selling point or operates in a market where all businesses operate responsibly will suffer a reduction in its competitiveness if it fails to operate responsibly. This in turn is likely to mean that customers will purchase from competitors rather than from that business.

Challenges from pressure groups

If a business is not operating responsibly, e.g. waste is polluting a local river, then pressure groups may campaign against the business in an attempt to influence it to change its processes. This campaign is likely to be reported in the media, either locally or nationally. This adverse publicity will then impact on customer confidence and the business's reputation.

Lack of compliance with relevant legislation and codes of practice

If a business fails to comply with legislation, e.g. the Health and Safety at Work Act, then it is likely to be prosecuted. This may result in fines, which will reduce the finance available within the business, as well as poor publicity. If staff are injured due to legislation not being adhered to then the business may also face compensation claims.

Similarly, if codes of practice are not complied with, membership of professional bodies can be revoked. In some industries, such as chartered surveying and accountancy, this will mean that the business cannot continue to offer such services to customers and therefore is likely to cease trading.

LO2 assessment activities

Below are suggested assessment activities that have been directly linked to the Pass, Merit and Distinction criteria in LO2 to help with assignment preparation. These are followed by top tips on how to achieve the best results.

To complete the activities you will need to research a specific business using primary research. It would also be beneficial if you could gather the necessary information to complete the assessment activities for LO3 and LO4 at the same time.

Activity 1 Pass criteria *P2*

Choose and research a business that has adopted responsible business practices. Use your research to produce a report. The first section of your report should explain why the business has chosen to adopt responsible business practices.

TOP TIPS

✔ The quality of the research undertaken will influence the quality of the final report you write. Make sure that you choose a business to investigate that will be able to help you with all of the information that is required.
✔ It would be useful to describe the responsible businesses practices used by the business to set the scene for your explanation. This will also help you to complete the LO3 assessment activity.

Activity 2 Pass criteria *P3*

The second section of your report should either:

● describe any consequences your chosen business has experienced of failing to operate responsibly, or
● describe any consequences the business believes may result from failing to operate responsibly.

Activity 3 Merit criteria *M1*

The third section of your report should describe and assess the processes your chosen business went through when selecting which responsible business practices to implement.

TOP TIPS

✔ In your assessment you could consider the advantages and disadvantages of the processes used, and reach a justified conclusion as to whether you believe that these processes were appropriate for this business.

Activity 4 Distinction criteria *D1*

The final section of your report should justify the choice of responsible business practices that your chosen business has implemented.

TOP TIPS

✔ To fully justify the choice of responsible business practices implemented, you could consider alternative practices to assess whether these would have been more appropriate.

LO3 Be able to review the impact of responsible business practices on different stakeholders *P4*

GETTING STARTED 👤 ·····················

(15 minutes)

Read the statement 'Fashion with Integrity' on the ASOS website: www.asosplc.com/corporate-responsibility

In pairs, discuss:

- which stakeholders will be affected by the ASOS corporate responsibility programme
- how each stakeholder may be affected – and whether this is a positive or negative impact

Feed back your ideas to the rest of the group.

3.1 Sources of information for a review

Social and environmental audits

Employment indicators

See Figure 17.5 for examples of employment indicators.

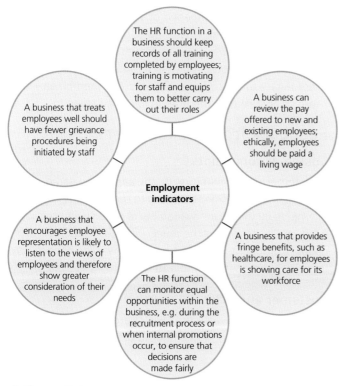

▲ **Figure 17.5** Employment indicators of the impact of responsible business practices

Human rights indicators

- **Child labour:** in recent years, a number of UK businesses have faced allegations of the use of child labour in the production of products and raw materials used by them, particularly in developing countries. For example, Primark suppliers were accused of using child labour in southern India to sew its clothing, as were cocoa farms in Ivory Coast that supply cocoa to Nestlé factories. However, due to increased awareness of such issues, and the resulting poor publicity within the media, many businesses, such as Primark, now state within their code of conduct that they will not use child labour.
- **Ethical supplies:** in addition to ensuring that child labour is not used within the supply chain, businesses can also monitor their use of ethical supplies in other ways – for example, whether tea and coffee served to visitors is fair trade or ensuring that the supply chain is free from corruption or bribery.

> ### ❓ THINK ABOUT IT
>
> The link below shows Primark's Code of Conduct, which includes a section relating to child labour:
>
> www.primark.com/en/our-ethics/workplace-rights/code-of-conduct
>
> The following link explains Sainsbury's ethical trading policy:
>
> www.j-sainsbury.co.uk/suppliers/ethical-trading/
>
> Many businesses, such as Primark and Sainsbury's, publish policies relating to ethical behaviour. Do you think that having such policies means that a business will always operate responsibility? Justify your answer.

Product responsibility

- Social impact of product/service: an ethical business should consider the social impact of the product or service it provides. For example:
  - Are suppliers using sustainable resources?
  - Will there be any impact on the environment when the product is disposed of?
  - Are there potential impacts on society from the sale of the product, e.g. alcohol?

A business can look to minimise social impacts wherever possible. However, if, as in the case of businesses producing and selling alcohol, not selling the product will significantly lower the revenue received by the business, then this may not be possible.

- **After-sales service:** providing good after-sales service will help to ensure customer satisfaction and, it is hoped, customer loyalty. However, this also provides a business with the opportunity to review whether customers believe it to be operating responsibly, as feedback can be obtained. A business should have a record of all complaints made and may also have information about how long it takes for each complaint or enquiry to be responded to. This information can be reviewed to decide whether any policies or practices should be improved.
- **Advertising:** a business can assess how responsible its advertising is based on the number of complaints received either direct or via the Advertising Standards Authority (ASA). For example, a Paddy Power plc newspaper advertisement was banned by the ASA in 2014 after complaints were received, as it advertised incentives to bet on the outcome of the Oscar Pistorius murder trial.
- **Data protection:** a business has a legal obligation to protect all personal data held relating to employees and customers, e.g. address, date of birth and bank details. Any breaches of data protection legislation would require investigation, and instances where this does occur are often reported in the media. For example, in 2015 the media reported on a data breach where the personal details of up to 2.4 million Carphone Warehouse customers had been accessed.

Environmental indicators

- **Amount/type of energy used:** a business can review the amount of energy used within the workplace and aim to reduce usage as far as possible, e.g. by using energy-efficient equipment, making sure that equipment is switched off at the end of the day rather than left on standby, and insulating offices to reduce heat loss. Similarly, the type of energy used can be reviewed. Today, there are options available such as wind and solar power, which are more environmentally friendly than traditional methods. Businesses may choose to install their own solar panels, for example, to reduce energy costs and to be more environmentally friendly.

▲ **Figure 17.6** Sign at Marks & Spencer, Monks Cross, York

- **Chemicals used:** businesses have a legal obligation to monitor the use of chemicals within the workplace and to ensure that employees are appropriately trained in their use; whether these are chemicals used in the production process or in the day-to-day running of the business, e.g. cleaning materials. They should therefore maintain records of all chemicals purchased and used, as well as all relevant training undertaken by staff.
- **Waste management:** businesses should have a waste management plan that details how any waste generated will be disposed of. Producing a plan provides the business with an opportunity not only to consider any environmental issues or whether any waste is hazardous, but also to ensure that all staff are aware of procedures. Checks can then be carried out to ensure that the plan is being adhered to.

Feedback from stakeholders

Customer complaints

If customers are unhappy with any part of the selling process, then a business is likely to receive complaints. Examples include poor availability of advertised products, poor-quality service or the inaccurate description of goods. Complaints provide a business with an opportunity to review its processes and amend them if necessary.

Customer enquiries

If a business receives a number of enquiries about the same matter then this should draw attention to the fact that customers are not being provided with the information they need. For example, if a number of customers enquire about whether the bananas in a supermarket are fair trade, then the business should review its advertising and/or labelling of the product.

Surveys

Surveys can be carried out to gather information about whether stakeholders perceive the business to be operating responsibly. For example, many businesses carry out an annual employee survey. As part of this, the business could gain feedback on whether employees believe that they receive fair treatment in the workplace. Similarly, customers could be surveyed to assess their perception of the business. This could be done in a range of ways, including online questionnaires and in-store surveys.

Research articles

Research articles are written to provide the public, businesses and professional bodies with information relating to a specific subject. Such articles have been written regarding ethical behaviour and businesses operating responsibly. Businesses can use this information to review their own practices and to assess whether they could make improvements.

Media and press releases

The media are likely to report instances where it is suggested that a business has failed to operate responsibly as this makes an interesting news article, particularly if the company is a well-known name. For example, in January 2016 Apple was accused of failing to check whether minerals used in its products were mined using child labour.

However, if a business has operated responsibly then it is likely to be the business itself that promotes this via a press release. For example, in 2014 Marks & Spencer plc announced that it was to begin installing the UK's largest single roof-mounted solar panel array at its East Midlands distribution centre.

PAIRS ACTIVITY

(20 minutes)

Choose one of the statements below. Draw a flow chart showing possible positive and negative consequences of the statement.

- A clothing retailer wins an award for using sustainable materials.

- It is announced in the media that a factory supplying a clothing retailer provides poor and dangerous working conditions for employees.
- An electrical company builds a warehouse using eco-friendly materials, although the cost was higher than using traditional construction methods.
- A call centre introduces new lighting systems that use less energy, but some workers have complained that it is more difficult to see their computer keyboards.
- In 2015, a plastic carrier bag charge was introduced in England.
- A business is accused of paying bribes to guarantee contracts from overseas companies.

Explain your flow chart to the rest of your group.

3.2 Business practices to be reviewed

Finance

Bribery

A dilemma that a business may face is clarifying the distinction between bribes and gifts. For example, a supplier may give a manager tickets to an event in return for the manager agreeing to purchase materials from them; this would be bribery. However, if the manager regularly orders materials from the supplier and the supplier buys the manager a bottle of champagne at Christmas, this could be viewed as a gift. In some instances the distinction between the two may become blurred. As such, many businesses do not allow any of their staff to accept gifts from other businesses.

Insider trading

Insider trading is where an individual uses business information for personal financial gain. For example, if a manager has access to information regarding the takeover of a competitor, they could buy shares in the business and wait for the value of these to increase once the announcement of the takeover has been made. They could then be sold at a profit. This is an illegal practice as the individual is benefiting from the use of information that is not in the public domain.

🔑 **KEY TERM**

Insider trading – using information gained from within a business, i.e. not in the public domain, for personal financial gain.

Executive pay

Executives within a business are often paid large salaries, plus bonuses and other benefits. It could be argued that, as they are responsible and accountable for decision making, this warrants high pay. However, it could also be argued that if employees who carry out vital day-to-day tasks, such as producing the product or dealing face to face with the customer, are paid only the minimum wage rate then this is unfair.

Human resources

Discrimination

A business in which any form of discrimination exists is not operating responsibly. Not only would legislation such as the Equality Act be breached, but the workplace would not be an acceptable working environment for staff.

Worker surveillance

The use of modern technology has resulted in a dilemma for businesses. The use of email and computers to carry out workplace activities has given workers the opportunity to do things such as send personal emails and use social media during working hours. Management also have the opportunity to monitor computer usage, but the ethical dilemma is whether they should be doing so as this may suggest they do not trust workers.

Many workplaces have CCTV installed. This is usually for security purposes, but also allows businesses to view the movement and activities of staff in any location where it is installed. It could be argued that this is intrusive and allows managers to 'spy' on their employees.

Production

Animal testing

Businesses can review research and production processes to assess whether any ethical issues may arise. One such issue is whether materials/products have been tested on animals as there are pressure groups set up to campaign against this.

Some businesses, such as Lush and The Body Shop, have used their beliefs against testing on animals as a selling point. However, products such as medicines and vaccines must still be tested on animals before they can be licensed for human use.

Genetic modification

This involves changing the genetic material of an organism, including crops and animals. For example, crops can be genetically modified to be more resistant to disease. However, debates have taken place about the safety and the ethics of genetic modification. Some consumers will buy only those products that do not contain any genetically modified (GM) ingredients.

Planned obsolescence

This is when a product is designed to have a specific life span. The idea is that a customer buys the product, gets used to having/using it, the business replaces it with an improved model and therefore the customer wants to buy the replacement. This ensures that a business will continue to have customers for its products.

For example, Apple regularly updates its iPhone, which creates desire among owners of the previous model to own the new one. Similarly, once Apple updates its products there comes a time when new apps etc. will not download on to an older model, which means that the product has to be replaced.

> ### CLASSROOM DISCUSSION
> **(5 minutes)**
> Is Apple operating responsibly by planning the obsolescence of older models of its iPhone when introducing new models?

Sales

Spamming

This involves sending emails or text messages to large numbers of people indiscriminately in an attempt to sell a product or service. Although this is a lower-cost method of trying to increase awareness than sending leaflets to individual homes, for example, many consumers find spamming a nuisance and delete the emails or texts without reading them.

Product placement

This is an advertising method whereby products are marketed subtly. A business pays for its product/brand to be shown in a film or television programme. It could be argued that the public are being exposed to advertising without realising that this is the case but it is hard to measure the proportion of viewers who are encouraged to buy the product.

▲ **Figure 17.7** This still from the film 'The Roommate' (2011) clearly shows a Sony Vaio laptop

Intellectual property

Software piracy

This is the illegal use, copying or distribution of software. Businesses must ensure that all software installed on workplace computers has a multi-user licence so that it can legally be installed on all computers.

Counterfeiting

Counterfeiting occurs when a business deals in 'fake' products, e.g. using the Rolex logo on a watch that is not made/designed by Rolex. Sometimes the consumer will be aware that they are buying a fake product but at other times may believe they are purchasing the 'real' item. Counterfeiting can include the manufacture, importing, exporting, distribution or selling of such products.

KNOW IT

1 Outline two ways in which employment indicators can be used to review whether a business is operating responsibly.
2 Explain how human rights indicators can be used to assess whether a business is operating responsibly.
3 Describe two ways in which customer feedback can be used to assess whether a business is operating responsibly.
4 Explain why insider trading is an illegal practice.
5 Identify one advantage and one disadvantage to a business of using spamming as a marketing tool.

LO3 assessment activity

Below is a suggested assessment activity that has been directly linked to the Pass criteria in LO3 to help with assignment preparation. This is followed by a top tip on how to achieve the best results.

Activity 1 Pass criteria *P4*

Based on your investigation into a selected business for the LO2 assessment activities, produce a presentation that reviews the responsible business practices used by your chosen business to determine whether the practices used meet the needs of its stakeholders.

You could divide your presentation into three sections, as follows.

1 Outline the responsible business practices used by the business.
2 Identify who the main stakeholders in the business are.
3 Review whether the practices used meet the needs of the stakeholders.

TOP TIPS
✔ Writing detailed notes to accompany your presentation will help to confirm your understanding.

LO4 Understand the difficulties and potential conflicts businesses face when implementing responsible business practice(s) *P5 P6 M2 D2*

GETTING STARTED

(15 minutes)

● In pairs, list the potential conflicts or disagreements that you think a business might face when implementing responsible business practices. Think about different stakeholders, and what their needs or wants might be.
● Compare your ideas with those of another pair.

4.1 Difficulties faced by businesses in operating responsibly

Cost implications

There will be cost implications associated with operating responsibly. These can range from the time costs of planning and producing policies to the financial costs of providing good working conditions and purchasing materials from sustainable sources.

Training needs

Any new operating procedure will require training for employees. This could be raising awareness of the importance of equality in the workplace or ensuring that staff are aware of all company policies, such as not accepting gifts from suppliers. Training may have a direct cost if it is provided by a third party, but there will always be time implications as, while undertaking training, staff are not completing their day-to-day duties.

Expected impact not achieved or outcomes are negligible

Businesses will implement responsible practices with good intentions, however the outcomes may not be as expected. This may be that staff are unwilling to accept changes, e.g. they may choose not to buy fair trade coffee for the workplace because the local shop does not sell it, or the use of ethical behaviour as a marketing tool may not result in an increase in customer numbers because customers place greater importance on price.

Consumer cynicism

Consumers may be sceptical about a business's true motivations for operating responsibly. Corporate responsibility is often highlighted in the media and businesses that are not seen to operate responsibly may have their reputations tarnished. As such, some businesses may choose to introduce new policies or methods purely to be seen to operate responsibly. Some consumers may therefore question a business's motivations for ethical decisions and ethical behaviour.

Social media has also provided businesses with the opportunity to use good causes to promote their business or their brand, which may result in consumer cynicism. For example, rather than donate £1,000 to a charity, they may tweet that they will donate £1 to the charity for every re-tweet. This therefore raises the online profile of the business/brand.

Keeping up to date with external policies

Policies and legislation change over time. A business must keep up with these changes to ensure that it is not in breach of any changes. A large business that employs specialist staff is more likely to be aware of any such changes than a smaller business where the owner is more involved in the day-to-day running of the business.

> **PAIRS ACTIVITY**
>
> **(10 minutes)**
>
> What are the penalties faced by businesses for failing to comply with legislation such as the Equality Act or the Health and Safety at Work Act?

4.2 How businesses deal with conflicts of interest

Potential conflicts of interest that may exist between different stakeholder groups

There is a range of potential conflicts of interests that may arise between different stakeholder groups.

Examples of conflicts may include those described below.

> **KEY TERM**
>
> **Conflicts of interest** – differing interests that cannot both be satisfied, e.g. owners may aim for high profits whereas customers may want low prices.

Better pay for employees versus increased salary costs/less dividends

Employees will strive for better pay, however this will increase a business's salary costs. Some businesses will aim to improve efficiency by minimising all costs, so increased salary costs will conflict with this aim. Similarly, if a business has shareholders, an increase in costs will lower profits and therefore result in a lower dividend payment. Some shareholders will be more interested in the value of their dividend each year than in the long-term success of the business.

> **KEY TERM**
>
> **Dividend** – a share of a business's profits that is paid to the owners/shareholders.

Cleaner environment versus costly production processes

The local community will desire a clean local environment, but this may result in increased production costs for a business, e.g. because filters have to be installed or specialist waste management processes utilised. The business owners may not want this increase in costs as it will lead to lower profits. However, if the environmental measures are required to meet legislation then the business must implement them or face the consequences.

How businesses deal with potential conflicts of interest

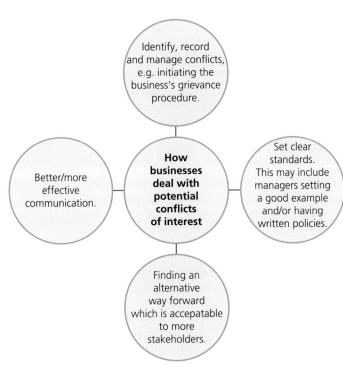

▲ **Figure 17.8** How businesses deal with potential conflicts of interest

How businesses manage ongoing conflicts of interest

Attempt to balance needs of stakeholders

The first step is for a business to recognise that stakeholders have conflicting interests. Once this has been established then an attempt can be made to balance the needs of the stakeholders involved. For example, if a customer wants low prices and the owners/shareholders want to earn high profits, then the business could consider special offers to balance the needs of the two stakeholder groups rather than reducing prices on an ongoing basis.

Set expectations

By setting clear expectations, a business may avoid ongoing conflicts of interest. For example, if a business has a clear customer returns policy then this should help to avoid conflict between customers and employees in a store. Similarly, if a business has a clear corporate strategy document, which has been approved by the shareholders, then this should help to avoid conflict between the shareholders and the directors.

Phased implementation of new practices

A sudden change in policy or practices within a business is more likely to result in conflict than if changes are phased in more slowly. For example, if a manufacturer decided to make its products using new eco-friendly technology that is different from the existing technology, staff may be unhappy about the change to their roles or the additional time needed to learn how to use it. The new processes could be introduced in stages so that employees can feel comfortable with the change.

Negotiation with stakeholders

The involvement of a neutral third party can sometimes help to resolve conflict. For example, the Advisory, Conciliation and Arbitration Service (ACAS) offers a process to act as a third party to try to resolve any dispute between an employee and her or his employer.

Collaborative working

Working together helps stakeholders to understand the interests of other stakeholders. This shared understanding should help stakeholders to work together better to achieve a goal or complete a task.

KNOW IT

1. Outline two ways in which providing training for employees may help a business to operate responsibly.
2. State four examples of legislation a business must adhere to if it is to operate responsibly.
3. Describe one conflict of interest that may occur between the owners of a business and its customers.
4. Explain how setting clear standards will help a business to overcome any conflicts of interest between stakeholders.
5. Explain how the use of collaborative working can help a business to manage ongoing conflicts of interest.

LO4 assessment activities

Below are suggested assessment activities that have been directly linked to the Pass, Merit and Distinction criteria in LO4 to help with assignment preparation. These are followed by a top tip on how to achieve the best results.

Activity 1 Pass criteria *P5*

You are to write a report that includes four sections, as outlined below.

● Section 1: using your research into a selected business, explain the difficulties that this business may face, or has faced, when implementing responsible business practice(s).

Activity 2 Pass criteria *P6* Merit criteria *M2*

You now need to add two more sections to your report. These should be based on your primary research and your earlier discussions.

● Section 2: explain the impact of conflicts of interest that your chosen business has faced or might face when implementing responsible business practices.

● Section 3: explain how your chosen business tried to reach a compromise when dealing with conflicting stakeholder needs.

Activity 3 Distinction criteria *D2*

You should now add a final section to your report, as follows.

● Section 4: if you have considered more than one compromise in Section 3 of your report, choose one of these to evaluate here. You need to evaluate the success or failure of the compromise that your chosen business reached when dealing with conflicting stakeholder needs.

TOP TIPS
✔ Consider the benefits and drawbacks of the compromise for each stakeholder involved to then draw a justified, supported conclusion as to the overall success or failure of the compromise.

Read about it

Business Ethics for Dummies, by Norman E. Bowie and Meg Schnieder, John Wiley & Sons, 2011

The Right Thing: An Everyday Guide to Ethics in Business, by Sally Bibb, John Wiley & Sons, 2010

Useful websites

Financier Worldwide Magazine – 'The importance of corporate social responsibility': www.financierworldwide.com/the-importance-of-corporate-social-responsibility/#.VxTk_2rHzIU

Frontstream blog – 'Why Corporate Social Responsibility is So Important': www.frontstream.com/why-corporate-social-responsibility-is-so-important/

Department for Business, Energy and Industrial Strategy: www.gov.uk/government/uploads/system/uploads/attachment_data/file/300265/bis-14-651-good-for-business-and-society-government-response-to-call-for-views-on-corporate-responsibility.pdf

ACCA blog – 'Why is ethics important to business?': https://blogs.accaglobal.com/2014/11/25/why-is-ethics-important-to-business/

Unit 20

Business events

ABOUT THIS UNIT

Business events are important to the continued success of a business. They can take many different forms, from simple to complex activities, which should achieve the overall aim of generating interest in the business. Organising any event will involve a variety of different people, who may be employees from the business or from external businesses who may supply products or services for the event. Without a combined approach, the event may not be run successfully, so an individual should be responsible for taking charge of the event, who is accountable and troubleshoots when required.

Organising a business event requires a number of different skills. This unit will give you the opportunity to learn and develop these skills in a variety of different ways. You will have the opportunity to plan and prepare for an actual event, as well as play a supportive role when the event takes place. The event will be reviewed and analysed afterwards, giving you the opportunity to evaluate all aspects of the event and to learn from the experience.

LEARNING OUTCOMES

The topics, activities and suggested reading in this unit will help you to:

1 be able to prepare for a business event
2 be able to support the running of a business event
3 be able to review a business event.

How will I be assessed?

You will be assessed through a series of assignments and tasks set and marked by your tutor.

How will I be graded?

You will be graded using the following criteria, which are in the specification produced by OCR for the qualification.

Learning outcome	Pass	Merit	Distinction
You will:	**To achieve a Pass you must demonstrate that you have met all the pass assessment criteria**	**To achieve a Merit you must demonstrate that you have met all the pass and merit assessment criteria**	**To achieve a Distinction you must demonstrate that you have met all the pass, merit and distinction assessment criteria**
1 Be able to prepare for a business event	**P1** Outline your proposal for allocation of responsibilities and use it to agree who does what		
	P2 Set objectives and success criteria for the business event	**M1** Describe the factors influencing the decisions made when planning the business event	**D1** Justify the decisions made when planning the business event, giving reasons why alternative options were rejected
	P3 Prepare a plan for the business event, including evidence of consideration of legal, ethical and budget requirements		
	P4 Produce documents and resources to aid the running of the business event		
	P5 Carry out pre-event tasks in line with the business event timeline		
2 Be able to support the running of a business event	**P6** Provide support to both attendees and support staff during the running of the business event		
3 Be able to review and evaluate if the business event met its objectives	**P7** Select method and format(s) for obtaining feedback and use your chosen method and format(s) to collect it	**M2** Assess the effectiveness of the method, format and timing used to gather feedback for the business event	**D2** Recommend and justify improvements to the planning and running of future business events
	P8 Evaluate the business event against its success criteria	**M3** Analyse the influence of factors on the outcomes of the business event	
	P9 Review own performance in supporting the event, identifying strengths and areas for improvement		

LO1 Be able to prepare for a business event *P1 P2 P3 P4 P5 M1 D1*

GETTING STARTED 👤

(15 minutes)

Business events can include conferences, product and service launch events, exhibitions and training events. Write a list of examples of the kinds of event you think a business may run. Ensure that your list involves a variety of small, medium-sized and large events. Compare your list with that of another member of your class, then feed back your results to the group.

1.1 The roles and accountabilities of staff involved in organising and running business events

The success of an event depends on the skills and attributes of the people involved in the process. Examples of key individuals are detailed in Table 20.1, which highlights the tasks, responsibilities and skills required for the key roles when planning an event.

Table 20.1 Roles and accountabilities of staff involved in business events

Who?	Responsibility	Skills required
Senior management	Monitor the event, reviewing its impact; accountable for its overall success	Co-ordination, leadership, organisational and communication skills
Budget holders	Allocation and monitoring of budgets to specific areas of the event, as well as post-event analysis	Communication, monitoring and co-ordination skills relevant to finance
Event organiser	Planning and organisation of the event, as well as post-event analysis	Co-ordination, delegation, leadership, motivational and communication skills
Event delivery staff	Complete tasks allocated to their roles	Good communication skills and specific skills relevant to tasks set

Another essential role is that of the supporting staff required for the event to run smoothly. **Support staff** are individuals who support specific elements of an event but are in the background. They could be tasked with roles that involve IT support, such as ensuring that internet access is available, or **troubleshooting** if there are hardware or software issues. Support staff also provide logistical support in the form of maintenance, reprographics and catering, all of which are important. Other support role tasks include:

- venue and facilities information
- front- and back-of-house duties
- catering
- publicity
- required documentation for employees, event staff and event guests
- general event troubleshooting.

🔑 **KEY TERMS**

Support staff – staff that perform a supporting role at an event to ensure that it runs smoothly.

Troubleshooting – a method of problem solving, giving specific stage-by-stage instructions to resolve the problem or issue.

PAIRS ACTIVITY 👥

(30 minutes)

Imagine you are going to organise a meeting for your year group to discuss the introduction of a new facility into your social space at your school or college. You have been allocated a budget of £500 to spend on the new item(s) but need to decide what it or they will be, taking into consideration the thoughts of your peers.

Discuss in pairs the different aspects that need to be considered in order for the event to run successfully, with the overall aim of deciding how the budget should be spent.

1.2 Who event organisers liaise with

An event organiser will need to liaise with three main groups of people, discussing various elements to ensure that the event runs successfully.

Internal customers

Internal customers are employees of the organisation providing the event, but who are attending the event in another role. They may be a delegate representing the business and participating in all aspects of the event in a customer role.

They could also be support staff at the event. Their support role may be slightly different from their everyday job within the business – they could be assisting with the catering, meeting and greeting delegates, providing IT support or troubleshooting problems that arise on the day.

An internal customer may also be one of the event deliverers. This role could range from front-of-house duties such as meeting and greeting delegates, to presenting various aspects of the event to delegates attending the event.

As you can see, being an internal customer can give employees various opportunities to demonstrate and develop their different skills, and give variety to their role within the business. This could lead to further opportunities in the future.

External customers

External customers are people from outside the company who will attend the event. They could have been invited to attend the event as a delegate, but there will also be external customers who are specially invited guests (VIPs – very important people). The type of delegate will be decided upon when devising the list of invited guests. The business may decide that the VIPs should be potential customers, to create a good impression, or they could decide to treat existing customers as the VIPs. They may choose not to have any type of guests and treat all delegates in the same way.

Suppliers

Event organisers must liaise with suppliers ahead of the event. The planning of events can take several months, or even years, depending on the event. Consider the time-frames involved in planning the football World Cup or the Olympic Games. Decisions about these major sporting events take years, from the bidding stages to the events taking place.

The number of suppliers the event organiser will need to communicate with will vary according to the size of the event. Many aspects need to be considered, which is why good co-ordination, delegation, leadership, motivational and communication skills are required in such a role.

Some examples of event suppliers are listed below.

- Hotel and conference facilities: a business organising a small launch event would have to consider and perhaps view several locations to assess their suitability and then book the venue to ensure the event can be run.
- Caterers: if food is not provided by the venue, suitable catering needs to be booked separately.
- Equipment suppliers: the events may require equipment not held by the business, e.g. specialist IT hardware, sound facilities, stages, stands.
- Transport providers: if the event is on more than one site, coaches or taxis may be needed to transport delegates.
- Designers and marketing agencies: creative services for promoting and running the event may be required, e.g. if employees are to wear uniforms or T-shirts so that delegates can spot them easily, then these will need to be designed and ordered.

1.3 How event organisers liaise with internal and external customers and suppliers

Event organisers will need to use a variety of different communications skills to liaise with internal and external customers and suppliers. The choice of communication method will depend on the information being sent.

Verbal communication

A face-to-face meeting with suppliers to negotiate the catering package may be the most suitable method, as it could involve tasting the food! Financial negotiating may also be best done face to face (although agreements should be confirmed in writing afterwards). Telephone conversations may be considered the best form of communication when updating senior management on the progress of the planning – for example, as a conference call where more than two people can participate in the conversation. This could take place in several locations in the UK, Europe or around the world.

Written communication

Written communication can include emails, contracts, SMS, schedules of activities, minutes of meetings, etc. The type of communication will be determined and agreed by the parties involved. It is useful to have plans and agreements in writing so that everyone is clear about what is expected of them. For example, supplier contracts will normally be written and could be sent via email, attaching the contracts to the email as written confirmation.

1.4 The factors influencing the effectiveness of business event management teams

The management of an event is key to its success. Having a clear structure in place, identifying individuals who have been allocated specific roles, can ensure that information is passed and reported to the right people so they can monitor the team's progress. It may be helpful for the team to produce an organisation chart when planning the event, which shows:

- roles and job titles clearly defined
- navigation of how decisions are made
- who is accountable to whom
- the relationships between the different positions.

If a business has a clear organisational structure in place for the event, the team will know and understand who to ask if they have a question or issue, which will help with the team's communication, ownership and loyalty. Equally, if the manager needs to speak to the team, they can gather everyone together with ease, communicate the relevant information relating to their role, and reiterate the business's aims and objectives for the event. Managers should communicate information that the team need to know. Too much irrelevant information could have a detrimental effect on the overall event. The manager must have the ability to resolve any conflicts that may occur within the team, using their leadership and management skills. All these different factors can influence the overall effectiveness of performance during and after the event.

Managers will also be required to be aware of a business's procedures and policies, such as **corporate social responsibility (CSR)** and resource management, which could include the budget allocated to the different elements of the event, the staffing, etc. These are management issues addressed within the management role and will directly impact on the planning of an event, which in turn will influence the team.

KEY TERM

Corporate social responsibility (CSR) – the way in which a business approaches and responds to economic, social and environmental issues for the good of the wider world.

THINK ABOUT IT

Case study: JTOJ Ltd

JTOJ Ltd planned an event for its shareholders to inform them of changes in the future direction of the business. The event was planned for mid-December to coincide with a Christmas celebration.

The event's organiser visited several hotels to assess the suitability of venues, and sampled the potential food, discussing catering packages and delegate accommodation with the hotel management. The business specified that it wanted several magicians to provide entertainment, and a string quartet to provide background Christmas music while the delegates were eating.

Finally, the venue was booked, with contracts agreed and signed by both parties, including the extra entertainment requirements. Invitations were sent out to 100 shareholders requiring them to confirm their attendance by a certain date. Once collated, the numbers were confirmed with the venue. In the meantime, the business worked on the presentations and information to be given out at the event.

On the day of the event, extra support staff were at the venue to ensure that all equipment was in place and the rooms were as they wanted. The event organiser liaised with the various suppliers as required.

On the evening of the event, the pre-booked string quartet did not appear and the hotel did not have enough desserts for one table of delegates. Some equipment supplied by the hotel failed, including the projector, which was connected to a laptop and the interactive whiteboard. These problems were fixed quickly by the internal team but the event organiser felt that these issues may have a negative impact on shareholders' loyalty. They checked the contracts, which stated that the hotel would organise the music and checked the confirmation numbers of the catering.

1 Write a suitable letter to the manager of the hotel, informing them of the issues.
2 Do you consider that these issues will have had a detrimental effect on the business? Explain your reasons.

KNOW IT

1 Identify three skills that you may require as an event organiser.
2 Why do you think these skills are needed?
3 What is the difference between an internal and an external customer at an event?

1.5 How to identify event objectives and success criteria

INDIVIDUAL ACTIVITY

(10 minutes)

You are going to organise a dinner event for prominent stakeholders associated with your business. What preparations do you think you will need to consider and complete when planning this event? Write a list detailing the plans, to ensure the event is successful.

Every event has to have a purpose, which will be measured by the success of the event. It is therefore important that the business has clear SMART objectives to focus the team to achieve the common goal.

In general, events bring together people who have a common interest. For example, a Doctor Who convention would generally be attended by people who are fans of the long-running TV programme, and the Gardeners World Live show will attract people who are interested in gardening. In both cases, attendees will find out more about their interest and perhaps purchase associated merchandise. A charity fundraising event would be attended by stakeholders who have an association with the charity, from businesses and donors, to recipients of the charity's work or money. The purpose of many events is to provide entertainment for the people attending and, if successful, the event could be staged again in the future.

▲ **Figure 20.1** The Glastonbury Festival is an example of a successful and long-running entertainment event

Business objectives

An event must have clear business objectives for the selected team to achieve, as a measure of its success. Business objectives will provide the team with a focus, motivation and clarification of what it is trying to achieve – for example, informing and increasing awareness of the product portfolio, awareness of a particular brand.

Event objectives

Event objectives are slightly different as they focus on the event in particular rather than business objectives. Event objectives could include:

- ensuring that delegates are satisfied with the event
- building on customer relationships
- creating new channels of support for the business
- generating sales and interest
- improving the PR profile.

SMART objectives

Any objectives should be SMART (Specific, Measurable, Achievable, Realistic, Time-bound) so that the business can set high-quality standards that can be reviewed after the event.

- Specific: objectives are easier to achieve if team members understand what they are aiming for – for example, inviting 40 specific key business clients to a launch event within a two-day period.
- Measurable: objectives need to be measured to evaluate the performance of both individuals and the team as a whole. This is not to say that the objective has to be easy – some have to be worked for – but as long as performance can be measured against the objective it can be reviewed.
- Achievable: if objectives are impossible to achieve this can be demotivating for the individual(s) involved, which may have a negative impact on the event. Objectives, then, should be neither too easy nor too hard. Too easy and the team may become too relaxed about their work; too hard and the team may lose focus or interest.
- Relevant: individuals' roles in planning a business event must be clear and within the objectives set – for example, if a person is tasked with considering the travel logistics for delegates, as that is their expertise, their skills would be better used in this role than in selling merchandise.

- Time-bound: giving individuals a time allocation to complete tasks in the form of a deadline creates a focus. This can be reviewed easily with the team member accountable for the set task.

All objectives – whether business or event objectives – should be SMART as this creates a focus for the team, which can then be reviewed successfully before, during and after the business event.

(20 minutes)

The case study on page 314 is about a business called JTOJ that organised a shareholders' Christmas meeting but encountered some problems during the event. Take on the role of the event manager and identify some objectives that JTOJ will have set when planning this important event again. Share your ideas with the class and justify your objectives.

1.6 How to plan for a business event

Clarifying event requirements

A business that is planning an event will need to ensure that it considers many different aspects, to ensure that the event is successful.

Agreeing objectives and success criteria

The first task when planning a business event is to clarify the event requirements as a team. This will include devising and agreeing the main business and event objectives, ensuring they are SMART, with the individuals involved. This will include (for example) the senior event management team, line managers, event sponsors (depending on the size of the event) and team colleagues involved in the event.

Determining constraints

The team will need to consider budget requirements carefully. Having a set budget will make the team focus on planning, co-ordination, wastage and efficiency, as well as controlling the spending. There may be various budgets for the different elements of the event (such as food, drinks, stationery, entertainment, etc.), which all need to be kept under control. Ensure there are sufficient funds to pay deposits if required to secure bookings of items for the event.

Contracts with suppliers will be legally binding. This will demonstrate a commitment to the event from both parties. The business will need to consider that all health and safety requirements are fulfilled to ensure that all people involved in the event – including employees, suppliers, contractors and delegates – are safe during the event. All laws, regulations and guidelines that are designed to protect people will have to be planned for. Sufficient public liability insurance will need to be in place to cover any payments relating to an accident.

The business event will also need to consider the ethical constraints, which will involve promoting an honest and trustworthy business that engages in fair practice in any given situation – for example, if delegates were made to feel uncomfortable due to a speaker's inappropriate comments.

(20 minutes)

Consider the following situation that a business may face.

Your business has accepted an invitation to a small business event. However, the day after accepting the invitation the business has an opportunity to attend a much bigger event, which will potentially create more exposure and publicity for your business. What do you do?

Identifying support documents needed

The business will need to identify, supply, create and distribute any supporting documents required for those involved with the event in any capacity. Examples include planning documents for employees, promotional materials such as emails, social media posts, posters, information leaflets, invitations and agendas for delegates, joining and travel instructions if required, and post-event evaluation forms, which could be printed or devised through online means. All individuals should be informed of the details that are relevant to them. There is no point in distributing documents or information that is irrelevant to the individual's specific role as too much information may lead to the specific information required being missed, which could have a consequence for the event or individual.

Identifying suitable venue and establishing booking arrangements

Identifying a suitable venue for a business event is an important business decision. The venue should be determined by the type of event and the resources that will be required as part of the event. For example, if an AGM is to take place at a suitable location, the business may want to consider the following questions.

- Is the venue big enough?
- Is the venue available?
- Is there sufficient parking?
- Is the venue easily accessible for all who will be attending?
- Are all fire regulations supported?
- Are the facilities on offer suitable?
- Are there suitable transport links?
- Will local residents be affected by the event?
- Will all delegate needs be met?

If the business is confident that the selected venue is right for the event, it can establish and enter into a booking agreement with the venue, which will be legally binding when both parties agree by signing to the terms and conditions set out in the agreement. The venue may be required to pay a deposit to secure the booking, which may be lost if the agreement is broken.

Identifying resources

The business organising the event will need to consider other forms of physical resources needed to run the event successfully.

Personnel

This includes the people required to help plan and support the event, from events management to support staff, as well as the specific smaller roles given to individuals. The business may want to create an event organisation chart, which would detail the structure of the organisation in terms of the individuals involved, their roles, accountability, chain of command and span of control specifically for the event. Having such a structure in place should enable the team to communicate with the right individuals regarding specific information at all times – provided that they understand the organisation chart!

Equipment

Planning the right equipment for the event is a key element. Most events require some sort of equipment, such as tables, chairs or display screens, with some events requiring specialist IT resources that may be limited in supply. It is important to identify the equipment requirements, particularly if something is hard to obtain, so that it can be booked in advance. For regular or annual events, management may decide to purchase specific items to be used over a number of years rather than hiring the equipment each time. Some businesses hire equipment for each event on a short-term basis so they do not need to purchase every item required. For example, did you know that you could hire VIP ropes, poles and red carpet for an event (Figure 20.2)?

▲ **Figure 20.2** What items can you hire?

🔍 **INDEPENDENT RESEARCH ACTIVITY**

(20 minutes)

Research an event hiring business and identify ten unusual products that you did not know you could hire. Share these items and the costs with the rest of the group.

Delegate requirements

Catering and refreshments must remain within budget. Questions to think about could include those listed below.

- Will delegates be offered drinks (tea, coffee, wine) when they arrive?

- What food will be supplied by the venue?
- How many delegates need to be catered for?
- What are the likely dietary requirements?
- How many breaks for refreshments will be required during the event?
- Is it a one-, two- or three-day event?

Transport will need to be considered by the event planning team, for both delegates and the staff running the event. For example, will delegates require taxis from train stations if they are arriving at the event by train? It really will depend on the scale and size of the event, but all travel requirements should be considered and planned for by the team, as any problems can directly impact on a business's reputation – for example if taxis are not available at the right time.

Delegate packs

Delegate packs should contain the relevant supportive documentation required for them to know what will be discussed and presented at the event.

Schedule activities

The time and date of the event will provide a crucial deadline for all tasks and plans to be achieved. Once these decisions are made, it will be hard for them to be moved to another date or time, so once decided upon these should not change. This will give the team the ability to focus and work backwards from the end goal of the date and time, and plan accordingly. Planning aids like online project management software can be used to help the team when planning the various elements of the event.

Timelines (Figure 20.3) include particular timescales and specific deadlines for various activities in a chronological order, which is displayed in a straight line. The line can either be horizontal or vertical. Timelines are advantageous because they can show the team how long the event will take to plan, the order in which activities and tasks should be completed and how they correspond to the deadlines. However, sometimes timelines do not show how long each task may take – just the deadline or the current status of the activities.

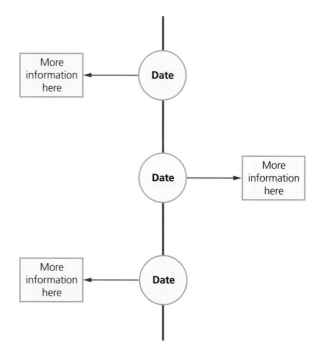

▲ **Figure 20.3** An example of a vertical timeline

1.7 How to produce guidance to help others resolve potential problems during the operation of a business event

The majority of business events are successful because all planning elements have been considered carefully. However, even the best-laid plans can run into difficulties that cannot be controlled or predicted. Unforeseen circumstances can cause difficulties for events so, in these situations, the event should have contingency plans just in case.

Method, format and content

Such a plan will outline the actions that should take place, including any help sheets, handouts or verbal briefings that should be given to relevant individuals, who will then act upon the actions. Such documents should contain pre-prepared content that is based on any emergency procedures, troubleshooting methods or **communication protocols**.

Communication protocols – formal descriptions that are specific to digital message formats. They are needed to exchange messages from one computer system to another when using telecommunication methods.

Potential problems

A business can plan for potential problems. These could include:

- non-arrival of delegates
- late arrival of delegates
- lack or late delivery of specific resources
- IT equipment failure
- emergencies, including fire, first aid and health issues
- transportation disruption
- bad weather
- last-minute document requirements, such as extra photocopying.

(45 minutes)

Using the JTOJ case study on page 314, imagine that you have taken on the role of event manager and are responsible for producing guidelines for your team about how to handle any issues or problems that may occur during the event.

Produce guidance for your staff that explains how to resolve any issues. Include who should make the decisions on how to resolve the situation so that it does not affect the overall running and success of the event.

1.8 How to prepare for a business event

Preparing for a business event will require the business to make final decisions based on the planning that has already been completed. The business will be required to secure facilities that are needed at the event; these are detailed below.

Book facilities

Organising an event will involve the business entering into contracts; these are legally binding agreements between two or more different parties. When the business wants to book a venue, a contract will be drawn up stating the terms and conditions of the agreement, which both parties will sign and therefore agree to, making it legally binding. This means that both parties will be legally obligated to fulfil their part of the contract. For example, if the contract states that a deposit of £1,000 is required within seven days of contracts being signed, to secure the booking for the designated date, the business must pay £1,000 within seven days to fulfil the contract and retain its booking.

As well as booking the venue, the business will need to consider the catering arrangements for both delegates and employees at the event. A hotel's contract may include details about the catering arrangements. However, the business may decide to use a specialised caterer that needs its own contract.

Specialist contractors could also be used for transporting the delegates to the venue. Individuals may arrive from abroad and will need transport from an airport or railway station to the venue. Coaches or taxis need to be booked in advance. The people requiring transport need to know what to expect, to reduce stress for all involved.

The business may also require specialist transportation for certain equipment – for example, art works for an exhibition would need to be transported with care to ensure they are not damaged.

The event organiser must be involved in these decisions so that all facilities that are required on the day are booked, with contracts agreed and signed, and nothing missed, so that the event is a success.

Create and distribute documentation

When all aspects of the event have been booked, the business needs to create and distribute a variety of different documents to give those attending the information they need. These could be printed or sent out via email attachments. All delegates will need the joining instructions, which normally contain vital information such as the start time of the event, the venue address and directions, details of facilities and an overview of the event.

Otherwise, the documentation will vary according to the type of event – for example, an **annual general meeting (AGM)** for shareholders needs an agenda detailing the topics that will be covered. Delegates may be required to use a booking form to attend a particular workshop. Promotional materials such as posters, leaflets and emails may also be distributed direct to stakeholders and media outlets.

Evaluation forms are used after the event to gain the views of those who attended. They are a good way to obtain direct feedback on the various aspects of an event. They need to be devised and produced before the event so that they (or online links to them) can be distributed to delegates while they are there.

Health and safety protocols

Once facilities like the venue, transport and catering have been booked and documentation has been produced, the organisers need to consider health and safety. This includes referring to the Health and Safety at Work Act 1974 and the Management of Health and Safety at Work Regulations, which require the business to carry out risk assessments. Risk assessments allow the business to identify risks or hazards that may occur as a result of people attending or participating in the event. The business should follow five main steps.

1 Identify the hazard or risk: key individuals identify the potential hazards by considering the event, the site, location, structure and the activities delegates will participate in.
2 Consider who could be exposed to the risk or hazard: this would be specific groups, people or individuals, with a focus on those more vulnerable – people with disabilities, the elderly, children, etc.
3 Evaluating the risks: the likelihood of harm to people, so that every precaution is taken into account to reduce or eliminate risk. Risks are usually classified as low, medium or high, and measures to act on them are decided before the event. If this still does not eliminate the risk, then the event may be deemed to be too high risk and therefore unfeasible.
4 Document findings: recorded findings should be clearly documented, so that these can be checked and any actions completed. It is the responsibility of event management to ensure that all risks are identified and evaluated appropriately, adhering to all related health and safety legislation.

5 Monitor and review risks: the final stage of the risk assessment process is to continually monitor the situation and monitor potential risks during the event. Afterwards, the risk assessment should be reviewed, with identified risks being analysed and any new risks considered for future risk assessments.

The event organisers should also ensure that emergency procedures are rehearsed, with staff being clear of their roles in such situations – for example, having trained first aiders available. Large venues, such as the NEC in Birmingham, will often have trained staff onsite who can deal with emergency situations.

Data security

All legal requirements must be fulfilled, which will include data security. The Data Protection Act 1998 states that companies must legally prove how they handle personal information. Anyone attending or associated with a business event will provide confidential and personal details, and it is the business's responsibility to ensure that this information is:

- adequate, relevant and not excessive
- processed fairly and lawfully
- obtained only for one or more specified and lawful purposes, and shall not be further processed in any manner incompatible with that purpose or those purposes
- accurate and up to date
- processed in accordance with the rights of data subjects under this act
- not kept for longer than is necessary
- secure, i.e. measures shall be taken against unauthorised or unlawful processing of personal data and against accidental loss or destruction of, or damage to, personal data
- not transferred to other countries without adequate protection.

Source: http://tinyurl.com/jgr6476

Businesses must also ensure that data remains secure when using any form of electronic communications.

Determine and accommodate delegate requirements

The business should also take into account any particular requirements that delegates make the organisers aware of – for example, special diets, access needs (such as wheelchair access) or **assistive technologies**.

> **KEY TERM**
>
> **Assistive technologies** – equipment that individuals may require to assist with their participation during an event.

KNOW IT

1 What are the main differences between business objectives and event objectives?
2 Why is it important for a business to produce thorough plans for any business event?
3 Giving clear and realistic deadlines to a team can have both a positive and negative impact on a team. Why may this be the case? Explain your answer.
4 Why must risk assessments be completed by a business before running a business event?

LO1 assessment activities

Below are suggested assessment activities that have been directly linked to the Pass, Merit and Distinction criteria in LO1 to help with assignment preparation. These are followed by top tips on how to achieve the best results.

Activity 1 Pass criteria *P2*

P2 Write clear objectives for a business event of your choice that will measure whether it is successful.

Activity 2 Merit criteria *M1*

M1 Complete detailed descriptions that highlight why certain decisions were made in the planning stages of a business event.

Activity 3 Distinction criteria *D1*

D1 Justify, with detailed reasoning, the decisions that have been made when planning a specific business event. These justifications should also cover any alternative options that were discussed but consequently rejected.

Activity 4 Pass criteria *P1* and *P3*

P1 P3 Prepare a suitable plan for a business event, including details of legal, ethical and budget requirements which are clearly evidenced Include the allocation of responsibilities for the event.

Activity 5 Pass criteria *P4*

P4 Produce realistic guidance that focuses on resolving the potential problems that may occur during a specific business event, to help others.

Activity 6 Pass criteria *P5*

P5 Perform relevant preparations for a particular business event you are involved in.

> **TOP TIPS** ✔
>
> ✔ Ensure that the business event you choose fully meets all requirements of the assessment criteria. Use an event that you are involved in.
> ✔ Ensure that relevant documentation is completed, evidenced and explained within your work.
> ✔ Make sure that all documentation looks professional.

LO2 Be able to support the running of a business event *P6*

GETTING STARTED

(10 minutes)

Write a list that identifies the types of activity that you think will need to be completed by the employees who are going to be running a large business meeting at a local hotel.

2.1 Provide support and help resolve problems

A business event gives an organisation the opportunity to present itself to various stakeholders. The business must be able to present a well-run event, supporting all participants in their various roles. Remember that the roles will vary, so management will need to know the identities of the key individuals if and when seeking information. Some employees may require specific training ahead of the event, which should be planned for earlier on in the process.

Use appropriate verbal and non-verbal communication

The main forms of communication that will be used at an event will be face to face, telephone conversations and email. This will be determined by the situation and the time-frame – for example, if an item of essential equipment is not delivered to the location as specified within the contract, a team member will most likely telephone the supplier to speak to someone direct to find out where the item is and if it can be delivered within the required timescale. In this situation an email would not be suitable as it may not be read or could be missed; if the business is several miles away from the venue, speaking face to face may also not be the best choice of communication.

Further information on verbal and non-verbal communication methods can be found in Unit 4, page 116.

Management may choose to brief the whole team in a face-to-face meeting before the event starts. If the event is large then this briefing may be held within sub-teams, with the leaders of each team briefing each team. The reason for a final briefing is to:

● ensure that all employees and staff are there on the day
● pass on any last-minute changes that may have occurred as a result of unforeseen circumstances
● answer any questions that individuals may have
● motivate the team to create a positive experience for all involved in the event, in order for it to be a success.

Within the team briefing, management may inform staff of the procedures on how to deal with particular issues and who to inform. If delegates encounter any problems, they must know who to approach, so staff should be easily identifiable (e.g. by wearing a uniform or identity badge). Even if the team members are not able to answer a question, they should actively seek the answer.

Apply appropriate responses to problems

On the day of the event, staff in all roles will be providing some form of customer service support. Looking after the delegates and meeting their needs is an important aspect of running a successful business event. Customer service issues must be dealt with appropriately. A problem of any size must have an adequate solution.

Figure 20.4 could help with the decision-making process if a problem arises.

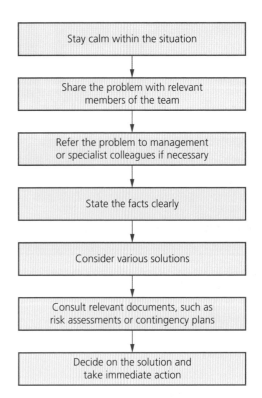

▲ **Figure 20.4** Problem solving on the day of the event

PAIRS ACTIVITY

(15 minutes)

One table of shareholders at the JTOJ event did not receive their desserts as the hotel had miscalculated the number of guests. Jenny, one of the staff at JTOJ, was made aware of the situation and needed to resolve it as quickly as possible to satisfy the shareholders. If you were Jenny, what would you do?

Give appropriate administrative support

Customer service will include offering and completing administrative support if required, which could include:

● checking delegate documentation on arrival, and handing out badges and delegate packs
● taking an attendance register
● collecting feedback about the event (e.g. post-event surveys), which is subsequently summarised and reviewed as part of the reviewing process
● taking notes.

▲ **Figure 20.5** Business events of all sizes require support systems for their smooth running

INDIVIDUAL ACTIVITY ....

(30 minutes)

Consider the situations below that could occur at a business event.

- One of the guest speakers is delayed due to traffic and has telephoned to inform you that she is going to be one hour late.
- During part of a presentation, the projector starts to give off smoke, which is followed by a small 'bang'.
- Some delegate packs do not contain all of the resources and documents required for the event.
- Some coffee is accidentally spilt on one of the delegates.

Explain how a business should respond to each of these situations and what the potential impact could be on the overall success of the event.

KNOW IT

1 Why is customer service an important aspect of running a business event?
2 How can management determine the most appropriate form of communication in any given situation?
3 Identify two different administrative tasks that should be completed when running an event.

LO2 assessment activity

Below is a suggested assessment activity that has been directly linked to the Pass criteria in LO2 to help with assignment preparation. This is followed by top tips on how to achieve the best results.

Activity 1 Pass criteria *P6*

P6 Produce all relevant documentation and provide support to the staff during the business event, as well as supporting the people attending the specific business event.

TOP TIPS

✔ Ensure that you are aware of the support that staff may need during the event.
✔ Consider the needs and wants of the attendees who are attending the business event.
✔ Good customer service is the key to a successful event.

● ● ● ● ● ● ● ● ● ● ● ● ● ● ● ● ● ● ● ●

LO3 Be able to review a business event *P7 P8 M2 M3 D2*

GETTING STARTED ....

(10 minutes)

Imagine that a number of issues occurred when your company ran an event at a local hotel. Why would it be important to review the event?

3.1 How to appraise own performance in supporting business events

The team and individuals should review their own performance when supporting a business event.

To review or appraise your own or someone else's performance, you will need to focus on several elements, which may include the:

- strengths of your performance during the event, with specific examples given to illustrate where you or they were particularly good

- weak areas of your performance, e.g. poor timekeeping, controlling nerves
- identification of skills that could be improved in the future through specific training or CPD activities
- various skills that you used and applied to the activities you completed while supporting the event; this could include different communication skills (such as verbal and face-to-face team briefings), teamwork, leadership activities and problem solving (depending on your role)
- way your performance contributed to the main business and event objectives that were set at the planning stage of the process.

3.2 How to gather feedback for a review

Once the event has been completed, the business should evaluate whether or not it was successful. The review process will assess a variety of different sources, and measure the outcomes against the original business and event objectives. Feedback is a good form of evaluation, with the overall goal of making improvements for the future.

Identify objectives for gathering feedback

The first stage of the review will be to identify the objectives that were initially set. These could include meeting delegate needs and wants, measuring delegate satisfaction and measuring the messages that delegates learned during the event. The business will already have decided during the planning stage how the data would be sourced and the methods that would be used. This means that the processes should be in place on the day to collect the necessary data.

Sources

These include delegate and support staff feedback.

Delegate feedback

Delegate feedback will give the people attending the event the opportunity to give specific feedback on various elements of the event, which could include the venue, transport, catering, general facilities at the venue, the presentations, usefulness of the workshops attended, quality of resources and information, etc.

Support staff feedback

As well as written feedback, team meetings can determine how successful the planning and running of the event was in general. The team will refer to the objectives, and discuss how the group and individuals contributed to them. Specific examples will help illustrate the feedback.

The most important aspect of any review is to remain unbiased: discussion should be based upon facts rather than individual views. Any recommendations for improvement can be discussed, which could involve specific training and development for the team and individuals.

Methods

Ways of gathering feedback from the event could include asking delegates to complete feedback at the venue or at a later date, using a suitable format.

- Response cards ask several short questions about the event. Delegates either hand in the completed card at the event or post the card to the team afterwards.
- Delegates could be emailed a link to an online survey after the event so that they can answer questions on different elements. Delegates should be given an idea of how long the survey will take to complete, so that they are aware of the time commitment. Responses to online surveys can be tracked and analysed in real time.
- Social media forums allow delegates to leave comments, messages and information for organisers and other delegates.
- Direct discussions with delegates and support staff at or after the event provide qualitative, if anecdotal, feedback, and allow for more detail to be explored.

Question and response format

If an online or traditional questionnaire is going to be used, then the types of questions and formats need to be discussed at the planning stage. This is because the questions need to be devised, reviewed and tested prior to the event, to ensure that the required information will be gathered from the review process. Types of questions may include:

- open-ended questions, which give the respondent the opportunity to offer their opinion, e.g. What were the best elements of the conference?
- closed questions, which require the respondent to respond with, for example, a yes or no answer, e.g. Were the objectives of the event made clear to you?
- multiple choice questions, which give respondents the opportunity to choose an answer to a question that has already been written, e.g. How suitable do you consider the chosen venue to be for the event?
  - Excellent venue
  - Good venue
  - Fair venue
  - Disappointing venue

- the Likert scale, which enables respondents to consider a statement and then use the given scale to rate their response, e.g.

	Disagree				Strongly agree
I enjoyed the event	1	2	3	4	5

Whatever the method of review, the aim is for each delegate to complete it fully, giving constructive criticism and praise as appropriate. The comments and information can then be analysed, processed and discussed as part of the whole event review.

INDIVIDUAL ACTIVITY

(20 minutes)

Devise a series of questions that a company could give to employees who recently had a role 'front of house' at a conference. The team were responsible for meeting and greeting delegates, giving out delegate packs, serving refreshments, etc. Ensure that a variety of questions give the employees the opportunity to explain how their role supported the conference.

3.3 How to analyse feedback

The final stage in reviewing a business event is to analyse the feedback that either delegates and support staff (or both) have given in this important aspect of review.

The method of evaluation will determine how the information is collated and summarised. For example, if an online survey is used to gain feedback, the business will be able to utilise web analytical tools to review the responses. A team may be tasked with the evaluation, which will involve presenting and summarising their

findings in the most suitable form to the individuals or groups who require the information. Specific review criteria make the review process effective and relevant. For example, if the evaluations gave the respondents the opportunity to recommend ideas for future workshops or experiences, the business could investigate using these suggestions if another similar event were to take place in the future. This would, of course, depend on issues such as relevance, budget, time constraints, and fulfilling and supporting current or future business and event objectives.

PAIRS ACTIVITY

(15 minutes)

Refer to the JTOJ case study on page 314. The guests were asked to complete an online evaluation of the event, which covered the information they were given, the speakers, the venue, entertainment, quality of the catering, etc. Overall the feedback was positive but there were many negative comments about the technical issues and the missing or small portions of dessert.

Discuss in your pair how you think the business should use this feedback to plan future events. Could the issues have been predicted and therefore prevented?

KNOW IT

1 Why is appraisal an important form of reviewing a business event?
2 Explain three different methods of gathering information that a business may use after an event has taken place.
3 Explain two different types of question that can be used within a survey.

LO3 assessment activities

Below are suggested assessment activities that have been directly linked to the Pass, Merit and Distinction criteria in LO3 to help with assignment preparation. These are followed by top tips on how to achieve the best results.

Activity 1 Pass criteria *P7*

P7 Complete a detailed review of your performance when you supported the running of a business event, focusing on your strengths and weaknesses.

Activity 2 Pass criteria *P8*

P8 Considering the success of the event, review it against the initial objectives that were set in the planning stages of the event to determine if the objectives were fully met.

Activity 3 Merit criteria *M2*

M2 Consider and analyse how the different factors you encountered during the business event influenced the overall outcomes.

Activity 4 Merit criteria *M3*

M3 Consider the methods used, the timings and how information was gathered for evaluation purposes, and assess how effective and relevant these methods were for the specific business event.

Activity 5 Distinction criteria *D2*

D2 If another business event were to take place, recommend some improvements to both the planning stages and running of the event, and justify these suggested improvements.

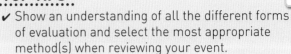

TOP TIPS
✔ Show an understanding of all the different forms of evaluation and select the most appropriate method(s) when reviewing your event.
✔ Show evidence of an 'objective approach' to the review process, meaning that it is factual rather than from a certain viewpoint.

Read about it

Event Planning Tips: The Straight Scoop on How to Run a Successful Event, by Natalie Johnson, ebook, MCJ Publishing, 2014

Events Management (3rd edn), by Glenn A.J. Bowdin and Johnny Allen, Routledge, 2010

The Business of Events Management, by John Beech, Sebastian Kaiser and Robert Kaspar, Pearson, 2014

Unit **22**

Delivering a business project

LEARNING OUTCOMES

The topics, activities and suggested reading in this unit will help you to:

1 be able to scope a project
2 be able to collaborate to deliver a project
3 be able to evaluate the effectiveness of the project against its objectives and own contribution to the project.

How will I be assessed?

You will be assessed through a series of assignments and tasks set and marked by your tutor.

How will I be graded?

You will be graded using the following criteria, which are in the specification produced by OCR for the qualification.

Learning outcome	Pass	Merit	Distinction
You will:	**To achieve a Pass you must demonstrate that you have met all the pass assessment criteria**	**To achieve a Merit you must demonstrate that you have met all the pass and merit assessment criteria**	**To achieve a Distinction you must demonstrate that you have met all the pass, merit and distinction assessment criteria**
LO1 Be able to scope a project	**P1** Carry out primary and secondary research to inform the project		
	P2 Set SMART objectives and success criteria for the project		
	P3 Assess and record the feasibility and viability of the project and recommend next steps		
	P4 Calculate costs against the project budget		
	P5 Identify and record risks to the project		
	P6 Produce project documentation to cover: • purpose • key stakeholder requirements • desired outcomes • legal requirements • ethical issues • budget constraints • timeline(s) • tasks • Key Performance Indicators (KPIs) • risk register • decisions log	**M1** Explain factors influencing the decisions made when planning the project	**D1** Justify the decisions made when planning the project, giving reasons why alternative options were rejected
LO2 Be able to collaborate to deliver a project	**P7** Outline your proposal for allocation of roles and responsibilities and collaborate with others to agree who does what		
	P8 Create an individual plan to achieve own responsibilities for the delivery of the project		
	P9 Demonstrate ability to adapt behaviour for different roles and situations when collaborating to deliver the project	**M2** Analyse how the team responded to changing events or circumstances that impacted on the project	**D2** Evaluate the quality of the collaboration demonstrated by stakeholders
	P10 Demonstrate the ability to work collaboratively with others to achieve stated project goals		
	P11 Liaise with project stakeholders in an appropriate and timely manner		

	P12 Review and update progress against: • own individual plan • project plan and agree with others any proposed changes to the project plan		
	P13 Monitor and report progress against the plan with reference to KPIs, risks, budget and key decisions	**M3** Make recommendations for changes to the project plan based on monitoring of progress	
LO3 Be able to evaluate the effectiveness of a project against its objectives and own contribution to a project	**P14** Select method(s), format(s) and timing for obtaining feedback and use your chosen method(s) and format(s) to collect it	**M4** Assess the effectiveness of the method, format and timing used to gather feedback for the project	**D3** Recommend and justify improvements to the planning and running of future projects based on the feedback gathered
	P15 Collate feedback collected from stakeholders and present your analysis in a form that is easily understood to summarise trends		
	P16 Use feedback and review the outcome of the project against its original objectives, making any recommendations for improvement	**M5** Analyse the impact of factors not originally planned for, on the desired project outcomes	
	P17 Provide constructive feedback to project stakeholders on their performance		
	P18 Review own performance in delivering the project, identifying strengths and areas for improvement		

LO1 Be able to scope a project *P1*
P2 P3 P4 P5 P6 M1 D1

GETTING STARTED 👤

(15 minutes)

In pairs, discuss why it is important for a business to research the likely success of a business project before embarking on the whole project. Share your ideas with the rest of the group.

1.1 How to carry out research and the tools to use

For every business considering any kind of business project, it is important that research is completed to ensure that there is a need and want for the outcome of

the project. If businesses are going to make a financial investment or commitment, they need to be confident that the project will meet the outcomes that are set. Businesses should gain a variety of different data to ensure that as much information as possible is taken into account. For this reason, two forms of research should be completed: quantitative and qualitative research. For more information, see also Unit 3, LO1.3, Unit 5, LO4.3, and Unit 15, LO5.2.

Quantitative research

Quantitative research is often data led, which can provide a business with statistical and numerical data to help with decision making, e.g. gaining the opinions of others regarding a new product or service that may be launched. The types of question a business may ask could start:

- How many?
- How often?
- Who?
- When?
- Where?

Quantitative research methods include online surveys, face-to-face discussions, telephone interviews, emails, questionnaires sent via the post, etc. The questionnaires or surveys could have a variety of questions and answers that respondents tick or circle from a predefined selection. It is important that the questions enable the business to gain meaningful answers.

Some businesses offer incentives such as cash, vouchers or free products to encourage customers to answer the questions. Once the results have been compiled, the research can be analysed and used to help determine if the project is viable.

Qualitative research

Qualitative research gathers the opinions, views and attitudes of participants, who may have been interviewed individually or have been part of a focus group where recordings or notes have been taken on a variety of different open-ended questions posed to participants. The types of questions that may be asked could start:

- Why?
- Would?
- How?

The results of both the quantitative and qualitative research will enable a business to determine if the proposed project should go ahead, or if alterations and/ or revisions should be made to the original idea. It is also good practice to review what went well about the research, what did not work and the outcomes of the research. This could be judged against the original set of research objectives.

INDIVIDUAL ACTIVITY

(30 minutes)

A new 'garden city' development has been built to address housing shortages, provide green spaces and encourage eco-friendly living. A small business that has just opened there wants to hold a street party on the May Day bank holiday weekend to celebrate the community, involving as many local businesses as possible and raising money for nearby charities. It wants to gauge interest from different stakeholders including local businesses, local residents who may wish to attend the street party and those who live on

the proposed street. Local businesses could be invited to have stalls promoting their products and services or, in the case of larger businesses, to sponsor the event.

Produce examples of both quantitative and qualitative research materials that could be used to gain the opinions of these stakeholders, and describe how the examples would be used to help to move the proposed project forward.

1.2 How to investigate the feasibility and viability of a project

When reading this section, keep in mind the street party at the new garden city development, and how the team might arrange a charity fundraising event, complete market research for a specific purpose, and consider other important aspects including the purpose, different stakeholders, outcomes, budgets, various resource requirements and constraints.

Purpose

The purpose of the project should be established early on, so that those on the project team (whether internal or external to the organisation) are working towards the same business goals. Having a clear objective or purpose will ensure that the team members are focused. The team will look to the project manager for reassurance and guidance, so it is important that this individual communicates the purpose of the tasks required, delegates tasks and gives the team confidence.

Often the core purpose of a project is lost or shifts as the project progresses, resulting in extra work that makes the project fall behind schedule. This is why **scope control** is important to prevent the project from losing its focus.

> **KEY TERM**
>
> Scope control – preventing too many changes and additions to a business project that may disrupt the project schedule.

Key stakeholder requirements

The business project team should consider the needs of all stakeholders that the project will affect, from local residents to suppliers. The key stakeholders are those who will be directly involved with, and affected by, the project. The business must identify these key stakeholders and approach them to gain their support and understanding.

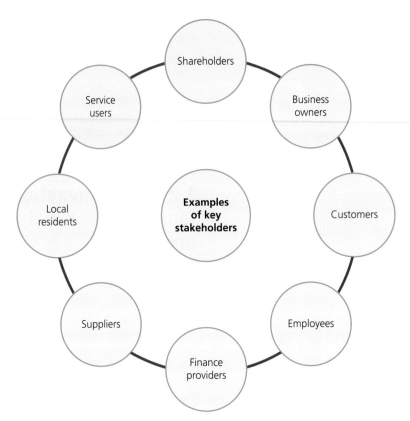

▲ **Figure 22.1** Key stakeholders need to be consulted about how the project may affect them

Desired outcomes

A business project should have a clearly defined purpose that details realistic objectives that can be achieved, which could be in the form of SMART objectives (see Unit 20, LO2, page 315). Members of the team should share the same desired outcomes, as this could be a key element in the success of the project.

Resource requirements

Specific resources may not be realistic in terms of the available budget but a list could be compiled detailing resource needs and wants, and used to identify which resources are actually required rather than simply wanted (desired). These could be prioritised and included in the budget.

If you consider the resources required for the street party at the new garden city development, tables and chairs will be needed due to the type of event, but paying for tablecloths would be a desirable, not essential, element. The project management team may try to obtain as many resources as they can from businesses for free. Businesses would in turn want some recognition for this, such as an official mention in the 'thanks', both verbal and written.

Legal requirements

All legal requirements must be considered and met. These will include health and safety legislation, employment laws, data protection, etc. Considering all stakeholders, the business must analyse and ensure that all legal aspects are identified to meet the requirements of the law.

For a street party, the local authority would have to approve any road closures. Often, several weeks' notice is required so the project team would need to complete the necessary paperwork as early as possible.

Ethical issues

Any business project must consider whether the process and outcome will be ethically sound and not cause offence or harm to others in any form. If ethical issues are not considered, stakeholders could be upset or injured, negative media attention could result in the business project being abandoned, or employees may not be motivated to work on the project. Ethical issues can vary from cultural values to the thoughts and beliefs of specific individuals. It is vital that a business considers these important aspects while planning a business project.

For example, consideration would need to be given to the local residents living where the party is going to be held, especially if they are not participating in the event. The project team should consider the impact of noise levels, especially at night, as well as ensure that residents are inconvenienced as little as possible.

Budget constraints

Any project will have some form of financial or budget constraints, so the team must justify their spending requirements for the project. The constraints are often grouped together to form a concept called 'The Triple Constraint', which identifies the main constraints as being cost, time and scope, ensuring that any projects are delivered within the budget (cost), on time and meeting the agreed scope (purpose).

▲ **Figure 22.2** The quality triangle

The quality triangle (Figure 22.2) focuses the project team on three main areas, as follows, that in turn can impact upon the overall quality.

1 **Cost:** projects are limited by budget and should incorporate the many different aspects of producing a product or service, including how much potential customers will be willing to spend. If the team has to reduce the project's cost this will impact on the overall quality.

2 **Time:** projects have an overall deadline and, if this has to be reduced, it can impact the quality of the product or service that a potential customer receives. Equally, if a project overruns, the business may be fined for this delay, which will impact directly on the cost. If a project's time is reduced, costs may increase or the other option is to reduce its scope. Either way, this can impact on the quality. Time is money.

3 **Scope:** some projects fail because the project scope is either not fully defined or really understood from the start. If a project's scope has increased, this will affect the cost or running time of the project, which in turn will impact on the overall quality.

Tasks

The business must identify the different and individual tasks that need to be completed for its overall project, as this can help determine whether a project is worth considering.

- Is it **feasible**? Has the business considered the legal, economic, technological, ethical and scheduling aspects of a project before committing time and money to it?
- Is it **viable**? How will the project benefit the business in terms of its strategic goals by adding value over a substantial period of time?
- What is the skills set of the proposed team? Will other skills be required? If so, how will these be acquired? Will some services need to be outsourced?

Once tasks have been identified, they could be allocated and delegated to specific roles, which would aid the planning in terms of internal and external staffing requirements.

> ### 🔑 KEY TERMS
>
> **Feasibility** – analysis and evaluation of a proposed project to determine specific factors regarding the legal, economic, technological and scheduling aspects of a project, allowing the business to investigate the positive and negative elements before committing time and money to the proposed project.
>
> **Viability** – an investigation into how a proposed project will benefit the business in terms of its strategic goals and adding value to achieve the maximum potential over a sustainable period of time.

Timeline(s)

Sufficient time should be given to planning and running the project, as well as for reflection and evaluation at the end of the project.

For example, when planning a street party, the project management team will need to arrange the tasks and deadlines to gain the support of specific stakeholders, to meet deadlines for administrative and application tasks relating to street closures, to book entertainment and equipment in good time, etc. The team will also need to prioritise the tasks. Businesses will use planning aids such as fishbone/Ishikawa diagrams, critical path analysis flow diagrams and Gantt charts to help plan the timelines (see Table 22.1, as well as Unit 3, LO5, page 95, and Unit 16, LO4, page 285).

Key performance indicators

Key performance indicators (KPIs) enable a business to measure itself in terms of how it is achieving its business objectives (see Unit 1, LO8, and Unit 15, LO5). The project team can identify KPIs that apply during the project and when measuring its outcome. An example from the street party idea could be to gain the commitment of ten local craft and food makers and confirm their attendance. Another example could be that a business may need to purchase a new piece of machinery to replace an old system that is not as economical as newer alternatives. This could address a very different KPI.

Project management tools

Business projects involve many different tasks that have to be completed over a period of time, involving different groups or individuals, and often with specific deadlines and budgets. Project management tools enable team members to plan and monitor these tasks, and to take action when required. Table 22.1 shows some examples, giving more detail on project management tools.

Table 22.1 Examples of project management tools

Name of tool	Explanation
Critical path analysis (see Unit 3, LO5.3)	Based on the idea that you cannot start some activities until others are finished, so tasks are completed in a sequence
Gap analysis	Helps to identify what needs to be completed in order to meet the project's objectives
Gantt charts (see Unit 16, LO4)	Enables teams to schedule medium and large projects, so that they are completed in the most efficient way
Project charters	Sets out the purpose of a project, explaining the expectations for each member of the team
Risk impact	Helps to identify the risks involved in the project, and estimates how likely it is that these risks will occur

Recommendations

Clear recommendations are vital to the successful planning of a business project. Recommendations will form the basis for moving the business project forward, concluding with whether the project is deemed to be feasible and viable. Management will be interested in the details of the recommendations, as this could ultimately make key people decide if the project should go ahead.

INDIVIDUAL ACTIVITY

(30 minutes)

A local bakery has recognised that it is producing too much waste and is keen to reduce this. It is a very competitive market and the business has experimented with various new product lines over the past 18 months, with varying success. The bakery produces traditional sweet and savoury bakery products, organic product ranges, a world foods range and a 'twists' range, which is a twist on traditional bakery products.

Research the fishbone diagram planning aid and use this to help the business plan how to reduce its wastage rates.

1.3 How to identify risks to a project

Business projects have an element of risk, ranging from risks to the safety of those involved to those that cannot be controlled, such as the weather. For example, if it rained during the street party, this could have an adverse effect on the desired outcomes as fewer people may attend so passing trade for the craft and food stalls may be reduced. Equally, if council permission was not sought to close the street for the party, then the party could be stopped on the day. If potential risks are not identified early in the planning process, the project could ultimately be at a high risk of not being completed according to the agreed schedule, staying within the allocated budget or meeting the expected quality.

In order to alleviate the element of risk associated with the project, the project manager should:

- ensure that the team members share common goals during the project
- have realistic expectations
- have a good skills mix within the team
- not be over-reliant on one member of the team
- ensure that adequate resources are allocated
- have good and open communications with all the team
- monitor the project's progress at regular intervals
- plan, plan, plan.

How can a business identify risks?

Having clear aims will ensure that the team members remain focused. If subsequent objectives are SMART (Specific, Measurable, Achievable, Realistic and Time-bound), this will give the team a greater understanding of how their aims will be achieved. If the aims and objectives are changed, then the team members are informed immediately as this could cause confusion, frustration and maybe stress on the team, which could have an adverse effect on team morale and/or performance.

It is important to recognise that risks are associated with any project. If management is 'too positive', it may not be in a position to recognise that risks could be associated with the business project. This could impact on the overall outcomes if the project managers are not able to identify or recognise problems. Any problems would come as a shock if due consideration had not been given to the elements of risk. Therefore, being 'too positive' could be classed as a risk for any project. Examples of negative risks could involve underestimating or overestimating the timescales and resource requirements of the project.

Positive risks are also possible. For example, referring again to the street party, if the weather is very hot, more people may attend and stallholders might run out of drinks, which could result in disappointment for the customers attending. Good weather and lots of people are a positive thing, but it would create a potential risk of disappointing customers if stocks of drinks run out.

It is important for the team delivering a business project to also consider **contingency planning**. This is when a business considers certain events that may occur and therefore how they would deal with them. Examples could be a main supplier going out of business or the loss of key data from an IT fault relating to the project. Such issues will cause disruption to the project process, so the project managers must consider and plan for potential outcomes.

KEY TERM

Contingency planning – developing appropriate responses in advance for potential situations that might arise during a business project and that may impact on the overall outcomes.

KNOW IT

1 What are the main differences between qualitative and quantitative data?
2 Why is it important for a business to consider if a project is both feasible and viable?
3 Identify five important elements that should be considered when embarking on a business project.
4 Why is it important for a business to identify potential risks when planning a business project?

LO1 assessment activities

The aim of this unit is for you to undertake a team project that will meet all of the required learning outcomes and assessment criteria. For this reason, the assessment activities for LO1 and LO2 have been combined for this unit only and can be found on pages 342–44.

LO2 Be able to collaborate to deliver a project P7 P8 P9 P10 P11 P12 P13 M2 M3 D2

GETTING STARTED

(10 minutes)

Write down four key elements that you consider to be the most important to ensure that your proposed business project is a success, e.g. the need for team members to have a common aim.

Review your key elements from the task above and reach a conclusion as to which one you consider to be the most important and why. Share your ideas with the rest of the group.

2.1 How to agree roles of project team members

In any team, there are individuals who have different strengths, weaknesses and interests. Having a mixture of different skills and knowledge within a team is important, as this will contribute to a good balance and a successful team.

The first element of agreeing roles is to identify the roles that will need to be filled during the project. Some typical roles are described in Table 22.2.

Table 22.2 Typical roles in project teams

Role	Description	Duties
Project manager	Plays a key role in the project, and is responsible for its completion Ensures that the project proceeds within the specified timeframe and budget, and achieves its objectives; will have an overview of the project to ensure that it is delivered on time Ensures that sufficient resources are allocated Must have good working relationships at all levels with the team and other internal and external stakeholders	Develops a clear project plan Leads the project team Sets the expectations of the team Establishes a project schedule, monitors its progress and reschedules if required Solves problems related to the project by dealing with any unexpected issues Ensures that sufficient resources are allocated at specific times Delegates tasks to specific members of the project team in order to set individual targets Provides regular updates to the team/management
Project team member	Individuals who work on different elements of a project; may be a mixture of internal and external individuals Specific roles within the team will be allocated according to the individual's skills set as well as the time allocated to the roles	Contributes to the project objectives Completes individual and group project tasks Provides expertise within their role Works with stakeholders to establish and meet the business's needs Documents the process at specific times Meets deadlines Feeds back any issues to project manager initially
Project sponsor	Often a member of senior management working closely with the project manager Works towards the project's overall objectives Influences the project's planning stages May resolve conflicts and remove any obstacles that may prevent progress within the project	Influences key decisions Helps to allocate or agree the budget Communicates the project's aims and objectives with specific stakeholders, e.g. senior managers, suppliers, customers, financial institutions
Business analyst (optional as this role is not always required so the duties will be fulfilled by the project manager; it will depend on the nature of the project)	Identifies needs and wants Recommends solutions Tries to ensure that the project's objectives solve existing problems or enhance the business's performance by adding value	Helps achieve the aims and objectives of the project Gathers the requirements of each individual stakeholder, e.g. the financial information that needs to be provided to banks Provides documented evidence of technical and business requirements for the management team Reviews the overall project deliverables to meet the stakeholder requirements Tests any solutions needed to meet the objectives

When a team is presented with a business project, the roles should be allocated to people with the necessary skills and knowledge to complete the tasks successfully. Skills could include:

- communication skills
- problem-solving skills
- numeracy skills
- decision-making skills
- leadership skills
- IT skills
- conflict resolution skills
- project-specific skills, e.g. understanding processes.

When agreeing the method in order to allocate roles, teams may want to consider these other methods in order to reach a consensus:

- rotating the roles so that everyone takes a turn at a different role and gaining experience of the different roles
- allocate the main roles within the team to the people who would like to fulfil them or are best qualified to carry them out because of their prior or current experience
- allocate roles to people who would like to take on an unfamiliar role in order to gain valuable experience.

Whichever method the team members decide to use, it is important that all agree, so that the team dynamics start in a positive way.

INDIVIDUAL ACTIVITY

(10 minutes)

Complete a SWOT analysis on yourself that considers your own Strengths, Weaknesses, Opportunities and Threats. Share your findings with another team member to see if they agree.

Belbin Team Roles

One well-known method of identifying effective teams was created by Dr Meredith Belbin, who identified nine behaviours that individuals can often display in their place of work – known as the **Belbin** Team Roles. These are as follows.

1 **Shaper:** likes to drive work forward and gets things done, while having a clear idea of the desired direction.
2 **Implementer:** likes to get tasks completed and looks for ways to turn talk into an action that generates practical activity.
3 **Completer-finisher:** driven by completing tasks, making sure that all loose ends are tied up.
4 **Co-ordinator:** likes to manage the group dynamics in a leadership role.
5 **Team worker:** likes to help the team to work effectively by supporting all staff.
6 **Resource investigator:** likes to gather resources and information in order to help the team reach its given goals.
7 **Plant:** likes to generate a variety of different ideas and creative solutions for the team.
8 **Monitor-evaluator:** good at analysing and critically assessing ideas and proposals in order to help make team decisions.
9 **Specialist:** brings expert knowledge to a group for the good of the team.

Further information on the Belbin Team Roles can be found at:

www.belbin.com/about/belbin-team-roles

> **KEY TERM**
>
> **Belbin** – a team-building theory that identifies the different elements of an effective team.

INDIVIDUAL ACTIVITY

(15 minutes)

Using the information on the following website, complete the team roles test:

www.123test.com/team-roles-test

Do the results surprise you? Share your thoughts with the rest of the class.

Four Dimensions of Relational Work

The Four Dimensions of Relational Work concept was advanced by Timothy Butler and James Waldroop. It can help managers to match team members' natural aptitudes and skills to specific tasks or projects within their work. The four dimensions were identified as follows.

1 **Influence:** individuals who are strong in this area tend to enjoy being able to influence others. They are often good at negotiating and persuading others, enjoy sharing their knowledge and skills, and often can create networks, connections and strategic business friendships with ease.
2 **Interpersonal facilitation:** individuals who have a real strength in this area are often 'in the background' workers who are good at sensing people's emotions and motivations. They often have skills that can help others with emotional issues or conflict. They may have strong intuition.
3 **Relational creativity:** these individuals are often good at using illustrations and words in order to create emotion, build relationships or motivate others to act for the good of the project. This is very different from influencing others, as that is person to person whereas this is often done from a distance. For example, they might use a famous quote to change the outlook, approach and motivation of a team.
4 **Team leadership:** individual members who have strong leadership skills often succeed through their interactions with others and working with other people in order to achieve their goals. They are often interested in the individuals and the processes involved in reaching the final goal of a successful business project.

Management matches current job roles and skills to the skills needed for the project, selecting the most reliable and hardworking individuals. Management may consider giving individuals roles that they do not currently undertake, as they may recognise that specific team members may not be utilising all of their strengths within their current role.

> **KEY TERM**
>
> **Four Dimensions of Relational Work concept** – a tool to aid managers to match team members' natural aptitudes and skills to specific tasks or projects within their work.

2.2 How to agree responsibilities of project team members

Once team roles have been identified, the responsibilities associated with each role, as well as the skills and knowledge, should be made clear to all team members and agreed. The team members might want to draft brief responsibilities associated with each role so that all are aware of the specific elements relating to each role. This could then be agreed and will aid this important process. See Table 22.2 for more details of roles and responsibilities.

Creating a good working team relationship is vital to ensure that individuals feel:

- supported
- valued
- confident in using communication channels to report any issues or concerns
- fully informed of the progress of the business project
- able to solve problems in a professional manner
- able to resolve and diffuse conflict.

All of these points are important to the workings of a successful team on any given business project. In turn, the management of the project will expect all team members to:

- work towards the overall aims of the business project
- support and adhere to the SMART objectives
- work to their set targets
- show fairness and consideration to others within the team
- keep lines of communication open
- solve problems if and when they occur
- deliver given tasks and activities according to the devised schedule
- provide documentation when appropriate
- comply with procedures and policies relating to the business and the business project, e.g. health and safety regulations, Data Protection Act, employment legislation.

Tuckman Theory

In 1965, Bruce Tuckman developed a theory that focused on the way in which a team tackles a task or a project, from the initial idea through to completion.

Tuckman Theory relates to fulfilling responsibilities by focusing on what the team does, how it does it and how the team members relate to one another. For example, if fairness and consideration is not shown towards team members, some of them may feel aggrieved, which could affect their work and the team's dynamics.

The theory investigates the different stages described below.

Tuckman Theory – a theory that focuses on the way in which a team can potentially tackle a task or a project from the initial idea through to completion.

Forming

This first stage is when team members are very positive and polite towards one another. Some may be slightly anxious, while others may be overly excited at the prospect of a new challenge. The leader will then confirm the team members' roles and responsibilities so all are aware about the lines of communication as well as the **chain of command**. It is important that these are established. This first stage will involve the team getting to know the way in which individuals work, so that routines and expectations can be established.

Chain of command – the levels of authority in an organisation where communication and instructions flow down the hierarchy and accountability flows upwards.

Storming

Storming is the next phase of the process, where the team members are more comfortable with their roles but potentially may start to push the boundaries. This could result in various forms of conflict – for example, clashes over different working styles, challenges over authority, excessive workloads and time pressures. Individuals could become frustrated, which could in time affect their work and the balance of the team. At this stage, the team dynamics may alter.

Norming

This third stage occurs when the team settles after resolving any differences and the strengths of specific team members will emerge with the team starting to utilise these. The team members will know one another much better, be more willing to help one another, and will show real commitment to the overall aims and objectives. Progress will be made at a rapid pace.

Performing

This is when the team reaches the performing stage of this theory, when work is being completed well, any friction has been resolved, targets are being met and management is clearly seeing the project progress.

Adjourning

This final stage will be met at the end of the project when the team is disbanded as the project has been completed in full. Hopefully, the team members will regard their work as successful by its purpose being fulfilled. From a management perspective, recognition should be given to deserving members, and there should be an awareness that some members of the team may be nervous about the future and feeling insecure. Team members may find this stage hard, particularly if they have enjoyed and thrived during the experience.

GROUP ACTIVITY

(45 minutes)

This activity focuses on a team's ability to work together and then relates the experiences to two different theories.

In small groups, create a spaghetti bridge to support a small item. The following website contains further information:

www.jamesdysonfoundation.co.uk/resources/

INDIVIDUAL ACTIVITY

(45 minutes)

Once completed, review your group's overall performance and the roles that individuals played before, during and after the activity.

Relate your findings to two of the following: Belbin Team Roles, Four Dimensions of Relational Work and Tuckman Theory.

Share your thoughts with the rest of the group.

2.3 How to collaborate with others towards achieving common project activities

Figure 22.3 illustrates the importance of teamwork. It highlights the important skills that people should demonstrate if they are to work together successfully.

Collaboration is the key to delivering a business project. Some examples are given in Table 22.3.

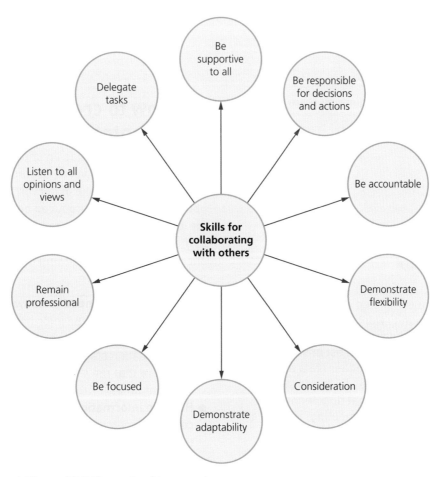

▲ **Figure 22.3** Elements of teamwork

Table 22.3 Examples of collaborating for success

Item	Example	Reasoning
Prepare for meetings	Agendas, scheduling events and activities	Such documentation is vital in order to ensure that meetings have a clear reason and outcome, for the good of the project
Adapt behaviours	Behaviour or approaches may need to be altered depending on the situation or circumstances; team members need to be aware of what is appropriate at specific times	Being able to judge a situation and react in an appropriate way is vital when working with others.
React to unforeseen circumstances	Respond to internal or external changes to the business and/or environment, e.g. the budget being cut or a key team member leaving	Teams must be able to adapt to any number of circumstances that may have an impact on the project
Use appropriate forms of communication	Verbal (face-to-face, telephone) or non-verbal (email) communication methods	All team members must be able to judge the most suitable form of communication for any situation
Apply appropriate responses to problems or issues	Being able to identify issues and solutions, and resolve problems; also to delegate tasks to appropriate members of the team	Management and team members must respond professionally to problems and work together to resolve the issue
Give administrative support when required	Preparing any documents required; organising, collating and evaluating when required	The administrative team must try to ensure that all team members complete the required documents when needed in a timely manner, so that everything is up to date, enabling stakeholders to have an accurate snapshot of the project's progress at any time

Any business project will also require all team members to be:

- accountable
- considerate
- focused
- flexible
- responsive
- responsible.

PAIRS ACTIVITY

(30 minutes)

Earlier in this unit, you completed a task relating to a local business community wanting to plan a street party on the May bank holiday weekend. Several businesses have expressed an interest in supporting this local event. You want to invite them to a meeting to discuss the aims and objectives for the local community. In pairs, consider what documentation should be prepared ahead of this meeting, including items to be discussed.

Share your ideas with the rest of the group, giving justifications as to why suggested documents items should be prepared.

2.4 How to create project documentation

Project documentation is an important aspect of any business project. However, documentation should not be created for the sake of it, even if it is contractually obliged; it should be produced because there is a need for it, adding value and meaning to the project in terms of the information that it contains. An organisation should consider the following factors when creating project documentation.

- **What individuals need to know:** project managers need to determine the information that is required at specific points during the planning, implementation and evaluation stages of the business project, in order to ensure that the team receives the information at the right time.
- **How the information should be presented, and the content:** creators should consider the audience or the user of the information. Should it be formal or informal? What writing style should be used? How should it be delivered, e.g. within a presentation, a meeting, an email?

- **Updates:** if the requirements change for any reason, the project manager must be able to issue information updates to the key members of the team this could affect. This is particularly important in terms of changes to deadlines or if further information is required in order to complete a task in full according to the new requirements. It is important that all documents are accurate, including the **risk register** and **decisions log**, as well as minutes of meetings.

🔑 **KEY TERM**

Decisions log – a document that details all the key decisions that have to be made on any given business project. It should be kept up to date.

Risk register – a document and management tool that is created within the planning stages of any business project to identify any risks.

Documentation is a good form of communication. It does, however, need to be accurate, relevant in terms of the content, presented well and given to those who require the information at the required intervals (frequency). All documentation represents the organisation so it is important that everything is proofread as, if mistakes are made, it could affect the reputation of the business. Examples of documentation that may be required for a business project will include agendas, minutes of meetings, market research results, decisions log, risk register, etc.

Considering the street party at the new garden city development, what documentation is required and should be completed by the project management team? Write down your ideas and justify them.

Discuss your thoughts with the rest of the group.

2.5 How to create, complete and maintain a risk register, issues log and decisions log

Risk register

A risk register is a document and management tool intended to aid the planning stages of a project, to determine any risks (issues) that may occur. It also shows how the project team will manage the risks, giving the actions required in order to reduce or prevent risks occurring. Risk management is a critical element, which can ultimately determine the success or failure of any project. The project manager will complete the risk register, with key team members and stakeholders, seeking input when required, to ensure that all aspects of the project are considered. Once created, the risk register should be issued to all stakeholders as they may also have other risk ideas that may not have been considered.

A typical risk register could contain the sections shown in Table 22.4.

Table 22.4 Sample sections in a risk register

Risk register section	Function
Risk description	A brief description of the identified potential risk
Risk category	Specifies different categories of risk such as time, cost, resource, environmental, etc.
Risk identification	Tracks and identifies the risk using a code
Project impact	A description of the impact of the risk on the project, e.g. a delay of three days on delivery of the project will make it go over budget
Likelihood	An estimate of the likelihood or probability that the risk will occur and its impact on the project; some risk registers document this in either qualitative (e.g. high, medium or low) or quantitative terms (a description) if enough information is available
Impact	Identifies what effect the risk will have
Risk rank	A number indicating the level of the risk; it must be made clear what the numbers mean, e.g. 1–10 indicates low to high
Risk trigger	Describes warning signs that the risk has occurred or is likely to occur
Response/prevention and contingency plan	Explains, often in the form of an action plan, how to try to prevent the risk from occurring and what to do if risks occur; it could include the functional areas and details of key individuals that should be contacted
Risk owner	States who is accountable for the risk and the implementation of prevention and contingency planning; this is important as the risk owner should be aware of the activities that need to take place in the fastest possible time
Residual risk	Identifies the likelihood and/or impact of the risk after it has been addressed; ideally, this should be 'low'

Table 22.5 shows an example of a risk register for the street party.

Table 22.5 Example risk register

| Risk identification | | Qualitative rating | | | | Risk response | | |
Risk description	Risk category	Likelihood	Impact	Risk score	Risk rank	Risk trigger	Risk response	Risk owner
Fire	1	Medium	High	7	7	A stallholder will be barbequing at the street party	Ensure that stallholder has fire regulatory equipment to put out a fire were it to occur	O&J Barbeques

Table 22.6 Example decisions log

Reference	Decision made	Agreed by	Person to action	Date agreed	Action taken	Date completed	Further info
SP003	Contact Mr Balloon, street entertainer	All team	Anita	03.02.17	Emailed Mr Balloon, who agreed to perform for £100 Contract sent	04.02.17	Email trail saved in 'Street party' folder

Further information about risk registers can be found in Unit 3, LO5 (page 95).

Issues log

An issues log is a tool for reporting and communicating what is happening during a project. This ensures that any potential issues are raised then subsequently investigated, and resolved quickly and efficiently so that they do not have a negative effect on the overall project.

An issues log enables you to:

● have a reliable method in order to raise issues
● delegate responsibility to specific team members for each issue
● prioritise issues
● record the issue resolution
● monitor the overall project status.

An example of an issues log can be found at:

www.projectmanagementdocs.com/project-documents/ issue-log.html#axzz49HpzZSVw

Decisions log

A decisions log lists all the key decisions that have to be made on a project. Information might include:

● a reference number for the decision
● the decision made
● the date that the decision was made
● an identification of who agreed the decision

● the name of the person responsible for carrying out the decision
● the action taken and outcome, with reasoning
● where further information can be found if required and who is responsible for the decision.

A decisions log like the one shown in Table 22.6 should detail all decisions that are made so that they are documented in one place, which can be referred to as necessary. Users are reliant on all individuals updating this document when decisions are made otherwise it will not work. The log can potentially solve any disputes as long as accountability is clear on the documents.

2.6 How to monitor and report progress against a plan

Monitoring and reporting the progress of a project is an important aspect of ensuring that the project will be delivered on time. Not meeting deadlines can have direct consequences for a business, ranging from financial implications to team morale and the business's reputation being damaged. Therefore plans must be reviewed frequently to monitor:

● progress towards, and achievement of, KPIs
● spend against project budget
● the action taken to mitigate risks and address issues if they occur
● timing and sequencing of activities to identify whether the project is running to schedule.

Ideally – at least every week – the project should be monitored and reviewed to ensure that KPIs can be tracked, as it is often clear from the planning stages that the size of tasks has been underestimated and new tasks are identified that need to be added to the plan. Equally, the team should be told when key deadlines are met, and this should be celebrated as a motivational tool for team morale. Potential risks that have been identified within the risk register should also be actioned and reviewed.

In order to monitor the timing and sequencing of the different aspects of a project, managers can use critical path analysis (CPA). You can find out more about CPA in Unit 3, LO5.3 (page 96), which also includes information on critical path network diagrams, earliest start times (EST), latest finish times (LFT), float time for an activity and how to identify a project's critical path.

> **KNOW IT**
>
> 1 What are the key concepts and categories of the Belbin theory?
> 2 Why is important for team members to have a variety of different skill and knowledge sets?
> 3 Identify three expectations that a project manager might place on their team to ensure that the project is delivered.
> 4 What project tools could a project manager use to document the business project process?

LO1 and LO2 assessment activity

Below is a suggested assessment activity that has been directly linked to the Pass, Merit and Distinction Criteria in LO1 and LO2 to help with assignment preparation. This is followed by top tips on how to achieve the best results.

Activity 1 Pass criteria *P1 P2 P3 P4 P5 P6 P7 P8 P9 P10 P11 P12* and *P13* Merit criteria *M1 M2* and *M3* Distinction criteria *D1* and *D2*

You are required to complete a business project in a team of between three and eight people. It is important that your team members demonstrate a variety of different skill sets and knowledge to help you justify some of the decisions that you make, either individually or as a team.

Once your team is established, you will need to consider different ideas for your business project. You could brainstorm some ideas, but ensure they are realistic (feasible and viable). For instance, you could consider:

- setting up, running and closing down a business enterprise
- holding an event in your local community, which could be affiliated with your school or college
- organising and running a charity event
- researching a specific marketing campaign and carrying out the launch event.

Whatever you choose, it must be complex enough for you to complete the following assessment criteria, which will also help you to plan and structure your project. As evidence you could include development ideas and you could individually make notes (minutes) on your discussions to choose a project to provide this evidence.

Although you will be working as a team, you need to be able to demonstrate your own role by providing evidence such as emails, documentation and photographs. You can complete some of the criteria individually and then decide as a team which elements you will use for the overall project.

P1 Once you have decided on an idea, or if you are trying to decide between two ideas, carry out primary and secondary research to determine if the idea is viable and feasible. The results should then inform the basis of the proposed business project.

P2 Individually, devise clear SMART objectives and detailed success criteria for delivering the selected business project.

P3 Produce an assessment of the feasibility and viability of the business project that provides recommendations for how the team can move the project forward.

Once you have completed this element of the criteria, if your business project is not feasible or viable, you should review the project and try a different approach until it is deemed to be viable so that the planning stages can then take place.

P4 Calculate costs against the project budget.

Now that the project is established, you may be given a budget. Provide detailed costings to show how you will use this budget. If you do not have a budget, calculate your costs and consider how you could cover these costs, e.g. by gaining sponsorship or asking businesses to donate items free of charge.

P5 Identify different risks that may be associated with the business project and record these using appropriate documentation, such as a risk register.

P6 Complete detailed documentation appropriate for the business project. You could complete a detailed progress report that outlines the purpose, key stakeholder requirements, desired outcomes, legal requirements, ethical issues, budget constraints and KPIs (key performance indicators). You must use an appropriate project management tool(s), which could include decisions log, issues log, risk register, Gantt charts, CPA, etc.

M1 Explain the factors that will potentially influence the decisions that will be made when planning the business project.

D1 Justify the decisions made when planning the project, giving reasons why alternative options were rejected by you or the team.

In your teams, you should discuss how specific roles and responsibilities will be allocated. You may want to use the results of any team tasks you have completed as part of your learning for LO1 and LO2.

P7 Outline your proposal for the allocation of roles and responsibilities among team members. Collaborate with team members to agree who does what.

P8 Prepare an individual plan that details how you intend to achieve the responsibilities that have been allocated to you for the duration of the project.

P9 When delivering the business project, note down when you have had to adapt your behaviour when completing specific roles with team members. This must be clearly evidenced so that you can demonstrate your ability to adapt your behaviour.

P10 When delivering the business project, you are required to demonstrate your skills and ability to work together with others collaboratively in order to achieve the project goals. Document specific examples of when this has happened, which include your views as well as evidence from your fellow team members.

P11 Liaise with project stakeholders in an appropriate and timely manner by interacting with them

professionally. You will need to provide evidence, which could be in the form of witness statements, videos, recordings, etc. You could also provide evidence of emails, minutes of meetings, etc.

P12 Review and update progress against:

● own individual plan
● project plan

and agree with others any proposed changes to the project plan. If any changes are needed as a result of the review process, seek agreement from the team and document it. You could use the working documents that are required for the planning of the project, such as a decisions log. If changes are not needed, this could also be documented.

P13 Monitor and report progress against the plan with reference to KPIs, risks, budget and key decisions, as well as any important deviations from the plan, e.g. timings, sequencing.

M2 In any project, changing events or circumstance will occur that as a team you have no control over. Consider the different situations that occurred and analyse how the team responded to these events or circumstances. Analyse how they impacted on the business project.

M3 Recommend changes to the project plan based on the outcome of the monitoring of your project progress.

D2 Evaluate the quality of the collaboration demonstrated by all stakeholders.

Your business project will have involved a variety of different stakeholders. Some of these stakeholders will have enabled you to make key decisions. You are required to consider the stakeholders (e.g. anyone involved in the project) and assess the quality of the interaction and collaboration by all stakeholders that were involved in the project. You could consider, for example, the meetings and the various forms of communication methods, and evaluate how each stakeholder directly impacted on the overall quality of the business project.

- ✔ Try to be clear in the overall aims and objectives of your chosen project
- ✔ Ensure that you can gain the relevant information to fulfil every aspect of the criteria in this section of the specification from your chosen business project.
- ✔ Consider how your team will be divided and how to allocate specific tasks in order to be fair to all team members. You could use any previous team-building tasks that have been completed as part of LO1 and LO2 to help with such decisions.
- ✔ Provide high-quality documented evidence of each stage of the project, which is stated in the various assessment criteria.
- ✔ Keep track of any changes within your portfolio, which can be identified within the specific assessment criteria (e.g. P9 when you have demonstrated the ability to adapt your behaviour for different situations or liaising on timescales with project stakeholders, which relates to P11), so that these can be discussed at certain times.
- ✔ Be as organised as you can, as this will make the reviewing process easier to complete.

LO3 Be able to evaluate the effectiveness of a project against its objectives and own contribution to a project *P14 P15 P16 P17 P18 M4 M5 D3*

GETTING STARTED

(10 minutes)

Consider the following situations and discuss in pairs the most suitable form of gaining feedback from stakeholders when reviewing the event:

- a school or college summer ball
- a local recruitment fair
- a training course for the finance department in a medium-sized business on how to track payments
- an initial consultation meeting informing the local community, about a proposed new housing development in a small village
- a 'gaming' event at the NEC in Birmingham where gamers can experience the latest games, meet game creators and take part in panel discussions.

Share your ideas with the rest of the group, using clear reasoning.

3.1 How to gather feedback for a project review

Reviewing a business project provides the team with the opportunity to analyse both the positive and negative aspects of the project once it has taken place. By completing a **project review**, future projects could be improved as the experiences and thoughts of individuals and stakeholders can be scrutinised. Lessons can be learned from any situation.

Significant consideration should be given to gathering feedback so that it is a useful, efficient and effective process. Stakeholders can offer their unique perspective, and their feedback can help develop future projects, for example, their aims and objectives. However, asking stakeholders for feedback without providing some form of documentation could lead to confusing and, ultimately, useless feedback.

The project manager must decide how to gather specific feedback from the review process, which could focus on the aspects described below.

🔑 KEY TERM

Project review – an evaluation of a specific project that details different elements of success and areas for improvement. The outcomes could influence future projects.

Identify feedback objectives

This will focus on gaining feedback regarding stakeholder satisfaction, recognise successes and failures, as well as focusing on identifying lessons learned, etc. It is important that feedback is sought from the different stakeholders involved so that all views are considered. Feedback could include gaining specific information from key stakeholders involved in the project from interviews, meetings or questionnaires.

Identify sources of feedback

The project manager must consider the different parties that will be involved in the review process. Ideally, this should include all the stakeholders who have had an input but this may not always be feasible.

Identify methods of gathering feedback

The team and project manager should analyse the different forms of feedback and determine which will be the most suitable for the process, e.g. questionnaires, surveys, response cards, interviews (face to face, telephone), group discussions or focus groups.

Timing

Often a review will happen at the end of the project, but reviews can also happen at the end of a specific phase of the project. For example, considering the street party, if sponsorship were wanted, the project management team could approach businesses to determine their interest. If several businesses were interested, then they could be asked them to pitch their sponsorship ideas, with the project manager selecting the most suitable, all within specific timescales. Once all contracts and agreements have been signed, this part of the project could be deemed to have been completed. In this situation, the objectives will have been achieved and a review could take place in order for the next phase to be completed. Reviews can take place while the project is ongoing, as well as post-project.

Question and response format

Decisions will need to be made with regard to the way in which the questions or responses will be written – for example, open or closed questions, open-ended questions, multiple-choice suggestions or Likert scale items (ranking items using a scale from 1 to 5 or 1 to 10, say). Thought must be given to the design of the review, including testing the process before involving the relevant stakeholders. The team will also need to consider the format, e.g. email attachment, online survey. The review process should not be time consuming for the respondents or they may not complete the answers.

Collate feedback

This aspect of the process will be determined by the method and format of the review. Closed or multiple-choice questions can be quantified easily. However, open-ended questions enable a more personal view to be sought, with a wider range of responses which could prove more useful to the review process. In such situations, these responses will need to be reviewed individually. These views, if significant, could then form a crucial part of the planning of future business projects.

INDIVIDUAL ACTIVITY

(1 hour)

Look at the following website, which describes a variety of small- and large-scale projects that have won APM (Association of Project Management) Awards:

www.apm.org.uk/project-case-studies#EXE

Select two smaller-scale projects and consider how you would aim to gain feedback from specific stakeholders associated with them. Devise one form of feedback for each project.

3.2 How to analyse feedback from stakeholders

An analysis of the responses must be completed. This analysis could have a direct impact on future projects in terms of the team, resources, budgets and timing. It can also help to identify whether patterns and trends occur within feedback data.

Stakeholder feedback can provide details that relate to various roles, the services that were provided, as well as behavioural factors relating to attitudes. It is important that a variety of different levels within the business hierarchy and different types of stakeholder participate in the review to ensure that the data collected is meaningful, giving consideration to the following aspects.

Certain types of feedback can sometimes be hard to hear, such as open and honest comments. It is therefore important that the criteria for analysis are clearly established so you are aware of how the process will work.

What tools you will use in order to analyse the results; numerical data may be more appropriate than detailed descriptive reviews completed by stakeholders in certain circumstances. This could be as a result of a lack of time as managers may require the data quickly, which may influence the form of feedback.

Ensuring that the stakeholders are aware of any ethical, equality and confidentiality issues when taking part in the review process.

Reviewing the feedback will enable management to identify any similar patterns, thoughts or trends. If there are similar findings from a variety of stakeholders (positive or negative), the team will be able to focus on these and prioritise them accordingly.

By utilising the feedback and analysis, project managers will be able to make specific recommendations for future projects – for example, about:

- suitable budgets
- what is achievable
- project aims
- SMART objectives.

3.3 How to appraise own performance in delivering a project

All team members need to spend time **appraising their own performance** by considering the different contributions they have made. A simple way of completing a review is to complete a SWOT analysis, which focuses on the Strengths, Weaknesses, Opportunities and Threats on a specific project (see Unit 1, LO8, page 43, for more information about this).

(see Unit 1, LO8, page 43, for more information about this)

KEY TERM

Appraise own performance – the opportunity for individuals to consider the different contributions they have made during a business project.

A self-appraisal should focus on a number of core elements:

- your strengths and weaknesses
- areas for improvement
- what skills you have applied and how
- how your performance contributed to the project, its objectives and success criteria.

A self-evaluation form could enable you to consider other elements of the roles you played when completing your project. The self-evaluation could include the details shown in Figure 22.4.

Project self-evaluation form
Name:
Team:
Project:
Individual role for the project: Describe the role you were allocated
Individual targets: A range of targets associated with the project as well as personal targets, e.g. improve communication skills, have the ability to delegate tasks to others
How your role enabled you to contribute to the feasibility and viability of the project:

Your contribution to the planning of the project: Explain your input into the planning stage of the project, with specific examples of the tasks that were completed.
Your contribution to the overall project, its objectives and success criteria: Details of the different elements you contributed to during the project, referring to the objectives and success criteria for the specific project
Individual skills you have developed by participating in the project: Details of the skills you have learned and/or developed, focusing on the positive elements you have gained from this work, e.g. communication skills, team-working skills
Knowledge you have gained: Specific details about information you have learned while working on the project
What further individual development and improvements could contribute and enhance future projects? Focus on personal development for the future; this should be seen as a positive analysis, as recognising where you need to develop will improve your skills and knowledge
What would you do differently if you were to complete the project again? Revisit what happened during the project and concentrate on how some elements could have been completed differently

▲ **Figure 22.4** An example of a self-evaluation form

3.4 How to provide feedback to others on their performance as part of a project team

We have established the importance of reviewing the business project, and individual team members completing self-evaluations with regard to their own contributions, but it is also important that overall feedback be given to the whole team. This can be done in several ways, as described below.

Through discussion

A senior member of the project team, in a supervisory or management role, could talk to each team member on a one-to-one basis. The discussion could include positive feedback and specific examples of their input, as well as the opportunity to recognise where development may be required to help them work effectively within a team situation for other projects. The team member would also have the opportunity to discuss how they felt they contributed.

Through an interview

An individual interview could be arranged, where specific notes could be taken and documentation completed. The individual may want to prepare some form of documentation prior to the meeting, which would then aid and prompt the discussion. Management may decide to ask each team member the same questions, enabling it to collate the opinions of all, which could help it improve how it co-ordinates and runs future projects.

By 360-degree feedback

This gathers anonymous opinions about an individual from eight to ten people who have been involved in the project, e.g. other team members, supervisors, managers, customers or clients. This individual also completes a self-evaluation.

Management analyses the feedback about, for example, the individual's skills, performance, knowledge, working relationships, delegation and interpersonal skills. We behave or act in different ways according to the situation or who we are communicating with, so by using this method of feedback, management can gain a real insight into the person and their performance within a team project.

A **360-feedback** survey can gain information about:

- someone's behaviours and competencies
- how others perceive the person
- the person's skill sets, such as communicating, listening, planning, setting aims and SMART objectives, achieving goals, review success criteria, etc.

- other people's opinions about someone's teamwork, leadership effectiveness, etc.

> ## 🔑 KEY TERM
>
> **360-degree feedback** – a method of feedback gaining the opinions of others (e.g. peers, managers) to enable management to form an understanding of an individual in relation to their performance, knowledge, skills, etc.

By using this method of feedback, management can encourage each individual to:

- increase their self-awareness
- gain a balanced view of their input into the project
- be aware of their strengths
- uncover blind spots with regard to their performance during the project, which can then be addressed
- develop their skills.

Use of interpersonal skills

Any form of feedback will focus on a variety of different interpersonal skills, which will include:

- verbal communication
- non-verbal communication
- evidence-based information that has been gathered
- a focus on competency
- the ability to praise
- the ability to provide constructive criticism.

All of the stakeholders involved in the feedback process must ensure that they know that it is a professional discussion, interview or review, and not personal criticism. It is for development purposes and should provide opportunities to improve for future project work.

> ## ❓ THINK ABOUT IT
>
> ### Case study: London 2012 Olympics
>
> The London 2012 Olympics has left a lasting legacy in the UK. The original bid, planning and staging of the games took many years and many thousands of people. Read the following article:
>
> www.theguardian.com/public-leaders-network/2013/jan/22/lessons-london-2012-government-projects
>
> 1 What are the main points raised in the article?
> 2 Using this knowledge, investigate how certain facilities created for the games will continue to be used for years to come.
> 3 What specific elements of project management will be used? Give current examples of this in practice.

KNOW IT

1 Why would a project team want to review the project?
2 Identify and explain three examples of different stakeholders who may be involved in the review process.

3 Why is it important to review your own performance in a project team?
4 What are the main features of the 360-degree feedback method?

● ●

LO3 assessment activity

Below is a suggested assessment activity that has been directly linked to the Pass, Merit and Distinction Criteria in LO3 to help with assignment preparation. This is followed by top tips on how to achieve the best results.

Activity 1 Pass criteria *P14 P15 P16 P17* and *P18*, Merit criteria *M4* and *M5*, Distinction criteria *D3*

P14 Select method(s), format(s) and timing for obtaining feedback, and use your chosen method(s) and format(s) to collect it.

Using the knowledge you have gained from completing LO3, select the feedback methods, formats and timings that you will realistically be able to complete. You should consider such factors as the availability of the stakeholders and use your chosen suitable method(s) of feedback for the stakeholders, e.g. online survey, paper-based survey, telephone survey, as well as the timescales you are working towards.

P15 Collate the feedback you have gained from your stakeholders, and analyse and present your results in a suitable format that includes and summarises the trends. You will need to consider your audience and use the most suitable form of presentation for the task.

P16 Use feedback and review the outcome of the project against its original objectives, making any recommendations that could improve the overall project. You may want to combine this task with P15, and present your review and recommendations as part of a joint task.

P17 Deliver constructive feedback to stakeholders involved in the project based on their performance

in various different tasks and roles. Ensure you have evidence to support this feedback.

P18 Review your own performance related to delivering the project, which focuses on your strengths and areas that you consider could be improved.

M4 Assess how effective the chosen method, format and timings (that you selected for P14) have been in order to gain the required feedback about the project.

M5 Analyse how unplanned factors have influenced the project outcomes.

D3 Recommend and justify improvements to the planning and running of future projects based on the feedback gathered. Ensure that your justification is related to the feedback collated for assessment criteria including P15, P16 and P18.

TOP TIPS ✔

- ✔ When devising the types and forms of feedback, it is important that these are 'tested' on others prior to sending them out to the identified stakeholder. This should ensure that they are clear and will achieve the feedback you need to assist with this important process.
- ✔ If considering an online survey as part of your feedback, you could read the following advice: www.surveymonkey.com/blog/2012/04/13/10-online-survey-tips; www.smartsurvey.co.uk/articles/10-tips-for-designing-an-effective-online-survey; www.marketingprofs.com/articles/2014/24219/six-tips-for-creating-an-effective-online-customer-survey
- ✔ Consider the most suitable form of collating and presenting the feedback results. Think about the audience that will need to use the results and ensure that they can easily be interpreted and used for the desired purpose.

Read about it

Project Management: Efficient & Effective: The Beginners Pocket Guide to Successful Project Completion, by Greg F. Myers, CreateSpace Independent Publishing Platform, 2015

Project Management Step by Step: How to Plan and Manage a Highly Successful Project, by Richard Newton, Pearson Business, 2007

Useful websites

Project Smart case studies – 'Project management in practice': www.projectsmart.co.uk/case-studies.php

APM case studies: www.apm.org.uk/case-studies

Glossary

360-degree feedback – a method of feedback gaining the opinions of others (e.g. peers, managers) to enable management to form an understanding of an individual in relation to their performance, knowledge, skills, etc.

Accountability – the responsibility that someone has for actions that are carried out.

Accounting cycle – the process of recording and processing the accounting events within a business.

Adverse variance – where the actual figure is worse than the budgeted figures, e.g. if costs are higher than budgeted or revenue is lower than budgeted.

Annual general meeting (AGM) – a meeting that a public limited company must hold every year, inviting specific shareholders, official bodies and associations involved in the business, to review the business year and to inform the delegates of future plans.

Annual report – a comprehensive report of a company's activities throughout the last year.

Appraise own performance – the opportunity for individuals to consider the different contributions they have made during a business project.

Appropriation account – shows the distribution of net profit.

Asset-led strategy – assessing the strengths and needs of a specific market, producing the product and highlighting the product's attributes as part of a marketing campaign.

Assets – resources owned by a business, e.g. cash, motor vehicles, premises, machinery.

Assistive technologies – equipment that individuals may require to assist with their participation during an event.

Audience – the people or other businesses that communication is aimed towards.

Bank statement – a record of the balance in a bank account, and the amounts that have been paid into the account and withdrawn from it.

Belbin – a team-building theory that identifies the different elements of an effective team.

Body language – a form of non-verbal communication in which thoughts, feelings and intentions are expressed.

Branding – the processes involved in creating a unique name and image for a product or organisation that a consumer will be able to identify easily.

Break-even – the point at which the level of sales allows total costs to equal total revenue; at the break-even point a business makes no profit or loss.

Budget – planned income and expenditure over a period of time.

Business activities – tasks completed by a business to achieve its objectives, e.g. buying, selling and producing products or services.

Business aims – a summary of what the business wants to achieve in the future.

Business customers – businesses that purchase products or services from another business.

Business objectives – targets set by a business that detail the steps involved in achieving the overall aims of the business.

Business performance – how a business judges if it is succeeding and in which areas it needs to improve, to maintain or gain in terms of market share.

Business profile – a summary of a business; what it does, who it is and what its values are.

Capital and current accounts – used by partnerships, to record individual partners' day-to-day transactions and finance invested.

Capital expenditure – business spending on non-current assets.

Capital income – money invested either in the initial setting up of the business or for the purchase of non-current assets.

Capital/equity – how much a business is worth. It represents how much the owner(s) have invested in the business.

Cash book – a book in which receipts and payments are recorded.

Cash discount – a reduction in the amount owing to a supplier when the customer pays the amount owing before the due date.

Cash flow – the movement of money into and out of a business.

Cash flow forecast – a management accounting report that outlines predicted future cash inflows and cash outflows per month over a given period of time.

Cash flow forecasting – estimating the expected cash inflows and outflows for a period of time in the future to identify likely surpluses or shortages.

Cash flow statement – a financial accounting statement that shows the actual cash inflows and outflows for a business over the previous 12 months.

Centralised structure – a structure where decision making is kept at the top of the hierarchy.

Chain of command – the levels of authority in an organisation where communication and instructions flow down the hierarchy and accountability flows upwards.

Code of conduct – a set of guidelines outlining rules and responsibilities.

Commercial advantage – to gain an advantage over other businesses through particular marketing methods.

Communication protocols – formal descriptions that are specific to digital message formats. They are needed to exchange messages from one computer system to another when using telecommunication methods.

Competitors – other businesses in the same market that provide similar products and services, and so try to gain the same customers.

Conflict resolution – the methods a business may implement to resolve any major issues that affect the way in which business is performed.

Conflicts of interest – differing interests that cannot both be satisfied, e.g. owners may aim for high profits whereas customers may want low prices.

Constraints – restrictions that are imposed on individuals or businesses.

Consumables – resources that will be used and replaced on a regular basis, e.g. printer cartridges, stamps and paper.

Contingency planning – developing appropriate responses in advance for potential situations that might arise during a business project and that may impact on the overall outcomes.

Corporate governance – the concept that businesses should follow rules and principles that balance the interests of stakeholders. In a limited company the directors are responsible for the governance of the company, i.e. ensuring that principles are followed.

Corporate social responsibility (CSR) – the way in which a business approaches and responds to economic, social and environmental issues for the good of the wider world.

Corruption – using power for individual gain, e.g. a buyer for a supermarket chain accepting bribes from a supplier to stock its product in the stores.

Cost of sales – the total amount the business has paid to create or make available a product or service that has been sold.

Costs – the expenses a business incurs when producing and supplying products and services to customers.

Customer expectations – the perceived value a customer will gain from the purchase of a product or service.

Customer needs – the solutions to problems that a customer is aiming to solve with the use of the product or service.

Customer service – the support and guidance supplied to a customer before, during and after the purchase of a product or service.

Data – information, normally in numerical form, that can be analysed to help plan a product or service going to market.

Day books/journals – account books from which financial transactions are transferred to the ledgers.

Decentralised structure – a structure where decision making is more spread out and filtered down the hierarchy.

Decisions log – a document that details all the key decisions that have to be made on any given business project. It should be kept up to date.

Depreciation – the cost of an asset consumed over its useful life, e.g. due to wear and tear.

Digital marketing – the marketing of products or services using digital channels or media to reach consumers, e.g. email, social media.

Direct debit – an instruction given by an account holder to the bank to allow another account holder (usually a business) to withdraw funds from that account.

Direct report – a subordinate to a member of staff.

Disciplinary procedure – a specified process for dealing with alleged employee misconduct, e.g. poor performance.

Discount allowed – a discount a business offers to a customer when it settles its bills promptly.

Discount received – a discount a customer receives from a supplier for settling their bills promptly.

Diseconomies of scale – when a business becomes too large, the cost per unit may increase and the business may become more inefficient, e.g. communication becomes slower as more employees join the hierarchy.

Dishonoured cheque – a cheque that a bank will not pay because there is not enough money in the account.

Diversification – a strategy for expansion into new markets, and/or developing and selling new products.

Dividend – a share of a business's profits that is paid to the owners/shareholders.

Double-entry bookkeeping – records based on the assumption that every financial business transaction has opposite effects on two different accounts: one debit and one credit.

Economic factors – changes in the economy that affect the price and cost of goods and services – the level of interest rates, exchange rates, unemployment rate and taxation.

Economies of scale – cost advantages gained when the size of a business increases, e.g. suppliers may offer discounts to those placing larger orders.

Embezzlement – theft by an employee of assets that belong to the employer; this may include money, stock and stationery.

Environmental factors – green or sustainability issues that exist in a business's surrounding area.

Ethical and cultural constraints – restrictions for ensuring that individuals, groups or other businesses are not adversely affected by the conduct of others.

Ethical factors – moral issues, doing what is right.

Ethical values – principles that an individual chooses to live by or a business chooses to operate by, such as honesty, fairness and responsibility. For example, 'We put our customers first everyday' and 'We care for our colleagues everyday' (George clothing).

Ethics – moral judgements about what is right and what is wrong.

Executive summary – a section at the start of a large business document that briefly summarises the main points made within the main report, to ensure that readers get an insight into the content (a summary) of the document without having to read it all immediately.

Explicit – communication that is fully and clearly expressed or explained.

External customers – those who do not belong to the business but conduct a transaction with the business to purchase its products or services, e.g. a customer visiting a supermarket.

External influences – factors outside of a business that are beyond the owner's control.

External source – information from outside of the organisation.

External stakeholder – a person or group of people with links to the business, e.g. because of their personal location or that of the business they are connected with the organisation directly. They can be shareholders, customers, suppliers, potential investors, lenders, local community, pressure groups, and central and local government (e.g. HMRC, environmental health, planning department).

Favourable variance – where the actual figure is better than the budgeted figures, e.g. if costs are lower than budgeted or revenue higher than budgeted.

Feasibility – analysis and evaluation of a proposed project to determine specific factors regarding the legal, economic, technological and scheduling aspects of a project, allowing the business to investigate the positive and negative elements before committing time and money to the proposed project.

Financial analysis – a variety of different tools that enable a business to review its current financial arrangements, make improvements and future plans for the organisation.

Financial constraints – restrictions relating to money.

Financial information – data and monetary information about an individual or business, e.g. account balances, credit card numbers, loan transactions.

Flat structure – a company structure containing few levels.

Forecast – a financial prediction or estimate.

Four Dimensions of Relational Work concept – a tool to aid managers to match team members' natural aptitudes and skills to specific tasks or projects within their work.

Functional area – a division of a business where employees have similar roles, skills and expertise, e.g. marketing function, human resource function.

Grievance procedure – a specified process for dealing with a complaint made by an employee about their treatment at work, e.g. discrimination or receiving lower pay than stated in their employment contract.

Gross profit – revenue minus cost of sales.

Hierarchical/tall structure – a pyramid-shaped structure with many levels.

Ice breakers – activities used to introduce individuals to one another.

Implicit – communication that implies a certain meaning but this is not expressed openly.

Imprest system – a form of financial accounting system, most commonly used in the petty cash system.

Income statement – a financial statement that shows the revenue and expenses a business has received and paid over a period of time; the statement will show the profit the business has made during this time.

Insider trading – using information gained from within a business, i.e. not in the public domain, for personal financial gain.

Insolvent – when a business is unable to pay its debts.

Interim deadline – projects can be broken down into smaller tasks/targets, each of which can be allocated a deadline; these interim deadlines, if completed on time, will help to meet the final deadline.

Internal customers – a member of a business or organisation who relies on others within the business to do their job, e.g. an employee is an internal customer of the IT function.

Internal source – information from within the organisation.

Internal stakeholder – an individual or group who are involved in a business directly by being or representing members of the workforce; this includes owners (sole trader, partners), employees (e.g. chief executive, directors, managers, supervisors, assistants) and trade unions.

Key performance indicator (KPI) – a measure that a business judges itself against based upon the goals it has set itself.

Leasing – a method of financing a fixed asset whereby the lessee pays to rent (lease) the asset from the leasor.

Legal constraints – restrictions relating to laws that apply within the markets in which the product or service is produced and sold.

Legal factors – anything to do with the law.

Legislation – a law or set of laws that a government has suggested and that have been made official by Parliament. Once approved, individuals and business organisations are bound to abide by the content.

Liabilities – the debts owed by an organisation.

Limited liability – when the owners of a business are liable for the debts incurred by the business only to the value of their investment in the business.

Line manager – the superior to whom an employee reports; usually this is the person directly above the employee on an organisation chart.

Living wage – the minimum level of income needed by workers to meet their basic needs.

Loss – the deficit of revenue after paying total costs.

Margin of safety – the amount a business sells in excess of its break-even point.

Market – a defined area in which consumers, businesses and organisations are involved in the manufacture, purchase and use of a specified product.

Market analysis – marketing research that produces data about the current market, enabling a business to compete in a particular sector.

Market penetration – when a business increases the market share of a product by using different marketing strategies.

Market research – collecting information about a particular market for a specific purpose.

Market research proposal – suggesting ideas or methods to collect relevant market research material for a given purpose.

Market segmentation – splitting customers into different categories (segments) to enable the targeting of specific products or services to that particular group or category.

Market share – the percentage of a market's total sales or revenue that a particular company contributes.

Market structure – an overview of a market's characteristics, e.g. the amount and types of competitors, the products and services these produce, the size of the market.

Market-led/market orientation – focusing on meeting the needs and wants of potential customers.

Marketing – the management process responsible for identifying, anticipating and satisfying customer requirements profitably (source: Chartered Institute of Marketing (CIM)).

Marketing campaign – a defined series of steps or activities to promote or create awareness of a new or existing product or service.

Marketing mix – a key marketing tool that allows a business to consider the product, price, place and promotion of its goods.

Marketing objective – a specified and measurable goal or reason for carrying out a marketing activity.

Marketing strategies – methods that a business introduces to fulfil its marketing aims and objectives.

Marketing strategy – how marketing messages and activities will be combined with sales objectives to contribute to a business's overall objectives.

Mass marketing – aiming a product at all, or most, market segments.

Matrix structure – where employees are grouped by function and product/project.

Net cash flow – the difference between money coming into a business and money going out of a business.

Net profit – gross profit minus expenses.

Niche marketing – targeting a product or service at a small segment of a larger market.

Non-current assets – items acquired for use within the business that are likely to be used for a considerable amount of time (usually more than 12 months), e.g. motor vehicles, premises, machinery.

Operational decisions – day-to-day decisions made by staff at all levels that help the business to run smoothly.

Opportunity cost – a benefit, profit or other advantage that must be given up to acquire or achieve something else.

Overseas marketing – investing in either producing or selling products abroad.

Payment terms – when payment should be made by the buyer/customer to the supplier.

Petty cash – a small amount of cash held in a business to purchase minor items (e.g. stationery, coffee) reducing the need to write a cheque or pay on credit.

Plagiarism – using someone else's work and leading others to believe that it is your own.

Press release – an announcement that issues information to the media, e.g. regarding an award or a new innovation.

Pressure group – a group made up of individuals with a common concern or objective. They join together in an attempt to influence decision making by business organisations or the government.

Pricing strategies – methods a business may adopt to determine the ideal price(s) of its products and services.

Pricing strategy – the method used to determine the price of a product/service, taking into consideration the market, competitors' pricing, customer incomes, etc.

Primary research – collecting data that has not been researched before, so that the data is original.

Probability – the likelihood of consumers completing an action, such as purchasing an item.

Product life cycle – a theoretical method that businesses use to focus on six main areas of a product's life: development, introduction, growth, maturity, saturation and decline.

Product-led/product orientation – when a business focuses on a product before it decides on its target market.

Profit – the surplus left over from revenue after paying total costs.

Project – a set task or series of tasks to be completed. A project is temporary because it has defined beginning and end times. The outcome of a project is the end product, result or goal that the project is planned to achieve. Projects can take place in and across various departments, e.g. filling a skills gap in human resources, researching and developing a new product, constructing a new building, installing a new IT system.

Project management – the process of planning, organising, monitoring and applying resources to achieve an end goal.

Project manager – the person in charge of initiating, planning, executing and monitoring activities scheduled to achieve a planned outcome.

Project review – an evaluation of a specific project that details different elements of success and areas for improvement. The outcomes could influence future projects.

Project stakeholders – anybody who has an interest in a project. They could be internal or external to a business, e.g. client, customers (internal and external) or users, project manager, team members, suppliers, consultants, project sponsors and contractors. They might gain from a successful project or they might have an influence on how projects are completed.

Protocol – procedures or rules that must be followed.

Public relations – methods used to communicate a business's messages, to maintain its reputation and to build relationships with stakeholders.

Public relations (PR) – the relationship between a business, the general public and other organisations. The PR function within a business is responsible for maintaining a positive relationship and minimising the impact of any poor publicity.

Qualitative research – information that includes consumer opinions, attitudes and views.

Quantitative research – factual, often numerical, information such as sales figures, number of enquiries, number of emails opened, etc.

Questioning – a method of seeking information that requires a response.

Receipts and payments account – a summarised cash book for a specific period, prepared by non-profit organisations at the year end.

Recession – a period of economic decline where demand and output fall.

Reliability – determining whether the information is consistent and therefore will aid the research.

Retail customers – customers who buy finished products, e.g. frozen peas from a supermarket.

Retained profit – the money remaining within a business once all costs, taxes and dividends have been deducted.

Revenue – the money earned from selling manufactured output, goods purchased or services offered; the total revenue of a business is based on both the level of output and the selling price per unit.

Revenue expenditure – business spending on regular or day-to-day items.

Revenue income – money that comes in to a business from its day-to-day operations.

Risk register – a document and management tool that is created within the planning stages of any business project to identify any risks.

Scope control – preventing too many changes and additions to a business project that may disrupt the project schedule.

Secondary research – information and research that has been collated about or by other businesses or individuals and government organisations.

Skills audit – a review of the existing skills of employees, which is then compared to the skills the business needs currently and expects to need in the future.

SMART objectives – Specific, Measurable, Achievable, Realistic and Time-bound objectives that ensure the business focuses on the key areas within each objective stated.

Social factors – things that affect our lifestyle, e.g. demographic issues, attitudes to work, disposable income, social trends, cultural beliefs.

Social values – values that impact on the way society behaves, such as individuality, respect and equality.

Source document – a document or form designed to provide details of a business transaction.

Span of control – the number of subordinates a supervisor manages.

Stakeholder – any person, group or organisation that has an interest in a business because they are, or may be, affected by the activities of that business.

Standing order – an instruction given by an account holder to the bank to pay a specific amount to another account on a regular basis, e.g. annually or monthly – for example, to pay a monthly gym membership.

Statement of financial position – a summary statement on a particular date that shows a business's assets, liabilities and owner's equity.

Strategic decisions – decisions made by top management that affect the long-term direction of a business.

Support staff – staff that perform a supporting role at an event to ensure that it runs smoothly.

Sustainability – considering the economic, environmental and social impact of business operations, e.g. by using the resources that we need now but trying to ensure that there will still be sufficient remaining for future generations.

SWOT analysis – a tool that enables a business to analyse the Strength, Weaknesses, Opportunities and Threats of its current operations.

Tactical decisions – decisions made by middle management that aim to meet strategic objectives.

Target audience – the type of customers who are likely purchase the product or service.

Technical constraints – restrictions relating to technology or equipment.

Technological factors – these include machines used to automate the production process in a factory, hardware and software used for communication, purchasing and sales, and mobile technology.

Trade discount – a reduction in price charged by suppliers when a trade customer buys in bulk.

Trial balance – a statement of all debits and credits from a business's double-entry accounts.

Troubleshooting – a method of problem solving, giving specific stage-by-stage instructions to resolve the problem or issue.

Tuckman Theory – a theory that focuses on the way in which a team can potentially tackle a task or a project from the initial idea through to completion.

Unique selling point (USP) – a specific factor that makes a business stand out from its competitors, e.g. excellent customer service.

Unlimited liability – when the owners of a business are personally liable for all debts incurred by the business if the business itself does not have the funds to repay them.

Validity – whether the research that has been collated is accurate and genuine.

Viability – an investigation into how a proposed project will benefit the business in terms of its strategic goals and adding value to achieve the maximum potential over a sustainable period of time.

Voluntary constraints – restrictions that are not legally required but that a business can choose to adopt – for example, to ensure best practice.

Zero-hours contract – an agreement to hire an employee on varying numbers of hours, with no guarantee of work.

Index

INDEX

356